THE PSYCHOLOGY OF HIGH-PERFORMANCE SPORTS ORGANIZATIONS

The Psychology of High-Performance Sports Organizations: Culture, Safety, and Leadership provides a step-by-step guide to managing a professional sports organization through the principles of organizational psychology and psychological safety. It offers insights on how to manage sports organizations effectively, covering team operations, culture, and performance design. Readers will gain a deep understanding of psychological safety and learn how to cultivate it in diverse team settings.

Although focused on professional sports, many of the key takeaways are applicable to elite amateur sports organizations and general businesses. Some of the topics covered in the book include transformational leadership, values-based decision-making, talent development, psychological safety, and leadership, which can all be applied outside of the sport organization. While these topics have been explored extensively individually, this is one of the first books to bring all of them together with a focus on sports and in an easy-to-digest format. Each chapter provides the what, the why, and the how: what is the concept, why is it important, and how can it be applied in the real world?

Whether the reader is preparing for a career in sports management or is already in that world, *The Psychology of High-Performance Sports Organizations: Culture, Safety, and Leadership* delivers practical, research-backed insights for fostering psychological safety and improving team performance and is key reading for students, researchers, and practitioners in the fields of sport psychology, sport management, organizational behavior, organizational psychology, and related subdisciplines.

Marie Claire Bourque, MD, MSc, FRCPC, is an award-winning psychiatrist, educator, clinician, and public speaker who specializes in working with high-performing individuals. Known for blending mental health expertise with insights from her own athletic background, Marie Claire Bourque offers a performance-enhancing approach to therapy. Her professional experience spans from working with patients struggling with polysubstance use disorder and experiencing homelessness to professional athletes and business executives at top companies. She serves as a National Hockey League (NHL) Mental Health and Peak Performance Expert for the Toronto Maple Leafs and the Toronto Marlies and holds a Certificate of Additional Training in Sports Psychiatry from the International Society for Sports Psychiatry. Marie Claire Bourque is a clinical instructor at the University of British Columbia School of Medicine and an adjunct assistant professor at the University of Calgary's Cumming School of Medicine, and she maintains a virtual psychiatry practice in British Columbia.

Madeline Antony earned a Bachelor of Science in biology and psychology with honors at the University of Victoria, Canada, and a Juris Doctor at the University of Calgary. Throughout her academic career, Madeline Antony has worked alongside Marie Claire Bourque as a research assistant specializing in mental toughness in elite athletes and developing culture in professional organizations. Madeline Antony is a passionate advocate for community and culture building, as reflected in her diverse academic and professional pursuits. She has volunteered in the fields of international relations, politics, healthcare, literacy, environmental protection, and athletics.

THE PSYCHOLOGY OF HIGH-PERFORMANCE SPORTS ORGANIZATIONS

Culture, Safety, and Leadership

Marie Claire Bourque and Madeline Antony

Routledge
Taylor & Francis Group
NEW YORK AND LONDON

Designed cover image: Getty Images

First published 2027
by Routledge
605 Third Avenue, New York, NY 10158

and by Routledge
4 Park Square, Milton Park, Abingdon, Oxon, OX14 4RN

Routledge is an imprint of the Taylor & Francis Group, an informa business

ISBN: 978-1-041-05063-6 (hbk)
ISBN: 978-1-041-05062-9 (pbk)
ISBN: 978-1-003-63121-7 (ebk)

DOI: 10.4324/9781003631217

Typeset in Times New Roman
by Apex CoVantage, LLC

To sport and to everyone whose life is richer because of it.

CONTENTS

FIGURES

TABLES

ABBREVIATIONS

AAR	After-Action Review
ABQ	Athlete Burnout Questionnaire
ACGME	Accreditation Council for Graduate Medical Education
AI	Artificial Intelligence
AP	Associated Press
CART-Q	Coach–Athlete Relationship Questionnaire
CBA	Collective Bargaining Agreement
CCBS	Controlling Coach Behaviours Scale
CEO	Chief Executive Officer
CFIR	Consolidated Framework for Implementation Research
COVID-19	Coronavirus Disease 2019
CTE	Chronic Traumatic Encephalopathy
CVF	Competing Values Framework
DARVO	Deny, Attack, and Reverse Victim and Offender
DLQ	Destructive Leadership Questionnaire
DSM-5-TR	Diagnostic and Statistical Manual of Mental Disorders, Fifth Edition, Text Revision
EBM	Evidence-Based Medicine
EBP	Evidence-Based Practice
EI	Emotional Intelligence
EU	European Union
FIFA	Fédération Internationale de Football Association
GAD-7	Generalized Anxiety Disorder Seven-Item Scale
GLOBE	Global Leadership and Organizational Behavior Effectiveness (Study)

GM	General Manager
GPS	Global Positioning System
HPCOS	High-Performance Culture Operating System
HR	Human Resources
IAP2	International Association for Public Participation
ICS	Implementation Climate Scale
IDP	Individual Development Plan
ILI	Identity Leadership Inventory
ILS	Implementation Leadership Scale
IOC	International Olympic Committee
KPI	Key Performance Indicator
LGBTQ+	Lesbian, Gay, Bisexual, Transgender, Queer, and related identities
LMA	League Managers Association
MAC	Mindfulness-Acceptance-Commitment (approach)
MCB	Marie Claire Bourque (Psychology Sidelines with Dr. MCB)
MLB	Major League Baseball
MLSPA	Major League Soccer Players Association
NASA	National Aeronautics and Space Administration
NBA	National Basketball Association
NCAA	National Collegiate Athletic Association
NFL	National Football League
NHL	National Hockey League
NIL	Name, Image, and Likeness
NPT	Normalization Process Theory
NWSL	National Women's Soccer League
OCAI	Organizational Culture Assessment Instrument
PCDEQ2	Psychological Characteristics of Developing Excellence Questionnaire, Version 2
PHQ-9	Patient Health Questionnaire, Nine-Item
RACI	Responsible, Accountable, Consulted, Informed
RE-AIM	Reach, Effectiveness, Adoption, Implementation, Maintenance
RED-S	Relative Energy Deficiency in Sport
ROI	Return on Investment
TAP	Transition Assistance Program (Military)
TSN	The Sports Network
UK	United Kingdom
UNICEF	United Nations Children's Fund
US/USA	United States/United States of America
VRIN	Valuable, Rare, Inimitable, and Non-Substitutable

PREFACE

I came to professional sport from academic medicine.

In that world, difficult questions keep people alive. In grand rounds, you ask uncomfortable questions to your colleagues. You poke holes in treatment plans. You challenge because the alternative is missing something that matters. I assumed that culture of questioning would translate directly to sport—and in many ways, it does, but the structures look different, the pressures are different, and the dynamics around speaking up operate in ways I hadn't encountered before.

I started working in professional sport in 2018. I'd grown up as a competitive athlete—sport was not new to me. But working inside professional sport organizations was. I'm a sports psychiatrist, and I was fascinated by what I was seeing—the complexity of how these environments operate, the dynamics between coaches and athletes and front offices, the way information moves (or doesn't) under pressure. I kept noticing moments where things worked beautifully—where people trusted each other, where problems got solved early, where talent flourished—and moments where the same organizations struggled with the same patterns. I wanted to understand what made the difference.

In academic medicine, when you want to understand something, you ask questions and you look at the research. So that's what I did. Partly because curiosity has always been how I'm wired—I need to understand why things work the way they do. But mostly because I wanted to be genuinely useful to the organizations and people I was working with, and that meant going beyond intuition. I asked Madeline Antony—who was studying and researching sport psychology at the time, and who would become the co-author of this book—to find out. "I'm seeing this pattern—what does the literature say about it?" She'd come back with a five-page researched document. Sometimes, it was a robust evidence base from sport psychology. More often, it was a finding from organizational psychology, aviation human factors, healthcare team science, or military transition research that hadn't been widely applied to sport. Sometimes, the answer was: "There's no evidence in sports—but here's what they found in healthcare" or "here's what organizational psychology says." And sometimes the answer surprised us both.

So I'd ask another question. And another. What does the evidence say about silence under selection pressure? About decision-making during losing streaks? About what happens to staff who report concerns upward? About how organizations handle athlete transitions—and what happens when they don't? Madeline kept producing. I kept asking. The cycle ran for years. Every answer opened new questions. Every application in the field taught us something that the literature alone couldn't.

By 2022, something had shifted. We'd accumulated years of evidence reviews, applied frameworks, and documents tracking what worked and what didn't across multiple environments. At some point—neither of us remembers exactly when—one of us said, "We should just write a textbook." It was half a joke. We'd been building one without realizing it.

But the material wasn't just a pile of research summaries. The questions had started to organize themselves. They had a dependency logic. I couldn't answer the question about decision architecture until I'd answered the question about whether anyone could tell the truth. I couldn't address sustainability until I'd addressed what happens when external stakeholders start screaming. The questions had an order—and that order kept proving itself in practice. When organizations tried to skip a layer, the intervention struggled. When they worked through the layers in order, the architecture held under pressure, and good things followed.

What we had wasn't a collection of tips or a leadership philosophy. It was an operating system. Seven questions. Seven layers. A way of thinking about organizational culture that helped us—and the organizations we worked with—make sense of what was happening and what to do about it.

This book is what that cycle of observation and evidence review produced. It's built practice-up—not theory-down. Every chapter starts with what practitioners see in the field, then asks what the evidence says about it, and then translates the answer into something an organization can use on Tuesday morning. It's a reflection of how the architecture was actually built: one observation at a time, chased through the literature, tested in application, refined, and repeated.

I'm constantly learning, and I feel enormously grateful to do this work. The people I get to work with—the athletes, the staff—are some of the best in the world at what they do, and they're constantly teaching me. Every environment I enter, I learn something I didn't know before. The frameworks in this book are better because of the people who trusted me enough to be honest about what they were experiencing. That generosity runs through every page, even where confidentiality means I can't name them.

* * *

A word about the partnership that produced this book. Madeline and I represent two sides of what we call the prac-ademic stance. I'm a clinician. I'm in the room. Madeline found out whether what I was seeing was backed by evidence—and when it wasn't, she told me.

Madeline is relentlessly curious. I'd hand her a half-formed observation, and she'd disappear into the literature and come back with a five-page document and three follow-up questions I hadn't thought to ask. She worked extraordinarily hard on this—nights, weekends, across years—and she pushed back when the evidence didn't support what I thought I was seeing. That made the book better at every stage.

Since we began this work, Madeline has gone on to become a lawyer—which, if you've read this far, probably doesn't surprise you. She builds arguments carefully, interrogates assumptions, and doesn't let anything through that hasn't earned its place. That rigor is on every page of this book. What a practitioner sees and what the evidence says don't always agree—and we tried to be honest about that throughout the book.

* * *

The question underneath this entire book is a simple one: what does it take to build a high-performance sport organization that actually works—for everyone in it? That question is what drove us to write it.

Marie Claire Bourque (Dr. MCB)

DATA AVAILABILITY STATEMENT

No original datasets were generated or analyzed. The work synthesizes peer-reviewed literature from sport psychology, organizational psychology, neuroscience, and adjacent fields, alongside practitioner-developed frameworks derived from clinical observation across multiple high-performance sport environments. All case studies presented are composite vignettes constructed from recurring patterns observed across the authors' applied work, conversations with colleagues, and accounts shared by athletes and staff across international high-performance settings; identifying details have been altered or blended to protect confidentiality, and no vignette represents a specific individual or organization. Practitioner tools included in the book carry per-tool status labels designating them as empirically supported, theoretically grounded, or practitioner-derived, each with supporting citations. No unpublished datasets underlie their construction. All referenced sources are cited in the chapter reference lists.

ACKNOWLEDGMENTS

The authors thank Meg Graham for invaluable assistance in preparing and organizing the manuscript files for submission.

We are also eternally grateful to the many teachers—formal and informal—whose influence shaped the thinking in this book: the mentors, colleagues, athletes, and staff who challenged our assumptions, sharpened our questions, and taught us things the literature alone never could.

STATEMENT ON THE USE OF GENERATIVE AI TOOLS

This book was conceived, researched, written, and revised by its authors. The theoretical framework, clinical observations, applied recommendations, and all editorial decisions reflect the authors' own professional judgment, shaped by years of applied work in high-performance sport, study of brain and behavior, and sustained engagement with the research literature.

Generative AI tools assisted at specific stages of the preparation process, always under direct author supervision. Claude (Anthropic; versions 3.5 Sonnet through Opus 4.6) supported developmental editing, refinement of pedagogical elements (learning objectives, abstracts, discussion questions, and composite case studies), citation formatting and cross-referencing, and structural consistency checks across chapters. Gemini (Google; versions 2.5 Pro and 3.0 Pro, including Research mode) supported research synthesis, source verification, and fact-checking. Perplexity AI (Research mode) was used for literature search and citation verification. NotebookLM (Google) supported source organization and management. No tool operated autonomously or generated content that was published without substantive human editorial judgment.

The authors take full responsibility for the accuracy, originality, and integrity of the final published content. Every empirical claim was verified against primary sources. All citations were audited for accuracy. No AI tool is listed as an author. No images, figures, or original research data were generated using AI tools.

INTRODUCTION

The High-Performance Culture Operating System

The Structural Thesis

Elite sport is one of the most sophisticated performance environments on the planet. Organizations invest extraordinary resources in physical preparation, tactical analysis, and talent identification—and the results are visible in the precision and intensity of modern competition. But the organizational environment inside which that performance occurs—the information pathways, the decision architecture, and the systems that determine whether people speak up or stay silent—has not received comparable structural attention. The investment in the athlete's body far outpaces the investment in the system around the athlete.

This book closes that gap. It treats organizational culture as a system—something that must be designed, built, maintained, and repaired with the same rigor applied to physical conditioning, tactical preparation, and talent identification. That architecture is the High-Performance Culture Operating System (HP-COS), and every chapter in this book builds, tests, or protects a specific layer of it.

The starting premise is structural: when culture problems arise in elite sport, they almost always trace to a layer that was missing—not a person who was deficient. Organizations often treat culture as a people problem: replace the coach, train the athlete, and workshop the front office. Those interventions can help, but they rarely hold, because the diagnosis is incomplete. The coach who narrows under pressure is operating without decision architecture. The athlete who conceals an injury is making a rational calculation inside a system where disclosure has historically produced punishment. The staff member who filters bad news upward learned, by watching what happened to others, that unfiltered honesty costs more than strategic silence.

DOI: 10.4324/9781003631217-1

The central reframe of this book: **dysfunction is adaptation, not failure.** The silence, the concealment, and the short-term thinking—these are not breakdowns of individual character. They are rational responses to structural conditions. Diagnose the structure before labeling the person. If you accept that reframe, the intervention target shifts: you stop trying to make individuals braver and start redesigning the architecture that makes silence rational. If you do not accept it, the tools in these chapters can still be useful—but they will work harder and hold less well without the structural foundation underneath them.

Figure 0.1 is the map.

The Architecture: Seven Questions, Seven Layers

Take a moment with Figure 0.1. It is the single most important visual in this book. Every chapter opens with a "You Are Here" version of this diagram, highlighting the layer being addressed. Every tool, protocol, and framework in the chapters that follow lives inside one of these layers. When implementation stalls or an initiative fails, the answer is almost always visible here: a layer was skipped, a dependency was unmet, or the work was launched above an unstable foundation.

The architecture is organized around seven questions. Each corresponds to a structural layer. The layers are dependency-logical: each depends on those beneath it. Answer the questions honestly—from the executive suite to the locker room—and the architecture supports sustained performance. Skip a layer, and everything built above it eventually degrades.

The three phases visible in the figure each serve a different structural function:

Diagnostic (Layers 1–3) is where the work begins. Before building anything, the organization maps its pressure terrain (Layer 1), determines whether truth can travel safely through the system (Layer 2), and diagnoses—with precision—what is actually broken and where (Layer 3). Layer 2 is load-bearing: it establishes psychological safety—the team-level operating condition in which people can speak without punishment (Edmondson, 1999). If the answer to *Can anyone here tell the truth?* is no, then the outputs of every layer above it are unreliable. The organization is navigating on bad data and does not know it.

Operational (Layers 4–5) is where the organization builds how it functions. Diagnosis is complete; now the architecture gets installed. Layer 4 constructs the decision pathways, leadership infrastructure, and consequence architecture that determine what happens when values compete under pressure. Layer 5 designs the people systems—athlete transitions, staff coordination, selection, and lifecycle architecture—that make culture visible in the daily interactions where trust is built or broken.

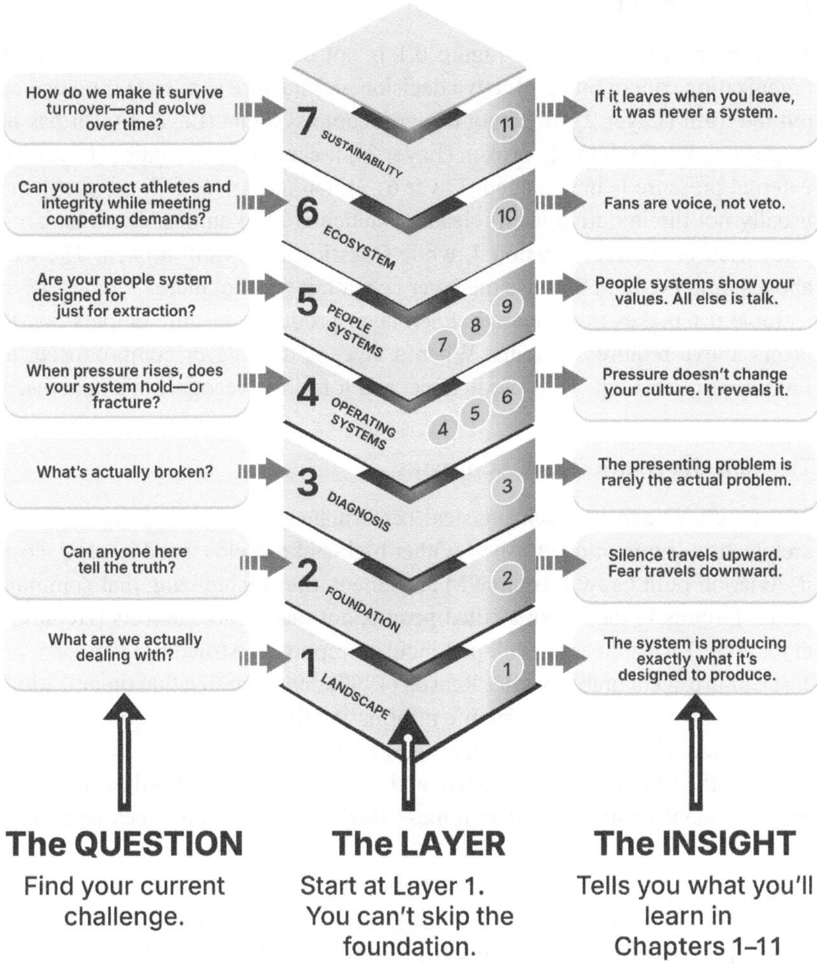

FIGURE 0.1 The HPCOS.

The seven-layer architecture that organizes this book. Each layer answers a structural question. Each depends on those beneath it. The three phases—Diagnostic, Operational, and Protective—group the layers by function. Read bottom to top: nothing built above a missing layer holds under pressure.

Protective (Layers 6–7) is where the organization defends and sustains what it has built. Layer 6 governs the interface with external stakeholders—sponsors, media, families, fans—because unmanaged external pressure degrades internal architecture from the outside in. Layer 7 ensures the whole system survives leadership transitions, budget shifts, and the quiet drift back to threat-based defaults that happens in ordinary weeks when no one is watching.

The Dependency Logic

The vertical arrangement in Figure 0.1 is not decorative—it is structural. An organization cannot build effective decision architecture (Layer 4) if no one can tell the truth (Layer 2). It cannot design people systems (Layer 5) if it has not diagnosed what is actually broken (Layer 3). It cannot sustain gains (Layer 7) if external pressure is unmanaged (Layer 6). When initiatives fail, the problem is usually not the initiative itself—leaders launched it on an unstable foundation. They tried to answer Question 4, while Question 2 was still broken. The work above could not hold because the layer beneath it was not there.

Table 0.1 makes this concrete. Each layer produces specific outputs that the layers above require as inputs. When a layer is missing or compromised, the failure is not abstract—it is predictable, and it follows recognizable patterns.

The Gap the Architecture Addresses

The structural gap between physical performance systems and organizational architecture is not unique to sport. Other high-stakes fields faced it—and closed it. Aviation built Crew Resource Management after recognizing that communication failures in the cockpit killed people, not mechanical defects (Helmreich et al., 1999). Healthcare developed incident reporting, structured handoffs, and Just Culture accountability after Reason (1997) demonstrated that organizational accidents are produced by systemic information flow failures, not individual incompetence. These fields learned, at significant human cost, that when the stakes are high, the timeline is compressed, and the consequences of failure are public, organizational architecture determines whether pressure produces learning or silence.

Elite sport operates under comparable structural conditions—high stakes, compressed timelines, public visibility, and complex interdependencies between specialized roles—but has been slower to build comparable infrastructure (Fletcher & Wagstaff, 2009). The HPCOS adapts proven structural principles from these fields for sport's specific pressure landscape, integrating organizational psychology, safety science, implementation research, and sport-specific evidence into a single layered architecture.

How Culture Actually Operates

The mechanism that drives the failures described in Table 0.1—and that connects every layer of the architecture—is reinforcement.

Behavior is maintained by its consequences (Skinner, 1953), and those consequences are learned vicariously by everyone watching (Bandura, 1977). People repeat what gets reinforced. They stop doing what gets punished or ignored.

TABLE 0.1 What Each Layer Produces—And What Breaks Without It

Layer	*The Question*	*What It Produces*	*What Breaks Without It*
1—Landscape	What are we actually dealing with?	A structural map of the pressure terrain: which dimensions are loaded, whose silence calculus is steepest, and where truth is slowest.	Subsequent interventions are designed for an environment that does not exist. Leaders build psychological safety programs for a culture they have not diagnosed, install voice channels that miss the populations most silenced, and interpret resistance as defiance rather than rational adaptation.
2—Foundation	Can anyone here tell the truth?	Voice infrastructure, meeting protocols, accountability structures, and a measurable baseline for how fast truth travels. The operating condition on which every layer above depends.	The organization navigates on bad data—and does not know it. Diagnosis (Layer 3) runs on sanitized inputs. Decision architecture (Layer 4) enforces values no one will challenge. People systems (Layer 5) collect feedback that no one trusts enough to give honestly. The silence calculus goes uninterrupted.
3—Diagnosis	What is actually broken?	Three outputs: environment classification (demanding vs. damaging), cascade source (coaching-tier or executive-level origin), and Toxic Triangle analysis (Padilla et al., 2007). These are required inputs for Layer 4.	Interventions target the wrong level. The organization replaces the coach when the problem is executive, runs culture workshops when the problem is a single destructive leader, or applies generic programming to an undiagnosed system—the organizational equivalent of prescribing without a differential.

(Continued)

TABLE 0.1 (Continued)

Layer	*The Question*	*What It Produces*	*What Breaks Without It*
4—Operating system	How do we decide when it matters?	Decision architecture: values-in-use excavated through conflict archaeology, safeguarding gates, discipline decision trees, documentation standards, and leader infrastructure for regulation under pressure. The consequence architecture that teaches the organization what is real.	Decisions default to status, convenience, and improvisation under pressure. The same behavior produces different consequences depending on who did it. Inconsistency erodes trust. Staff learn that stated values do not reliably govern decisions—and update their silence calculus accordingly. The gap between the wall words and Tuesday morning behavior widens.
5—People systems	Are we listening—and using what we hear?	Structured systems for the moments where culture becomes visible: rookie integration, veteran transitions, injury and mental health disclosure, staff role clarity, selection and deselection pathways, and lifecycle architecture from entry to exit.	Transitions become crises—not because the events are unpredictable, but because the system has no structural resources to meet predictable demands. Rookies optimize for invisibility. Veterans disengage. Injuries go undisclosed. Staff filter information upward. The acquisition–extraction cycle runs unchecked: heavy investment in talent identification, performance extraction, and systemic neglect of every seam between.

6—Ecosystem	How do we stay grounded when everyone is screaming?	Governance infrastructure for the organization's interface with external stakeholders: ecosystem mapping, crisis communication protocols, digital safety systems, and boundary frameworks for agents, families, and sponsors.	External pressure degrades internal architecture from the outside in. A sponsor overrides decision rights. A media pile-on collapses psychological safety. A fan campaign shifts the silence calculus. An agent's threat produces a selection decision no one can explain. Unmanaged stakeholder relationships become structural bypasses of the operating system—and important conversations move to car parks and text messages.
7—Sustainability	Will this survive us?	The ownership spine, custodianship cycle, measurement-to-action feedback loops, and governance frameworks that ensure that the architecture outlasts any single leader, budget cycle, or performance streak.	The system works—until it doesn't. A key champion is promoted. A sporting director leaves. A budget squeeze folds the culture custodian role into "general responsibilities." Nobody cancels the systems; they just stop being maintained. Pulse survey response rates drop from 84% to 41%. Default drift returns the organization to threat-based defaults, and the next leader starts from scratch—inheriting scar tissue they cannot see and a transition report no one wrote.

The HPCOS layers degrade top-down. When a lower layer fails, every layer above it produces unreliable outputs—not because the tools are wrong, but because the information feeding them is incomplete.

They learn the rules not from what leaders say but from what happens to the last person who spoke up, the last person who challenged a decision, and the last person who reported a problem.

This is why similar patterns appear across organizations that share little else in common—different sports, different countries, different leadership, and similar structural failures. When silence is reinforced (the person who raised a concern was excluded from the next meeting), silence spreads. When voice is reinforced (the person who flagged a problem saw the organization act on it), voice normalizes. The patterns are produced by the consequence architecture operating underneath the stated values.

The diagnostic expression of this logic is the Culture Hypothesis: a testable prediction, framed in behavioral terms, about what will change if a specific consequence changes. "If we change this consequence, this behavior will change in this domain within this timeframe." That converts culture from an abstraction ("we need more accountability") into something an organization can design, test, and track.

Three Leading Indicators

If the HPCOS is functioning, three things become observable:

Speed of Truth measures the elapsed time between someone knowing something and the organization being able to act on it. In high-functioning systems, problems surface in hours. In dysfunctional ones, they fester for months until they become crises that could have been prevented.

Voice Normalization measures whether concerns, bad news, and dissenting perspectives are raised before problems escalate—without the person who raises them paying a social or career cost.

Decision clarity measures whether decision rights are specified, honored, and transparent—whether people know who decides what, on what basis, and what happens when values collide.

These are not three separate metrics. They are three readings of the same underlying construct: information flow under pressure. Together, they function as the system's vital signs. All three are practitioner-derived heuristics, not validated instruments—they operationalize research on voice behavior (Morrison, 2011), information flow in high-reliability organizations (Weick & Sutcliffe, 2015), and procedural justice (Colquitt, 2001), but they have not been independently validated in sport settings. They are tracked because they are observable, because they respond to structural change, and because they degrade before outcome measures do. If they are improving, performance and welfare outcomes are more likely to follow. If they are declining, the underlying architecture needs attention—regardless of what other initiatives are running.

The Evidentiary Stance

Three sources of evidence inform this book: peer-reviewed research from sport psychology, organizational psychology, neuroscience, and adjacent fields; practitioner expertise developed through pattern recognition across multiple high-performance environments; and contextual factors specific to the organization, culture, and competitive environment in which the work takes place. Evidence-based practice integrates all three. It does not mean "only do what is in journals." It means weighing evidence appropriately, acknowledging uncertainty, and tracking whether interventions work in your context.

The direct evidence base for elite sport interventions is thinner than most assume. Bernier and colleagues' (2025) systematic review found only 11 studies over 12 years meeting the inclusion criteria for elite athlete psychological interventions—11 studies. For the population organizations most want to serve, the sport-specific evidence is remarkably sparse. This does not mean flying blind. It means adapting rigorously from adjacent fields—organizational psychology, military performance, healthcare team science, and aviation human factors—where the evidence base is stronger, while building evaluation into implementation so organizations can track what works in their specific context.

Throughout the book, every tool carries a validation status declaration: either a *validated instrument* with citation or a *practitioner-developed heuristic* with the theoretical tradition it synthesizes. Where the evidence is strong, we say so. Where it is thin, we say that too. Where practitioner consensus is the best available guide, we name it as such and build in mechanisms to test whether it holds. This transparency is not a weakness—it is the honest accounting that allows practitioners to calibrate confidence appropriately.

The central stance is prac-ademic: every theory earns its place by answering one question—*what does this change on Tuesday morning?* That is not a dismissal of foundational research—the architecture depends on it. It is a filter for which research gets operationalized in these chapters and how.

What Makes the Architecture Survive

The gap between "what works" and "what stays" is the central problem addressed by the final layer of the HPCOS. Initiatives fail not because the plan is wrong but because ownership disappears when the plan competes with daily performance priorities. Measurement disconnects from action. Leadership transitions produce institutional amnesia. Under load, systems revert to their pre-intervention defaults—a pattern this book calls default drift.

The sustainability layer (Chapter 11) addresses this through three mechanisms. The ownership spine specifies minimum roles, decision rights, cadence, and escalation triggers so that implementation survives the departure of any single champion. The custodianship cycle—capture, store, transfer, and audit—ensures that cultural knowledge survives turnover. And the measurement-to-action system closes the feedback loop: if people provide input and nothing visibly changes, they learn that voice is not taken seriously, and the silence calculus shifts accordingly. Measurement without action trains silence. The system must demonstrate, repeatedly, that speaking up produces a response.

How the Chapters Work

Each chapter follows a consistent structure designed for practitioner use:

A composite case study opens each chapter. All vignettes are composites; names, roles, and details have been altered to prevent identification. Examples of public cases are used for learning purposes and are drawn from publicly available reporting. If a story feels familiar, treat it as a mirror for your system—not a claim about anyone in particular. The views expressed are the authors' own and do not represent any employer or affiliated organization.

A "You Are Here" figure appears near the opening of every chapter, locating that chapter's layer within the full HPCOS architecture from Figure 0.1. These figures are navigation tools. When you are deep in the details of decision trees, transition protocols, or stakeholder governance, they remind you what layer you are working on, what it depends on, and what depends on it.

Psychology Sidelines with Dr. MCB boxes provide a clinical perspective—first-person observations from applied practice that connect theoretical frameworks to the patterns practitioners encounter in the field.

TIMEOUT boxes isolate key concepts for quick reference.

Skeptic's Corner boxes address common objections and resistance points directly because the strongest counterarguments deserve engagement rather than avoidance.

Every diagnostic tool includes a validation status declaration (validated instrument or practitioner-developed heuristic), scope notes addressing cultural adaptation and context limitations, and guidance on what each tool can and cannot claim. Tables, figures, and decision trees are designed to be used operationally—not just read.

Chapters conclude with learning objectives, key takeaways, discussion questions, and references.

Who This Book Is For

Sport psychologists, performance directors, head coaches, welfare leads, front-office executives, board members, and anyone responsible for the organizational environment inside which athletic performance occurs. It is also written for graduate and advanced undergraduate students in sport psychology, sport management, kinesiology, and related fields—those who will inherit these systems and need to understand their architecture before they are inside them. The learning objectives, discussion questions, and case studies in each chapter are designed to support both classroom use and independent professional development. The principles cross levels—professional, collegiate, and developmental—though the primary context is professional team sport, with adaptation notes throughout. The architecture covers everyone: the locker room, the front office, the boardroom, and the classroom. The principles do not change based on job title or career stage. The applications do.

Scope and Limitations

This book is built from a specific vantage point, and its limitations should be named before the reader commits to the architecture.

Context. The primary evidence base and practitioner experience draw from professional team sport in Western, English-speaking governance structures. The structural logic—dependency layers, information flow, and reinforcement architecture—is designed to transfer across settings, but the entry points, facilitation strategies, and implementation sequences may need significant adaptation for centralized government sport models, collegiate systems operating under NCAA oversight, or organizations embedded in high power-distance cultural norms. Chapters include adaptation notes where specific tools require contextual modification, but those notes are starting points, not comprehensive adaptation guides.

Individual sport. The architecture assumes multi-tiered organizational hierarchies: athletes, coaches, support staff, front office, and board. In individual sport, many of these layers compress into the coach–athlete dyad, and decision architecture looks fundamentally different. The principles apply; the structures need reworking. This book does not do that reworking comprehensively.

Diversity of sport populations. Para-sport amplifies every power gradient described in these chapters through dependency relationships and access barriers. International athletes navigating second-language environments, athletes from low-resource backgrounds, and athletes whose demographic identity compounds the silence calculus all experience the architecture differently. The book flags these dynamics throughout but does not claim to address them with the depth each deserves. Practitioners working with these populations should treat the frameworks as scaffolding that requires further specification—not as finished structures.

Evidence. As the Evidentiary Stance section acknowledges, much of the architecture adapts research from adjacent fields rather than drawing on sport-specific validation. The practitioner-developed tools in this book are operational heuristics, not validated instruments. They are designed to be useful, not to be treated as psychometric measures. Where validated alternatives exist, the book cites them. Where they do not, the book is transparent about the gap and encourages organizations to build evaluation into implementation.

Scope of practice. This book addresses organizational architecture—not individual clinical intervention, not coaching technique, and not tactical preparation. It does not replace clinical supervision, safeguarding training, or specialist mental health support. Where clinical and organizational boundaries intersect (mental health disclosure, injury reporting, and welfare escalation), the book draws the line explicitly and directs readers to the appropriate professional domain.

Implementation constraints. The architecture requires organizational willingness. It cannot be fully implemented from below by practitioners without positional authority, though Chapter 2 offers harm-reduction strategies for that reality. It cannot be imposed from the outside by consultants without internal ownership, though Chapter 11 addresses how to build that ownership. Some organizations are not ready—and the readiness assessment in Chapter 11 is designed to surface that honestly rather than encourage premature implementation.

Practitioners should weigh these boundaries against their own context before implementing. The architecture is a starting point, not a finished product—and treating it as one would contradict everything in it.

Where to Begin

Start with Chapter 1 and work sequentially. The dependency logic builds: each chapter assumes the reader understands what came before, and each layer assumes the layers beneath it are in place.

But practitioners rarely have the luxury of starting from scratch. Mid-crisis, start with Chapter 3, and then loop back to Chapter 1. Examining your own leadership under pressure, start with Chapter 5. Managing a coaching transition, Chapters 6 and 7. Working without positional authority, Chapter 2. Trying to understand why the last culture initiative failed, the Introduction, Chapter 11, and then Chapter 4. Wherever you enter, check what sits beneath the layer you are working on. If the foundation is unstable, the work above it will not hold.

The work starts with the landscape.

References

Bandura, A. (1977). *Social learning theory*. Prentice-Hall.

Bernier, M., Bagot, P., Sondt, N., Levillain, G., Vacher, P., Doron, J., Martinent, G., Fournier, J. F., & Kermarrec, G. (2025). The effectiveness of psychological interventions in elite sport: methodological issues and opportunities to gather evidence. *Frontiers in Psychology, 16*, 1516760. https://doi.org/10.3389/fpsyg.2025.1516760

Colquitt, J. A. (2001). On the dimensionality of organizational justice: A construct validation of a measure. *Journal of Applied Psychology*, *86*(3), 386–400. https://doi.org/10.1037/0021-9010.86.3.386

Edmondson, A. C. (1999). Psychological safety and learning behavior in work teams. *Administrative Science Quarterly*, *44*(2), 350–383. https://doi.org/10.2307/2666999

Fletcher, D., & Wagstaff, C. R. D. (2009). Organizational psychology in elite sport: Its emergence, application and future. *Psychology of Sport and Exercise*, *10*(4), 427–434. https://doi.org/10.1016/j.psychsport.2009.03.009

Helmreich, R. L., Merritt, A. C., & Wilhelm, J. A. (1999). The evolution of crew resource management training in commercial aviation. *The International Journal of Aviation Psychology*, *9*(1), 19–32. https://doi.org/10.1207/s15327108ijap0901_2

Morrison, E. W. (2011). Employee voice behavior: Integration and directions for future research. *Academy of Management Annals*, *5*(1), 373–412. https://doi.org/10.5465/19416520.2011.574506

NCAA Research. (2023). *NCAA coach well-being study*. NCAA. https://www.ncaa.org/sports/2023/5/24/ncaa-coach-well-being-study.aspx

Padilla, A., Hogan, R., & Kaiser, R. B. (2007). The toxic triangle: Destructive leaders, susceptible followers, and conducive environments. *The Leadership Quarterly*, *18*(3), 176–194. https://doi.org/10.1016/j.leaqua.2007.03.001

Reason, J. (1997). *Managing the risks of organizational accidents*. Ashgate.

Skinner, B. F. (1953). *Science and human behavior*. Macmillan.

Weick, K. E., & Sutcliffe, K. M. (2015). *Managing the unexpected: Sustained performance in a complex world* (3rd ed.). John Wiley & Sons.

1

THE PRESSURE LANDSCAPE

Learning Objectives

By the end of this chapter, the reader will be able to:

1. Analyze how misaligned temporal incentives produce organizational incoherence and identify which stakeholder time horizon is driving a specific dysfunctional decision.
2. Differentiate between fear-based, architecture-based, and network-based silence and determine the appropriate intervention pathway for each.
3. Assess how compounding power gradients—role hierarchy, demographic identity, gender, and legal precarity—differentially weight the silence calculus for different populations.
4. Trace the cascade failure pathway from weak signal to organizational crisis and identify intervention points where structural redesign can interrupt the sequence.

Every layer of the HPCOS architecture depends on the one beneath it. This is the first layer—and the first question: *what are we actually dealing with?* The answer requires a structural read, not an instinct. Without it, organizations can end up building psychological safety programs for a culture they have not yet diagnosed, installing voice channels that miss the populations most affected, or designing interventions for an environment they assumed rather than mapped. This chapter maps the environment. Figure 1.1 shows where it sits in the architecture.

DOI: 10.4324/9781003631217-2

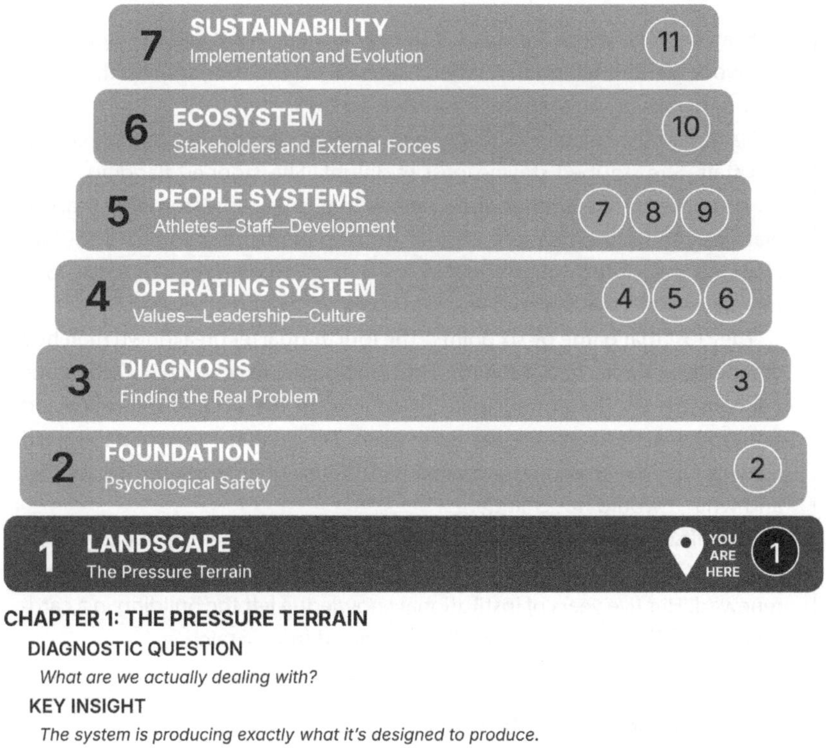

FIGURE 1.1 You Are Here—Landscape.

The HPCOS seven-layer architecture with Layer 1 (Landscape) highlighted. This chapter answers Question 1—what are we actually dealing with?—by mapping the eight pressure dimensions that shape every system built above. Getting this layer right shapes whether subsequent interventions fit the environment they are entering.

BOX 1.1 CASE STUDY — THE VIDEO COORDINATOR WHO STOPPED STAYING LATE

Composite vignette. Details changed to protect privacy.

Nadia had been the video coordinator for five seasons—outlasting three head coaches and a full front-office restructure. She was the longest-tenured person in the building who was not on the maintenance crew.

The new head coach arrived in July with his own analytics staff. His first week, he told Nadia her overnight clip packages—tactical breakdowns she had built over four years—were "not what we need going forward." He did not say what he needed instead. The new analytics lead began duplicating her work without telling her. When Nadia raised the overlap with the director of operations, he told her not to step on toes.

Nadia ran the calculus. She stopped sending packages to the full coaching staff. She stopped staying past midnight. She stopped flagging cross-game patterns—the kind of observations that only came from five years of watching the same division. One of those patterns: a divisional rival had changed their fourth-quarter defensive scheme three games in a row. She mentioned it to the analytics lead. He said, "We've got it covered."

They lost that game by six points. The fourth-quarter breakdown matched the pattern Nadia had flagged. The post-game review cited "schematic adjustments we didn't anticipate." Nadia sat in the back of the room and said nothing. Her contract was up in April. The analytics lead had the head coach's ear. The structure had already told her what speaking would cost and what it would not change.

The offseason review recommended "better opponent tendency tracking." The analytics lead was given additional staff. Nadia's contract was not renewed. Her five years of institutional knowledge left the building in a cardboard box. The next video coordinator started from scratch.

1.1 The Landscape of Elite Sport

Before mapping the pressures, it is worth standing still long enough to see the environment clearly (see Figure 1.1). Elite professional sport is a fundamentally different kind of organizational system—one that operates under conditions most industries would consider unmanageable, and most organizational theories were not designed to explain.

1.1.1 What Makes Elite Sport Structurally Distinct

Organizational psychology has produced strong frameworks for understanding workplace culture, leadership, and team dynamics. Most of those frameworks assume conditions that elite sport violates. Corporate models assume relatively stable employment, incremental performance evaluation, private feedback channels, and decision timelines measured in weeks or months. Elite sport offers none of these. The result is not simply that sport is a *harder* version of conventional work. It is that several foundational assumptions of organizational design do not hold.

Consider what an organization looks like when its workforce's primary productive asset—the human body—depreciates with every use (Nixon, 1992); when career viability is measured in years, not decades, and the end is not a planned retirement but a physical inevitability that arrives on a schedule the person does not control (Wylleman & Lavallee, 2004); when the core product is performance under uncertainty, delivered in public, evaluated in real time by millions of people with access to slow-motion replay but no access to context (Sanderson, 2011); when the labor force turns over at rates that would trigger regulatory concern in healthcare or aviation (Massey & Thaler, 2013); when salaries within a single locker room range from the league minimum to figures that exceed the operating budget of the entire support staff combined; and when roster decisions can be made overnight, trades executed mid-season, and contracts terminated with mechanisms that have no parallel in conventional employment law.

These are not complications layered on top of an otherwise normal organization. They are the foundational conditions. Any intervention—whether in leadership development or culture change—works better when it accounts for them, and risks missing its target when it does not.

1.1.2 The Building, the Season, and the Seasonal Rhythm

To read a pressure landscape, one must first understand the physical and temporal structure of the system producing it.

A professional sports organization is typically housed in a training facility that functions as a small, self-contained village. Within that building, an athlete may interact with 15–25 professionals in a single day: coaches, athletic trainers, strength and conditioning (S&C) staff, medical personnel, sport psychologists, nutritionists, equipment managers, video coordinators, communications staff, and operations personnel. Each of these roles carries different reporting lines, different professional obligations, and different relationships to the information the athlete produces. The athletic trainer who tapes an ankle hears things the head coach never will. The equipment manager who notices a player has stopped caring for his gear is reading a behavioral signal that no performance metric will capture. The video coordinator who has watched four years of an opponent's tendencies holds institutional knowledge that no analytics dashboard can replicate. The building is dense with expertise and information—and the organizational architecture determines whether that information reaches the people who need it or dies in the hallway where it was spoken (Becker, 1981; Thaler & Sunstein, 2008).

The season imposes a temporal rhythm that structures everything. Preseason compresses roster decisions into weeks. The regular season runs for months of accumulated fatigue, travel, and performance evaluation. The trade deadline collapses long-term strategy into 48-hour windows. The postseason intensifies every dynamic—the stakes, the scrutiny, the physical toll, and the emotional load—while simultaneously narrowing the cognitive bandwidth available to navigate them (Arnsten, 2009; Starcke & Brand, 2012). And then the offseason arrives, bringing its own pressures: contract negotiations, roster turnover, coaching changes, and the organizational amnesia that follows when the people who understood how things worked are replaced by people who must learn from scratch (Bridgewater, 2010). There is no period of equilibrium. The system cycles through distinct phases of pressure, each demanding a different organizational response, and the transitions between phases are themselves destabilizing.

1.1.3 Why This Terrain Resists Structural Analysis

The environment produces experiences that are genuinely extraordinary: mastery at the edge of human capacity, belonging inside a shared mission under conditions that cannot be simulated, flow states that most people will never access, and financial compensation that can change a family's trajectory for generations. These rewards are real, and they matter. They are also what makes people willing to tolerate conditions they would reject in any other workplace (Brewer et al., 1993; Meyer & Allen, 1991). The person who stays inside a dysfunctional system is not weak. The system satisfies fundamental needs—belonging, mastery, identity, and financial security—at an intensity that cannot be replicated elsewhere. That intensity is what makes the environment resistant to critique: the very people best positioned to identify structural problems are the people most invested in the system that produces them.

The resistance runs deeper than individual investment. Elite sport operates inside powerful narratives—glory, sacrifice, toughness, and exceptionalism—that can make structural critique feel like softness, and systemic analysis feel like an attack on the thing that makes sport meaningful. The refrain is familiar: *pressure is the job.* And the refrain is partly right. Pressure is inevitable in elite competition. But the question is not whether pressure exists. The question is whether the organizational systems built to operate under that pressure are designed to catch what they need to catch, protect what they need to protect, and surface information at the speed the environment demands.

Aviation did not build its safety infrastructure because flying was terrible. It built it because flying was valuable enough to justify the investment in making it survivable. Healthcare did not develop nonpunitive reporting systems because hospitals were failing. It developed them because patient outcomes mattered enough to warrant honest accounting of how errors occurred (Reason, 1997; Weick & Sutcliffe, 2015). Elite sport shares many of the structural features that led those industries to invest in safety architecture—tight coupling between units, compressed decision windows, high consequences for error, and intense public accountability—and is still building the organizational infrastructure to match. The gap between the operating conditions and the maturity of the systems designed to manage them is where the problems described in this chapter live.

1.1.4 A Note on Scope

This chapter draws primarily from professional team sport, where structural features are most visible and entrenched. Women's professional sport as a structurally distinct system—with different economic conditions, pipeline structures, and collective bargaining agreement (CBA) protections—is addressed in a subsequent chapter, not as an addendum to the analysis presented here.

Youth sport and developmental pathways are addressed in Chapter 9. Non-Western professional systems—where government funding models, centralized selection, and different collective bargaining structures reshape the pressure landscape—require adaptation of several frameworks presented here. Para-sport introduces dependency dynamics that compound the power gradients described in this chapter.

1.1.5 The Eight Dimensions: A Map Before the Territory

The rest of this chapter maps the terrain through eight pressure dimensions that define much of the operating environment of elite sport. They are not exhaustive—other dimensions exist, and the weight of each shifts across contexts, sports, and national systems. But these eight recur with enough consistency across the research and applied literature to serve as a diagnostic starting point. They are as follows:

1. **Temporal incentive misalignment**—the key stakeholders operate on conflicting time horizons, and the system has no structural mechanism to reconcile them.
2. **Zero-sum resource scarcity**—there are always more people than positions, and the competitive structure makes information hoarding and concealment rational.
3. **The body as workplace**—the athlete's body is simultaneously employee, instrument, and asset, and pain is a variable in a career calculation rather than a straightforward warning signal.
4. **Permanent selection pressure**—evaluation never stops, and the pipeline that produces elite athletes systematically rewards compliance over challenge.
5. **Asymmetric power gradients**—the people with the most information about organizational functioning are often the people with the least structural power to surface it.
6. **Cultural inheritance**—norms transmit across generations through coaching lineages, family systems, and normalization processes that are invisible from the inside.

7. **Chronic transience**—nothing is permanent, and the constant turnover of people degrades trust, erases institutional memory, and resets organizational learning.
8. **Neurobiological degradation under sustained stress**—the operating conditions narrow the cognitive capacity of the people navigating them, at precisely the moments when complex thinking matters most.

These dimensions do not operate independently. They stack. And the mechanisms through which they suppress voice, distort decisions, and degrade organizational functioning—the silence calculus, the golden handcuffs problem, and the cascade failure pathway—are mapped in Section 1.3, after the dimensions themselves have been described. The rest of the book tracks these dynamics through a core diagnostic metric: Speed of Truth—the elapsed time between someone recognizing a problem and that information reaching a person with the authority to act on it. Every pressure dimension in this chapter can be read through that metric. The landscape determines how fast truth travels—and this chapter is where that speed gets diagnosed.

1.2 The Eight Pressure Dimensions

1.2.1 Temporal Incentive Misalignment

Everyone in elite sport is on a clock. The clocks do not synchronize. The athlete's body is running out. The coach's record is being counted. The owner's investment is compounding on a timeline that has nothing to do with either. March (1991) describes the broader pattern: organizations under performance pressure consistently weigh short-term optimization over long-term adaptation because the returns on exploitation are more certain, more immediate, and more proximate than the returns on exploration. Elite sport is a particularly clear expression of that tendency. The coach in a contract year does not have the luxury of a developmental timeline. The GM who believes in a three-year rebuild may not survive two losing seasons to reach it. The athlete whose body is breaking down cannot wait for the organization to settle on its long-term strategy. Everyone acts rationally inside their own window. The resulting system reflects the sum of those individual logics, which do not add up to a coherent organizational strategy—and the system has no built-in mechanism to reconcile them. Table 1.1 maps the four primary stakeholder clocks operating simultaneously.

The misalignment compounds with stakeholder salience. Mitchell et al.'s (1997) salience framework identifies three attributes—power, legitimacy, and urgency—that determine whose interests dominate organizational decision-making (see Figure 1.2). In most industries, these attributes are distributed unevenly but remain relatively stable. In elite sport, urgency shifts with the calendar.

TABLE 1.1 Stakeholder Time Horizons in Elite Sport

Stakeholder	*Clock Type*	*Time Horizon*	*Primary Driver*
Athlete	Biological	10–15 years	Physical capacity, injury accumulation, age-related decline (Wylleman and Lavallee 2004)
Coach	Results	2–4 years	Win–loss record, playoff appearance, owner patience (Bridgewater 2010; Hughes et al., 2010)
Owner	Investment	Decades	Franchise valuation, revenue growth, private equity returns (Nauright and Ramfjord 2010)
Agent	Commission	Transaction-based	Contract size, deal frequency, client retention (Shropshire and Davis 2008); Dunn 2021)

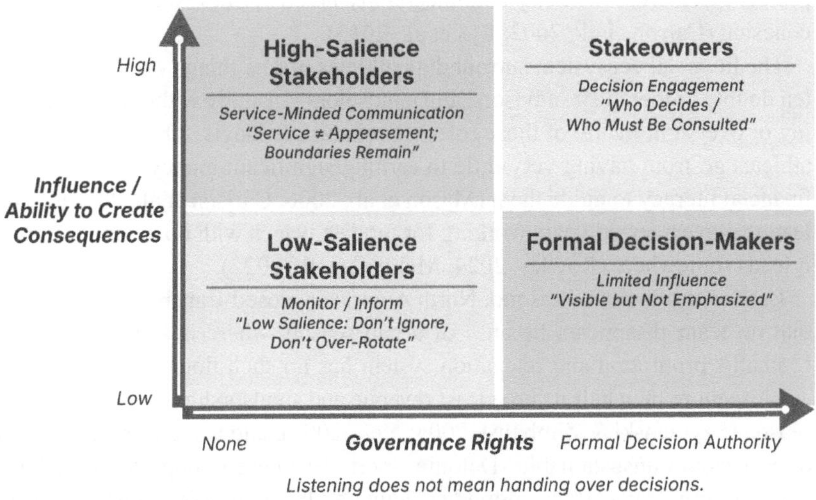

FIGURE 1.2 Stakeholder Salience in Elite Sport.

Four stakeholder groups mapped against Mitchell et al.'s (1997) salience attributes—power, legitimacy, and urgency. In elite sport, urgency almost always belongs to the actor with the shortest clock, which is why short-term thinking dominates even when long-term strategy is formally endorsed.

During a playoff push, the coach's two-to-four-year clock becomes the loudest voice in the room. During the offseason, the owner's investment horizon reasserts itself. The agent's transaction clock spikes at the trade deadline and in free agency. The athlete's biological clock ticks underneath all of it, unheard until something breaks. Short-term thinking does not dominate because people lack vision. It dominates because urgency, by its nature, is more salient than patience—and the system has no built-in mechanism to counterbalance that reality.

1.2.2 Zero-Sum Resource Scarcity

There are always more players than roster spots. That fact alone is enough to reshape every relationship in a locker room. Teammates are also competitors. Information gets hoarded rather than shared, because what you know might be the thing that keeps you employed (Deutsch, 1949; Connelly et al., 2012).

The instability is constant. NFL rosters turn over by as much as 40% each offseason (Massey & Thaler, 2013). In Major League Soccer, the gap between a Designated Player's salary and a minimum-salary athlete's can be sevenfold, with some players earning near poverty-level wages (MLSPA, 2024; AP, 2023). Whether contracts are guaranteed or not changes the entire feel of a locker room—how much risk people take, how much they share, how carefully they protect themselves. Scarcity and uncertainty breed cliques, silos, and fractured cohesion (Carron et al., 2002; Eys et al., 2015).

The financial ecosystem surrounding athletes makes things worse. Agents often double as therapists, advisors, and counselors—usually without formal training or oversight in any of those roles (Shropshire & Davis, 2008). Many young athletes go from having very little to earning significant money with almost no financial literacy to guide them (Mason et al., 2006; Carlson et al., 2015). Minor league players spend years working for modest wages with no guarantee any of it leads somewhere (Rowley, 2024; McLeod et al., 2022).

League structure matters too. North America's closed-franchise model means that no team disappears because of a bad season—there is a floor. European football's promotion and relegation system has no such floor. A relegated club can lose more than half its broadcast revenue and sponsorship income in a single season (Szymanski & Zimbalist, 2005; Noll, 2002), and wage-to-revenue ratios often become unsustainable (Deloitte Sports Business Group, 2023). When a club's future is uncertain, individual vulnerability gets worse—especially for players on expiring contracts who are fighting for their own careers while the organization around them may be collapsing.

None of this, though, compares to the thing every professional athlete eventually faces: the cliff. The average career ends before the age of 30 years. When it does, income, daily structure, identity, and physical capacity all change at once—often alongside decades of chronic pain (Wylleman & Lavallee, 2004; Weir et al., 2009; Mez et al., 2017). These transitions are especially difficult because elite sport tends to narrow an athlete's sense of self around a single role—what the literature calls identity foreclosure—leaving limited psychological infrastructure for life after the game (Brewer et al., 1993; Marcia, 1966; Park et al., 2013; Gouttebarge et al., 2019).

And the cliff doesn't wait for retirement. It shapes behavior long before then—in every contract year, every injury decision, every moment an athlete weighs whether being honest is worth the risk to the only professional identity they have ever had.

1.2.3 The Body as Workplace

In most industries, the employee uses tools to produce value. In elite sport, the employee *is* the tool. The body is simultaneously the worker, the instrument, the asset, and the product—and it is the one thing in the system that cannot be replaced without replacing the person. In this context, pain is less a warning signal than a variable in an ongoing calculation about availability, contract status, and competitive position (Nixon, 1992). Athletes routinely make decisions about injury disclosure based on what is at stake professionally, and the research on this point is consistent (Nixon, 1992; Kerr et al., 2014; Kroshus et al., 2015).

That calculation is shaped by a structural tension that no individual created, but everyone inside the system navigates: the medical staff are employed by the team. The physician whose clinical judgment determines whether an athlete returns to play reports, directly or indirectly, to the same organization that benefits from that athlete being available. Most people in these roles are doing careful, conscientious work under genuinely difficult conditions. The issue is not the quality of their judgment but the architecture they are asked to exercise it within. Athletes underreport concussion symptoms not because they fail to understand the risk but because the incentive structure around disclosure is ambiguous at best (Kroshus et al., 2015; Kerr et al., 2014). The NFL illustrates the structural pattern clearly: injury incidence in professional football exceeds that of other major collision sports, including ice hockey and rugby, yet the NFL remains the only major North American league where the majority of player contracts are not fully guaranteed (Staudohar, 1996; league CBA provisions as of the 2023–2024 season). The resulting gap between physical toll and contractual protection shapes how athletes think about disclosure. No one designed it to suppress information. The structure produces that effect regardless of intent.

Meanwhile, the body has become increasingly visible to the organization through global positioning system (GPS) tracking, wearable technology, and biometric monitoring that can detect fatigue, workload thresholds, and recovery deficits in real time (Bourdon et al., 2017). These tools offer genuine performance and safety benefits. They also shift the information asymmetry: the data flows to the organization rather than to an independent advocate for the athlete's long-term health, meaning that the organization may know more about the body's condition than the athlete chooses to disclose.

In contact sports, the shadow of brain injury is part of the daily psychological landscape. The evidence of pervasive chronic traumatic encephalopathy (CTE) pathology in contact sports is well established (Mez et al., 2017; McKee et al., 2023), and the risk is compounded by early youth exposure and the accumulation of sub-concussive impacts long before the professional contract is signed (Stamm et al., 2015; Alosco et al., 2017). Grashow et al. (2024) found that longer career duration in professional football was associated with elevated rates of later-life health conditions—meaning that the body that earns the paycheck is also the body accumulating the cost of earning it. Athletes in contact sports are broadly aware of this reality, but that awareness does not typically change the decision to play. What it changes is the willingness to talk openly about what hurts and what worries them.

1.2.4 Permanent Selection Pressure

Elite sport operates as a continuous evaluation environment. At every level, more people are filtered out than advance—and the filtering does not stop at the professional level. Youth sport in high-performance countries functions as a sorting pipeline that selects for early physical maturation, coachability, and family resources sufficient to support the investment (Green, 2005). Some of these systems overweight early physical development at the expense of late-blooming talent—in most professional leagues, players born just after the age-group cutoff date are dramatically overrepresented (Cobley et al., 2009).

The pipeline does not only sort for physical capacity—it also shapes behavioral norms. Athletes who advanced through the system learned, at each stage, that continued selection depended on alignment with institutional expectations. By the time they reach the professional level, the population has been shaped by a decade of selection pressure that systematically rewarded compliance over challenge (Jacobs et al., 2017). The introduction of Name, Image, and Likeness (NIL) deals in collegiate and developmental sport has shifted intense financial pressures further upstream, compounding the selection pressure at an earlier developmental stage. The cost–benefit calculation around speaking up does not begin at the professional contract. It begins at the first academy tryout.

BOX 1.2 PSYCHOLOGY SIDELINES WITH DR. MCB — THE LINE BETWEEN DEMANDING AND DAMAGING

The question I get asked most often: *how do I make sure I do not mess up my kid?*

The honest answer: care more about the kid than the performance. Kids learn quickly, and they repeat what gets rewarded. High standards, honest feedback, and real consequences are not inherently damaging. Young athletes can thrive in demanding environments–when those environments are also characterized by safety, support, and genuine care for the person behind the performance.

The line gets crossed when the message shifts from *I believe you can do better* to *your value here is conditional on results,* when feedback becomes humiliation, and when the coach's emotional regulation becomes the athlete's responsibility.

The parent who raises a concern risks their child's access. The parent who stays silent risks their child's welfare. There is no cost-free choice.

The developmental pathway also filters for compliance, coachability, and the ability to suppress needs that conflict with team demands. When a child shows promise, the family restructures. The investment is financial, emotional, and logistical—and increasingly, it becomes identity (Dorsch et al., 2015). The parent who enters the system learns its norms—not from a handbook, but from other parents, from coaches, and from what gets rewarded and what gets punished. The parent faces a version of the silence calculus mediated through their child: the deeper the investment, the harder it becomes to challenge the system. Over time, the culture reproduces itself by selecting for people who fit its existing norms—which means that the people who might have offered a different perspective are disproportionately the ones who did not advance through the pipeline (Jacobs et al., 2017).

1.2.5 Asymmetric Power Gradients

Coaches hold career-determining authority over athletes—selection, playing time, role, and contract recommendations all flow through their judgment. That authority reaches past hierarchy into livelihood and identity. Research consistently finds that power asymmetry predicts silence (Morrison, 2014; Morrison & Milliken, 2000; Sherf et al., 2021). When the perceived cost of speaking exceeds the expected benefit, people stay quiet. This is not a character deficit; it is a rational calculation.

The power map has shifted in ways that complicate simple hierarchical assumptions. Star athletes now often hold more organizational leverage than their support staff. Guaranteed contracts, social media platforms, salary cap structures that undervalue elite talent, and free agency have reshaped organizational power dynamics (Coon, 2019). Micropolitical research confirms that coaches' effectiveness and longevity depend not only on win–loss records but also on their ability to gain the approval of "contextual power brokers" (p. 229)—athletes, other coaches, and owners—whose informal influence shapes organizational decisions (Potrac & Jones, 2009). A star's informal influence can affect whether support staff keep their positions. The staff are aware of it. The direction of the power gradient has shifted, but the suppressive effect on voice has not—it has simply moved to a different set of people.

Above the team, above the league, sits another tier of structural authority: national sport organizations, international federations, and governing bodies such as the International Olympic Committee (IOC), the Fédération Internationale de Football Association (FIFA), and the National Collegiate Athletic Association (NCAA). These entities set policy, control eligibility, distribute funding, and manage reputational consequences that extend beyond any single team. For athletes whose identity and income depend on access to elite-level competition, the governing body holds structural leverage that makes most other power gradients look negotiable by comparison (Tuakli-Wosornu et al., 2021).

Some of the most consequential psychological safety failures in sport have occurred at this layer—cases where structural conditions created the environment for harm to persist because reporting mechanisms were absent, inadequate, or subordinated to institutional reputation. The USA Gymnastics case involved reports of sexual abuse by a team physician that went unaddressed for years (Kwiatkowski et al., 2016; Armour & Axon, 2018). Hockey Canada settled sexual assault cases through a confidential fund without public disclosure (Westhead & Strashin, 2022). The National Women's Soccer League (NWSL) investigation revealed systemic patterns in which complaints were handled through quiet separations that allowed abusive coaches to move to new organizations (Yates, 2022; Brackenridge, 2001; Mountjoy et al., 2016; Vertommen et al., 2022). These cases share a structural signature: insufficient independent reporting channels, institutional reputation interests competing with individual welfare, and power gradients steep enough to make silence the rational calculation for anyone considering disclosure.

1.2.6 Cultural Inheritance

Norms transmit across generations. The head coach learned from the previous one, who learned from the one before that. Practices that would be flagged as harmful in other professional contexts can survive as "tradition" because the people who transmit them experienced them as formative (Kerr & Stirling, 2012). The refrain—"When I played hockey, we did not have all of these extras and we were fine"—reflects survivorship bias (Denrell, 2003): the people still in the system are disproportionately the people for whom the system worked. Those who left—whether by choice, by injury, or by exclusion—are not in the room to offer a different account of the same experience. This is not an indictment of any individual coach's intentions. It is a structural observation about how norms persist unchallenged when the feedback loop is incomplete. *The diagnostic question:*

which current practices in your organization are justified by the phrase "that is how we have always done it"—and what information would the organization need to evaluate whether those practices still serve performance?

The cultural inheritance pathway has a specific transmission vehicle: hazing. In the most comprehensive NCAA data, 80% of athletes reported experiencing activities that qualify as hazing—yet only 12% identified themselves as having been hazed (Hoover, 1999; Allan & Madden, 2008). Notably, 80% percent experienced it, and 12% recognized it. The gap between experience and recognition is itself diagnostic: it illustrates what successful normalization looks like from the inside.

The team-building justification does not survive empirical scrutiny. Van Raalte et al. (2007) found a negative relationship between hazing severity and task cohesion, and Waldron and Kowalski (2009) documented how the ambiguity of hazing rituals allowed participants to reframe harmful experiences as bonding. At the governing body layer, Hockey Canada's sexual assault cases revealed the institutional architecture that normalization can produce: a confidential fund used to settle sexual assault claims without public disclosure (Westhead & Strashin, 2022). The fund was not a breakdown of the system. It was a product of the system's internal logic—an architecture that prioritized institutional continuity over transparency. *The diagnostic question: if 80% of your athletes have experienced something but only 12% recognize it, what does your organization's normalization look like from the inside—and who would be in a position to name it?*

1.2.7 Chronic Transience

Nothing is permanent. Rosters turn over. Coaches are hired and fired. Ownership changes hands. Every investment in the system carries an expiration date: trust built with a coach who will be replaced, development invested in an athlete who will be traded. High-turnover organizations stay stuck in the earliest stage of trust—where reliability has not yet been demonstrated (Mayer et al., 1995). Coaching transitions are where this hits hardest—in English football, median tenure for managers is three years or less (Audas et al., 2002; Bridgewater, 2010), and comparable churn characterizes most professional leagues.

Nadia's five years of cross-game pattern recognition—the kind of institutional knowledge that takes seasons to accumulate and cannot be transferred in an onboarding document—left the building when her contract was not renewed. The incoming coach faces a difficult diagnostic problem: the information system that would reveal what is and is not working is the system the previous regime built. Most new coaches address this by bringing their own people—which makes short-term sense but resets the trust clock organization-wide.

International athletes carry the full weight of transience—plus legal precarity. Work permits and residency often depend on continued employment with the sponsoring organization. A termination does not just end the job—it can end the right to remain in the country. Cultural and language barriers compound this: the informal networks where real organizational intelligence moves are already difficult to access for anyone outside the dominant culture.

1.2.8 Neurobiological Degradation Under Sustained Stress

The structural pressures described in this chapter do not remain external. They get inside.

Under acute stress, the brain shifts resources from the prefrontal cortex—responsible for complex reasoning, long-term planning, and integrating conflicting information—to subcortical systems optimized for rapid threat response (Arnsten, 2009). This is adaptive when the threat is immediate and physical. It is maladaptive when the threat is a contract negotiation or a staff conflict that requires nuance and tolerance of ambiguity.

The cognitive effects are well documented: attentional narrowing reduces the number of cues a decision-maker can process (Easterbrook, 1959; Staal, 2004), risk assessment shifts toward threat avoidance, and the capacity to hold multiple perspectives simultaneously—exactly the capacity that complex organizational decisions require—is the first thing to go (Starcke & Brand, 2012).

Under chronic stress, the degradation becomes structural. Sustained cortisol exposure weakens prefrontal connectivity, reducing working memory capacity and impulse regulation as an operating baseline (Woo et al., 2021; Arnsten, 2009). Chronic circadian disruption from the professional travel schedule compounds the impairment (Leota et al., 2023). The coach in month 14 of a losing season is not making decisions with the same brain that started in September—and is unlikely to recognize the degradation because the metacognitive capacity to monitor one's own cognitive state is itself prefrontal and therefore itself degraded.

The hardest implication is recursive: the leaders who need to recognize that the system is degrading their judgment are using the degraded judgment to assess whether they are impaired. Metacognitive monitoring—the capacity to evaluate one's own cognitive state—is itself a prefrontal function, and it is offline under exactly the conditions that would make it most necessary. This is why structural safeguards matter more than individual insight. The system must be designed to catch what the people inside it can no longer see—not because they are incompetent, but because the operating conditions have narrowed what competent people can process.

1.3 The Structural Mechanisms

The eight pressure dimensions do not produce dysfunction in isolation. They produce it through shared mechanisms—structural patterns that operate across dimensions and determine how pressure converts into silence, concealment, and organizational failure. This section maps those mechanisms: the silence calculus, the demographic and gender dynamics that load it differently across populations, the architecture of disclosure and health access, the populations the system is least structured to hear, and the structural traps—the golden handcuffs problem and the cascade failure pathway—that hold the pattern in place.

1.3.1 The Silence Calculus

Every structural feature described so far converges on a shared mechanism: the silence calculus. The cost side of the equation stacks career risk, identity threat, power gradient steepness, demographic credibility, and legal precarity against a benefit side that depends entirely on the organization's structural capacity to respond. When the cost exceeds the expected benefit, silence is the rational output—and the structure, not the person, is the primary variable.

Nadia's calculation illustrates the pattern: she flagged the opponent's schematic change to the analytics lead, received a dismissive acknowledgment, and stopped pushing—not because she lacked conviction, but because the structure had already communicated what speaking further would cost and what it would not change.

The silence calculus becomes self-reinforcing under the conditions described in Section 1.2.8: stress narrows attention, narrowed attention misses signals, missed signals produce crises, and crises produce more stress. The system does not select for people who make bad decisions. It creates conditions under which good decision-makers make worse ones and then evaluates them as though the conditions did not exist.

> **BOX 1.3 TIMEOUT — THE CALCULUS HAS A DIRECTION**
>
> Notice what the silence calculus predicts: the people with the most direct information about organizational functioning are often the people with the least structural power to surface it. The athlete knows about the injury. The athletic trainer knows about the culture. The international player knows about the exclusion. The information exists in the system—it tends to concentrate in positions the system is least structured to hear. The diagnostic question is not "why don't people speak up?" It is "what about the structure makes staying silent the more rational choice?"

1.3.2 Three Types of Organizational Silence

Before fear enters the calculation, the structure has already determined who has access to the conversation and who does not. The performance staff are not in the room when selection is discussed. The medical team is not consulted when the travel schedule is set. The sport psychologist hears about trades through the news. No one can speak up in a meeting they were not invited to. Some silence has nothing to do with fear. The architecture produced it before anyone had the chance to feel afraid.

Hiring and promotion pipelines in sport tend to be familiarity-based—coaches hire coaches they played with, and general managers hire people they worked under—which produces predictable exclusionary effects. In men's professional sport, these networks are overwhelmingly male because the generations that produced today's leadership were overwhelmingly male (Cunningham, 2010; LaVoi, 2016; Norman, 2010). This distinction matters diagnostically because the intervention for each type of silence differs. Table 1.2 maps the three types for diagnostic reference.

TABLE 1.2 Three Types of Organizational Silence—Diagnostic Differentiation

Type	*Mechanism*	*Diagnostic Question*	*Required Intervention*
Fear-based silence	Person could speak but calculates that cost exceeds benefit—career risk, retaliation, and identity threat	"Do people here believe speaking up is safe?"	Build psychological safety infrastructure—reporting systems, nonpunitive escalation, ad leadership modeling
Architecture-based silence	Person is structurally excluded from the conversation—not in the room, not on the distribution list, not consulted	"Who is missing from the rooms where decisions are made?"	Change who is in the room—restructure meeting access, decision-input protocols, consultation requirements
Network-based silence	Person cannot enter the informal channels where real information and influence flow—familiarity-based pipelines, homogeneous networks	"How do people enter the influence network here—and who cannot?"	Restructure access pipelines—mentorship, sponsorship, hiring practices, network diversification

Status: Theoretically grounded. Integrates organizational silence research (Morrison, 2014; Morrison & Milliken, 2000) with structural exclusion literature (Cunningham, 2010). Sport-specific three-type differentiation and diagnostic questions are original to this chapter. Not a validated instrument.

The three-type taxonomy does not replace the silence calculus—it specifies its scope. The silence calculus applies to fear-based silence, where a person could speak but calculates that the cost exceeds the benefit. Architecture-based and network-based silence operate upstream: the person never reaches the point of deciding whether to speak because the structure has already excluded them. Where CBAs exist, they set a floor beneath the power gradient (Staudohar, 1996). Where they are absent—individual sports, many women's leagues—the gradient steepens further.

1.3.3 The Demographic Power Map

The silence calculus does not load equally across the people inside the system. Demographic identity—race, gender, sexuality—adds weight to the cost side of the equation before any individual decision about speaking is made.

Race. In North American professional sport, the playing population in the highest-revenue leagues is disproportionately Black—approximately 70% in the NBA and 57% in the NFL—while ownership, front offices, and head coaching positions remain disproportionately white (Lapchick, 2024). The people generating the labor and the people making career-determining decisions about that labor do not share the same demographic profile. This is a structural fact with measurable consequences for voice.

Research on racial dynamics in sport organizations documents the pattern across coaching hires, leadership pipelines, disciplinary actions, and media framing (Cunningham, 2010; Singer, 2005). Race adds weight to the cost side of the silence calculus: an athlete whose credibility is already discounted by systemic patterns carries additional cost into every decision about whether to speak. The evidence is direct: concerns raised by Black employees are evaluated as less legitimate and more threatening than identical concerns raised by white employees (Ashburn-Nardo et al., 2003; see also Cunningham, 2010, on leadership pipeline exclusion). In sport, where disciplinary actions, fines, and suspensions fall disproportionately on Black athletes (Singer, 2005), the cost of speaking is not hypothetical—it is empirically documented.

Gender. Men's professional team sport was built within male institutional traditions. The locker room, the team bus, the coaching offices, and the informal networks through which real information moves—these spaces carry the social codes of male-dominant institutions. Women working inside these environments navigate a constant ambient negotiation that their male colleagues do not experience: how to be present without being perceived as intrusive, authoritative without being perceived as threatening, warm enough to build rapport without being sexualized, and direct enough to be taken seriously without being labeled "difficult" (Norman, 2010; LaVoi, 2016). This is the double bind: the traits required for credibility—directness, confidence, and willingness to challenge—are evaluated differently when they come from a woman (Eagly & Karau, 2002; Heilman, 2012). The informal channels described in Section 1.3.2 are often inaccessible to women—not through explicit exclusion but through social dynamics that make participation awkward or professionally risky.

The high-profile cases documented in Section 1.2.5 are not isolated incidents. They represent the visible surface of a broader structural pattern of sexual harassment (Brackenridge, 2001; Fasting et al., 2004; Mountjoy et al., 2016). For a woman reporting sexual harassment in men's professional sport, the calculus carries a specific weight: *if I report, I become the disruption. My career in this environment ends. His likely does not.* Retaliation risk and career consequences for reporting are higher in environments with steep power gradients and few women in leadership (Fitzgerald et al., 1997; McLaughlin et al., 2012). Professional sport meets both criteria.

BOX 1.4 PSYCHOLOGY SIDELINES WITH DR. MCB — WHAT IT IS ACTUALLY LIKE TO BE THE WOMAN IN THE ROOM

You learn the codes fast. You learn that the way you dress matters more than it should. You learn that there is a volume at which you can speak and be heard, and it is narrower than the range available to your male colleagues. You learn that certain hallway conversations stop when you approach—not because anyone dislikes you, but because the social calculus of the space has not updated to include you.

You learn to pick your battles with precision because every battle costs more when you are the one who "made it about gender." You learn to channel your expertise through people the room already trusts—which sometimes means watching someone else present your idea and accepting that the idea reaching the decision-maker matters more than the attribution.

And here is the part that does not get said enough: most of the men you work with are decent people—great people. They are not deliberately exclusionary. They are operating inside a system that was built before you arrived, and they do not see what the system does because it was designed for them. The system is not hostile. It is habitual. And habits are harder to change than hostility because no one thinks they need to.

The toughness premium and gendered masculinity. In elite sport, mental toughness is treated as the price of entry. The popular definition—suppressing doubt and pain by sheer force of will—narrows the construct considerably from what the research describes (Gucciardi et al., 2015). Toughness defined this way prioritizes the appearance of invulnerability over the adaptability and psychological safety that high-performance systems require (Edmondson, 1999). In men's sport environments, toughness is inextricable from heteronormative masculinity norms (Anderson, 2011). When toughness functions as an identity marker rather than a performance capacity, it stigmatizes help-seeking and emotional disclosure (Bauman, 2016). The silence calculus already includes identity threat as a cost variable. The toughness premium explains why that variable carries so much weight in sport contexts: when vulnerability is incompatible with the self-concept the environment has constructed, the calculus is no longer purely about career survival. It becomes about psychological coherence. The athlete who conceals a struggle is protecting not only their roster spot but their identity. The career calculation says *I will lose my spot.* The identity calculation says *I will lose myself.*

The scale of LGBTQ+ exclusion illustrates the point concretely. As of 2024, the number of male athletes who have come out as gay while actively competing at or near the top tier of North American professional sport remains vanishingly small—Jason Collins in the NBA (2013), Carl Nassib in the NFL (2021), and Luke Prokop, who came out publicly in 2021 while in the NHL prospect pipeline. The brevity of the list is itself the data point. The Denison and Kitchen (2015) international study found that 80% of respondents had witnessed or experienced homophobia in sport. That silence is structural. Table 1.3 maps the three pathways through which the toughness premium loads the silence calculus.

Self-medication and the road culture. When formal help-seeking carries a significant identity cost, self-medication becomes a predictable adaptation. Alcohol use in professional team sport is not merely tolerated—it is culturally embedded as bonding ritual, stress release, and performance of toughness. The toughness premium means that admitting a problem with alcohol carries the same identity cost as admitting any other vulnerability (Reardon & Factor, 2010; Reardon et al., 2019; Gouttebarge et al., 2015). The prescription pipeline compounds this: treatment for sport injuries often begins with legitimate medical intervention inside an environment that incentivizes return-to-play over full recovery. The transition from prescribed use to dependency is gradual and structurally predictable (Cottler et al., 2011). The self-medication pathway persists because the formal one is functionally inaccessible—not because individuals lack the will to use it, but because the cost of accessing it is loaded by the same cultural variables. *The diagnostic question: when someone in your organization describes a colleague as "mentally tough," are they describing adaptability under pressure—or the suppression of information the organization needs?*

TABLE 1.3 The Toughness Premium—Three Pathways to Silence

Pathway	*Mechanism*	*Silence Calculus Effect*	*Diagnostic Question*
Career survival	Pain and doubt are economic calculations—disclosure risks deselection, reduced playing time, or contract non-renewal Nixon (1992); Kerr et al. (2014)	Cost variable: career risk. The athlete concealing a struggle is protecting their roster spot.	"What happens to athletes here who admit they are struggling?"
Identity coherence	Toughness functions as an identity marker; vulnerability is incompatible with the self-concept the environment has constructed (Brewer et al., 1993)	Cost variable: identity threat. The athlete is protecting not their position but their psychological coherence—*I will lose myself.*	"Is toughness here a performance capacity or a membership requirement?"
Gendered masculinity norms	In men's sport, toughness is inextricable from heteronormative masculinity; emotional disclosure and LGBTQ+ identity carry compounded identity costs (Anderson, 2011; Denison & Kitchen, 2015)	Cost variables: identity threat + demographic credibility discount. Disclosure risks both self-concept and social standing within the dominant culture.	"Who in this environment would pay the highest price for showing vulnerability—and why?"

1.3.4 The Architecture of Disclosure and Health Access

To read the landscape, one must read the physical building. The training facility is not a neutral container. It maps social systems onto a floor plan, and the floor plan quietly shapes what gets said and to whom.

The training room functions as the organization's true information hub—not because it was designed for that purpose, but because the architecture of the interaction removes the formality of seeking help. Getting an ankle taped is a daily routine. Sitting on a table while someone works on a hamstring creates a conversational context that no office can replicate. The athlete is physically still, the interaction is expected, and the social cost of talking is near zero. This is where athletes tend to open up. The sport psychologist's office, by contrast, is frequently placed near coaching suites or isolated in medical wings, meaning that a visit requires a deliberate, visible choice in an environment where that visibility carries weight (Becker, 1981; Thaler & Sunstein, 2008).

This creates an interesting structural tension. The training room's architectural advantage—its informality, its daily access, and its low barrier to conversation—makes it the space where athletes are most likely to share what is going on. But the person receiving that information—the athletic trainer—operates within the same organizational structure described above, where the boundaries around how that information can be held or shared are not always clear. The information flows to a natural and trusted place. The question is whether the organizational architecture around that place is designed to protect both the person who shared and the person who received it.

Any clinical or professional staff member providing care to athletes sits in a structural trap. Whether employed by the team, contracted independently, or shared across multiple organizations, the core problem is the same: the person providing support is embedded in a system with competing interests in the information that support might surface. Contractual agreements may require reporting of substance use or fitness-affecting conditions to management, regardless of whether the athlete consented to disclosure (Moore, 2003; Andersen et al., 2001). In a survey of New Zealand sports medicine physicians, most identified confidentiality as their primary area of ethical conflict; half reported having disclosed sensitive player health information to the organization (Anderson & Gerrard, 2005).

In English football academies, this plays out as the structure predicts: coaches attempt to extract confidential information, clinicians self-censor to protect the therapeutic relationship, and invisible walls form between staff members (Bickley et al., 2016). The NFL's 2020 CBA addressed one layer of this problem by mandating that every team employ a licensed behavioral health clinician—a structural intervention that changed staffing, not just culture. But the conflict of interest persists across employment models and across leagues: the employer of the clinician is also the employer of the patient.

1.3.5 The Invisible and Shadow Staff

The pressure landscape is typically described through the experience of athletes and coaches. A complete picture includes the people who hold the organization together and are almost never included in the conversation about it.

Athletic trainers arrive before the players and leave after them. They hold more clinically sensitive information about more people than anyone else in the building. They are rarely consulted on organizational decisions that directly affect their work. Equipment managers often know which players are struggling before anyone else does—because a player who stops caring about his equipment has stopped caring about something larger. Video coordinators spend more hours in the building than most coaches. These roles sit low in the formal hierarchy, high in informational access, and almost entirely outside the culture conversation.

The silence calculus for support staff is among the steepest in the organization: less job security, more exposure to dysfunction, fewer channels for raising concerns. These positions function as early-warning indicators. When support staff turnover is high, when the video coordinator who has been there for eight years leaves unexpectedly—the organization is producing information about its own internal conditions. The diagnostic question is whether anyone is structured to read it.

A parallel population operates outside the organization without formal accountability. Private performance coaches, physical therapists, chefs, and consultants hired directly by athletes or agents exist outside the formal organizational structure but can wield considerable influence over the athlete's daily choices. When a private trainer's protocol conflicts with the team's official medical directives, it creates a friction point where internal staff hold formal responsibility but lack functional authority.

1.3.6 The Visibility Problem

Elite sport is evaluated in real time by millions of people with no professional obligation to be accurate or fair. A mistake in the 53rd minute is on social media before the final whistle. The psychological consequences are measurable: public scrutiny and social media abuse are associated with increased anxiety, reduced well-being, and avoidance behavior in elite athletes (Geurin, 2017; Kavanagh et al., 2021).

The social media economy operates on a logic that rewards speed and provocation over accuracy: a 10-second clip becomes a narrative, and a difficult week becomes a character assessment. Athletes learn to give answers that contain no information. The public narrative about an athlete or a team may bear little resemblance to what is actually happening inside the building—and yet it shapes front-office decisions, affects contract negotiations, and alters the athlete's standing in real time (Sanderson, 2011). The legalization of sports gambling (*Murphy v. National Collegiate Athletic Association*, 2018) has added a financial layer to this visibility: prop bets on individual performance mean a single athlete's output is someone's money, and when that money is lost, the abuse follows—often targeted along racial and gender lines (Kavanagh et al., 2021). *The diagnostic question: when a public narrative about your organization diverges from the internal reality, how long does it take for the internal reality to reach the people making decisions—and does the external narrative change the decision before the internal data arrives?*

1.3.7 The Golden Handcuffs

The rewards of elite sport—belonging, mastery, identity, and financial security—are powerful enough to hold people inside a system whose structural costs are measurable at the population scale. Table 1.4 consolidates the available prevalence data.

Roughly one in three current elite athletes reports anxiety or depression symptoms; prevalence among former athletes remains elevated relative to general population estimates (Gouttebarge et al., 2019). Grashow et al. (2024) found that longer career duration in professional football predicted elevated rates of later-life health conditions—meaning that the structural features that keep athletes competing longer may also be associated with the greatest downstream health costs. Coaches and high-performance support staff meet probable clinical caseness at comparable rates—and 80% of coaches were unaware of available mental health resources, a structural access gap rather than an individual awareness deficit (Pilkington et al., 2022).

The clinical data illustrate the golden handcuffs problem at the population scale. The diagnostic question is what structural changes would reduce the cost—without dismantling the features that make elite sport worth pursuing.

TABLE 1.4 Population-Level Mental Health Prevalence in Elite Sport

Population	*Domain*	*Prevalence*	*Source*
Current elite athletes	Anxiety/depression symptoms	~34%	Gouttebarge et al. (2019)
Current elite athletes	Psychological distress	19.6%	Gouttebarge et al. (2019)
Current elite athletes	Alcohol misuse	18.8%	Gouttebarge et al. (2019)
Current elite athletes	Suicidal ideation	6.9–18%	Gill et al. (2024)
Former elite athletes	Anxiety/depression symptoms	~26%	Gouttebarge et al. (2019)
NFL players	Later-life health conditions	Inverted U-shape (highest in intermediate careers)	Grashow et al. (2024)
Coaches	Clinical caseness	43.6%	Pilkington et al. (2022)
High-performance support staff	Clinical caseness	40.1%	Pilkington et al. (2022)
Coaches/support staff	Risky alcohol consumption	41.8%	Pilkington et al. (2022)
Coaches	Discussing athlete mental health more than pre-pandemic	>80%	NCAA Research (2023)

FIGURE 1.3 The Cascade Failure Pathway.

A weak signal enters a system without detection infrastructure, sits unowned long enough to compound, and escalates into an organizational crisis. The figure traces this sequence and marks the intervention points where structural redesign can interrupt it.

1.3.8 The Cascade Failure Pathway

Industries such as aviation, healthcare, and nuclear power operate under conditions that make failure both likely and costly: tight coupling between units, compressed decision windows, high consequences for error, and intense public accountability (Weick & Sutcliffe, 2015). They responded by building safety infrastructure to match—nonpunitive reporting systems, structured escalation protocols, and independent oversight (Reason, 1997; Westrum, 2004).

Professional sport shares every one of those structural features. The gap is not in the severity of outcomes but in the maturity of the safety architecture built to prevent them. That mismatch is where weak signals sit long enough to become crises. Figure 1.3 traces this cascade and highlights the intervention points where the sequence can be interrupted.

BOX 1.5 SKEPTIC'S CORNER — PRESSURE IS THE JOB

The objection: "Elite sport is supposed to be hard. People need thicker skin. The system is not the issue."

The answer: Pressure is inevitable, but it shouldn't impact truth. When incentives punish bad news, truth slows down. When time horizons are misaligned, decisions tilt toward optics over outcomes. These are not personality problems–they are predictable system effects. Toughness helps individuals tolerate stress, but it does not fix information bottlenecks, governance ambiguity, or the cost of speaking. HPCOS starts by naming the environment so later layers (safety, diagnosis, decision architecture) are designed for reality–not for speeches.

What to observe now: Before the next pressure-point moment on your calendar–selection, trade window, and playoff push–ask one question: *what truth is most likely to get stuck, and where?* You are not intervening yet. You are learning to read the landscape. The intervention comes later. The observation starts now.

1.4 Reading Your Own Landscape

The eight pressure dimensions described in this chapter do not operate at equal intensity in every organization. Some organizations are dominated by temporal misalignment, and others by power gradient steepness or cultural inheritance that has never been examined. The specific combination matters because it determines where silence concentrates, where information gets stuck, and where the cascade failure pathway is most likely to ignite. Two organizations can share every structural feature described in this chapter and still produce entirely different patterns of dysfunction—because the dimensions are loaded differently, and the loading determines which intervention points are live and which are irrelevant.

That loading cannot be inferred from the outside or assumed from the literature. It has to be read—structurally, in context, before any intervention is designed. The Pressure Landscape Audit that follows is the diagnostic tool for that read.

1.4.1 The Pressure Landscape Audit

This is a diagnostic tool, not a reading exercise. It is structured as a series of questions rather than a summary table because the act of answering—and discovering where you cannot answer—is the diagnostic. A table presents information to be absorbed. These questions require you to retrieve specific observations from your own organization: who is affected, what you are seeing, and what structure exists to catch it. Where you can answer precisely, you have visibility. Where you hesitate, hedge, or realize no one is tracking the signal, you have found the gap. The gaps are the audit's primary output.

Status: Practitioner diagnostic tool. Synthesizes the eight pressure dimensions mapped in this chapter, drawing on stakeholder salience theory (Mitchell et al., 1997) and organizational silence research (Morrison, 2014). Not a validated instrument.

For each of the eight pressure dimensions, answer the questions that follow. If you cannot, that finding belongs on the map.

Temporal misalignment. When was the last time a short-term roster or personnel decision contradicted a stated long-term strategic plan—and did anyone flag the contradiction in real time? Who bears the cost when the timeline shifts: mid-career athletes on expiring contracts, development coaches whose player pipelines are raided for short-term needs, or both? Does your organization have any formal mechanism to surface when short-term decisions undercut long-term strategy, or does the misalignment only become visible in retrospect?

Zero-sum scarcity. Where in your organization are two or more people competing for the same finite resource—roster spot, playing time, budget allocation, access to a key decision-maker—while simultaneously expected to collaborate? Are athletes in contract years or on non-guaranteed deals disclosing injury status to shared support staff, or is the competitive structure making concealment rational? Does any protocol exist for managing resource conflicts at the team level, or does the organization rely entirely on individual performance reviews to surface problems that are structural?

Body as workplace. Who clears your athletes for return to play after non-concussion injuries, and who evaluates that clinician's job performance? If the answer to both questions involves the same chain of command, the dual-loyalty problem is live. Are medical staff navigating pressure to return athletes that originates from coaching or front-office personnel? Does an independent review exist for return-to-play decisions beyond the concussion protocol, or does the governance structure assume that one category of brain injury requires oversight while all other clinical judgments do not?

Permanent selection. Is injury disclosure dropping during contract years, camp cuts, or free agency windows? Are your training staff observing compensatory movement patterns that athletes deny when asked directly? What mechanism exists to link biomechanical observation by training staff to medical follow-up when the athlete does not self-report—and if no such mechanism exists, what does the organization do with the gap between what the training staff can see and what the medical staff are permitted to act on?

Power gradients. Are support staff—athletic trainers, video coordinators, and sport psychologists—raising concerns directly to coaching and management, or are they routing concerns through athletes because the direct channel feels unsafe or structurally blocked? Does a structured upward feedback mechanism exist, or does the organization rely on an open-door policy that the people lowest in the hierarchy experience as decorative? Which roles, demographics, or contract statuses in your organization have the steepest cost-of-speaking relative to the expected benefit?

Cultural inheritance. When leadership changes, which practices from the previous regime survive—and does anyone distinguish inherited tradition from current policy? Are "optional" activities being tracked informally and used in personnel decisions without a written framework? How are newer players, international players, or staff who did not experience the previous regime supposed to decode cultural signals that no one has made explicit?

Transience. What happened to the institutional knowledge held by the last person who left—the opponent-tendency data, the relationship maps, and the undocumented procedural knowledge? Does your onboarding process focus exclusively on integrating new arrivals, or does it also capture what departing personnel know before they leave? When leadership turns over, is the incoming regime consulting existing staff who hold institutional memory, or does each new administration start from scratch while the people who outlast the transition watch their expertise go unasked?

Neurobiological degradation. Who in your organization has been under sustained performance pressure for more than twelve months—and who is monitoring the quality of their decision-making, not just their outcomes? Are assistant coaches, medical staff, or support personnel noticing patterns of increasingly reactive or narrowed decision-making in leaders under chronic stress? Does any structured peer-review process exist for decision quality during high-stress periods, or does the organization wait for the post-season review to assess decisions that were made under conditions where the decision-maker's prefrontal capacity may have been compromised?

Three Questions That Sharpen the Audit

1. **Where is truth slowest?** Identify the decision or disclosure that takes the longest to travel from the person who knows it to the person who needs it. That pathway maps the silence calculus in your organization.
2. **Whose silence calculus is steepest?** Identify the role, demographic, or contract status for which the cost of speaking is highest relative to the expected benefit. That population is your canary.
3. **What is the organization's dominant response to weak signals—symptom management or root-cause inquiry?** The answer predicts whether the cascade failure pathway (Figure 1.3) will repeat.

This audit does not produce a score. It produces a map.

> **BOX 1.6 TIMEOUT — FIVE SIGNALS THAT YOUR LANDSCAPE IS PRODUCING PATHOLOGY**
>
> You do not need a survey to read a pressure landscape. You need to know what to watch. Five observable signals indicate that structural pressures are converting into organizational dysfunction:
>
> 1. Support staff turnover exceeds coaching staff turnover—the canaries are leaving.
> 2. Injury disclosure drops during contract years—the silence calculus is active.
> 3. New hires repeat the same mistakes as their predecessors—Institutional memory has left the building.
> 4. Athletes seek help from the athletic trainer for problems outside the trainer's scope—the formal channels are structurally blocked.
> 5. Post-incident reviews consistently name the symptom and miss the root cause—the cascade failure pathway is running uninterrupted.

1.4.2 Chapter Synthesis

The pressure landscape is an interlocking architecture. Temporal misalignment, power asymmetry, identity foreclosure, cultural inheritance, and neurobiological degradation compound one another—making silence, concealment, and short-term thinking structurally rational. The eight pressure dimensions do not operate independently; they stack, and the silence calculus captures their cumulative weight on any individual's decision about whether to speak. The three-type silence taxonomy and the Pressure Landscape Audit provide the diagnostic precision required to read that architecture before committing resources to change it. The central reframe—dysfunction is adaptation, not failure—establishes the foundation for every layer of the operating system that follows.

Key Chapter Takeaways

1. **Dysfunction is structural, not individual.** Silence, injury concealment, and short-term thinking are rational adaptations to architecture—diagnose the structure before labeling the person.
2. **The silence calculus compounds across variables.** Career risk, identity threat, power gradient steepness, demographic credibility, and legal precarity stack—single-lever interventions leave most of the math untouched.
3. **Three types of silence require three different interventions.** Fear-based silence needs safety infrastructure; architecture-based silence needs different people in the room; and network-based silence needs restructured access pipelines. Misdiagnosis wastes effort.
4. **Chronic stress degrades the capacity to respond to it.** Prefrontal shutdown under sustained pressure narrows attention and impairs judgment at precisely the moments when complex thinking matters most—structural safeguards must compensate for what individuals can no longer self-correct.

Discussion Questions

1. Select one structural pressure from this chapter and trace how it differentially weights the silence calculus for an athlete, a coach, and a support staff member within the same organization. Where does the calculus diverge most—and what does that imply for intervention design?
2. The chapter distinguishes fear-based, architecture-based, and network-based silence. Identify a situation in your professional context where the wrong type was diagnosed. What intervention was applied, and why did it miss?
3. If chronic stress degrades the prefrontal capacity of leaders responsible for fixing organizational problems, what structural safeguards could an organization design that do not depend on individual self-awareness?

References

Allan, E. J., & Madden, M. (2008). *Hazing in view: College students at risk.* University of Maine. https://www.stophazing.org/hazing-in-view/

Alosco, M. L., Kasimis, A. B., Stamm, J. M., Chua, A. S., Baugh, C. M., Daneshvar, D. H., Robbins, C. A., Mariani, M., Hayden, J., Conneely, S., Au, R., Torres, A., McClean, M. D., McKee, A. C., Cantu, R. C., Mez, J., Nowinski, C. J., Martin, B. M.,

Chaisson, C. E., . . . Stern, R. A. (2017). Age of first exposure to American football and long-term neuropsychiatric and cognitive outcomes. *Translational Psychiatry*, *7*(9), Article e1236. https://doi.org/10.1038/tp.2017.197

Andersen, M. B., Van Raalte, J. L., & Brewer, B. W. (2001). Sport psychology service delivery: Staying ethical while keeping loose. *Professional Psychology: Research and Practice*, *32*(1), 12–18. https://doi.org/10.1037/0735-7028.32.1.12

Anderson, E. (2011). *Inclusive masculinity: The changing nature of masculinities*. Routledge.

Anderson, L., & Gerrard, D. F. (2005). Ethical issues concerning New Zealand sports doctors. *Journal of Medical Ethics*, *31*(2), 88–92. https://doi.org/10.1136/jme.2002.000836

Armour, N., & Axon, R. (2018, January 26). USA Gymnastics in turmoil as leadership crisis deepens amid Nassar fallout. *USA Today*.

Arnsten, A. F. (2009). Stress signalling pathways that impair prefrontal cortex structure and function. *Nature Reviews Neuroscience*, *10*(6), 410–422. https://doi.org/10.1038/nrn2648

Ashburn-Nardo, L., Knowles, M. L., & Monteith, M. J. (2003). Black Americans' implicit racial associations and their implications for intergroup judgment. *Social Cognition*, *21*(1), 61–87. https://doi.org/10.1521/soco.21.1.61.21192

Associated Press. (2023). 2023 baseball payrolls, list. *AP News*. https://apnews.com/article/mlb-sports-compensation-in-baseball-944ba0b4b6ba9b58e898f0c9bcc7d095

Audas, R., Dobson, S., & Goddard, J. (2002). The impact of managerial change on team performance in professional sports. *Journal of Economics and Business*, *54*(6), 633–650. https://doi.org/10.1016/S0148-6195(0200120-0)

Bauman, N. J. (2016). The stigma of mental health in athletes: Are mental toughness and mental health seen as contradictory in elite sport? *British Journal of Sports Medicine*, *50*(3), 135–136. https://doi.org/10.1136/bjsports-2015-095570

Becker, F. D. (1981). *Workspace: Creating environments in organizations*. Praeger.

Bickley, J., Rogers, A., Bell, J., & Thombs, M. (2016). "Elephant spotting": The importance of developing shared understanding to work more effectively with talented but challenging athletes. *Sport & Exercise Psychology Review*, *12*(1), 43–53. https://www.changingmindsuk.com/wp-content/uploads/2025/06/Elephant-spotting-paper.pdf

Bourdon, P. C., Cardinale, M., Murray, A., Gastin, P., Kellmann, M., Varley, M. C., Gabbett, T. J., Coutts, A. J., Burgess, D. J., Gregson, W., & Cable, N. T. (2017). Monitoring athlete training loads: Consensus statement. *International Journal of Sports Physiology and Performance*, *12*(Suppl 2), S2-161–S2-170. https://doi.org/10.1123/ijspp.2017-0208

Brackenridge, C. H. (2001). *Spoilsports: Understanding and preventing sexual exploitation in sport*. Routledge.

Brewer, B. W., Van Raalte, J. L., & Linder, D. E. (1993). Athletic identity: Hercules' muscles or Achilles heel? *International Journal of Sport Psychology*, *24*(2), 237–254.

Bridgewater, S. (2010). *Football management*. Palgrave Macmillan.

Carlson, K., Kim, J., Lusardi, A., & Camerer, C. F. (2015). *Bankruptcy rates among NFL players with short-lived income spikes* (NBER Working Paper No. 21085). National Bureau of Economic Research. https://doi.org/10.3386/w21085

Carron, A. V., Brawley, L. R., & Widmeyer, W. N. (2002). *The Group Environment Questionnaire test manual*. Fitness Information Technology.

Cobley, S., Baker, J., Wattie, N., & McKenna, J. (2009). Annual age-grouping and athlete development: A meta-analytical review of relative age effects in sport. *Sports Medicine*, *39*(3), 235–256. https://doi.org/10.2165/00007256-200939030-00005

Connelly, C. E., Zweig, D., Webster, J., & Trougakos, J. P. (2012). Knowledge hiding in organizations. *Journal of Organizational Behavior*, *33*(1), 64–88. https://doi.org/10.1002/job.737

Coon, L. (2019). NBA salary cap FAQ. *CBA FAQ*. http://www.cbafaq.com/salarycap.htm

Cottler, L. B., Ben Abdallah, A., Cummings, S. M., Barr, J., Banks, R., & Forchheimer, R. (2011). Injury, pain, and prescription opioid use among former National Football League (NFL) players. *Drug and Alcohol Dependence*, *116*(1–3), 188–194. https://doi.org/10.1016/j.drugalcdep.2010.12.003

Cunningham, G. B. (2010). Understanding the under-representation of African American coaches: A multilevel perspective. *Sport Management Review*, *13*(4), 395–406. https://doi.org/10.1016/j.smr.2009.07.006

Deloitte Sports Business Group. (2023). *Annual review of football finance 2023*. Deloitte. https://www2.deloitte.com/uk/en/pages/sports-business-group/articles/annual-review-of-football-finance.html

Denison, E., & Kitchen, A. (2015). *Out on the fields: The first international study on homophobia in sport*. Repucom; Bingham Cup Sydney; Australian Sports Commission. https://outonthefields.com/wp-content/uploads/2020/11/Out-on-the-Fields-Final-Report-1.pdf

Denrell, J. (2003). Vicarious learning, undersampling of failure, and the myths of management. *Organization Science*, *14*(3), 227–243. https://doi.org/10.1287/orsc.14.3.227.15164

Deutsch, M. (1949). A theory of co-operation and competition. *Human Relations*, *2*(2), 129–152. https://doi.org/10.1177/001872674900200204

Dorsch, T. E., Smith, A. L., & McDonough, M. H. (2015). Early socialization of parents through organized youth sport. *Sport, Exercise, and Performance Psychology*, *4*(1), 3–18. https://doi.org/10.1037/spy0000021

Dunn, L. (2021). Agents in the sporting field: A law and economics perspective. *International Sports Law Journal*, *21*, 156–175. https://doi.org/10.1007/s40318-021-00197-7

Eagly, A. H., & Karau, S. J. (2002). Role congruity theory of prejudice toward female leaders. *Psychological Review*, *109*(3), 573–598. https://doi.org/10.1037/0033-295X.109.3.573

Easterbrook, J. A. (1959). The effect of emotion on cue utilization and the organization of behavior. *Psychological Review*, *66*(3), 183–201. https://doi.org/10.1037/h0047707

Edmondson, A. C. (1999). Psychological safety and learning behavior in work teams. *Administrative Science Quarterly*, *44*(2), 350–383. https://doi.org/10.2307/2666999

Eys, M. A., Bruner, M. W., & Martin, L. J. (2015). The dynamic group environment. In S. D. Mellalieu & S. Hanton (Eds.), *Contemporary advances in sport psychology* (pp. 51–75). Routledge.

Fasting, K., Brackenridge, C., & Sundgot-Borgen, J. (2004). Prevalence of sexual harassment among Norwegian female elite athletes in relation to sport type. *International Review for the Sociology of Sport*, *39*(4), 373–386. https://doi.org/10.1177/1012690204049804

Fitzgerald, L. F., Swan, S., & Magley, V. J. (1997). But was it really sexual harassment? Legal, behavioral, and psychological definitions of the workplace victimization of women. In W. O'Donohue (Ed.), *Sexual harassment: Theory, research, and treatment* (pp. 5–28). Allyn & Bacon.

Geurin, A. N. (2017). Elite female athletes' perceptions of new media use relating to their careers: A qualitative analysis. *Journal of Sport Management*, *31*(4), 345–359. https://doi.org/10.1123/jsm.2016-0315

Gill, V. S., Sullivan, G., Stearns, H., Tummala, S. V., Haglin, J. M., Economopoulos, K. J., Marks, L., & Chauhan, M. (2024). Mental health in elite athletes: A systematic review of suicidal behaviour as compared to the general population. *Sports Medicine*, *54*(6), 1499–1516. https://doi.org/10.1007/s40279-024-01998-2

Gouttebarge, V., Backx, F. J. G., Aoki, H., & Kerkhoffs, G. M. M. J. (2015). Symptoms of common mental disorders in professional football (soccer) across five European countries. *Journal of Sports Science & Medicine*, *14*(4), 811–818. https://pmc.ncbi.nlm.nih.gov/articles/PMC4657424/

Gouttebarge, V., Castaldelli-Maia, J. M., Gorczynski, P., Hainline, B., Hitchcock, M. E., Kerkhoffs, G. M., Rice, S. M., & Reardon, C. L. (2019). Occurrence of mental health symptoms and disorders in current and former elite athletes: A systematic review and meta-analysis. *British Journal of Sports Medicine*, *53*(11), 700–706. https://doi.org/10.1136/bjsports-2019-100671

Grashow, R., Tan, C. O., Thomas, J. D., DiGregorio, H., Lee, H., Rotem, R. S., Marengi, D., Terry, D. P., Eagle, S. R., Iverson, G. L., Whittington, A. J., Zafonte, R. D., Weisskopf, M. G., & Baggish, A. L. (2024). Career duration and later-life health conditions among former professional American-style football players. *Occupational and Environmental Medicine*, *81*(10), 498–506. https://doi.org/10.1136/oemed-2024-109571

Green, B. C. (2005). Building sport programs to optimize athlete recruitment, retention, and transition: Toward a normative theory of sport development. *Journal of Sport Management*, *19*(3), 233–253. https://doi.org/10.1123/jsm.19.3.233

Gucciardi, D. F., Hanton, S., Gordon, S., Mallett, C. J., & Temby, P. (2015). The concept of mental toughness: Tests of dimensionality, nomological network, and traitness. *Journal of Personality*, *83*(1), 26–44. https://doi.org/10.1111/jopy.12079

Heilman, M. E. (2012). Gender stereotypes and workplace bias. *Research in Organizational Behavior*, *32*, 113–135. https://doi.org/10.1016/j.riob.2012.11.003

Hoover, N. C. (1999). *National survey: Initiation rites and athletics for NCAA sports teams*. Alfred University. https://hazingpreventionnetwork.org/wp-content/uploads/2023/01/4.NationalSurvey_IntiationRites_Athletics_NCAA_Sports_Team.pdf

Hughes, M., Hughes, P., Mellahi, K., & Guermat, C. (2010). Short-term versus long-term impact of managers: Evidence from the football industry. *British Journal of Management*, *21*(2), 571–589. https://doi.org/10.1111/j.1467-8551.2009.00668.x

Jacobs, F., Smits, F., & Knoppers, A. (2017). "You don't realize what you see!": The institutional context of emotional abuse in elite youth sport. *Sport in Society*, *20*(1), 126–143. https://doi.org/10.1080/17430437.2015.1124567

Kavanagh, E. J., Litchfield, C., & Osborne, J. (2021). Sporting events and online abuse: Exploring victimization of athletes. In I. Saleem, T. Ahmad, & I. Iqbal (Eds.), *Athlete mental health and performance psychology* (pp. 75–94). Springer.

Kerr, G. A., & Stirling, A. E. (2012). Parents' reflections on their child's experiences of emotionally abusive coaching practices. *Journal of Applied Sport Psychology*, *24*(2), 191–206. https://doi.org/10.1080/10413200.2011.608413

Kerr, Z. Y., Register-Mihalik, J. K., Marshall, S. W., Evenson, K. R., Mihalik, J. P., & Guskiewicz, K. M. (2014). Disclosure and non-disclosure of concussion and concussion symptoms in athletes: Review and application of the socio-ecological framework. *Brain Injury*, *28*(8), 1009–1021. https://doi.org/10.3109/02699052.2014.904049

Kroshus, E., Garnett, B., Hawrilenko, M., Baugh, C. M., & Calzo, J. P. (2015). Concussion under-reporting and pressure from coaches, teammates, fans, and parents. *Social Science & Medicine*, *134*, 66–75. https://doi.org/10.1016/j.socscimed.2015.04.011

Kwiatkowski, M., Alesia, M., & Evans, T. (2016, August 4). A blind eye to sex abuse: How USA Gymnastics failed to report cases. *The Indianapolis Star*. https://web.archive.org/web/20160804172003/https://www.indystar.com/story/news/investigations/2016/08/04/usa-gymnastics-sex-abuse-protected-coaches/85829732/

Lapchick, R. E. (2024). *The racial and gender report card*. The Institute for Diversity and Ethics in Sport, University of Central Florida. https://www.tidesport.org

LaVoi, N. M. (2016). *Women in sports coaching*. Routledge.

Leota, J., Nash, C., & Muñoz-Arjona, C. (2023). Travel fatigue and sleep in professional sport: A systematic review. *Sleep Medicine Reviews*, *68*, Article 101760. https://doi.org/10.1016/j.smrv.2023.101760

Major League Soccer Players Association. (2024). *2024 spring-summer salary guide*. https://mlsplayers.org/resources/salary-guide

March, J. G. (1991). Exploration and exploitation in organizational learning. *Organization Science*, *2*(1), 71–87. https://doi.org/10.1287/orsc.2.1.71

Marcia, J. E. (1966). Development and validation of ego-identity status. *Journal of Personality and Social Psychology*, *3*(5), 551–558. https://doi.org/10.1037/h0023281

Massey, C., & Thaler, R. H. (2013). The loser's curse: Decision making and market efficiency in the National Football League draft. *Management Science*, *59*(7), 1479–1495. https://doi.org/10.1287/mnsc.1120.1657

Mason, D. S., Thibault, L., & Misener, L. (2006). An agency theory perspective on corruption in sport: The case of the International Olympic Committee. *Journal of Sport Management*, *20*(1), 52–73. https://doi.org/10.1123/jsm.20.1.52

Mayer, R. C., Davis, J. H., & Schoorman, F. D. (1995). An integrative model of organizational trust. *Academy of Management Review*, *20*(3), 709–734. https://doi.org/10.5465/amr.1995.9508080335

McKee, A. C., Mez, J., Abdolmohammadi, B., Butler, M., Huber, B. R., Uretsky, M., Babcock, K., Cherry, J. D., Alvarez, V. E., Martin, B., Tripodis, Y., Palmisano, J. N., Cormier, K. A., Kubilus, C. A., Nicks, R., Kirsch, D., Mahar, I., McHale, L., Nowinski, C., . . . Alosco, M. L. (2023). Neuropathologic and clinical findings in young contact sport athletes exposed to repetitive head impacts. *JAMA Neurology*, *80*(10), 1037–1050. https://doi.org/10.1001/jamaneurol.2023.2907

McLaughlin, H., Uggen, C., & Blackstone, A. (2012). Sexual harassment, workplace authority, and the paradox of power. *American Sociological Review*, *77*(4), 625–647. https://doi.org/10.1177/0003122412451728

McLeod, C., Agha, N., & Rosenbaum-Larson, S. (2022). Unrealistic expectations and future status coercion in Minor League Baseball players' future-oriented labor. *Sociology of Sport Journal*, *40*(4), 363–381. https://doi.org/10.1123/ssj.2022-0066

Meyer, J. P., & Allen, N. J. (1991). A three-component conceptualization of organizational commitment. *Human Resource Management Review*, *1*(1), 61–89. https://doi.org/10.1016/1053-4822(9190011-Z)

Mez, J., Daneshvar, D. H., Kiernan, P. T., Abdolmohammadi, B., Alvarez, V. E., Huber, B. R., Alosco, M. L., Solomon, T. M., Nowinski, C. J., McHale, L., Cormier, K. A., Kubilus, C. A., Martin, B. M., Murphy, L., Baugh, C. M., Montenigro, P. H., Chaisson, C. E., Tripodis, Y., Kowall, N. W., . . . McKee, A. C. (2017). Clinicopathological evaluation of chronic traumatic encephalopathy in players of American football. *JAMA*, *318*(4), 360–370. https://doi.org/10.1001/jama.2017.8334

Mitchell, R. K., Agle, B. R., & Wood, D. J. (1997). Toward a theory of stakeholder identification and salience: Defining the principle of who and what really counts. *Academy of Management Review*, *22*(4), 853–886. https://doi.org/10.5465/amr.1997.9711022105

Moore, Z. E. (2003). Ethical dilemmas in sport psychology: Discussion and recommendations for practice. *Professional Psychology: Research and Practice*, *34*(6), 601–610. https://doi.org/10.1037/0735-7028.34.6.601

Morrison, E. W. (2014). Employee voice and silence. *Annual Review of Organizational Psychology and Organizational Behavior*, *1*(1), 173–197. https://doi.org/10.1146/annurev-orgpsych-031413-091328

Morrison, E. W., & Milliken, F. J. (2000). Organizational silence: A barrier to change and development in a pluralistic world. *Academy of Management Review*, *25*(4), 706–725. https://doi.org/10.5465/amr.2000.3707697

Mountjoy, M., Brackenridge, C., Arrington, M., Blauwet, C., Carska-Sheppard, A., Fasting, K., Kirby, S., Leahy, T., Marks, S., Martin, K., Starr, K., Tiivas, A., & Budgett, R. (2016). International Olympic Committee consensus statement: Harassment and abuse (non-accidental violence) in sport. *British Journal of Sports Medicine*, *50*(17), 1019–1029. https://doi.org/10.1136/bjsports-2016-096121

Murphy v. National Collegiate Athletic Association, 584 U.S. 453 (2018).

Nauright, J., & Ramfjord, J. (2010). Who owns England's game? American professional sporting influences and foreign ownership in the Premier League. *Soccer & Society, 11*(4), 428–441. https://doi.org/10.1080/14660971003780321

Nixon, H. L. (1992). A social network analysis of influences on athletes to play with pain and injuries. *Journal of Sport and Social Issues, 16*(2), 127–135. https://doi.org/10.1177/019372359201600208

Noll, R. G. (2002). The economics of promotion and relegation in sports leagues: The case of English football. *Journal of Sports Economics, 3*(2), 169–203. https://doi.org/10.1177/152700250200300205

Norman, L. (2010). Feeling second best: Elite women coaches' experiences. *Sociology of Sport Journal, 27*(1), 89–104. https://doi.org/10.1123/ssj.27.1.89

Park, S., Lavallee, D., & Tod, D. (2013). Athletes' career transition out of sport: A systematic review. *International Review of Sport and Exercise Psychology, 6*(1), 22–53. https://doi.org/10.1080/1750984X.2012.687053

Pilkington, V., Rice, S. M., Walton, C. C., Gwyther, K., Olive, L., Butterworth, M., Clements, M., Cross, G., & Purcell, R. (2022). Prevalence and correlates of mental health symptoms and well-being among elite sport coaches and high-performance support staff. *Sports Medicine—Open, 8*, Article 89. https://doi.org/10.1186/s40798-022-00479-y

Potrac, P., & Jones, R. L. (2009). Power, conflict, and cooperation: Toward a micropolitics of coaching. *Quest, 61*(2), 223–236. https://doi.org/10.1080/00336297.2009.10483612

Reardon, C. L., & Factor, R. M. (2010). Sport psychiatry: A systematic review of diagnosis and medical treatment of mental illness in athletes. *Sports Medicine, 40*(11), 961–980. https://doi.org/10.2165/11536580-000000000-00000

Reardon, C. L., Hainline, B., Aron, C. M., Baron, D., Baum, A. L., Bindra, A., Budgett, R., Campriani, N., Castaldelli-Maia, J. M., Currie, A., Derevensky, J. L., Glick, I. D., Gorczynski, P., Gouttebarge, V., Grandner, M. A., Han, D. H., McDuff, D., Mountjoy, M., Polat, A., . . . Engebretsen, L. (2019). Mental health in elite athletes: International Olympic Committee consensus statement (2019). *British Journal of Sports Medicine, 53*(11), 667–699. https://doi.org/10.1136/bjsports-2019-100715

Reason, J. (1997). *Managing the risks of organizational accidents*. Ashgate.

Rowley, C. (2024). It's past time: Unionization and self-determinism in Minor League Baseball. *University of Colorado Law Review, 95*, 1157–1210.

Sanderson, J. (2011). *It's a whole new ballgame: How social media is changing sports*. Hampton Press.

Sherf, E. N., Parke, M. R., & Isaakyan, S. (2021). Distinguishing voice and silence at work: Unique relationships with perceived impact, psychological safety, and burnout. *Academy of Management Journal, 64*(1), 114–148. https://doi.org/10.5465/amj.2018.1428

Shropshire, K. L., & Davis, T. (2008). *The business of sports agents* (2nd ed.). University of Pennsylvania Press.

Singer, J. N. (2005). Understanding racism through the eyes of African American male student-athletes. *Race Ethnicity and Education, 8*(4), 365–386. https://doi.org/10.1080/13613320500323963

Staal, M. A. (2004). *Stress, cognition, and human performance: A literature review and conceptual framework* (NASA/TM-2004-212824). NASA Ames Research Center.

Stamm, J. M., Bourlas, A. P., Baugh, C. M., Fritts, N. G., Daneshvar, D. H., Martin, B. M., McClean, M. D., Tripodis, Y., & Stern, R. A. (2015). Age of first exposure to football and later-life cognitive impairment in former NFL players. *Neurology, 84*(11), 1114–1120. https://doi.org/10.1212/WNL.0000000000001358

Starcke, K., & Brand, M. (2012). Decision making under stress: A selective review. *Neuroscience & Biobehavioral Reviews, 36*(4), 1228–1248. https://doi.org/10.1016/j.neubiorev.2012.02.003

Staudohar, P. D. (1996). *Playing for dollars: Labor relations and the sports business.* Cornell University Press.

Szymanski, S., & Zimbalist, A. (2005). *National pastime: How Americans play baseball and the rest of the world plays soccer.* Brookings Institution Press.

Thaler, R. H., & Sunstein, C. R. (2008). *Nudge: Improving decisions about health, wealth, and happiness.* Yale University Press.

Tuakli-Wosornu, Y. A., Gouttebarge, V., & Engebretsen, L. (2021). Athlete health protection: Why qualitative research matters. *British Journal of Sports Medicine, 55*(6), 300–301. https://doi.org/10.1136/bjsports-2020-103467

Van Raalte, J. L., Cornelius, A. E., Linder, D. E., & Brewer, B. W. (2007). The relationship between hazing and team cohesion. *Journal of Sport Behavior, 30*(4), 491–507.

Vertommen, T., Kampen, J., Brackenridge, C., & Toftegaard Støckel, J. (2022). Interpersonal violence against children in sport: A systematic review and meta-analysis. *Sports Medicine, 52*(12), 2899–2929. https://doi.org/10.1007/s40279-022-01735-1

Waldron, J. J., & Kowalski, C. L. (2009). Crossing the line: Rites of passage, team aspects, and ambiguity of hazing. *Research Quarterly for Exercise and Sport, 80*(2), 291–302. https://doi.org/10.1080/02701367.2009.10599564

Weick, K. E., & Sutcliffe, K. M. (2015). *Managing the unexpected: Sustained performance in a complex world* (3rd ed.). Wiley.

Weir, D. R., Jackson, J. S., & Sonnega, A. (2009). *National Football League player care foundation: Study of retired NFL players.* Institute for Social Research, University of Michigan.

Westhead, R., & Strashin, J. (2022, May 26). Hockey Canada paid millions to settle sexual assault claims, used player registration fees for confidential fund. *TSN/CBC.* https://www.tsn.ca/hockey-canada-sexual-assault-settlement-fund-1.1809247

Westrum, R. (2004). A typology of organisational cultures. *Quality and Safety in Health Care, 13*(Suppl 2), ii22–ii27. https://doi.org/10.1136/qshc.2003.009522

Woo, E., Sansing, L. H., Arnsten, A. F. T., & Datta, D. (2021). Chronic stress weakens connectivity in the prefrontal cortex: Architectural and molecular changes. *Chronic Stress, 5*, Article 24705470211029254. https://doi.org/10.1177/24705470211029254

Wylleman, P., & Lavallee, D. (2004). A developmental perspective on transitions faced by athletes. In M. R. Weiss (Ed.), *Developmental sport and exercise psychology: A lifespan perspective* (pp. 507–527). Fitness Information Technology.

Yates, S. Q. (2022). *Report of the independent investigation to the U.S. Soccer Federation concerning allegations of abusive behavior and sexual misconduct in women's professional soccer.* King & Spalding LLP.

2

PSYCHOLOGICAL SAFETY—THE FOUNDATION

Learning Objectives

By the end of this chapter, the reader will be able to:

1. Differentiate psychological safety from trust, inclusion, and comfort, and explain why conflating them leads to misdiagnosed interventions.
2. Evaluate the evidence linking psychological safety to team performance, distinguishing meta-analytic claims from what sport-specific research has yet to establish.
3. Analyze how structural features of elite sport produce rational silence, and classify the dominant silence type operating in a given context.
4. Apply the Safety Diagnostic framework to assess psychological safety and translate findings into a prioritized intervention plan.
5. Design voice infrastructure and meeting protocols that scaffold lower-risk voice before higher-risk voice and structurally separate interpersonal process from performance evaluation.

2.1 What Psychological Safety Is

Most elite sport environments follow a predictable pattern: athletes who know exactly what is wrong but say nothing. The rookie stays quiet because speaking up feels like career suicide. The veteran hides a nagging hamstring because admitting pain means losing playing time. The physio notices a pattern in soft-tissue injuries but does not challenge the head coach's training load decisions. The video analyst sees a tactical mismatch in the opposition review but defers to

DOI: 10.4324/9781003631217-3

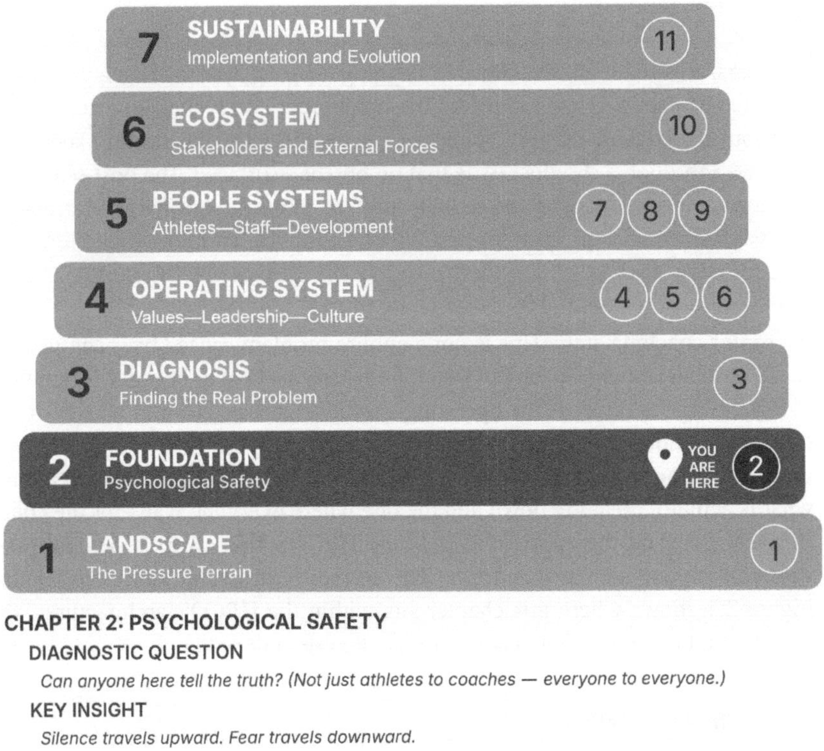

FIGURE 2.1 You Are Here—Foundation. The HPCOS Seven-Layer Architecture With Layer 2 (Foundation) Highlighted.

This chapter answers Question 2—can anyone here tell the truth?—by building psychological safety and voice infrastructure that keeps information moving under pressure. If this layer is weak, diagnosis is distorted and decision architecture becomes theater; strengthening it protects every layer above.

BOX 2.1 CASE STUDY — THE ASSISTANT COACH WHO STOPPED DISAGREEING

Composite vignette. Details changed to protect privacy.

Marta had been the assistant coach for three seasons, known for pushing back in staff meetings when the game plan had gaps. That changed after the club dropped four straight. The head coach, Marcus, cut a veteran midfielder by posting the squad list without telling the player first. Marta raised it in the next staff meeting: “We owe people a conversation before they see it on a list.” Marcus: “Selection is my call. If you want to coach your own squad, apply somewhere else." Marta stopped raising process concerns. Within weeks, the video analyst stopped flagging when player load data contradicted Marcus's rotation choices. The goalkeeper coach shelved a concern about the backup keeper's confidence. A month later, the starting keeper played through a shoulder issue that no one had surfaced. The post-season medical review cited "delayed disclosure" as a contributing factor. No one asked why disclosure had stopped. No one connected it to the squad list.

the senior coaching staff. This is not a culture problem caused by mean people. It is a rational response to an environment where the cost of honesty is too high.

Psychological safety is the operating condition that determines whether truth travels fast enough for pressure to produce learning rather than silence. In sport terms, it is the difference between the halftime debrief, where athletes name what is actually breaking down and the one where everyone waits for the coach to speak first and then agrees. This is the HPCOS framework's second question: can anyone here tell the truth? The answer is structural, not motivational. Figure 2.1 shows where this chapter sits within the HPCOS architecture—the foundation layer on which every subsequent system depends.

2.1.1 The Core Definition

Edmondson (1999) defined it precisely: "a shared belief held by members of a team that the team is safe for interpersonal risk taking" (p. 354). The concept has earlier roots—Schein and Bennis (1965) identified psychological safety as a precondition for organizational change, and Kahn (1990) linked it to the conditions under which people psychologically engage or disengage at work—but Edmondson's formulation anchored it at the team level.

Three elements matter for sport environments. It is shared—a team-level phenomenon, not one brave athlete willing to speak. A goalkeeper who challenges a defensive setup does not create psychological safety if the rest of the back line stays silent because the norm punishes dissent. It concerns interpersonal risk—admitting errors in training, questioning a game plan, flagging an injury, and challenging a coach's rotation. And it operates through belief: what athletes and staff expect will happen when they speak governs whether they speak at all.

When players and staff believe that speaking up will not result in benching, public humiliation, or marginalization, they share information earlier. Meta-analytic evidence links this to faster learning cycles, better coordination, and fewer preventable errors (Frazier et al., 2017). In sport, the performance advantage is concrete: the injury flagged before it becomes a season-ending rupture, the tactical adjustment identified in Tuesday's film review rather than discovered in Saturday's second half, the young player who asks for clarification on a set piece rather than guessing and getting caught out of position.

Sport-specific research is catching up to the broader organizational evidence. Fransen et al. (2020) linked psychological safety in elite sport teams to resilience and performance. Hurst et al. (2025) found that elite athletes report significantly lower psychological safety than recreational athletes—and are less likely to report interpersonal violence. Rice et al. (2022) validated a Sport Psychological Safety Inventory. Walton et al. (2024) proposed a theoretically informed model linking psychological safety to mental health outcomes in elite sport. The evidence base is emerging rather than definitive, but the direction is consistent: when athletes believe the environment punishes candor, information stops moving.

BOX 2.2 TIMEOUT — WHAT PSYCHOLOGICAL SAFETY IS NOT

Psychological safety is not permission to avoid hard tackles, lower selection standards, or tolerate mediocrity. It is the operating condition that allows accountability and high standards to function without producing silence. A single athlete who feels emboldened to speak does not create safety if the group norm punishes dissent. The team-level conditions that make honesty risky are what need to change. Psychological safety does not eliminate consequences for a poor performance on match day. It eliminates consequences for honesty—for flagging an injury, questioning a game plan, or telling a coach that something is not working.

A note on scope. Research shows that psychological safety is best supported in corporate knowledge-work teams (Edmondson, 1999; Frazier et al., 2017), with this chapter's frameworks based mainly on professional team sports in Western, English-speaking contexts. Individual sports, youth sports, para-sports (see Mountjoy et al., 2016), and high power-distance coaching cultures require different approaches and units of analysis. For instance, a figure skater's relationship with their coach differs structurally from a rugby squad's interactions with a coaching panel. While the main principles apply, implementation varies.

2.1.2 Performance Safety: The Operating Distinction

Here is the tension every leader in elite sport faces: real consequences exist. Selection, contracts, funding, and careers depend on results. A head coach cannot promise that "mistakes will not be held against you" when there are 40,000 people in the stands, a television audience, and a board reviewing win percentages.

A national team director cannot guarantee roster spots to athletes who speak candidly about tactical concerns. No leader in sport can eliminate performance consequences—nor should they.

The resolution is Performance Safety—separating interpersonal safety from performance accountability. The underlying distinction draws on Edmondson's (1999) original framing—that psychological safety concerns interpersonal risk specifically, not performance consequences—and her later clarification that psychologically safe environments are not "relaxed" or "easy" but rather enable candor alongside high standards (Edmondson, 2018, pp. 15–17). Taylor et al. (2026) have since formalized this, conceptualizing psychological safety specifically for contexts where errors carry real consequences—precisely the conditions that define elite sport. The existing literature describes this distinction without naming it. What remains unnamed tends to remain unimplemented.

In practice, leaders who understand psychological safety in the abstract still conflate interpersonal process with performance decisions. A named construct gives practitioners a shared referent: "Was the selection decision wrong, or was the way we communicated it harmful?" Without a term that separates the two, post-match debriefs collapse them. Performance Safety is not a new theory. It is an operational framework built on a distinction the literature has established (Edmondson, 1999, 2018; Taylor et al., 2026), but the field has not systematically operationalized.

You can deselect an athlete, but you should not humiliate them on the way out.

The structural conditions described throughout this chapter—squad lists posted without conversations, selection wielded as threat, public dressing-downs after losses—run on a shared assumption: you're lucky to be here. That orientation treats athletes as interchangeable and speaking up as ingratitude.

Performance Safety operationalizes the inverse: we're lucky to have you. Not as a slogan on the locker room wall, but as the foundation to the entire architecture. When athletes believe that they are replaceable, they protect themselves—hiding injuries, suppressing tactical concerns, and avoiding the difficult conversation with a coach—and the organization loses the information it needed most, usually without realizing it until the torn ligament, the blown lead, or the safeguarding crisis is already public.

Consider the practice: a head coach must cut a veteran midfielder from the squad. The decision and standards are identical in both environments. What differs is whether the athlete learns through the media, a leaked squad announcement on social media, or through a direct conversation with transparent criteria. That process is what the rest of the squad is actually watching. Social learning operates through observation of consequences (Bandura, 1977): when a teammate sees how a deselected player was treated—whether they were ghosted or given a conversation—the observer updates their own calculation of whether speaking up or disclosing problems is safe. Table 2.1 contrasts how the same high-standards decisions look with and without Performance Safety.

TABLE 2.1 High Standards With and Without Performance Safety

Observable Behavior	*High Standards, Low Safety*	*High Standards, High Safety*
Selection decisions	Opaque criteria, communicated through avoidance or public lists	Transparent criteria, communicated directly with rationale
Post-error response	Public humiliation or silent benching after a costly turnover	Direct debrief focused on the decision, not the player's character
Injury disclosure	Athlete hides injury; disclosure risks deselection	Athlete discloses early; medical pathway is separated from selection decisions
Challenging the game plan	Labeled "not a team player" or "not coachable"	Invited during designated tactical forums; debated on evidence from film
Delivering bad news upward	Sport scientist who flags overtraining data is sidelined	Sport scientist's data is reviewed; training load is adjusted

Performance Safety is operationalized throughout this chapter: in the voice infrastructure, the accountability architecture, and the sustainability mechanisms. It is what separates the Learning Zone from the Anxiety Zone.

2.1.3 The Learning Zone

Edmondson's (2018) Learning Zone framework resolves the tension between safety and standards. Map psychological safety against performance standards. Four zones emerge:

1. **Apathy Zone (low safety, low standards):** Nobody cares, nobody speaks. The end-of-season team is going through the motions, where the coaching staff has mentally moved on, and athletes are protecting their bodies for the off-season.
2. **Comfort Zone (high safety, low standards):** Pleasant but mediocre. Everyone gets along, training is relaxed, but no one is pushed. This is the "soft" environment that competitive coaches and performance directors rightly want to avoid—and the one they mistakenly assume psychological safety will create.
3. **Anxiety Zone (low safety, high standards):** The most common default in elite sport. Standards are visible—sprint times are posted, selection metrics are tracked, and performance reviews carry consequences. But the cost of candor is so high that athletes and staff protect themselves instead of the team. The player who sees a hole in the opposition's press does not mention it because

last time someone offered a tactical suggestion they were told to "just do your job." The physio does not push back on return-to-play timelines because the last one who did was removed from the touring squad. Information that could prevent a loss, an injury, or a crisis never reaches the people who need it.

4. **Learning Zone (high safety, high standards):** The target. The standards in the weight room, on the training pitch, and in competition remain non-negotiable. Selection is competitive. Performance expectations stay high. But the friction of communicating drops low enough that problems surface while they are still fixable—in the Tuesday film session rather than the Saturday post-mortem.

Table 2.2 maps these four zones.

Operating with high standards and high safety seems like a no brainer to strive for in professional and elite sports, so why is it so hard?

TABLE 2.2 Edmondson's Learning Zone Framework

	Low Standards	*High Standards*
High Psychological Safety	Comfort Zone. Pleasant but mediocre. Training is relaxed, everyone gets along, but no one is pushed. The pre-season camp where the coaching staff wants to be liked more than respected. This is the "soft" environment competitive leaders rightly want to avoid.	Learning Zone (Target). Pressure stays high. Selection is competitive. Fitness standards, tactical expectations, and match-day accountability are non-negotiable. But the friction of communicating drops low enough that problems surface while still fixable—in the Tuesday film session rather than the Saturday post-mortem.
Low Psychological Safety	Apathy Zone. Nobody cares, nobody speaks. The end-of-season squad is playing out dead rubbers, where the coaching staff has mentally moved on, and athletes are protecting their bodies for the off-season. Low investment from both the organization and individuals.	Anxiety Zone. Standards are visible—sprint times are posted, selection metrics are tracked, and performance reviews carry consequences. But the cost of candor is so high that athletes and staff protect themselves instead of the team. The midfielder who sees a gap in the opposition press stays quiet because the last person who offered a tactical suggestion was told to "just do your job." Common default in elite sport.

Adapted from The Fearless Organization: Creating Psychological Safety in the Workplace for Learning, Innovation, and Growth (p. 18), by A. C. Edmondson (2018), John Wiley & Sons. Copyright 2018 by Amy C. Edmondson.

The Learning Zone also shares structural features with self-determination theory (Deci & Ryan, 2000), suggesting that safety interventions may produce additional gains through motivational pathways beyond the information-flow mechanism emphasized here. In sport, this connection is intuitive: athletes who feel safe to ask questions and take interpersonal risks are also more likely to experience the autonomy, competence, and relatedness that sustain intrinsic motivation across a grueling season.

The difference between the Anxiety Zone and the Learning Zone is not whether consequences exist. Players get cut in both. Athletes get benched in both. Contracts expire in both. The difference is whether people believe they can be honest without being destroyed for it—whether the defender can tell the coach the press is not working, whether the physio can push back on a return-to-play timeline, whether the analyst can flag data the head coach does not want to see.

BOX 2.3 SKEPTIC'S CORNER — SAFETY IS NOT COMFORT

The pushback: "This sounds like coddling. Elite sport requires thick skin. You cannot compete at the highest level if you need permission to feel safe."

Comfort means "do not push me." Psychological safety means "I can tell you the truth without you punishing me for it." A rugby forward does not need comfort. They need to know that when they report a head knock, the medical staff—not the coaching staff—controls the return-to-play decision. A figure skater does not need a soft landing on the ice. They need to know that telling their coach that a training load is unsustainable will not end their competitive season.

Fear-based cultures do not eliminate pain, doubt, or mistakes. They suppress disclosure. Athletes still get injured, still struggle with form, still see tactical problems the coaching staff has missed. They just stop telling anyone—and the coaching staff ends up making selection, tactical, and load-management decisions with incomplete data.

The evidence: Psychologically safer teams share more information and learn faster, which raises the odds of performance under pressure (Edmondson, 1999; Frazier et al., 2017). Hard coaching is not the problem. Humiliating the messenger is.

What to try anyway: In your next staff meeting or post-match debrief, ask for one concern about the game plan, thank the first person who speaks, and make one visible change based on their input. The rest of the room is watching what happens to the person who went first.

2.1.4 Safety, Trust, and Inclusion

When safety, trust, and inclusion get collapsed into a single concept, the wrong fix often follows. This is one of the most common diagnostic errors in sport organizations.

The three constructs operate at different levels. Psychological safety is a group norm—the shared expectation about whether this team, this squad, or this staff room punishes people for speaking up. Trust is a one-to-one relationship—whether a specific person has proven reliable through repeated interactions. Inclusion is an individual experience—whether someone feels they belong. Each is built differently and changes on a different timeline. Safety can shift in weeks with consistent leader behavior. Trust builds slowly and breaks fast. Inclusion requires sustained structural change.

Each also comes with its own signature misdiagnosis in sport. "We are a tight squad" mistakes cohesion for safety—the most cohesive teams can also be the most punishing when someone breaks ranks. "I trust Coach" mistakes an individual relationship for a team-level norm—the captain's trust in the manager tells you nothing about whether the third-choice goalkeeper feels safe reporting a shoulder problem. "We hired diverse staff" mistakes demographics for belonging—a female S&C coach on a men's professional team has been included in the roster, but not necessarily in the room where tactical decisions are debated.

In practitioner settings, the conflation often stems from Lencioni's (2002) The Five Dysfunctions of a Team, whose vulnerability-based trust overlaps heavily with psychological safety. This chapter maintains the academic distinction: trust is dyadic (between two people), whereas psychological safety is a team-level norm.

Trust between the head coach and a veteran captain does not extend to the junior physiotherapist who sees a return-to-play decision being rushed—or to the academy coach who notices that a youth player's behavioral changes suggest a problem at home. That physiotherapist needs team-level norms that protect dissent, not dyadic trust with someone higher up the hierarchy (Rousseau et al., 1998). And when belonging is already fragile—the international player navigating a new language, the openly gay athlete in a hyper-masculine locker room, and the female coach in a historically male-dominated sport—speaking up becomes even riskier (Clark, 2020). Mistaking one construct for another sends the intervention in the wrong direction entirely.

The errors are predictable. Treating low safety as a trust problem leads to team-building retreats and one-on-one coaching sessions that strengthen dyadic relationships between the coach and individual players but leave the squad-level norm untouched—the norm that says you do not question the game plan, you do not flag a teammate's declining form, you do not tell the head coach what the assistant coaches already see. Treating it as an inclusion problem leads to diverse hiring and equity initiatives that get people into the building but do not change whether they can speak once they are in the performance meeting.

2.2 Why It Matters

The evidence for psychological safety is strongest where it matters most—in the processes that produce performance: information flow, learning speed, coordination, and error correction.

In organizational contexts, Frazier et al.'s (2017) meta-analysis of 136 primary studies found moderate-to-strong relationships between psychological safety and information sharing, learning behavior, and task performance. Moderator analyses confirmed that this relationship was most potent at the team level, predicting performance beyond what interpersonal trust alone could account for. At the organizational level, a climate of psychological safety directly predicts longitudinal changes in firm financial performance (Baer & Frese, 2003). Crucially, teams with higher psychological safety report more errors—not because they make more, but because they feel secure enough to surface and correct them without fear of retribution (Edmondson, 1999). Today, this evidence base robustly extends across healthcare, technology, and diverse organizational settings (Edmondson & Bransby, 2023).

However, a strict boundary condition applies when transferring this concept to elite sport. Most meta-analytic studies were conducted in traditional knowledge-work settings where job security is relatively stable, and failure is framed as a learning opportunity. Elite sport, by contrast, involves embodied performance under intense public scrutiny, compressed time horizons, and the constant, zero-sum threat of deselection (Taylor et al., 2026). These volatile conditions fundamentally alter—and sometimes actively suppress—how safety operates, often forcing athletes to "wear a mask" to conceal mental health struggles, injuries, or burnout out of fear that vulnerability will cost them their roster spot (Walton et al., 2024). In these environments, physical or tactical errors have immediate, punitive consequences, requiring a distinct conceptualization of "performance safety" rather than just interpersonal voice behavior (Taylor et al., 2026).

Sport-specific studies are beginning to capture this duality. While Rice et al. (2022) successfully validated a sport psychological safety inventory showing its protective benefits, the reality of the elite environment remains stark: Hurst et al. (2025) found that elite athletes report significantly lower psychological safety than recreational athletes, often silencing them from reporting interpersonal violence or injury to protect their careers. When successfully cultivated despite these pressures, psychological safety acts as a critical buffer; Fransen et al. (2020) demonstrated that leaders who foster it significantly enhance both team functioning and athlete well-being. Nevertheless, because most sport-specific research remains cross-sectional, relies on small samples, and wrestles with ambiguous conceptual definitions of "safety" in inherently exclusionary environments (Collins et al., 2022; Vella et al., 2024), current evidence in sports should be treated as a directional compass rather than a definitive map.

2.3 Why Sport Makes It Harder

Principle: Elite sport does not merely lack psychological safety. It contains structural features that actively produce silence. Building safety here requires overcoming forces that make silence rational.

2.3.1 Fear and the Top-Down Cascade

Many sport environments rely on anxiety as a performance lever. Benching decisions carry implicit threat, selection uncertainty is maintained rather than reduced, and public correction is treated as motivational—patterns that can overlap with forms of psychological abuse documented in elite sport (Mountjoy et al., 2016). The intent is often performance-driven, but the downstream effects are predictable: chronic fear narrows attention, degrades working memory, and triggers threat-rigidity (McEwen, 2017; Staw et al., 1981), producing defensive behaviors that interfere with learning (Argyris, 1990). Under sustained pressure, compliance without candor is what remains.

The effect cascades. Leader inclusiveness directly predicts psychological safety, and the relationship is stronger when status differences are large (Hirak et al., 2012; Nembhard & Edmondson, 2006). When leaders respond to voice with defensiveness or inaction, speaking up is suppressed regardless of stated policy (Detert & Burris, 2007). In sport, status differences are among the most extreme in any professional context, and what the leader models propagates through social learning (Bandura, 1977). A single defensive reaction at the top can reshape the silence calculus for an entire organization.

2.3.2 Power, Stakes, and Selection

Three structural forces combine to make silence rational in elite sport.

The first is power asymmetry. Coaches control playing time, contract renewals, and career trajectories. The person being challenged often holds material power over the person speaking. Status differences suppress voice (Nembhard & Edmondson, 2006), and in sport, the consequences of misjudging that calculus are public and immediate.

The second is selection anxiety. Athletes compete for roster spots, which means that teammates are simultaneously collaborators and rivals. Admitting uncertainty or limitation risks being seen as the weak link in a system that is always looking for one (Taylor et al., 2022).

The third is public evaluation and financial stakes. Athletes perform in front of thousands, with cameras capturing every decision and social media extending the evaluation window indefinitely (Kavanagh et al., 2019). The internal calculus is constant: if I admit I do not understand the defensive scheme, does that make me the liability?

Goffman's (1959) concept of impression management helps explain the pattern: athletes operating under intense scrutiny curate images of invulnerability and competence. When the cost of losing face is steep enough, defensive silence becomes the most logical available choice.

2.3.3 The Job Insecurity Trap

"Hired to get fired" is a saying heard often in professional sports, and it applies to coaches and staff as much as athletes. Chronic job insecurity is associated with threat-rigidity—a narrowing of attention, a retreat to safe behaviors, and a collapse of creative risk-taking (Staw et al., 1981). Meta-analytic evidence finds negative associations between job insecurity and task performance (Sverke et al., 2019), and chronic stress produces physiological wear that can outlast the stressor itself (McEwen, 2017).

The intervention is structural: predictability. Define performance expectations explicitly, hold evaluation criteria stable across winning and losing periods, and make the evaluation process transparent before results arrive. The job may still be insecure, but learnable rules allow calculated risk-taking that undifferentiated threat does not (Staw et al., 1981). Building organizational learning systems that outlast individuals ensures that knowledge survives coaching cycles rather than walking out the door with each transition.

2.3.4 Who Pays More for Candor

The cost of speaking up is not distributed equally. Multiple identity-based factors compound the silence calculus, each loading voice with additional risk that varies by who is speaking and who is listening.

In racially homogeneous leadership structures, speaking up can trigger racialized interpretations—"difficult," "attitude problem"—that carry a credibility discount disproportionate to content (Cunningham, 2019; Farrington et al., 2015). Organizations shaped by hegemonic masculinity norms can penalize women and gender-diverse athletes more heavily for the same behaviors coded as assertive in others (Walker & Sartore-Baldwin, 2013). Stereotype threat reduces working memory capacity (Schmader & Johns, 2003), consuming the cognitive resources that speaking up already demands. For LGBTQ+ athletes, identity concealment is itself a cognitive tax, and disclosure risks compounding identity costs on top of professional ones (Cunningham, 2019). Athletes navigating unfamiliar cultural systems, visa dependency, and language barriers face structural barriers to voice that go beyond interpersonal dynamics (Ryba et al., 2015; Schinke et al., 2011). And mental health disclosure carries stigma and perceived weakness in high-performance contexts, adding deselection risk to an already loaded calculation (Gouttebarge et al., 2017; Reardon & Factor, 2010).

These dynamics compound across identity dimensions. An athlete who is a woman of color navigating immigration status in a hegemonic-masculinity environment faces a silence calculus with multiple simultaneous cost multipliers. Track who speaks, who gets interrupted, whose concerns get acted on, and whether follow-through differs by group. If the same people consistently pay the price for candor, that is not psychological safety—that is a participation gap.

2.3.5 Building Safety Without Positional Authority

Many practitioners reading this book operate in roles where structural decisions are made above them. The strategies in Table 2.3 address that reality: they are harm-reduction measures that protect information flow within a bounded sphere, while the case for structural change is built upward. For readers with structural authority, these same strategies model the behaviors they should be looking for—and protecting—at every level below them.

Local safety pockets are harm reduction, not a substitute for senior accountability. If the problem is structural, name it with evidence and escalate.

2.4 Diagnosing the Foundation

Principle: Psychological safety shows up in language before it shows up in surveys. Listen to how people talk—then measure what formal tools can capture.

The HPCOS framework's core diagnostic metric is Speed of Truth: the elapsed time between someone recognizing a problem and that information reaching a person with the authority to act on it. Every tool in this chapter—the Safety Diagnostic, the voice infrastructure, the meeting protocols, and the quarterly pulse—exists to compress that interval. When Speed of Truth is fast, errors get caught early, decisions improve, and the system learns. When it is slow, the organization navigates on stale or missing data. The diagnostic question is not "Do people feel safe?" but "How long does it take for bad news to travel from the person who sees it to the person who can fix it?"

The sections that follow build the conceptual foundation for this chapter's primary assessment tool—the Safety Diagnostic (Section 2.4.4)—by identifying the linguistic, behavioral, and structural signals it is designed to detect.

2.4.1 The Language of Unsafe Cultures

Table 2.4 translates common phrases into what they reveal about safety.

TABLE 2.3 Building Safety Without Positional Authority—Five Harm-Reduction Strategies

Strategy	*What to Do*	*Boundary Condition*
Build a local safety pocket	Create a micro-climate within your sphere of influence—even when the broader culture is unsafe. Make it clear that truth-telling within your space will not be punished, and prove it repeatedly.	A local pocket protects information flow within your reach. It does not fix the structural conditions above you.
Create one clear channel and close the loop	Designate how concerns reach you and demonstrate what happens with the information. Acknowledge within 24–48 hours; report back what changed or why it did not.	If concerns go in and nothing comes back, the channel dies. Closing the loop is the mechanism, not the aspiration.
Protect confidentiality within your role boundaries	State the boundary clearly: "What you tell me stays between us unless someone is at risk."	Be honest about the limits of your confidentiality. Do not promise what your role cannot guarantee.
Escalate with evidence, not gossip	Document patterns with specifics: dates, behaviors, outcomes. Evidence-based escalation is harder to dismiss than "I think we have a culture problem."	Evidence-based escalation requires a system that receives evidence. If no such system exists, building one becomes the first advocacy task.
Model the behavior publicly	Admit your own mistakes, ask questions that reveal what you do not know, and thank people who challenge you.	Modeling works when it is visible and consistent. Sporadic vulnerability in private does not shift the calculus for others.

TABLE 2.4 Diagnostic Language of Unsafe Cultures

Phrase	*Translation*
"That is above my pay grade."	I have thoughts, but sharing them gets me trouble.
"Stay in your lane."	Do not bring information across boundaries. I have learned that speaking up gets people in trouble.
"Keep your head down."	Visibility is dangerous.
"Hired to get fired."	Job security is an illusion—do not take risks.
"I just work here."	I have disengaged.

When these phrases become common, the organization is displaying organizational silence (Morrison & Milliken, 2000): learned behavior shaped by leadership response patterns. Milliken et al. (2003) found that the issues employees most commonly withheld concerned supervisors and organizational processes. Detert and Edmondson (2011) found that employees carry implicit voice theories that operate below conscious awareness and persist even when leaders explicitly invite dissent.

2.4.2 The Silence Taxonomy

Not all silence is the same. The three silence types introduced in Chapter 1 (Table 1.3)—acquiescent, defensive, and prosocial—require different interventions (Van Dyne et al., 2003).

Return to Marta: Marta's silence was defensive—she had raised the process concern and been shut down. The video analyst moved to acquiescent silence—he had watched Marta's experience and concluded that flagging contradictions in load data was pointless. The goalkeeper coach was prosocially silent—protecting his working relationship by not forcing a confrontation about the backup keeper's confidence. Three types of silence operated in one environment, each requiring a different fix, and the organization was addressing none of them.

2.4.3 False Cohesion

Some teams mistake shared suffering for psychological safety. A toughness-only identity can create loud bonding and still be unsafe for truth. This chapter calls it false cohesion: a room that sounds confident but where no one says what they actually think (Schein, 2010). The behavioral markers are high energy and verbal participation combined with an absence of admissions of uncertainty, requests for help, or challenges to authority. False cohesion produces high energy in one register only—agreement, enthusiasm, and toughness—while the registers that require vulnerability (uncertainty, dissent, and disclosure) remain silent.

If the Sentence Test returns zero instances of upward challenge in 30 days and the team self-reports as "close," treat the cohesion as false until evidence contradicts it.

BOX 2.4 PSYCHOLOGY SIDELINES WITH DR. MCB — FALSE COHESION AND THE SAFETY TEST

Many teams and groups confidently rate themselves as having excellent chemistry—often giving themselves a 10 out of 10. The atmosphere is lively and energetic, with members enthusiastically finishing one another's sentences. However, when posed with the question, "When was the last time someone junior told someone senior they were wrong–and it went well?," the collective silence reveals an uncomfortable truth. Despite the outward signs of camaraderie and engagement, everyone is aware that the honest answer is embarrassing.

This dynamic is not limited to individuals; entire teams exhibit similar behavior. Instead of simply asking whether the room feels psychologically safe, a more useful diagnostic approach is to ask who has recently tested the safety of the environment and to examine what the outcome was when they did. This shift in questioning provides a clearer indication of true safety, beyond the surface-level energy and perceived closeness.

2.4.4 The Safety Diagnostic

The Safety Diagnostic is this chapter's primary assessment tool. It provides a structured process for evaluating whether psychological safety is functioning in a given environment, organized into three components: a rapid leadership test (the Sentence Test), behavioral observation markers, and a formal assessment layer. It is a practitioner-developed diagnostic derived from research synthesis (Edmondson, 1999; Morrison, 2011; Van Dyne et al., 2003), not a validated instrument. It functions as a diagnostic lens, not a scorecard—designed to identify where silence is concentrating, what type it is, and where intervention should be directed first.

How to Use the Safety Diagnostic. Run the Sentence Test first—it establishes whether safety has actually been tested recently. Then assess the behavioral indicators in Component 2 using observation, not self-report. Classify the dominant silence type using the taxonomy from Section 2.4.2. From there, identify the highest-priority intervention using Table 2.5 and the Diagnostic Questions (Section 2.4.5). Repeat quarterly (see Section 2.8.1).

- **Component 1: The Sentence Test.** The Sentence Test is the rapid-assessment entry point of this diagnostic, not a standalone instrument. The question it asks: can someone in the organization ask a powerful person an uncomfortable question this week—and have it go well? Not theoretically. Actually. To apply, identify the five most powerful people in the environment. For each, look back 30 days. Did anyone with less power challenge them, deliver bad news, disagree publicly, or admit confusion? If zero instances surface—or if instances went badly—that is the signal. Investigate.
- **Component 2: Behavioral Observation.** Three observation domains capture what surveys typically miss. In meetings: who speaks? What happens

after someone admits uncertainty? Do people check faces before answering? After errors: do teammates move toward the person who made a mistake or away? How the group responds in the immediate aftermath of an error reveals more about safety than retrospective self-report. In hallways: are complaints surfacing in formal channels or in parking lots? When side conversations increase, it often means that official venues are not functioning as safe spaces for candor.

- **Component 3: Formal Assessment.** Validated instruments include Edmondson's (1999) team psychological safety scale (seven items) and the Sport Psychological Safety Inventory (Rice et al., 2022; 11 items across three factors). Both require anonymous administration and disaggregation by subgroup. In low-safety settings, people often do not believe anonymity is real (Tourangeau & Yan, 2007), so formal assessment should be triangulated with the behavioral observation and system signals from Components 1 and 2.

2.4.5 From Diagnosis to Action

The sequence is: signal → hypothesis → targeted action → sustained change.

Things to consider while you're diagnosing:

- **Where does the silence concentrate?** Localized silence often points to a leader problem; organization-wide silence often points to a structural one.

TABLE 2.5 Diagnostic Signals and Interventions

Diagnostic Signal	*Root Cause*	*Immediate Action*	*Long-Term Fix*
Complaints route through parking lots	Formal channels are unsafe	Interview five people in 48 hours; identify a pattern	Install a confidential voice channel; close loops publicly
The same three people speak in every meeting	Power asymmetry or status norms	Add structured turn-taking; the leader speaks last	Train leaders on inclusive facilitation
Increased turnover in one department	Local toxicity or low leader safety	Interview departing staff; identify leader response pattern	Coach or replace the leader; install protective structures
Post-loss silence	Fear of blame	Name the pattern: "We went quiet—what are we not saying?"	Blameless post-mortem protocol
Medical staff hedging injury reports	Return-to-play conflated with selection	Separate medical reporting from selection decisions	Build a protected clinical channel

- **Which roles are most affected?** Are the people closest to the problem the ones least positioned to name it?
- **What is the dominant silence type?** Misdiagnosis produces wasted effort.
- **Has anyone tested safety recently?** If no one with less power has challenged a decision in the past 30 days, safety has not been tested.
- **What happened the last time someone spoke up?** This—not survey scores—is the ground truth of psychological safety.

2.4.6 Inheriting an Unsafe Culture

When you inherit a psychologically unsafe culture, expect a significant lag before people believe that safety is real. Organizational trust repair research suggests that rebuilding credibility after violation requires sustained, repeated, consistent behavior over time—and that the timeline scales with the severity and duration of the prior breach (Kim et al., 2004; Dirks et al., 2009). In practice, this means months rather than weeks because belief tracks behavioral consistency, not announcements. The Safety Diagnostic should be run at intake to establish a baseline and then repeated quarterly to track whether the lag is closing.

2.5 Voice Infrastructure

Telling athletes or staff to "just speak up" is not an infrastructure; in a high-stakes sports environment, it is asking them to take an unmitigated risk. Morrison's (2011) review identifies three conditions that predict whether people will actually use their voice: perceived efficacy (will anything actually change?), perceived safety (will I be punished or benched?), and channel availability (is there a clear route to speak?). A functioning voice infrastructure actively engineers all three.

2.5.1 What Voice Infrastructure Looks Like

In practice, telling an athlete their voice matters means nothing without the systemic plumbing to back it up. Effective voice infrastructure requires four distinct components:

- **Decoupled Channels:** Confidential input routes that are structurally separated from the coaches or managers who control roster selection and contract evaluation.
- **Rapid Response Protocols:** A system that closes the loop on feedback within 24–48 hours, proving to the athlete that their input did not go into a void.
- **Protected Listeners:** Designated roles (such as a welfare officer or ombudsman) that sit entirely outside the coaching hierarchy.

- **Explicit Boundaries:** Total clarity from day 1 about what stays confidential and what legally or ethically must be escalated (Devitt & McCarthy, 2010).

2.5.2 Confidentiality Boundaries

Sports medicine professionals and psychologists operate under immense dual-loyalty pressures—caught between the athlete's privacy and the organization's desire to know who is fit to perform (Devitt & McCarthy, 2010). Confidentiality should be the default, with limits defined in advance by applicable law, professional codes, and safeguarding policy (which vary by jurisdiction and role). Typical exceptions include imminent risk of harm, mandatory safeguarding reporting, and explicit informed consent. When information must be shared, share the minimum necessary and keep it functional (e.g., availability needs) rather than diagnostic detail.

2.5.3 When Voice Infrastructure Fails

The design principles of infrastructure matter far less than the follow-through. When sports organizations fail to build this correctly, they usually fall into one of three distinct traps:

- **The Ghost Channel:** An anonymous reporting app or form is installed with massive fanfare, but receives zero submissions six months later because the earliest inputs were never acknowledged.
- **The Broken Promise:** A practitioner promises an athlete absolute confidentiality, but fails to escalate when the athlete discloses severe misconduct or abuse. When nothing happens, trust evaporates, and the rest of the team quietly stops disclosing.
- **The Privilege Trap:** The infrastructure is structurally available, but functionally inaccessible. If the reporting channels are only utilized by veteran players, captains, or majority-group members, the system is failing the most vulnerable. Voice metrics must always be disaggregated by demographic group and roster status to ensure true accessibility.

2.6 The 90-Day Sprint and Meeting Design

Principle: Psychological safety is never built by a locker room announcement. It is built by repeated proof under pressure. When an organization attempts to change its culture, the first 90 days dictate whether the athletes and staff believe that the shift is real or just another passing management trend.

To bridge the gap between theory and reality, leaders can utilize the 90-Day Sprint. While not a scientifically validated psychometric instrument, the Sprint

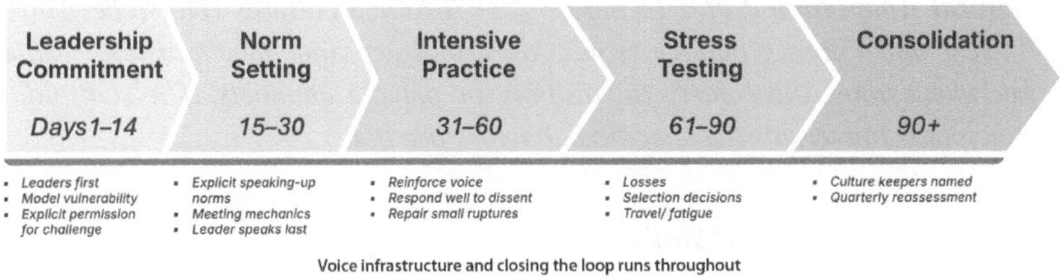

FIGURE 2.2 The 90-Day Psychological Safety Sprint. The Four Phases Mapped Alongside Key Actions, Measurement Points, and Common Failure Modes.

The sprint anticipates regression and builds correction into the process.

is a robust practitioner framework derived from leading implementation research (Clark, 2020; Detert & Burris, 2007; Nembhard & Edmondson, 2006). Its primary function is to deliberately scaffold lower-risk voice behaviors before demanding higher-risk vulnerability, closely following Clark's (2020) four-stage model of psychological safety. As outlined in Figure 2.2, the Sprint maps these four phases alongside key actions, measurement points, and the common failure modes leaders must navigate.

2.6.1 The Four Phases of the Sprint

- **Phase 1: Leadership Commitment (Days 1–14):** Executive alignment on specific behavioral changes—not values discussions, but behavior contracts. The most senior leader publicly shares a professional mistake. Concurrently, a baseline safety measurement is taken using strict anonymity and disaggregated by role and demographic. (Note: In hostile climates where public vulnerability would be weaponized, start with a smaller admission in a private leadership-team setting and scale outward.)
- **Phase 2: Norm Setting (Days 15–30):** Leaders explicitly articulate the new rules: "I expect you to tell me when something is not working." Structural changes begin by redesigning one meeting format at each level.
- **Phase 3: Intensive Practice (Days 31–60):** Teams introduce weekly 15-minute safety moments on genuine dilemmas and weekly three-question pulse checks. Middle managers and captains receive cascade training to embed status-flattening rituals, such as leaders deliberately speaking last or rotating facilitation (Detert & Burris, 2007; Nembhard & Edmondson, 2006).
- **Phase 4: Stress Testing (Days 61–90):** The true test of whether safety persists under pressure (e.g., post-loss meetings and selection decisions). Athletes get real input into tactical decisions and are held to the consequences; debriefs focus ruthlessly on decision quality, not character.

Cultural Adaptation Note: *In high power-distance cultures (Hofstede, 2001), Phase 1 and Phase 4 behaviors may need indirect voice mechanisms—written pre-submissions, third-party facilitation, or private channels. The scaffolding principle is universal; the specific behaviors are not.*

2.6.2 When the Sprint Stalls

Regression during the sprint is not a failure; it is an anticipated feature of the process. How leaders handle these stalls determines the ultimate success of the culture shift.

- **When Norms Do Not Stick (Phase 2):** The usual cause is leader reversion. The fix is a public correction: "I asked for honest feedback last week and I got defensive when I heard it. That is on me. Tell me what you held back." This public correction matters more than the original norm-setting because it proves the system can absorb a coach's mistake without collapsing.
- **When Safety Erodes Under Pressure (Phase 4):** This is the ultimate test. Leaders must name the erosion in real-time: "I notice we have gone quiet since the loss. That is the moment we need honesty most. What are we not saying?"

2.6.3 Meeting Design

To support the behaviors demanded in the Sprint, the architecture of team meetings and film sessions must change. This framework is theoretically grounded, integrating research on task conflict (Bradley et al., 2012), authentic dissent (Nemeth et al., 2001), and power-distance mitigation.

Before the Meeting

- **Circulate the question, not the answer:** Give athletes time to process.
- **Assign a rotating "Devil's Advocate":** Authentic dissent produces stronger tactical outcomes (Nemeth et al., 2001), but giving a player structural permission to disagree lowers the barrier.
- **Design for power-distance:** Invite two people who typically stay silent (e.g., rookies or junior staff) to prepare one specific observation. Use silent writing, pre-submitted questions, or small-group breakouts.

During the Meeting

- **Ask, then wait:** Count to 10 silently. Do not fill the void.

- **Go to the edges first:** Ask, "What are the junior staff/bench players seeing?" before the veterans speak.
- **Separate the idea from the person:** Discuss tactical proposals without attribution during the initial evaluation.

The Disagreement Protocol

Task conflict only improves performance when psychological safety is high enough to contain it; otherwise, it bleeds into relationship conflict (Bradley et al., 2012; De Dreu & Weingart, 2003; Jehn, 1995).

- Ask for the counterargument first.
- Anchor debates to video evidence or data, not locker room status.
- Challenge the ideas, never the motives.
- **The Rule: Once decided, debate stops, and execution starts.**

After the Meeting

Thank the challengers privately for speaking up. Most importantly, close the loop by reporting back on what happened as a result of their input. Silence after speaking up teaches silence.

2.7 Repair and Accountability

Principle: Safety breaks. Repair is part of the job. Under pressure, ruptures are contagious: people watch what happens next and decide whether to speak again.

2.7.1 Repairing Ruptures

When a rupture has already happened, speed matters. If the gap goes unfilled, people fill it with threat stories.

The protocol moves in five phases. Hours 0–4: acknowledge directly that something significant happened. No minimizing, no over-explaining. Hours 4–12: individual check-ins with affected people ("How are you doing with what happened?"). Hours 12–24: structured team meeting stating facts, values breached, and specific actions being taken. Hours 24–48: follow-up pulse check on whether people feel the situation was addressed. Days 3–7: return to routine with explicit safety messaging, referencing the rupture briefly in regular forums.

Common failure modes: minimizing ("it was not that bad"), over-explaining ("let me tell you the full context"), and disappearing for 48 hours while hoping it resolves on its own.

BOX 2.5 TIMEOUT — THE REPAIR IS THE MESSAGE

Every rupture is a live experiment in safety. The team is not watching the mistake–they are watching what happens next. A leader who names the rupture, owns it publicly, and changes a specific behavior teaches more about the culture in 48 hours than six months of values posters ever could. The correction is the credibility. Disappear after a rupture, and the silence becomes the organization's answer.

2.7.2 The Blameless Post-Mortem

High-reliability domains—aviation, healthcare, and nuclear power—investigate errors without scapegoating (Dekker, 2012; Reason, 1997; Weick & Sutcliffe, 2007). The Blameless Post-Mortem adapts that principle for sport. It is not a validated instrument but a practitioner-developed facilitation framework, structured around four After Action Review questions: what happened? What did we expect? What contributed to the gap? What will we change?

Three facilitation decisions shape whether the debrief produces learning or defensiveness. The session should be led by someone other than the head coach, and opened with an explicit frame: "We are here to understand the process, not assign blame." Each participant should identify one thing they personally could have done differently before discussing what others did—self-critique first reduces the defensive posture that blame-first sequencing produces (Dickerson & Kemeny, 2004). And video evidence should anchor the conversation to observable events rather than competing narratives. The session closes with two to three specific, owned action items.

If debriefs routinely produce silence or sarcasm, treat that as a signal that the process itself feels unsafe—a performance risk, not a personality problem (Dickerson & Kemeny, 2004).

2.7.3 Psychological Safety Versus Safeguarding

Some behaviors are cultural ruptures. Others are safeguarding/HR matters. Psychological safety supports earlier disclosure, but it does not replace formal reporting pathways. Coaches often serve as de facto gatekeepers for athlete disclosure of welfare concerns, which means that the line between safety-building and safeguarding must be clearly drawn. If the issue triggers safeguarding duties, follow policy and legal obligations (International Safeguarding Children in Sport Working Group, 2014; Mountjoy et al., 2016).

2.7.4 Accountability Without Fear: A Just Culture Lens

The Just Culture framework operationalizes one critical dimension of Performance Safety: accountability. Three structural requirements hold it together—clear expectations defined before evaluation occurs, fair process applied consistently, and protection from humiliation during the accountability process itself.

A Just Culture framework (Dekker, 2012; Marx, 2001; Reason, 1997) separates three categories:

Human Error: Inadvertent slips despite best intentions. Response: console, analyze system conditions, and fix contributing factors.

At-Risk Behavior: Shortcuts taken under production pressure—the athlete who skips the warm-up protocol because the schedule is compressed, and

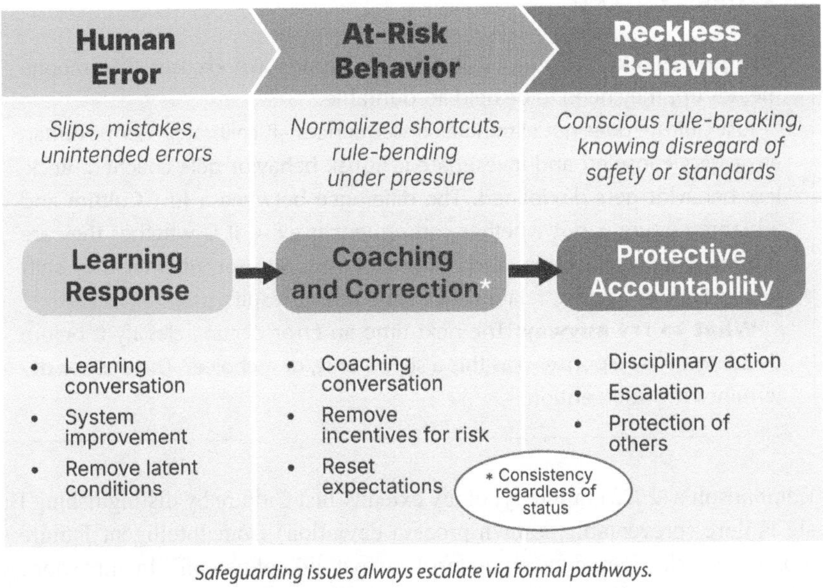

FIGURE 2.3 Just Culture Accountability Spectrum.

Adapted from Patient Safety and the "Just Culture": A Primer for Health Care Executives, by D. A. Marx (2001), Trustees of Columbia University; and Just Culture: Balancing Safety and Accountability (2nd ed.), by S. Dekker (2012), CRC Press. This figure maps human error, at-risk behavior, and reckless behavior alongside the appropriate response for each. A single "accountability" policy applied uniformly across all error types produces either excessive punishment for honest mistakes (destroying safety) or insufficient consequences for recklessness (destroying standards). The governance question is who classifies the behavior—and whether the classifier has a stake in the outcome.

the physio who clears someone faster than they should because the coach is asking. Response: coach, remove incentives to cut corners, and clarify expectations.

Reckless Behavior: Conscious disregard of clear rules and substantial risk. Response: discipline, restrict role, document, and escalate.

When people believe that honest disclosure will be met with investigation rather than punishment, the information system opens (Dekker, 2012; Reason, 1997). Elite sport has the same error taxonomy but has largely not built the classification infrastructure that aviation and healthcare now treat as standard. Figure 2.3 illustrates the accountability spectrum and the proportional response for each behavior category.

BOX 2.6 SKEPTIC'S CORNER — SO THERE ARE NO CONSEQUENCES?

The pushback: "This Just Culture stuff sounds like excuses. If someone messes up, they need to be held accountable."

Just Culture does not eliminate consequences—it calibrates them. Human error gets consoled and investigated. At-risk behavior gets coached. Reckless behavior gets disciplined. The difference between a Just Culture and a blame culture is not whether consequences exist. It is whether they are proportional, predictable, and applied consistently—or whether they shift depending on context, relationships, and recent results.

What to try anyway: The next time an error occurs, classify it before deciding on a response. Was this a slip, a drift, or a choice? The answer determines the intervention.

Edmondson's (2023) failure typology extends Just Culture by distinguishing Basic Failure (preventable, known-process deviation) from Intelligent Failure (a thoughtful risk taken in uncertain territory that did not pay off). In elite sport, an athlete who experiments with a tactical adjustment during a match and it fails has produced an Intelligent Failure. The Just Culture framework alone might classify this as at-risk behavior; Edmondson's lens asks whether the risk was taken thoughtfully in service of learning. Table 2.6 maps the two frameworks together. Punish Intelligent Failure, and people stop experimenting.

Governance note: *If the classifier has a stake in the outcome, the whole matrix collapses. In most elite sport environments, the head coach is both the person most affected by errors and the person who classifies them. The person classifying behavior should not be the person whose decisions are under review. Assign*

TABLE 2.6 Just Culture Categories Mapped Against Edmondson's Failure Typology

	Basic Failure (Preventable, Known-Process Deviation)	*Complex Failure (System Breakdown in Familiar Territory)*	*Intelligent Failure (Thoughtful Risk in Uncertain Territory)*
Human error (inadvertent slip)	Console; investigate system conditions; fix contributing factors.	Console; investigate compounding system elements; redesign workflow.	N/A—Intelligent Failure requires deliberate action; inadvertent slips do not qualify.
At-risk behavior (shortcut under pressure)	Coach; remove incentives to cut corners; clarify expectations.	Coach; investigate production pressure; redesign system incentives.	Protect and learn. Debrief the reasoning, extract the learning, adjust the approach—do not coach it away.
Reckless behavior (conscious disregard of clear rules)	Discipline; restrict role; document and escalate.	Discipline; investigate whether system signals made risk invisible.	Reclassify. Conscious disregard of clear rules is not Intelligent Failure. Apply standard reckless-behavior response.

Authors' synthesis. Just Culture categories adapted from Marx (2001) and Dekker (2012). Failure typology adapted from Edmondson (2023).

classification to someone with organizational standing but no direct involvement. If independent classification is not feasible, requiring written reasoning before consequences are applied provides a minimum safeguard.

2.8 Sustaining Safety Beyond Day 90

Principle: Psychological safety does not have a completion date. It has a maintenance schedule—measurement, repair, and recalibration on a recurring cycle.

2.8.1 The Quarterly Rhythm

Quarterly safety pulse: Administer a brief anonymous pulse (three to five items) disaggregated by role and demographics. Compare each cycle to baseline. The critical analytic move is subgroup comparison: an overall average that holds steady can mask regression in a single role group or demographic. If any subgroup declines on two or more items relative to the prior cycle, treat it as actionable—do not wait for a third data point.

Suggested pulse items, adapted from Edmondson's (1999) seven-item scale for brevity:

1. If I make a mistake in this environment, it is held against me (reverse-scored).

2. It is safe to take a risk in this team.
3. People in this environment sometimes reject others for being different (reverse-scored).

Add one to two context-specific items based on the previous cycle's findings—for example, "When I raised a concern in the past 30 days, something changed as a result."

Quarterly safety review: A 30-minute standing agenda item in the senior leadership meeting, facilitated with the following sequence. First, review pulse results by subgroup—where is the signal? Second, review voice channel metrics: submission volume, median response time, resolution rate, and disaggregation by channel type. Third, identify the single most concerning erosion signal. Fourth, assign one owner with a specific action and a 30-day timeline. Fifth, report the outcome of the prior quarter's action item—did the visible change happen?

The review must produce one visible, communicable change per quarter. If it does not, the review is theater.

Seasonal recalibration: Sport environments have natural pressure cycles—preseason, transfer windows, playoff pushes, post-loss sequences, and coaching transitions. Safety will be tested at each inflection point.

Schedule explicit check-ins at each transition: a 15-minute structured conversation with culture keepers asking three questions: what has gotten harder to say in the last two weeks? Who has gone quiet? What did the last rupture teach us about our response speed?

2.8.2 Culture Keepers

Identify three to five individuals across levels and roles who consistently model safety-enabling behavior—not an appointed committee, but the people who already do the work. This book calls them culture keepers. Invest in them: explicit recognition, regular access to senior leadership, and a standing channel for flagging erosion. Meet with them quarterly to gather the ground-level intelligence that pulse surveys miss. When leadership turns over—and in sport, it will—culture keepers are the continuity that prevents safety from resetting to zero.

Culture keepers are the people others already go to when something feels wrong (cf. Weick & Sutcliffe, 2007; Morgeson et al., 2010). Observable markers: they name problems without catastrophizing, they are trusted across status levels, and they challenge authority without being labeled as threats. The question "Who do people actually go to when something is off?" produces better candidates than "Who should represent us on a culture committee?"

Because culture keepers carry disproportionate emotional labor, they need explicit support: access to supervision, protection from retaliation, and a clear mandate from senior leadership.

2.8.3 Integration With the HPCOS Architecture

Psychological safety is Layer 2 of the HPCOS framework. The layers above it depend on it operationally: when this layer weakens, they produce misleading outputs because the information feeding them is incomplete.

A silence classification at the Foundation layer changes what the Diagnostic layer should look for. If voice channels surface information that never reaches decision-makers, the problem is routing; if it reaches them and nothing changes, the problem is decision structure. A subgroup regression on the quarterly pulse—particularly when concentrated in lower-status roles or specific demographic groups—is a leading indicator that the layers above are about to degrade.

Because no validated threshold exists for sport-specific safety pulse instruments, treat any directional decline in a subgroup as actionable. Organizations with stable baselines across two or more cycles can calibrate their own threshold.

2.8.4 When You Lose the Gains

Regression is not failure; it is signal. The most common triggers: leadership transitions, high-pressure periods, and success (winning masks erosion because nobody names problems during a streak). When regression appears, return to the Safety Diagnostic, apply the targeted intervention, and treat regression as expected. The question is not whether safety will erode but whether the organization detects the erosion early and responds within days rather than months.

2.8.4.1 Chapter Synthesis

Psychological safety is not a cultural nicety bolted onto a functioning system. It is the structural layer that determines whether the system functions at all. The tools in this chapter operationalize a shift from "you are lucky to be here" to "we are lucky to have you" as structural architecture, not sentiment. If the answer to Question 2—can anyone here tell the truth?—is no, the answers to Questions 3–7 are unreliable. The organization is navigating on bad data. And does not know it.

Key Chapter Takeaways

1. **Psychological safety is a team-level operating condition, not individual confidence or interpersonal trust.** Interventions that target dyadic relationships or individual courage miss the structural norms that govern whether anyone speaks. Diagnose at the team level; fix at the team level.
2. **Silence in elite sport is rational—produced by structural forces, not weak character.** Power asymmetry, selection anxiety, public evaluation, and

differential candor costs make self-protection the logical choice. Building safety means changing the structural calculation, not exhorting people to be braver.

3. **Performance Safety separates interpersonal process from performance accountability.** You can hold high standards and protect information flow simultaneously. The test is not whether consequences exist but whether people are humiliated in the process.
4. **Speed of Truth is the operational metric.** Measure the elapsed time between problem recognition and information reaching a decision-maker. Every tool in this chapter—the diagnostic, the sprint, the voice infrastructure, and the meeting protocols—exists to compress that interval.
5. **Safety requires a maintenance schedule, not a launch event.** Quarterly pulse checks, culture keepers, and seasonal recalibration sustain what the 90-Day Sprint builds. Expect regression under pressure; the question is detection speed and response quality.

Discussion Questions

1. Using the silence taxonomy, classify the dominant silence type in an organization you know. What structural feature made that silence rational, and what would need to change for the calculation to shift?
2. If adapting the 90-Day Sprint for a high power-distance context, which phases would you modify, and what alternative mechanisms would achieve the same information flow?
3. Design a measurement approach that would surface differential voice costs across demographic groups without creating surveillance dynamics that further suppress voice from the groups you are trying to hear.
4. In the opening case, the post-season review cited "delayed disclosure" without naming the structural cascade. Why do organizations default to surface-level process fixes when the root cause is a leader's defensive response?

References

Argyris, C. (1990). *Overcoming organizational defenses: Facilitating organizational learning*. Allyn & Bacon.

Baer, M., & Frese, M. (2003). Innovation is not enough: Climates for initiative and psychological safety, process innovations, and firm performance. *Journal of Organizational Behavior*, *24*(1), 45–68. https://doi.org/10.1002/job.179

Bandura, A. (1977). *Social learning theory*. Prentice Hall.

Bradley, B. H., Anderson, H. J., Baur, J. E., & Klotz, A. C. (2012). When conflict helps: Integrating evidence for beneficial conflict in groups. *Organizational Psychology Review*, *2*(4), 264–295. https://doi.org/10.1177/2041386612446407

Clark, T. R. (2020). *The 4 stages of psychological safety: Defining the path to inclusion and innovation*. Berrett-Koehler Publishers.

Collins, J., Cruickshank, A., & Carson, H. J. (2022). Psychological safety in elite sport: A critical review. *Journal of Sports Sciences*, *40*(15), 1735–1745. https://doi.org/10.1080/02640414.2022.2103507

Cunningham, G. B. (2019). *Diversity and inclusion in sport organizations: A multilevel perspective* (4th ed.). Routledge. https://doi.org/10.4324/9781315208572

De Dreu, C. K. W., & Weingart, L. R. (2003). Task versus relationship conflict, team performance, and team member satisfaction: A meta-analysis. *Journal of Applied Psychology*, *88*(4), 741–749. https://doi.org/10.1037/0021-9010.88.4.741

Deci, E. L., & Ryan, R. M. (2000). The "what" and "why" of goal pursuits: Human needs and the self-determination of behavior. *Psychological Inquiry*, *11*(4), 227–268. https://doi.org/10.1207/S15327965PLI1104_01

Dekker, S. (2012). *Just culture: Balancing safety and accountability* (2nd ed.). CRC Press. https://doi.org/10.4324/9781315251271

Detert, J. R., & Burris, E. R. (2007). Leadership behavior and employee voice: Is the door really open? *Academy of Management Journal*, *50*(4), 869–884. https://doi.org/10.5465/amj.2007.26279183

Detert, J. R., & Edmondson, A. C. (2011). Implicit voice theories: Taken-for-granted rules of self-censorship at work. *Academy of Management Journal*, *54*(3), 461–488. https://doi.org/10.5465/amj.2011.61967925

Devitt, B. M., & McCarthy, C. (2010). "I am in blood Stepp'd in so far . . .": Ethical dilemmas and the sports team doctor. *British Journal of Sports Medicine*, *44*(3), 175–178. https://doi.org/10.1136/bjsm.2009.067579

Dickerson, S. S., & Kemeny, M. E. (2004). Acute stressors and cortisol responses: A theoretical integration and synthesis of laboratory research. *Psychological Bulletin*, *130*(3), 355–391. https://doi.org/10.1037/0033-2909.130.3.355

Dirks, K. T., Lewicki, R. J., & Zaheer, A. (2009). Repairing relationships within and between organizations: Building a conceptual foundation. *Academy of Management Review*, *34*(1), 68–84. https://doi.org/10.5465/amr.2009.35713285

Edmondson, A. C. (1999). Psychological safety and learning behavior in work teams. *Administrative Science Quarterly*, *44*(2), 350–383. https://doi.org/10.2307/2666999

Edmondson, A. C. (2018). *The fearless organization: Creating psychological safety in the workplace for learning, innovation, and growth*. John Wiley & Sons. https://doi.org/10.1002/9781119477242

Edmondson, A. C. (2023). *Right kind of wrong: The science of failing well*. Atria Books.

Edmondson, A. C., & Bransby, H. (2023). Psychological safety comes of age: Observed themes in an established literature. *Annual Review of Organizational Psychology and Organizational Behavior*, *10*, 383–411. https://doi.org/10.1146/annurev-orgpsych-120920-055217

Farrington, N., Kilgour, L., & Reynolds, S. (2015). Race, representation, and media framing in sport organizations: A critical review. *Sport Management Review*, *18*(2), 190–202. https://doi.org/10.1016/j.smr.2014.08.002

Fransen, K., McEwan, D., & Sarkar, M. (2020). Psychological safety in elite sport teams: A critical factor for resilience and performance. *Psychology of Sport and Exercise*, *49*, Article 101704. https://doi.org/10.1016/j.psychsport.2020.101704

Frazier, M. L., Fainshmidt, S., Klinger, R. L., Pezeshkan, A., & Vracheva, V. (2017). Psychological safety: A meta-analytic review and extension. *Personnel Psychology*, *70*(1), 113–165. https://doi.org/10.1111/peps.12183

Goffman, E. (1959). *The presentation of self in everyday life*. Doubleday.

Gouttebarge, V., Jonkers, R., Moen, M. H., Verhagen, E., Wylleman, P., & Kerkhoffs, G. M. M. J. (2017). A prospective cohort study on symptoms of common mental disorders among Dutch elite athletes. *BMJ Open Sport & Exercise Medicine*, *3*(1), Article e000271. https://doi.org/10.1136/bmjsem-2017-000271

Hirak, R., Peng, A. C., Carmeli, A., & Schaubroeck, J. M. (2012). Linking leader inclusiveness to work unit performance: The importance of psychological safety and learning from failures. *The Leadership Quarterly*, *23*(1), 107–117. https://doi.org/10.1016/j.leaqua.2011.11.009

Hofstede, G. (2001). *Culture's consequences: Comparing values, behaviors, institutions and organizations across nations* (2nd ed.). Sage Publications.

Hurst, P., Kavussanu, M., & Stirling, A. (2025). Elite athletes report lower psychological safety and are less likely to report interpersonal violence compared to recreational athletes: A cross-sectional study. *Journal of Applied Sport Psychology*. Advance online publication. https://doi.org/10.1080/10413200.2025.2473403

International Safeguarding Children in Sport Working Group. (2014). *International safeguards for children in sport*. UNICEF. https://www.unicef.org.uk/wp-content/uploads/2014/10/International-Safeguards-for-Children-in-Sport-Final-version-October-2014.pdf

Jehn, K. A. (1995). A multimethod examination of the benefits and detriments of intragroup conflict. *Administrative Science Quarterly*, *40*(2), 256–282. https://doi.org/10.2307/2393638

Kahn, W. A. (1990). Psychological conditions of personal engagement and disengagement at work. *Academy of Management Journal*, *33*(4), 692–724. https://doi.org/10.2307/256287

Kavanagh, E., Litchfield, C., & Osborne, J. (2019). Athletes and cyberbullying. In G. Breslin & G. Leavey (Eds.), *Mental health and well-being interventions in sport: Research, theory and practice* (pp. 199–217). Routledge.

Kim, P. H., Ferrin, D. L., Cooper, C. D., & Dirks, K. T. (2004). Removing the shadow of suspicion: The effects of apology versus denial for repairing competence-versus integrity-based trust violations. *Journal of Applied Psychology*, *89*(1), 104–118. https://doi.org/10.1037/0021-9010.89.1.104

Lencioni, P. (2002). *The five dysfunctions of a team: A leadership fable*. Jossey-Bass.

Marx, D. A. (2001). *Patient safety and the "just culture": A primer for health care executives*. Trustees of Columbia University. https://psnet.ahrq.gov/issue/patient-safety-and-just-culture-primer-health-care-executives

McEwen, B. S. (2017). Neurobiological and systemic effects of chronic stress. *Chronic Stress*, *1*, 2470547017692328. https://doi.org/10.1177/2470547017692328

Milliken, F. J., Morrison, E. W., & Hewlin, P. F. (2003). An exploratory study of employee silence: Issues that employees don't communicate upward and why. *Journal of Management Studies*, *40*(6), 1453–1476. https://doi.org/10.1111/1467-6486.00387

Morgeson, F. P., DeRue, D. S., & Karam, E. P. (2010). Leadership in teams: A functional approach to understanding leadership structures and processes. *Journal of Management*, *36*(1), 5–39. https://doi.org/10.1177/0149206309347376

Morrison, E. W. (2011). Employee voice behavior: Integration and directions for future research. *The Academy of Management Annals*, *5*(1), 373–412. https://doi.org/10.5465/19416520.2011.574506

Morrison, E. W., & Milliken, F. J. (2000). Organizational silence: A barrier to change and development in a pluralistic world. *Academy of Management Review*, *25*(4), 706–725. https://doi.org/10.5465/amr.2000.3707697

Mountjoy, M., Brackenridge, C., Arrington, M., Blauwet, C., Carska-Sheppard, A., Fasting, K., Kirby, S., Leahy, T., Marks, S., Martin, K., Starr, K., Tiivas, A., & Budgett, R. (2016). International Olympic Committee consensus statement: Harassment and abuse (non-accidental violence) in sport. *British Journal of Sports Medicine*, *50*(17), 1019–1029. https://doi.org/10.1136/bjsports-2016-096121

Nembhard, I. M., & Edmondson, A. C. (2006). Making it safe: The effects of leader inclusiveness and professional status on psychological safety and improvement efforts in health care teams. *Journal of Organizational Behavior*, *27*(7), 941–966. https://doi.org/10.1002/job.413

Nemeth, C. J., Brown, K., & Rogers, J. D. (2001). Devil's advocate versus authentic dissent: Stimulating quantity and quality. *Journal of Applied Social Psychology*, *31*(1), 48–58. https://doi.org/10.1111/j.1559-1816.2001.tb00153.x

Reardon, C. L., & Factor, R. M. (2010). Sport psychiatry: A systematic review of diagnosis and medical treatment of mental illness in athletes. *Sports Medicine*, *40*(11), 961–980. https://doi.org/10.2165/11536580-000000000-00000

Reason, J. (1997). *Managing the risks of organizational accidents*. Ashgate.

Rice, S. M., Bendtsen, P., Purcell, R., & Stenling, A. (2022). Development and validation of the Sport Psychological Safety Inventory. *Journal of Sport and Exercise Psychology*, *44*(6), 444–456. https://doi.org/10.1123/jsep.2021-0204

Rousseau, D. M., Sitkin, S. B., Burt, R. S., & Camerer, C. (1998). Not so different after all: A cross-discipline view of trust. *Academy of Management Review*, *23*(3), 393–404. https://doi.org/10.5465/amr.1998.926617

Ryba, T. V., Stambulova, N. B., & Wylleman, P. (2015). The cultural turn in sport psychology. In S. D. Mellalieu & S. Hanton (Eds.), *Contemporary advances in sport psychology: A review* (pp. 310–333). Routledge.

Schein, E. H. (2010). *Organizational culture and leadership* (4th ed.). Jossey-Bass.

Schein, E. H., & Bennis, W. G. (1965). *Personal and organizational change through group methods: The laboratory approach*. Wiley.

Schinke, R. J., Blodgett, A. T., McGannon, K. R., & Ge, Y. (2011). Finding one's footing on foreign soil: A content analysis of cultural transition in sport. *Journal of Sport Psychology in Action*, *2*(1), 1–12. https://doi.org/10.1080/21520704.2010.531475

Schmader, T., & Johns, M. (2003). Converging evidence that stereotype threat reduces working memory capacity. *Journal of Personality and Social Psychology*, *85*(3), 440–452. https://doi.org/10.1037/0022-3514.85.3.440

Staw, B. M., Sandelands, L. E., & Dutton, J. E. (1981). Threat-rigidity effects in organizational behavior: A multilevel analysis. *Administrative Science Quarterly*, *26*(4), 501–524. https://doi.org/10.2307/2392337

Sverke, M., Hellgren, J., & Näswall, K. (2019). Job insecurity: A literature review. In C. Cooper & J. Campbell Quick (Eds.), *The handbook of stress and health: A guide to research and practice* (pp. 331–348). Wiley Blackwell. https://doi.org/10.1002/9781118993811.ch20

Taylor, J., Gretton, T. W., & Sweeney, L. (2026). Performance safety: Conceptualising psychological safety when errors have consequences. *Journal of Applied Sport Psychology*, *38*(1), 1–15. https://doi.org/10.1080/10413200.2025.2521261

Taylor, L., Cumming, S., & Briggs, D. (2022). Psychological safety as a mechanism for mental health disclosure in elite athletes. *Psychology of Sport and Exercise*, *58*, Article 102082. https://doi.org/10.1016/j.psychsport.2021.102082

Tourangeau, R., & Yan, T. (2007). Sensitive questions in surveys. *Psychological Bulletin*, *133*(5), 859–883. https://doi.org/10.1037/0033-2909.133.5.859

Van Dyne, L., Ang, S., & Botero, I. C. (2003). Conceptualizing employee silence and employee voice as multidimensional constructs. *Journal of Management Studies*, *40*(6), 1359–1392. https://doi.org/10.1111/1467-6486.00384

Vella, S. A., Swann, C., & Allen, M. S. (2024). Psychological safety in sports teams: A systematic review and meta-analysis. *Sports Medicine*, *54*(2), 315–332. https://doi.org/10.1007/s40279-023-01965-0

Walker, N. A., & Sartore-Baldwin, M. L. (2013). Hegemonic masculinity and the institutionalized bias in men's sport organizations. *Journal of Sport Management*, *27*(5), 369–383. https://doi.org/10.1123/jsm.27.5.369

Walton, C. C., Purcell, R., Pilkington, V., Hall, K., Kenttä, G., Vella, S., & Rice, S. M. (2024). Psychological safety for mental health in elite sport: A theoretically informed model. *Sports Medicine*, *54*(3), 557–564. https://doi.org/10.1007/s40279-023-01912-2

Weick, K. E., & Sutcliffe, K. M. (2007). *Managing the unexpected: Resilient performance in an age of uncertainty* (2nd ed.). Jossey-Bass.

3

WHEN CULTURES TURN TOXIC—DIAGNOSIS

Learning Objectives

By the end of this chapter, the reader will be able to:

1. Distinguish between demanding and damaging high-performance environments using specific diagnostic markers across feedback, standards, voice, and emotional regulation.
2. Analyze early behavioral, performance, and retention signals of organizational toxicity and evaluate whether observed patterns constitute isolated incidents or systemic syndromes.
3. Use the Triad's escalation pathway to trace whether the presenting dysfunction originates at the coaching tier or cascades from upstream executive-level conditions.
4. Evaluate the relative contribution of each corner of the Toxic Triangle—destructive leaders, susceptible followers, and conducive environments—to determine intervention priorities.
5. Design a first-week diagnostic response that differentiates between coaching-specific and system-wide toxicity using the Weekly Diagnostic Triad.

BOX 3.1 CASE STUDY — THE NEW COACH WHO INHERITED THE SILENCE

Composite vignette. Details changed to protect privacy.

Tomás was hired to fix the culture—explicitly. The previous head coach had been sacked after a safeguarding investigation, and the board wanted

DOI: 10.4324/9781003631217-4

a visible reset. He arrived with a 90-day plan, an open-door policy, and a genuine belief that trust would follow transparency.

Week 1, he told an all-staff meeting: "I want to hear what's not working. No consequences for honesty." The room was silent. He held one-on-ones with every staff member—polite, vague, and brief. He added a pre-match tactical input window for players. Nobody used it. By month 2, he had opened every door. No one was walking through. He started interpreting the silence as resistance.

What he couldn't see: senior players had tested speaking up under the previous regime and been punished for it. One was dropped for a month after questioning a tactical decision. The nervous system doesn't reset when the nameplate on the door changes. Staff had filed concerns through the sporting director's office and watched nothing happen. They were not going to file again, regardless of who was asking.

The operations manager had written a transition report documenting the patterns Tomás would inherit—flinch responses to raised voices, senior players policing younger ones, and assistants running the old playbook. Her line manager buried it: "Let's not poison the well. Give him a clean start."

Tomás never saw the report. He diagnosed resistance, where the real diagnosis was scar tissue. He responded to silence with more invitations to speak, when what the system needed was visible evidence that speaking had changed outcomes for someone.

His end-of-season review cited "limited buy-in from the senior group" and recommended leadership coaching for the captain. Nobody mentioned the transition report. Nobody asked what the environment had taught people about honesty before Tomás arrived.

The review named the leader. It missed the soil.

3.1 The Diagnostic Task

Principle: Toxicity diagnosis within the HPCOS requires understanding what to look for, where it originates, and what makes it durable—before attempting intervention.

3.1.1 What This Chapter Diagnoses

The diagnostic logic here parallels medicine. A patient presenting with fatigue, weight loss, and night sweats could have a dozen explanations—but a clinician who knows the pattern recognizes when those symptoms cluster into something that demands a specific workup. The same applies to organizational toxicity:

isolated complaints, rising turnover, and a culture of silence—the diagnostic skill is recognizing when they form a syndrome and knowing what to rule out before intervening.

Toxicity isn't a coach having a bad day. It's a system producing a predictable pattern of harm—reinforced by how consequences are distributed, how information flows, and how the operating environment protects what it should correct (see Figure 3.1).

Organizational toxicity is sustained behavior by leaders that degrades subordinates through hostility, manipulation, or neglect—combined with environmental conditions that make the behavior durable (Einarsen et al., 2007; Padilla et al., 2007; Tepper, 2000, 2007). The environment protects the leader, discourages dissent, and creates costs for anyone who surfaces problems. The meta-analytic evidence is consistent: destructive leadership degrades subordinate well-being, job satisfaction, and organizational commitment (Schyns & Schilling, 2013).

FIGURE 3.1 You Are Here—Diagnosis.

The HPCOS seven-layer architecture with Layer 3 (Diagnosis) highlighted. This chapter answers Question 3—what is actually broken?—by diagnosing toxic culture patterns and specifying containment outputs that feed the Operating System layer. The three diagnostic outputs—environment classification, cascade source determination, and triangle analysis—serve as required inputs for Layer 4.

Critically, toxicity degrades the organization's own capacity to detect and correct the problem—the system reinforces itself, and without a functioning diagnostic layer to interrupt that loop, it accelerates.

A note on scope: This chapter draws primarily from professional team sport; the frameworks apply broadly, but thresholds shift across individual sports, youth sport, and non-Western coaching contexts. Para-sport introduces dependency dynamics that amplify the power gradients described here—when physical dependency and career precarity intersect, reporting harm is not just a career risk but a risk to daily functioning and access (Mountjoy et al., 2016; Smith & Freyd, 2014).

If the diagnostic layer identifies institutional betrayal—where the organization minimizes, ignores, or retaliates against reports of harm—the required response is institutional courage: proactive commitment to truth and transparency, even when costly to the institution, naming systemic failures rather than managing reputation (Freyd, 2018; Harsey & Freyd, 2020; Smith & Freyd, 2014; Smidt & Freyd, 2018).

3.1.2 High Standards Are Not Toxic

One of the most common diagnostic errors in elite sport is confusing demanding environments with damaging ones. High standards do not produce toxicity. Structural exclusion, predictable retaliation, and unchecked power do. Table 3.1 clarifies the distinction.

TABLE 3.1 Demanding Versus Damaging—Key Diagnostic Markers

Feature	*Demanding (Not Toxic)*	*Damaging (Toxic)*
Feedback	Direct, specific, tied to controllable behaviors	Attacks character, uses public humiliation
Standards	High, clear, consistently applied	Arbitrary, shift without notice, applied selectively
Errors	Addressed as learning events	Weaponized for status punishment
Autonomy	Athletes given decision space within boundaries	Micromanagement or abandonment—no middle ground
Voice	Disagreement is expected, respected, and protected	Dissent is punished with exclusion or retaliation
Trust	Built through consistent behavior and follow-through	Eroded through unpredictability and broken promises
Emotion	Leaders regulate their own emotional state	Athletes manage the leader's emotional volatility

Authors' synthesis based on destructive leadership criteria (Einarsen et al., 2007), coaching abuse research (Stirling & Kerr, 2009), and meta-analytic outcomes evidence (Schyns & Schilling, 2013). Not a validated instrument.

The distinction is not subtle in its extremes. In practice, the same coaching behavior can read as demanding to one athlete and damaging to another depending on relationship quality, personal history, and cultural context. Table 3.1 provides diagnostic anchors, not a binary checklist—most environments contain elements of both columns. The diagnostic question is which column dominates, and whether the damaging features are addressed or tolerated.

One way to think about it: if the environment makes people sharper, it is demanding. If it makes them smaller, it is damaging. The line gets crossed when feedback targets identity rather than behavior, and when the athlete's emotional safety becomes subordinate to the coach's emotional regulation (Stirling & Kerr, 2009, 2014).

BOX 3.2 PSYCHOLOGY SIDELINES WITH DR. MCB — THE DIAGNOSTIC WORK ITSELF IS AN INTERVENTION

The diagnostic work itself is an intervention. Not because it changes things immediately—but because naming the pattern clearly and structurally makes the invisible visible.

When people can't name what they're experiencing, when they blame themselves for harm being done to them, the pattern continues. The diagnostic interrupts that. There's a reason for this. Neuroimaging work on affect labeling shows that putting emotional experience into words reduces amygdala activation (Lieberman et al., 2007)—a finding clinicians know as "name it to tame it." Naming isn't just metaphorically powerful—it's regulatory. The brain processes threat differently once the experience has language around it. It's a form of healthy externalizing.

What I see clinically maps onto this. Toxic environments produce a specific kind of learned helplessness: people stop trusting their own perception. They internalize the harm. They assume that the problem is their resilience, their attitude, or their fit. The diagnostic gives them back their perception. When someone can point to a cascade diagnostic and say, "This is not you—this is the system," the narrative shifts. When an athlete sees their experience matches a documented pattern, their reality is validated. When someone can finally see the structure grinding them down, they stop thinking they're broken. They start recognizing the system.

3.2 Early Signals—Behavior, Performance, Retention

Principle: Toxicity produces measurable signals across behavior, performance, and retention long before it becomes a crisis.

Toxicity does not announce itself. Toxicity accumulates. People adapt, and norms shift. In our experience, by the time someone raises a formal complaint, the culture has often been damaging people for months—a pattern consistent with research showing that employees typically endure sustained mistreatment before engaging formal reporting channels (Cortina & Magley, 2003). The diagnostic task is catching drift early, when structural intervention is still possible.

A methodological note: The markers below draw on evidence of varying strength—from meta-analytic findings to single-study results to practitioner-observed patterns. Where a marker rests on clinical observation rather than formal research, we flag it.

Here's what to look for. The markers below track degradation in two of the book's core metrics: **Speed of Truth** (how quickly accurate information reaches decision-makers) and **Normalization of Voice** (the proportion of people who believe speaking up is safe and productive). When behavioral markers spike, Speed of Truth is slowing. When retention markers cluster, Normalization of Voice has failed. The markers are the observable surface; the metrics are the underlying system state.

3.2.1 Behavioral Markers

Observable behavior shifts when pressure increases. Watch what happens after a loss, after a difficult conversation, and after someone challenges leadership. Chapter 1 categorized silence by structural source (fear-based, architecture-based, network-based); the three categories below (also in Table 3.2) go deeper into fear-based silence, distinguishing the psychological mechanisms within it.

- **Silence:** Silence is the most common early signal—but diagnosing it requires distinguishing its mechanism, because the intervention for each type runs in the opposite direction:
- **Quiescent silence:** Fear-based. People stay quiet because speaking costs them safety, status, or selection (Pinder & Harlos, 2001).
- **Acquiescent silence:** Futility-based. People stay quiet because they believe speaking changes nothing (Morrison, 2014).
- **Prosocial silence:** Loyalty-based. Staying quiet to protect teammates or the organization (Van Dyne et al., 2003). It is common in sport and can mask real harm under the guise of loyalty. The narrative must shift from "reporting is betrayal" to "concealment is the betrayal" before prosocial silence will yield to voice.

TABLE 3.2 Three Types of Organizational Silence—Differential Diagnosis

Feature	*Quiescent Silence*	*Acquiescent Silence*	*Prosocial Silence*
Mechanism	Fear: speaking costs safety, status, or selection	Futility: speaking changes nothing	Loyalty: silence protects teammates or the organization
Outward presentation	Silent in meetings, vocal in hallways and private conversations	Meetings are short, polite, and frictionless—no pushback even on low-stakes issues	Harm is known but framed as "not my place to report" or "we handle things internally"
Underlying belief	"It's not safe to speak"	"It doesn't matter if I speak"	"Speaking up would betray the group"
Diagnostic signal	The gap between public and private discourse	The absence of disagreement on issues that should generate it	Convergent exit interviews citing loyalty concerns alongside unaddressed harm
Intervention target	Psychological safety infrastructure—reduce the cost of voice (Edmondson 1999)	Demonstrated consequences of voice—show that input produces visible action	Reframe reporting as group protection—"concealment is the betrayal," not disclosure (Van Dyne et al., 2003)

Authors' operationalization built on Pinder and Harlos (2001), Morrison (2014), and Van Dyne et al. (2003). Not a validated instrument.

BOX 3.3 TIMEOUT — THE SILENCE THAT LOOKS LIKE COMPLIANCE

Silence is not one thing. The same outward behavior–no dissent in a team meeting–can reflect fear, futility, or loyalty, and each demands a different intervention. Fear-based silence needs safety infrastructure. Futility-based silence needs visible proof that voice changes outcomes. Prosocial silence needs the narrative reframed: concealment harms the group, disclosure protects it. Diagnosing the wrong type doesn't just waste resources–it deepens the problem. Ask: are people silent because they're afraid, because they've given up, or because they think silence is service?

Beyond silence, other behavioral markers reveal how the system is managing stress and conflict (see Table 3.3):

- **Emotional Contagion:** Emotion moves through groups fast—often outpacing formal information channels—and toxicity spreads through contagion (Barsade, 2002; Hatfield et al., 1994).

- **Passive-Aggressive Behaviors:** Healthy teams argue about ideas; toxic teams stay quiet or turn passive-aggressive (Edmondson, 1999).
- **Subtle Signs:** Small, repeated incivilities are harder to see and easier to dismiss (Smittick et al., 2019; Tepper, 2007).
- **Bystander Inaction:** When people witness harmful behavior and do nothing, normalization of deviance shifts the baseline of what is acceptable (Latané & Darley, 1968; Vaughan, 1996).

When individual voice calculus (Morrison, 2014) consistently favors silence across multiple people, the pattern becomes organizational—what we term *silence calculus*. The Weekly Diagnostic Triad's behavioral question is designed to detect exactly this shift: when silence calculus has moved from individual risk assessment to organizational default.

3.2.2 Performance Markers

Toxicity degrades performance—not always immediately, but consistently, and across everyone in the system, not just athletes.

- **Inconsistent Output:** Output becomes inconsistent in ways that don't track with ability. Athletes who perform well in practice but poorly in competition, or staff who underperform in team settings, indicate that the environment is likely activating fight-or-flight responses at the wrong times (Baumeister, 1984; Hill et al., 2010; Mesagno & Beckmann, 2017).
- **Risk Aversion:** Risk-taking disappears. Athletes stop trying new skills in training. Staff stop proposing ideas or flagging concerns. People play not to lose, protecting status over development (Elliot & McGregor, 2001). In a toxic system, failure is treated as exposure, so people stop risking it.
- **Error Concealment:** The data pipeline dries up when errors go underground. Athletes hide injuries and tactical mistakes. Staff stop surfacing operational problems or challenging decisions (Edmondson, 1999; Nixon, 1992). When psychological safety fails, the information flow stops.
- **Burnout Without Overload:** Athletes and staff show classic burnout markers—emotional exhaustion, depersonalization, and reduced sense of accomplishment (Maslach & Jackson, 1981)—but the training volume or workload hasn't changed. The source is environmental rather than physical (Gustafsson et al., 2011; Raedeke, 1997). The system is the stressor.

3.2.3 Retention Markers

People leave toxic systems—athletes and staff alike. The question is whether the pattern surfaces early enough to act on it.

- **Turnover Clustering:** Voluntary turnover that clusters deserves investigation, not explanation. When three or more athletes or staff leave within a short

TABLE 3.3 Behavioral Markers Beyond Silence—Differential Diagnosis

Marker	*Observable Behavior*	*Mechanism*	*What It Suggests*	*Intervention Direction*
Emotional contagion	Emotional flatness, withdrawal, or hyper-vigilance rippling across the group; athletes enter calm and leave agitated	Toxicity spreads through contagion (Barsade, 2002; Hatfield et al., 1994); chronic stress degrades prefrontal function (Arnsten, 2009)	The environment is activating stress responses that impair performance regulation	Identify the contagion source—is it a person, a practice, or a structural condition? Reduce activation first
Passive-aggressive behavior	No one challenges anyone; compliance without engagement; sabotage through omission	Fear suppresses direct conflict; disagreement goes underground rather than disappearing (Edmondson, 1999)	The absence of overt conflict is not harmony—it is fear. Harmony needs protecting, fear needs dismantling	Distinguish harmony from suppression; create low-stakes disagreement opportunities to test which is present
Subtle signs (incivility)	Dismissive comments, eye rolls, exclusion; individually minor, cumulatively corrosive	Microaggressions compound over time and follow demographic lines (Smittick et al., 2019; Tepper, 2007)	One microaggression is not toxicity. A pattern directed at specific people is—and the pattern is the signal	Track who the targets are; demographic clustering indicates structural bias, not interpersonal friction
Bystander inaction	People witness harmful behavior and do nothing; staff observe public humiliation without intervening	Diffusion of responsibility (Latané & Darley, 1968); normalization of deviance (Vaughan, 1996)	The silence reflects voice calculus: the perceived costs of speaking outweigh the perceived benefits (Morrison, 2014)	The problem is system architecture, not bystander courage. Reduce the cost of intervention; increase the cost of inaction

Authors' diagnostic format integrating cited research. Not a validated instrument.

window (outside natural contract cycles), that's a signal. Look across groups: athlete departures and staff departures may trace to the same upstream source even when they don't appear connected.

- **Adverse Selection:** The highest-agency athletes and the most marketable staff tend to leave first—sometimes called the "Dead Sea Effect" (Webster, 2008). When the people who remain are disproportionately those who tolerate or perpetuate harm, the system becomes self-reinforcing.
- **Exit Interview Convergence:** When multiple athletes and staff independently produce the same language—"not the right fit," "culture concerns"—that's convergent testimony. Identical language across five people is evidence, often reflecting a psychological contract violation (Robinson & Rousseau, 1994). *Note: Tracking who declines exit interviews can be as diagnostic as the interviews themselves.*
- **Rust-Out:** Skilled people who are systematically sidelined don't burn out—they rust out. Athletes benched without explanation and staff stripped of meaningful responsibilities follow the same arc: initial anger ("This is unfair"), then sadness ("I cannot change this"), and then withdrawal ("I will do the minimum and leave").

Table 3.4 outlines the difference between burnout-without-overload and rust-out. The diagnostic distinction is agency: the burned-out person is still trying and failing to cope; the rusted-out person has stopped trying because the system removed the point. Conflating the two produces interventions that miss the target.

Rust-out doesn't look like a crisis. It looks like someone doing their job—no complaints and no grievances. The mad-to-sad transition is invisible because organizations respond to noise, not silence. By the time you notice the disengagement, the person has already decided to leave. They just haven't told you yet. Track the decline in initiative, not just the rise in grievances.

3.3 Tracing the Cascade—Office to Field

Principle: The dysfunction visible at the athlete and staff level sometimes originates at the executive level. Trace it upstream before assuming that the coach is the root cause.

3.3.1 The Office-to-Field Pattern

Dysfunction at the executive level does not stay contained. Ethical and unethical leadership behavior at senior levels propagates through organizational tiers, shaping behavior at each subsequent level (Mayer et al., 2009; Mawritz et al., 2012; Wo et al., 2019). Pressure from above—board demands, ownership volatility, media scrutiny, and financial uncertainty—shapes how leaders at every tier

TABLE 3.4 Burnout-Without-Overload Versus Rust-Out—Differential Diagnosis

Feature	*Burnout-Without-Overload*	*Rust-Out*
Presentation	Exhaustion and cynicism despite manageable workload	Withdrawal and disengagement despite intact capability
Mechanism	The environment drains capacity—ambient threat, unpredictability, emotional labor	The environment removes purpose—sidelining, role stripping, exclusion from decisions
Diagnostic distinction	The person is still trying and failing to cope	The person has stopped trying because the system removed the point
Observable trajectory	Escalating frustration → emotional exhaustion → depersonalization	Anger ("This is unfair") → sadness ("I cannot change this") → withdrawal ("I will do the minimum")
What it looks like	Complaints, sick days, visible distress	Compliance, silence, invisible disengagement
Intervention target	Environmental repair: restore safety, reduce ambient threat, rebuild conditions for effort	Role restoration: return meaningful responsibility and decision-making authority
Common misdiagnosis	Treated as individual resilience failure → prescribed wellness programming	Treated as low motivation or poor attitude → managed out

Practitioner-derived. Burnout dimension draws on Maslach & Jackson (1981) and Gustafsson et al. (2011). Rust-out is a practitioner-observed term overlapping with bore-out (Rothlin & Werder, 2008) and underemployment (McKee-Ryan & Harvey, 2011). Not a validated instrument.

behave. The head coach absorbs it. So does the performance director, the head of medical, and anyone in a middle-management position sitting between executive pressure and frontline delivery.

When the executive tier operates through blame, secrecy, and short-term panic, the tiers below tend to mirror it—each in their own way. The cascade follows a predictable three-tier pattern:

- **Executive Tier:** Reactive decision-making and political maneuvering create chronic instability.
- **Management/Coaching Tier:** Coaches and managers absorb this as emotional volatility, inconsistent standards, and information hoarding.
- **Frontline Tier:** Athletes and staff experience the downstream result as anxiety, silence, and exit.

Coaches transmit the pressure to athletes; managers transmit it to staff. The mechanism is the same—the role determines the direction, not the content.

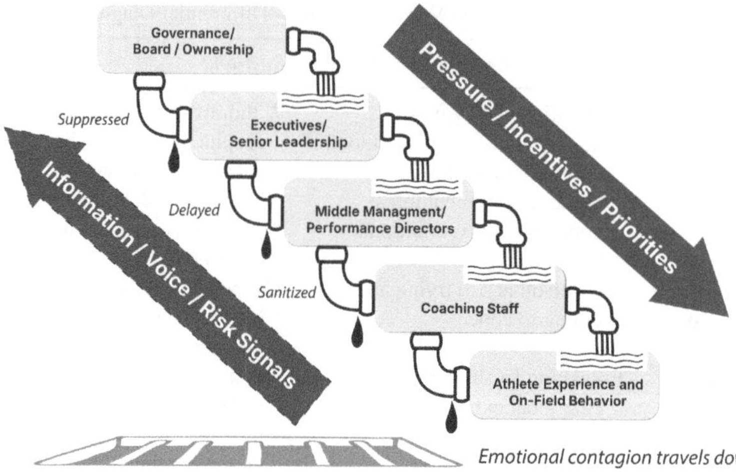

FIGURE 3.2 The Office-to-Field Cascade.

Dysfunction descends through organizational tiers, from governance to athlete experience, with each level absorbing and transmitting pressure. Upward information is filtered or blocked, giving top decision-makers a sanitized view of staff and athlete reality. Athletes and staff may not realize that they're experiencing the same upstream source because they rarely compare notes across the divide. That disconnect is itself a diagnostic marker. When both groups independently describe the same pattern without coordinating, the cascade is likely operating.

The most common diagnostic mistake is treating the coach or a mid-level manager as the problem without asking: *what are they responding to?* Sometimes, the answer is "they are the primary source" (Section 3.3.3). But the cascade diagnostic ensures that the question gets asked before the diagnosis settles. When the same dysfunction reappears under a different coach, that pattern points upstream, not at the coaching tier—and leader replacement alone is not the fix.

Note: This pattern assumes a multi-tiered hierarchy typical of professional team sport. In flatter structures or national team environments, the cascade operates across fewer tiers or crosses organizational boundaries—but the principle holds.

3.3.2 The Cascade Diagnostic (Three Questions)

- **Status:** Theoretically grounded. Derived from clinical diagnostic reasoning (Sackett et al., 2000) and trickle-down leadership research (Mayer et al., 2009; Mawritz et al., 2012). Scoring thresholds are rules of thumb. Not a validated instrument.

This diagnostic traces whether the coach or manager is the primary toxicity source or a transmission vector for upstream dysfunction. Three questions test for cascade. When these conditions converge, the presenting problem is unlikely to originate where it is most visible.

Question 1: Is the presenting problem isolated to one tier, or does it appear at multiple levels? If athletes report unpredictability from coaches and staff report the same from management—and both chains trace upward to executives—that suggests a cascade. If only one group reports it, the source may be localized. Check across both the athlete-facing and staff-facing chains before settling on an origin point.

Question 2: Does the problematic behavior intensify after board meetings, ownership changes, or media scrutiny? If the head coach's behavior deteriorates predictably after executive-level pressure events, the dysfunction is likely cascading downward. The same applies to managers. The coach or manager may be a transmission vector, not the origin. Map behavior shifts against the executive calendar—the temporal pattern is the tell.

Question 3: Do coaches and managers describe feeling unsupported, blamed, or excluded by the executive tier? If coaches report the same dynamics upward that athletes report about coaches—and managers report the same upward that staff report about managers—the pattern is systemic. The middle tier is experiencing from above what the frontline tier is experiencing from them.

When two or more of these questions point to "yes," the toxicity likely originates upstream. The intervention needs to address the executive tier, not just the coaching or management tier. *(Note: These thresholds are rules of thumb, not empirically validated cutoffs; convergence across two or more indicators increases the probability of a systemic pattern [Sackett et al., 2000].)*

3.3.3 When the Coach or Manager Is the Source

Tracing the cascade upstream does not absolve the coaching or management tier—it determines where additional intervention is needed. Sometimes, the coach or manager *is* the primary toxicity driver.

The diagnostic markers:

- The dysfunction is stable across executive changes (new board members/performance directors arrive, but behavior stays the same).
- Adjacent leaders operate normally, while this one does not.
- Athletes and staff report harm that is leader-specific, tied to this coach or manager, in this context, with these people.

When the pattern follows the person rather than the structure, the person is the variable. The sequence is: immediate containment, structural redesign, and the decision on whether the coach stays or goes. When a manager is the source, the same logic applies.

3.3.4 *What This Diagnostic Does Not Do*

The cascade diagnostic traces direction—upstream or localized—but it doesn't quantify severity, assign legal culpability, or replace a formal investigation. It's a triage tool, not a conclusion. And tracing the root cause upstream does not mean the downstream harm can be deprioritized. Athletes don't experience organizational cascades—they experience the person in front of them. Explaining that the coach was under executive pressure doesn't undo the damage in the locker room. Intervention runs in both directions: upstream to fix the cause and downstream to repair the harm.

3.4 The Toxic Triangle—Leaders, Followers, Environments

Principle: Toxicity is not just a bad leader. It is the interaction of destructive leaders, susceptible followers, and conducive environments (Padilla et al., 2007).

If the cascade diagnostic in Section 3.3 identifies *where* the dysfunction originates vertically (the executive tier versus the coaching tier), the Toxic Triangle identifies *what* makes it durable horizontally. Both frameworks are required: the cascade traces the origin, while the triangle diagnoses the structural ecosystem that allows the toxicity to survive.

The triangle helps diagnose which corner is doing the most work. When the environment has functioning oversight and follower agency is high, leader removal can be sufficient—but those conditions are precisely what make toxicity less durable in the first place. The more common presentation in sport: the environment is conducive, and follower susceptibility is elevated, making removal alone insufficient—the next leader inherits the same enabling conditions.

3.4.1 *Destructive Leaders*

Not all demanding leaders are destructive. Destructive leaders tend to display a recognizable pattern (Einarsen et al., 2007). Table 3.5 maps the four characteristics, their observable manifestations in sport, and why each persists.

One nuance on malignant personality features: the relationship between narcissism and leadership is curvilinear—narcissism predicts leadership emergence but degrades effectiveness beyond an optimal midrange (Grijalva et al., 2015). What moderates the risk is accountability. Dark personality features are a risk factor, not a diagnosis. The environment determines whether the risk materializes.

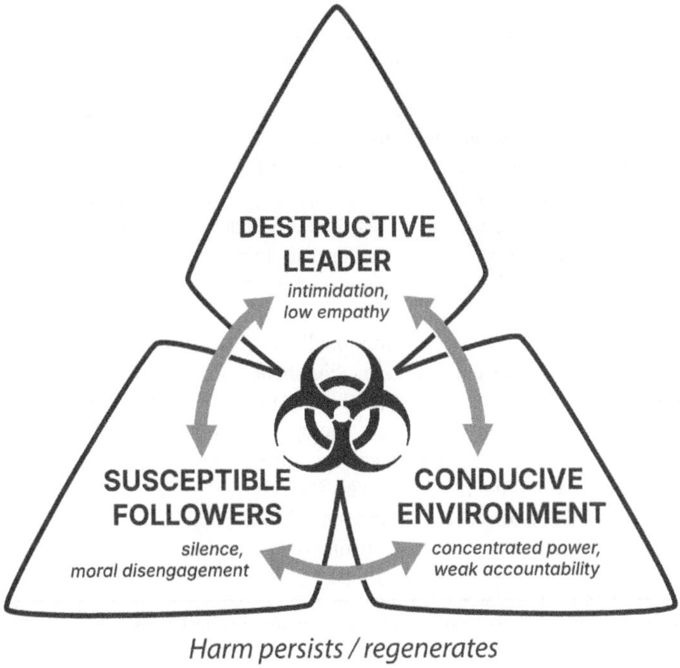

FIGURE 3.3 The Toxic Triangle.

Adapted from Padilla et al. (2007); extended by Thoroughgood et al. (2018). Three reinforcing elements sustain organizational toxicity: destructive leaders, susceptible followers, and conducive environments. The diagnostic value is identifying which corner is doing the most work—destabilize any one corner and the system begins to break down.

TABLE 3.5 Destructive Leader Characteristics—Diagnostic Reference

Characteristic	*Observable Pattern*	*Sport-Specific Manifestation*	*Why It Persists*
Charisma without integrity	Inspires and manipulates simultaneously; athletes and staff feel drawn in and trapped	Charisma generates loyalty that delays recognition of harm; early results justify tolerance	The leader's appeal creates a narrative shield—"they're tough but they get the best out of people"—that makes harm harder to name
Malignant personality features	Self-interest drives decisions; loyalty gets exploited; dissent is reframed as betrayal	Dark Triad traits (narcissism, Machiavellianism, psychopathy) override group welfare (Paulhus & Williams, 2002)	In sport, head coaches frequently operate with minimal supervision between results cycles—accountability structures that constrain these traits are often absent

(*Continued*)

TABLE 3.5 (Continued)

Characteristic	*Observable Pattern*	*Sport-Specific Manifestation*	*Why It Persists*
Lack of emotional regulation	Moods dictate the environment; athletes and staff end up managing the leader's emotional state	Emotional labor flows upward—subordinates regulate the leader rather than doing their own work	The system adapts around the volatility rather than addressing it; "managing up" becomes a survival skill
Sustained hostile behavior	Pattern of behavior that degrades well-being, satisfaction, and commitment—not isolated incidents	Emotionally abusive coaching behaviors produce lasting psychological harm across competitive levels (Gervis & Dunn, 2004; Stirling & Kerr, 2009)	Downstream propagation: leaders who experience abuse from above are more likely to reproduce it below (Mawritz et al., 2012)

Adapted from Einarsen et al. (2007) with sport-specific manifestations and persistence analysis added by the authors.

3.4.2 Susceptible Followers

Toxic leaders require followers who enable them. Not because followers are bad people, but because the environment makes enabling rational. Padilla et al. (2007) distinguish between "conformers" (who go along passively) and "colluders" (who actively participate in exchange for benefits). Both patterns emerge from structural conditions:

- **Unmet needs:** Athletes and staff who lack belonging, competence, or autonomy are vulnerable to leaders who promise those needs—then withhold them as control mechanisms.
- **Financial dependence and perceived upward mobility:** For many followers, the leader controls not just culture but livelihood. Economic dependency is a structural predictor of tolerance for abusive supervision (Tepper et al., 2009).
- **Conformity pressure:** When the group signals "this is normal," individuals suppress their own judgment. It's a survival strategy within the system as it currently operates.
- **Immature identification:** Athletes and staff who derive their identity primarily from the group or the leader are more susceptible to manipulation (Padilla et al., 2007; Tajfel & Turner, 1979).

Note on para-sport: These susceptibility dynamics compound. Athletes who depend on coaches or support staff for physical access or daily living needs face literal power asymmetry (Mountjoy et al., 2016). When the person you would report to is also the person who assists your daily functioning, the voice calculus is structurally different.

The intervention is changing the conditions that make susceptibility rational: alternative sources of belonging, low-cost voice mechanisms, and diversified pathways to financial security.

3.4.3 Conducive Environments

Toxicity survives when the environment protects it. The triangle cannot sustain itself without environmental enablers:

- **Lack of oversight:** No external checks, independent reporting channels, or consequences for harm create conditions where destructive leadership becomes durable (Mountjoy et al., 2016).
- **Cultural values that excuse harm:** "toughness" or "winning at all costs" sanitize abuse through moral disengagement mechanisms (Bandura, 1999; Boardley & Kavussanu, 2011). Organizations frequently deploy Deny, Attack, and Reverse Victim and Offender (DARVO) responses (Harsey & Freyd, 2020).
- **Instability and threat:** Organizations under threat are more likely to tolerate destructive leadership if it produces short-term results (Padilla et al., 2007).
- **Weak institutional memory:** High turnover produces two vulnerabilities: *institutional amnesia* (learning the same lesson from scratch) and *normalization of deviance* (Vaughan, 1996), where the baseline for acceptable behavior gradually shifts downward.

Table 3.6 synthesizes the three corners—diagnostic markers, the conditions under which each corner dominates, and the primary intervention target for each.

TABLE 3.6 Toxic Triangle—Diagnostic Markers and Intervention Targets

Triangle Corner	*Diagnostic Markers*	*When This Corner Dominates*	*Primary Intervention Target*
Destructive leader	Charisma without integrity; unchecked malignant traits; lack of emotional regulation; harm follows the person across contexts	Dysfunction is localized to one leader's sphere; adjacent leaders operate normally; pattern is stable across executive changes	Immediate containment → structural redesign → removal decision

(*Continued*)

TABLE 3.6 (Continued)

Triangle Corner	*Diagnostic Markers*	*When This Corner Dominates*	*Primary Intervention Target*
Susceptible followers	Unmet needs exploited for control; financial dependence tied to the leader; conformity pressure; self-concept fused with the leader	Enabling behavior persists even when leadership changes; dissent is suppressed by peers, not just by the leader	Redesign conditions: build alternative belonging, low-cost voice mechanisms, and diversified pathways to security
Conducive environment	Lack of independent oversight; cultural values that excuse harm; weak institutional memory producing amnesia and normalization of deviance	The same pattern reconstitutes around different leaders; removal produces a press release but not a culture change	Structural reform: independent reporting channels, accountability mechanisms, and external oversight

Adapted from Padilla et al. (2007) with sport-specific diagnostic markers added by the authors. Extended by Thoroughgood et al. (2018). Not a validated instrument.

BOX 3.4 TIMEOUT — DIAGNOSE THE TRIANGLE BEFORE YOU DIAGNOSE THE PERSON

When a toxic culture investigation lands, the instinct is to focus on the leader. The Toxic Triangle reframes the question: would a different leader behave identically under these structural conditions? If the environment lacks independent oversight, if follower susceptibility is structurally elevated, if the same pattern has reconstituted before—then removal is a press release, not a fix. Diagnose all three corners before you decide which one to intervene on. The corner you skip is the one that rebuilds the problem.

3.5 Diagnostic Tools

3.5.1 The Weekly Diagnostic Triad

- **Status:** Theoretically grounded. Derived from organizational silence research (Morrison, 2014; Pinder & Harlos, 2001), burnout literature (Maslach & Jackson, 1981), and trickle-down leadership models (Mawritz et al., 2012). Not a validated instrument.

- **Purpose:** Catch toxicity signals before they become patterns.
- **Cadence:** Weekly, 10 minutes, with a leadership triad (head coach, performance director, and senior medical/psych staff). *Note: Must include at least one member outside the direct coaching chain, and requires a quarterly independent external review.*

Three Questions

1. **Behavioral:** Did anyone go silent this week who is usually vocal? Did anyone escalate emotionally in a way that was out of character?
2. **Performance:** Did anyone's output shift suddenly—better or worse—without a corresponding training change?
3. **Retention:** Did anyone express doubt about staying, mention looking elsewhere, or withdraw from informal team activities?

If the answer to any question is "yes," flag it. One "yes" is not a crisis—it is a data point.

For example, a Triad log entry might read: *"Behavioral flag: The head physiotherapist, who normally pushes back on return-to-play timelines, agreed immediately today without making eye contact. Retention flag: Two academy coaches skipped the optional Friday staff breakfast for the third week in a row."*

Escalation Thresholds

- **Trigger 1—individual persistence:** When the same individual is flagged across three consecutive weekly triads, escalate to the source-tracing pathway.
- **Trigger 2—population-level convergence:** Two or more "yes" answers distributed across different people in a single week, or a clustering of retention signals (e.g., three departures within a contract window). Escalate regardless of individual continuity.

Escalation: Tracing the source when the triad flags a persistent pattern, answer the three cascade questions from Section 3.3.2 to trace the origin. Table 3.7 translates the count of "yes" answers into an interpretation and a recommended action.

3.5.2 Validated Instruments for Systematic Assessment

The aforementioned tool is built for speed. For organizations ready for systematic assessment, Table 3.8 maps each practitioner component to validated instruments assessing overlapping constructs.

TABLE 3.7 Cascade Diagnostic Scoring

"Yes" Answers	*Interpretation*	*Recommended Action*
0	Cascade indicators not present—problem may be coaching-specific, but gather corroborating data before concluding	Intervene at the coaching tier; continue monitoring for upstream signals
1	Unclear—insufficient convergence	Gather more data before deciding on the intervention level
2–3	Problem likely cascades from the executive tier	Expand investigation upstream; intervene at the executive tier

TABLE 3.8 Practitioner Tool Mapped to Validated Instruments

Practitioner Tool	*Construct*	*Validated Instrument*	*Key Reference*
Weekly Diagnostic Triad	Psychological safety	Edmondson's Psychological Safety Scale (7 items)	Edmondson (1999)
	Coach-athlete relationship	Coach-Athlete Relationship Questionnaire (CART-Q)	Jowett & Ntoumanis (2004)
	Athlete burnout	Athlete Burnout Questionnaire (ABQ; 15 items)	Raedeke & Smith (2001)
	Controlling behaviors	Controlling Coach Behaviours Scale (CCBS)	Bartholomew et al. (2010)
Triad (escalation pathway)	Abusive supervision	Abusive Supervision Scale (15 items)	Tepper (2000)
	Destructive leadership	Destructive Leadership Questionnaire (DLQ)	Shaw et al. (2011)
	Organizational culture	Organizational Culture Assessment Instrument (OCAI)	Cameron & Quinn (2006); sport validation: Choi et al. (2010)
Broad assessment	Athlete safety culture	U.S. Center for SafeSport Athlete Culture and Climate Survey	U.S. Center for SafeSport (2021, 2024)

3.5.3 *Diagnostic Layer Outputs*

The diagnostic layer produces three outputs that feed directly into the Operating System layer (Layer 4):

1. **A classification** of the presenting environment as demanding or damaging;
2. **A source determination** (coaching-tier origin or executive-tier cascade) based on the Triad's escalation pathway;

3. **An identification** of which corner of the Toxic Triangle is sustaining the pattern.

These outputs determine which operating system components need building, rebuilding, or protecting. Without them, Layer 4 defaults to generic culture programming—the organizational equivalent of prescribing antibiotics without a culture and sensitivity.

BOX 3.5 SKEPTIC'S CORNER — THIS PATHOLOGIZES NORMAL COACHING

"This pathologizes normal coaching. Every demanding coach looks toxic under this lens."

Legitimate concern–and the distinction matters. Table 3.1 exists to prevent that diagnostic error. Demanding coaching features high standards and direct feedback applied consistently. Damaging coaching features arbitrary standards, public humiliation, and selective consequences. The line isn't about intensity–it's about whether feedback targets behavior or identity, and whether the emotional regulation burden falls on the leader or the athlete (Stirling & Kerr, 2009). Meta-analytic evidence confirms that destructive leadership produces measurable harm across well-being, satisfaction, and commitment–effects not reducible to "high expectations" (Schyns & Schilling, 2013).

What to try anyway: Apply the cascade questions to a current concern. If the presenting behavior maps to the "Demanding" column and the three cascade questions return "no," the environment is intense, not toxic. If it maps to the "Damaging" column and the exit data corroborate, the framework is doing what it was designed to do.

3.5.3.1 Chapter Synthesis

Toxicity is not a personality problem with a structural alibi—it is a structural problem that expresses through personality. The diagnostic layer of the HPCOS exists because default interventions (replace the coach, survey the culture, and add a wellness program) fail without precision about what is actually broken and where. Demanding environments sharpen people; damaging environments silence them—and the cascade diagnostic reveals whether the source sits where it is most visible or upstream where it is most protected. Until diagnosis specifies the mechanism, intervention is guesswork.

Key Chapter Takeaways

1. **Read converging signals, not isolated complaints.** Behavioral markers, performance markers, and retention patterns form a syndrome—act on the convergence, not the individual data point.
2. **Distinguish demanding from damaging before intervening.** The diagnostic line is whether feedback targets behavior or identity, and whether emotional regulation falls on the leader or the athlete.
3. **Trace upstream before diagnosing downstream.** The Triad's escalation pathway determines whether the presenting dysfunction originates at the coaching tier or transmits from executive instability.
4. **Diagnose which corner of the Toxic Triangle sustains the pattern.** Leader removal resolves the problem only when the conducive environment and follower-susceptibility corners are not independently maintaining it.
5. **Match the intervention to the mechanism.** Fear-based silence needs safety infrastructure; futility-based silence needs demonstrated consequences of voice; burnout needs environmental repair; rust-out needs role restoration.

Discussion Questions

1. Apply the cascade questions to an organization you have observed. If two of three questions return "yes," how does that shift your intervention target—and what political resistance would you anticipate?
2. Design a two-week protocol using only observable indicators to differentiate rust-out from burnout-without-overload in an embedded sport psychology role.
3. Under what structural conditions would removing a destructive leader—without addressing the conducive environment corner—be a defensible standalone intervention? What would you need to verify first?

References

Arnsten, A. F. T. (2009). Stress signalling pathways that impair prefrontal cortex structure and function. *Nature Reviews Neuroscience*, *10*(6), 410–422. https://doi.org/10.1038/nrn2648

Bandura, A. (1999). Moral disengagement in the perpetration of inhumanities. *Personality and Social Psychology Review*, *3*(3), 193–209. https://doi.org/10.1207/s15327957pspr0303_3

Barsade, S. G. (2002). The ripple effect: Emotional contagion and its influence on group behavior. *Administrative Science Quarterly*, *47*(4), 644–675. https://doi.org/10.2307/3094912

Bartholomew, K. J., Ntoumanis, N., & Thøgersen-Ntoumani, C. (2010). The controlling interpersonal style in a coaching context: Development and initial validation of a psychometric scale. *Journal of Sport & Exercise Psychology*, *32*(2), 193–216. https://doi.org/10.1123/jsep.32.2.193

Baumeister, R. F. (1984). Choking under pressure: Self-consciousness and paradoxical effects of incentives on skillful performance. *Journal of Personality and Social Psychology, 46*(3), 610–620. https://doi.org/10.1037/0022-3514.46.3.610

Boardley, I. D., & Kavussanu, M. (2011). Moral disengagement in sport. *International Review of Sport and Exercise Psychology, 4*(2), 93–108. https://doi.org/10.1080/1750984X.2011.570361

Cameron, K. S., & Quinn, R. E. (2006). *Diagnosing and changing organizational culture: Based on the competing values framework* (Rev. ed.). Jossey-Bass.

Choi, Y. S., Seo, M., Scott, D., & Martin, J. J. (2010). Validation of the organizational culture assessment instrument: An application of the Korean version. *Journal of Sport Management, 24*(2), 169–189. https://doi.org/10.1123/jsm.24.2.169

Cortina, L. M., & Magley, V. J. (2003). Raising voice, risking retaliation: Events following interpersonal mistreatment in the workplace. *Journal of Occupational Health Psychology, 8*(4), 247–265. https://doi.org/10.1037/1076-8998.8.4.247

Edmondson, A. C. (1999). Psychological safety and learning behavior in work teams. *Administrative Science Quarterly, 44*(2), 350–383. https://doi.org/10.2307/2666999

Einarsen, S., Aasland, M. S., & Skogstad, A. (2007). Destructive leadership behaviour: A definition and conceptual model. *The Leadership Quarterly, 18*(3), 207–216. https://doi.org/10.1016/j.leaqua.2007.03.002

Elliot, A. J., & McGregor, H. A. (2001). A 2×2 achievement goal framework. *Journal of Personality and Social Psychology, 80*(3), 501–519. https://doi.org/10.1037/0022-3514.80.3.501

Freyd, J. J. (2018, January 11). When sexual assault victims speak out, their institutions often betray them. *The Conversation.* https://theconversation.com/when-sexual-assault-victims-speak-out-their-institutions-often-betray-them-87050

Gervis, M., & Dunn, N. (2004). The emotional abuse of elite child athletes by their coaches. *Child Abuse Review, 13*(3), 215–223. https://doi.org/10.1002/car.843

Grijalva, E., Harms, P. D., Newman, D. A., Gaddis, B. H., & Fraley, R. C. (2015). Narcissism and leadership: A meta-analytic review of linear and nonlinear relationships. *Personnel Psychology, 68*(1), 1–47. https://doi.org/10.1111/peps.12072

Gustafsson, H., Kenttä, G., & Hassmén, P. (2011). Athlete burnout: An integrated model and future research directions. *International Review of Sport and Exercise Psychology, 4*(1), 3–24. https://doi.org/10.1080/1750984X.2010.541927

Harsey, S. J., & Freyd, J. J. (2020). Deny, attack, and reverse victim and offender (DARVO): What is the influence on perceived perpetrator and victim credibility? *Journal of Aggression, Maltreatment & Trauma, 29*(8), 897–916. https://doi.org/10.1080/10926771.2020.1774695

Hatfield, E., Cacioppo, J. T., & Rapson, R. L. (1994). *Emotional contagion.* Cambridge University Press. https://doi.org/10.1017/CBO9781139174138

Hill, D. M., Hanton, S., Matthews, N., & Fleming, S. (2010). Choking in sport: A review. *International Review of Sport and Exercise Psychology, 3*(1), 24–39. https://doi.org/10.1080/17509840903301199

Jowett, S., & Ntoumanis, N. (2004). The Coach–Athlete Relationship Questionnaire (CART-Q): Development and initial validation. *Scandinavian Journal of Medicine & Science in Sports, 14*(4), 245–257. https://doi.org/10.1111/j.1600-0838.2003.00338.x

Latané, B., & Darley, J. M. (1968). Group inhibition of bystander intervention in emergencies. *Journal of Personality and Social Psychology, 10*(3), 215–221. https://doi.org/10.1037/h0026570

Lieberman, M. D., Eisenberger, N. I., Crockett, M. J., Tom, S. M., Pfeifer, J. H., & Way, B. M. (2007). Putting feelings into words: Affect labeling disrupts amygdala activity in response to affective stimuli. *Psychological Science, 18*(5), 421–428. https://doi.org/10.1111/j.1467-9280.2007.01916.x

Maslach, C., & Jackson, S. E. (1981). The measurement of experienced burnout. *Journal of Occupational Behaviour*, *2*(2), 99–113. https://doi.org/10.1002/job.4030020205

Mawritz, M. B., Mayer, D. M., Hoobler, J. M., Wayne, S. J., & Marinova, S. V. (2012). A trickle-down model of abusive supervision. *Personnel Psychology*, *65*(2), 325–357. https://doi.org/10.1111/j.1744-6570.2012.01246.x

Mayer, D. M., Kuenzi, M., Greenbaum, R., Bardes, M., & Salvador, R. (2009). How low does ethical leadership flow? Test of a trickle-down model. *Organizational Behavior and Human Decision Processes*, *108*(1), 1–13. https://doi.org/10.1016/j.obhdp.2008.04.002

McKee-Ryan, F. M., & Harvey, J. (2011). "I have a job, but . . .": A review of underemployment. *Journal of Management*, *37*(4), 962–996. https://doi.org/10.1177/0149206311398134

Mesagno, C., & Beckmann, J. (2017). Choking under pressure: Theoretical models and interventions. *Current Opinion in Psychology*, *16*, 170–175. https://doi.org/10.1016/j.copsyc.2017.05.015

Morrison, E. W. (2014). Employee voice and silence. *Annual Review of Organizational Psychology and Organizational Behavior*, *1*, 173–197. https://doi.org/10.1146/annurev-orgpsych-031413-091328

Mountjoy, M., Brackenridge, C., Arrington, M., Blauwet, C., Carska-Sheppard, A., Fasting, K., Kirby, S., Leahy, T., Marks, S., Martin, K., Starr, K., Tiivas, A., & Budgett, R. (2016). International Olympic Committee consensus statement: Harassment and abuse (non-accidental violence) in sport. *British Journal of Sports Medicine*, *50*(17), 1019–1029. https://doi.org/10.1136/bjsports-2016-096121

Nixon, H. L. (1992). A social network analysis of influences on athletes to play with pain and injuries. *Journal of Sport and Social Issues*, *16*(2), 127–135. https://doi.org/10.1177/019372359201600208

Padilla, A., Hogan, R., & Kaiser, R. B. (2007). The toxic triangle: Destructive leaders, susceptible followers, and conducive environments. *The Leadership Quarterly*, *18*(3), 176–194. https://doi.org/10.1016/j.leaqua.2007.03.001

Paulhus, D. L., & Williams, K. M. (2002). The dark triad of personality: Narcissism, Machiavellianism, and psychopathy. *Journal of Research in Personality*, *36*(6), 556–563. https://doi.org/10.1016/S0092-6566(02)00505-6

Pinder, C. C., & Harlos, K. P. (2001). Employee silence: Quiescence and acquiescence as responses to perceived injustice. In G. R. Ferris (Ed.), *Research in personnel and human resources management* (Vol. 20, pp. 331–369). JAI Press. https://doi.org/10.1016/S0742-7301(01)20007-3

Raedeke, T. D. (1997). Is athlete burnout more than just stress? A sport commitment perspective. *Journal of Sport & Exercise Psychology*, *19*(4), 396–417. https://doi.org/10.1123/jsep.19.4.396

Raedeke, T. D., & Smith, A. L. (2001). Development and preliminary validation of an athlete burnout measure. *Journal of Sport & Exercise Psychology*, *23*(4), 281–306. https://doi.org/10.1123/jsep.23.4.281

Robinson, S. L., & Rousseau, D. M. (1994). Violating the psychological contract: Not the exception but the norm. *Journal of Organizational Behavior*, *15*(3), 245–259. https://doi.org/10.1002/job.4030150306

Rothlin, P., & Werder, P. R. (2008). *Boreout!: Overcoming workplace demotivation*. Kogan Page.

Sackett, D. L., Straus, S. E., Richardson, W. S., Rosenberg, W., & Haynes, R. B. (2000). *Evidence-based medicine: How to practice and teach EBM* (2nd ed.). Churchill Livingstone.

Schyns, B., & Schilling, J. (2013). How bad are the effects of bad leaders? A meta-analysis of destructive leadership and its outcomes. *The Leadership Quarterly*, *24*(1), 138–158. https://doi.org/10.1016/j.leaqua.2012.09.001

Shaw, J. B., Erickson, A., & Harvey, M. (2011). A method for measuring destructive leadership and identifying types of destructive leaders in organizations. *The Leadership Quarterly*, *22*(4), 575–590. https://doi.org/10.1016/j.leaqua.2011.05.001

Smidt, A. M., & Freyd, J. J. (2018). Government-mandated institutional betrayal. *Journal of Trauma & Dissociation*, *19*(5), 491–499. https://doi.org/10.1080/15299732.2018.1502029

Smith, C. P., & Freyd, J. J. (2014). Institutional betrayal. *American Psychologist*, *69*(6), 575–587. https://doi.org/10.1037/a0037564

Smittick, A. L., Kuhn, K. M., Edwards, M. B., Danylchuk, K. E., & Babiak, K. (2019). The "I" in team: Coach incivility, coach gender, and team performance in women's basketball teams. *Sport Management Review*, *22*(3), 419–433. https://doi.org/10.1016/j.smr.2018.06.002

Stirling, A. E., & Kerr, G. A. (2009). Abused athletes' perceptions of the coach-athlete relationship. *Sport in Society*, *12*(2), 227–239. https://doi.org/10.1080/17430430802591019

Stirling, A. E., & Kerr, G. A. (2014). Initiating and sustaining emotional abuse in the coach–athlete relationship: An ecological transactional model of vulnerability. *Journal of Aggression, Maltreatment & Trauma*, *23*(2), 116–135. https://doi.org/10.1080/10926771.2014.872747

Tajfel, H., & Turner, J. C. (1979). An integrative theory of intergroup conflict. In W. G. Austin & S. Worchel (Eds.), *The social psychology of intergroup relations* (pp. 33–47). Brooks/Cole.

Tepper, B. J. (2000). Consequences of abusive supervision. *Academy of Management Journal*, *43*(2), 178–190. https://doi.org/10.5465/1556375

Tepper, B. J. (2007). Abusive supervision in work organizations: Review, synthesis, and research agenda. *Journal of Management*, *33*(3), 261–289. https://doi.org/10.1177/0149206307300812

Tepper, B. J., Carr, J. C., Breaux, D. M., Geider, S., Hu, C., & Hua, W. (2009). Abusive supervision, intentions to quit, and employees' workplace deviance: A power/dependence analysis. *Organizational Behavior and Human Decision Processes*, *109*(2), 156–167. https://doi.org/10.1016/j.obhdp.2009.03.004

Thoroughgood, C. N., Sawyer, K. B., Padilla, A., & Lunsford, L. (2018). Destructive leadership: A critique of leader-centric perspectives and toward a more holistic definition. *Journal of Business Ethics*, *151*(3), 627–649. https://doi.org/10.1007/s10551-016-3257-9

U.S. Center for SafeSport. (2021, July 14). *2020 athlete culture & climate survey: External report*. https://uscenterforsafesport.org/wp-content/uploads/2021/07/CultureClimateSurvey_ExternalReport_071421_Final.pdf

U.S. Center for SafeSport. (2024, July 18). *2024 athlete culture & climate survey report*. https://uscenterforsafesport.org/wp-content/uploads/2024/07/CultureClimateSurvey_ExternalReport_071824_v1.6.pdf

Van Dyne, L., Ang, S., & Botero, I. C. (2003). Conceptualizing employee silence and employee voice as multidimensional constructs. *Journal of Management Studies*, *40*(6), 1359–1392. https://doi.org/10.1111/1467-6486.00384

Vaughan, D. (1996). *The Challenger launch decision: Risky technology, culture, and deviance at NASA*. University of Chicago Press.

Webster, B. (2008, December 29). The Dead Sea effect. *The WetWare Crisis* [Blog]. https://brucefwebster.com/2008/12/29/the-dead-sea-effect/

Wo, D. X. H., Ambrose, M. L., & Schminke, M. (2019). Trickle-down, trickle-out, trickle-up, trickle-in, and trickle-around effects: An integrative perspective on indirect social influence. *Journal of Management*, *45*(6), 2263–2292. https://doi.org/10.1177/0149206318812951

4

VISION, VALUES, AND DECISION ARCHITECTURE

Learning Objectives

By the end of this chapter, the reader will be able to:

1. **Evaluate the gap** between an organization's stated values and its values-in-use by excavating past decisions made under pressure.
2. **Design behavioral anchors** that convert generic organizational values into fly-on-the-wall observable standards specific to a given sport context.
3. **Apply a discipline decision tree** with an integrated safeguarding gate to ensure consistent, status-blind processes across comparable incidents.
4. **Audit alignment** between recent high-stakes decisions and stated organizational values, identifying decorative values and structural fixes.
5. **Analyze decision architecture failure modes**—over-rigidity, gaming, weaponization, and false objectivity—and design safeguards against each.

BOX 4.1 CASE STUDY — THE WELFARE OFFICER WHO MAPPED THE PATTERN

Composite vignette. Details changed to protect privacy.

Sian was the player health officer—no selection authority, no coaching influence, and no seat in leadership meetings. But she had a clear view of every conduct incident that crossed her desk.

DOI: 10.4324/9781003631217-5

Three incidents in six weeks, same behavior: verbal abuse of support staff. When a senior player did it twice, the responses ranged from a private word to silence. When a young international player on a visa did the same thing, he was dropped for two matches.

Sian sent a briefing note to the head of performance: same behavior, three different responses, one obvious variable. The reply: *"These are football decisions. Context matters."* She requested a meeting. It was rescheduled twice, then cancelled. The sporting director told her it was a dressing room issue.

Two months later, the young player's agent filed a discrimination grievance—quoting the organization's own values statement. An external review found "insufficient documentation of disciplinary processes" and recommended a code of conduct revision. Sian's briefing note, which had identified the exact pattern, was never referenced. No one asked why the person hired to catch inconsistency had been told, twice, that it wasn't her concern.

The revised code of conduct was posted below the exact same three words that had been on the wall all along.

4.1 The Vision–Values–Decision Cascade

Principle: Values only matter when they cost something. If they do not change Tuesday morning behavior, they are decoration—and the room usually figures that out before leadership does.

This chapter answers the question: *how do we decide when it matters?* The diagnostic work in Chapter 3—environment classification, cascade source identification, and triangle analysis—told you what kind of culture you are operating in and where pressure enters. This chapter builds the decision pathways that keep your values in frame once that pressure arrives (see Figure 4.1).

Value statements fail not because organizations lack conviction, but because they lack architecture. Under pressure, decisions revert to status, convenience, and improvisation—and the gap between the words on the wall and Tuesday morning behavior widens without anyone making a deliberate choice to abandon what was stated.

The most dangerous failure mode is not hypocrisy. It is **ethical fading**—the cognitive process by which a values decision gets quietly recoded as a tactical one, so the brain stops registering the dilemma at all (Tenbrunsel & Messick, 2004). The head coach who tells the welfare lead, *"this is a football decision,"* has not rejected the organization's values; he has reclassified the situation so the values no longer apply. That reclassification is the architecture gap this chapter fills.

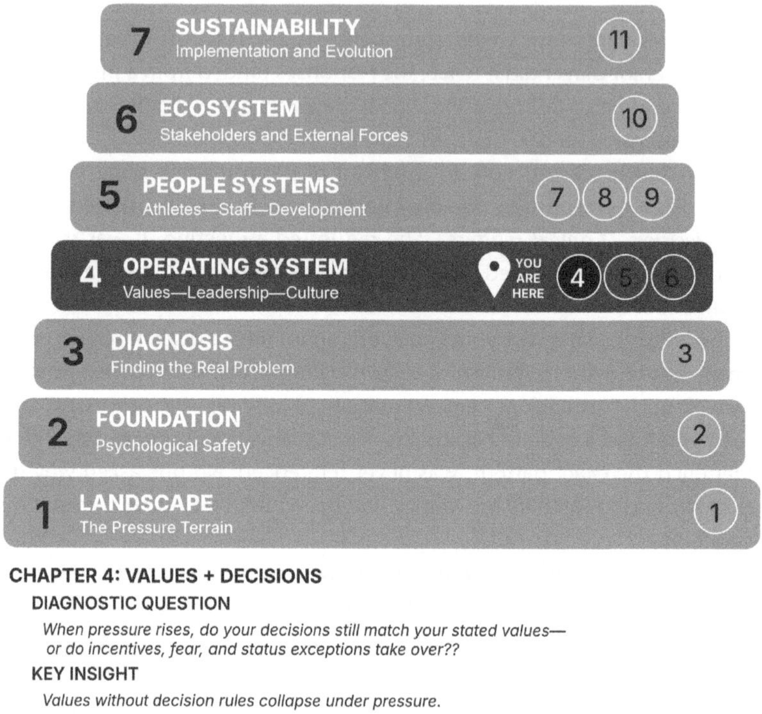

FIGURE 4.1 You Are Here—Operating System.

The HPCOS seven-layer architecture with Layer 4 (Operating System) highlighted. This chapter starts to answer Question 4—how do we decide when it matters?—by excavating values-in-use through conflict archaeology, building decision architecture with integrated safeguarding gates, and stress-testing both against the decisions that reveal whether stated values survive contact with pressure.

The chapter introduces *conflict archaeology*—a diagnostic method for excavating values-in-use from an organization's decision history—and then constructs the decision architecture required to close the gap:

- **Safeguarding gates** that hard-wire non-negotiable welfare checks before team-level processes begin;
- **Discipline decision trees** that make status-based exceptions visible and auditable;
- **Documentation standards** that create institutional memory;
- **Stress-testing methods** that identify architecture failures when the cost of discovery is a conversation rather than a crisis.

4.1.1 Map What You Are Actually Building

Walk into most locker rooms and weight rooms, and you will see the same wall words: Excellence. Integrity. Teamwork. Respect.

Walls are easy.

These statements are everywhere. They are also not doing the work. Corporate research has documented the pattern for decades (Collins & Porras, 1994), and sport culture change research tells the same story: espoused values routinely fail to translate into operational practice (Cruickshank & Collins, 2012).

Why? Because generic values justify almost any behavior (Weaver et al., 1999). "Respect" coexists comfortably with fear-based coaching and status exceptions because it never specifies what gets sacrificed. When an organization's espoused values diverge from its *theory-in-use*—the rules that actually govern decisions—the enacted pattern wins (Argyris & Schön, 1974). Behavior is maintained by its consequences (Skinner, 1953), and those consequences are learned vicariously by everyone watching (Bandura, 1977). The room does not read the wall. It reads what happens to people.

Before you touch values, make the cascade explicit:

- **Vision:** Where you are going (Collins & Porras, 1994)

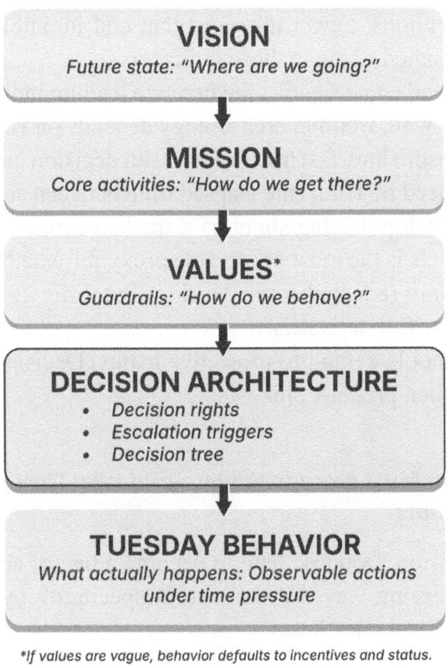

FIGURE 4.2 The Vision–Values–Decision Cascade.

From strategic intent to Tuesday morning behavior. The operational breakdowns happen below the mission line—in values-in-use and the decision architecture that translates them into action. For mission design, see David (1989).

- **Mission:** What you do to get there (David, 1989)
- **Values-in-use:** How you behave when it costs you
- **Decision architecture:** The repeatable pathways that translate intent into action (Thaler & Sunstein, 2008)

Most organizations invest heavily in the top two layers and leave the bottom two to improvisation.

Decision architecture is the missing link. People tolerate hard outcomes when the process is consistent and explainable—that is the core finding of procedural justice research (Colquitt, 2001; Lind & Tyler, 1988). Architecture also reduces decision noise by making similar cases run through the same standardized pathway (Kahneman et al., 2021). But the real test is simpler than either of those literatures suggests: if the answer to the fly-on-the-wall test changes depending on *who* is involved, your real value is status, not principle (Simons, 2002).

4.1.1.1 Linking to Leading Indicators

Decision architecture is the structural answer to the third leading indicator introduced in the Introduction: *do decisions get cleaner?* Fewer mystery reversals. Fewer status exceptions. Fewer meetings that end in ambiguity. Every tool in this chapter is designed to move those indicators.

Speed of Truth and *voice safety*—the first two leading indicators—run through the architecture as well. Conflict archaeology depends on voice, and documentation timelines measure how fast truth travels. But decision clarity is this chapter's primary target. Speed of Truth (the elapsed time between someone identifying a problem and leadership hearing about it) is tracked explicitly because the speed at which truth travels is the most observable proxy for whether the system is safe enough to speak into (adapted from Weick & Sutcliffe, 2015; Morrison, 2014; see Introduction for full derivation).

Under threat, people default to protective habits. Decision architecture keeps values in frame when pressure spikes.

4.1.2 Why Vision Must Precede Values—and Why They Must be Yours

Without a clear vision, "values" tend to become a bag of adjectives that people interpret in self-serving ways. Vision forces specificity by demanding honest answers to four critical questions:

- What does winning mean for us?
- What time horizon matters?
- What will we sacrifice, and what is non-negotiable?
- Who becomes disposable when resources tighten?

That last question often predicts whether values will protect people or merely extract from them. Test it: can your vision guide a hard call? "Be excellent" cannot. "Become the safest high-performance pathway in our region" can.

Yet, even a clear vision is insufficient if your values are borrowed. Borrowed values were not forged in your conflicts. They do not map to your recurring trade-offs, your incentive systems, or your governance lanes. Schein (2010) makes this case directly: durable cultural assumptions develop through an organization's *own* problem-solving history. Values imported from outside that history lack the experiential grounding required to make them self-reinforcing. When pressure hits, the organization will simply revert to status and convenience. If your leadership team cannot articulate the specific behaviors expected during recurring dilemmas, you do not yet have values. You have aspirations.

4.1.3 The Reinforcement Loop: How Values Become Observable

Values become real—or remain hollow—through a continuous reinforcement loop: **cue → behavior → consequence.**

As established in Section 4.1.1, consequences shape behavior, and everyone watching updates their internal model accordingly. When leaders' actions align

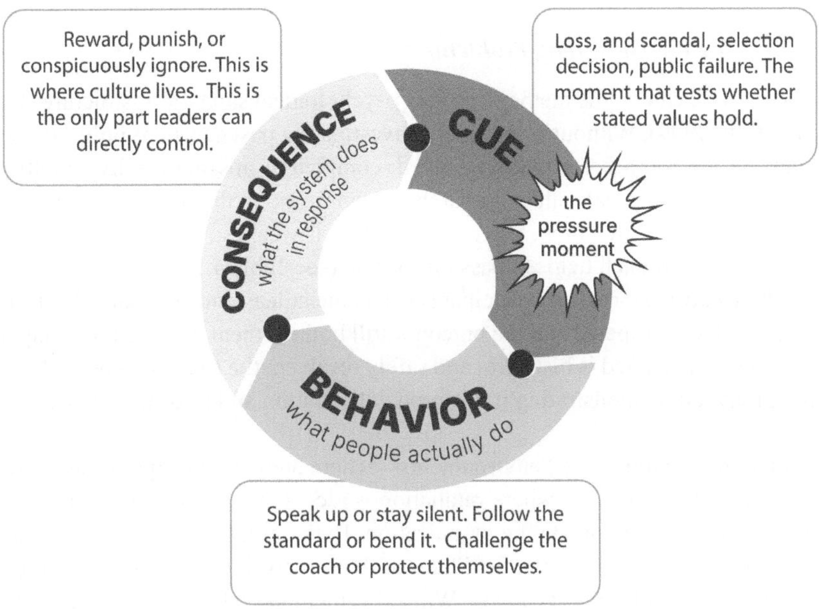

FIGURE 4.3 The Values Reinforcement Loop.

How consequences shape organizational behavior. Read the loop backward to diagnose which values the system is actually reinforcing; rewrite it forward to build a decision architecture that reinforces the right ones.

with their stated values, behavioral integrity builds trust. When their actions contradict their words, trust erodes (Davis & Rothstein, 2006; Simons, 2002).

This cascade defines your architecture: vision constrains mission, mission constrains values, and values constrain decision pathways. Building it requires knowing who you actually are, not who you wish you were.

4.2 Conflict Archaeology: Excavating Values-in-Use

Principle: Your real values live in the decisions you have already made under pressure. Mine your conflicts. The pattern reveals who you are.

Your organization has already shown you its values through what it protected and what it sacrificed when resources were tight, when people were angry, or when the media was watching. The gap between stated and enacted values predicts trust, commitment, and performance (Simons et al., 2015). *Conflict archaeology* is the practice of excavating those past decisions to extract the underlying pattern.

This process accelerates truth. By revealing the values that actually governed past decisions, an organization can close the gap between what is stated and what is enacted—precisely the gap that slows information flow and produces the "mystery reversals" flagged in the Introduction.

4.2.1 The Bootstrapping Problem

There is one catch: this method requires psychological safety infrastructure (Edmondson, 1999). Without voice safety, investigating past decisions only surfaces conflicts the room has already resolved, completely missing the live conflicts that contain your real values hierarchy. Organizations that most need conflict archaeology are often those where voice safety is weakest.

A staged approach helps bypass this hurdle (see Table 4.1).

The Readiness Test: If participants can name at least one unresolved conflict where values competed and the outcome still bothers them, the room is ready. If every conflict named is historical and safely resolved, the room may be performing safety, not demonstrating it. Proceed with caution and prioritize anonymous input.

In highly compromised environments—where anonymous input is suspected of being surveillance, or where retaliation is recent and visible—the staged approach must begin outside the organization. External interviews conducted under strict confidentiality by a facilitator with no reporting line to leadership can generate an initial conflict catalog. While this method is slower, more expensive, and filters data through a third party, it is the minimum viable approach when internal voice safety is entirely broken. The fact that external collection was necessary is, in itself, critical diagnostic data.

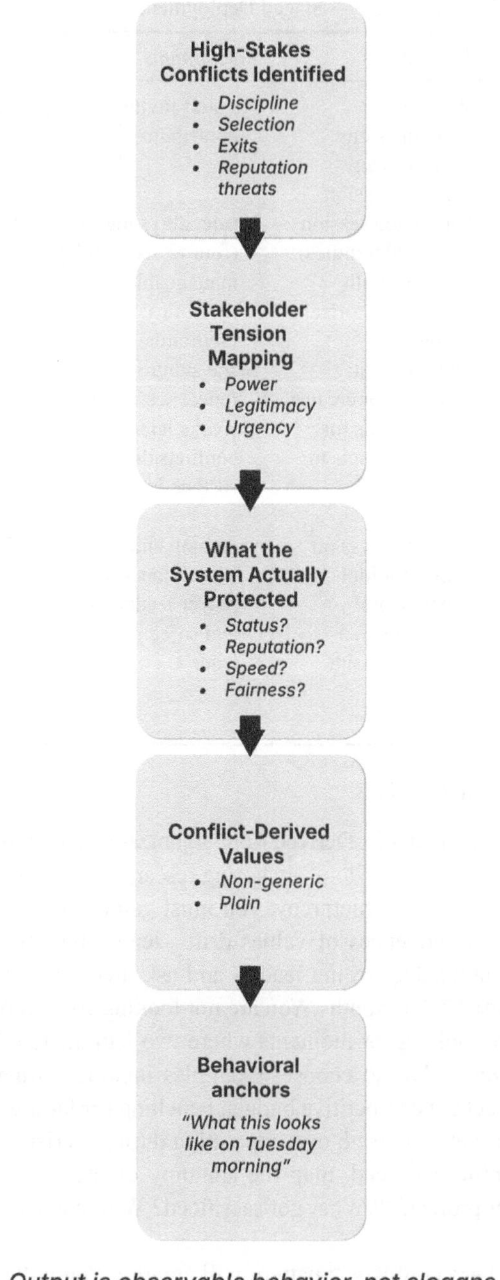

FIGURE 4.4 Conflict Archaeology Pipeline.

The staged process through which an organization surfaces past value conflicts, extracts the implicit hierarchy, and converts findings into decision rules.

TABLE 4.1 Conflict Archaeology—Staged Deployment

Stage	*Format*	*Participants*	*Readiness Signal*
1. Anonymous input	Written submissions prior to any group session	All staff invited to contribute	Generates a conflict catalog without forcing anyone to speak first
2. Small group, external facilitator	Facilitated session (60–90 minutes); begins with safely historical conflicts	Leadership subgroup (four to six people); manageable power dynamics; external facilitator	Participants can freely name trade-offs between legitimate values
3. Follow the room	Same format; facilitator creates conditions for live conflicts to surface	Same subgroup; repeat session 4–6 weeks later if live conflicts don't surface in Stage 2	Someone names an unresolved, current conflict—shifting the room from warm-up to real excavation
4. Broader group	Extended session using initial behavioral anchors as a starting point	Coaching and performance staff, player leadership, and safeguarding leads	The leadership subgroup has completed a full cycle and produced draft behavioral anchors

4.2.2 Mining the Conflicts

Status: Practitioner heuristic. Derived from organizational culture diagnosis methods (Schein, 2010) and behavioral anchoring research (Smith & Kendall, 1963).

To extract a true values hierarchy, you must gather the people who directly experience the consequences of values drift—leadership, coaching staff, performance staff, and safeguarding leads—and ask them to name genuine trade-offs from the past 12–24 months. You are not looking for complaints or process failures; you are looking for moments where two legitimate priorities collided, and the organization had to choose. Examples include cutting a development program to protect the competitive budget, benching (or failing to bench) a high-status player, or choosing truth over reputation during a crisis.

For each conflict surfaced, map the anatomy of the decision: what was at stake? What got protected? What got sacrificed? Who made the call, and under what pressure?

As you sort these conflicts, a pattern will emerge. You will see which values consistently won out and which were routinely sacrificed. You are not looking for perfection in this exercise; you are looking for the *actual* hierarchy visible in your decisions, rather than the idealized one printed on your wall.

TABLE 4.2 From Generic Values to Behavioral Anchors

Generic Value	*Behavioral Anchor (Fly-on-the-Wall Observable)*
Respect	We apply the same standards to high-status and low-status people. We correct public disrespect immediately, regardless of talent or tenure.
Accountability	When standards are violated, we document it, apply proportionate consequences, and clearly communicate the "why." We do not make quiet exceptions to avoid conflict.
Development	We protect long-term capability over short-term results. When forced, we prioritize decisions that build the next generation, even if it costs us this season.
Safety	Safeguarding issues route to an independent pathway before "team discipline" begins. We do not negotiate welfare under competitive or reputational pressure.
Truth	We speak the truth, even when uncomfortable, and reward early problem-surfacing. We track "Speed of Truth" (elapsed time between problem identification and leadership awareness) as a leading indicator.

Once the true hierarchy is clear, the generic values that actually govern your environment must be converted into **behavioral anchors**. Generic values like "respect" must be rewritten into operational language like, "we bench high-status players for the same violations that bench rotation players."

The benchmark for these anchors is the **fly-on-the-wall standard**: *if a neutral observer with no organizational history watched your team for a week, could they identify the value in action purely from observable behavior?* This practitioner standard ensures behavioral concreteness. If the observer needs someone to explain the value's meaning, the value is aspirational, not operational (Smith & Kendall, 1963). If the answer is vague or hypothetical, the value requires more work.

4.2.3 From Conflicts to Behavioral Anchors

These anchors are not universal; they are deeply specific to the organization that excavated them. Your anchors will differ based on your unique conflicts, governance structure, and stakeholder pressures. The ultimate test is not whether they sound inspiring, but whether they reliably guide decisions when values collide.

BOX 4.2 PSYCHOLOGY SIDELINES WITH DR. MCB — THE MOMENT THE ROOM GOES QUIET

The pattern in conflict archaeology sessions never varies. The first 15 minutes are comfortable. People list conflicts that feel safely historical—a budget decision from two years ago, a trade everyone already agreed was wrong. Sticky notes fill up with things the organization has already processed.

Then someone names the live one. Usually a mid-status person—not senior enough to have made the call, not junior enough to have missed it. They say something like: "What about when we kept [player] after the second incident because we needed him for the playoff push?"

The room shifts. Two people look at the table. The head coach's jaw tightens. The GM glances at the door.

That is the moment. The conflict the room doesn't want to name is the conflict that contains your actual values. Everything before it was a warm-up.

If you let the room retreat—"let's come back to that one," "that's a bit different"—you have signaled that the exercise is theater. Archaeology only works if the archaeologist is willing to dig where it hurts.

So I hold the silence. I say: "That one matters. Walk me through what happened. What got protected? What got sacrificed?" Then I shut up. What comes out is almost never comfortable. But it is always true.

The hardest part isn't the excavation. It's what happens after—when leadership sees the pattern and realizes the actual values hierarchy is not the one on the wall. The quiet moment where someone says, "So we say we value development, but we've sacrificed it every single time it competed with short-term results."

That is not a failure. That is where the real work starts. And you cannot build an architecture that protects what matters until you know what you've been willing to sacrifice.

4.2.4 Cultural Calibration

Behavioral anchors are not culture-neutral. What reads as "direct accountability" in one context may read as aggressive disrespect in another (Gelfand et al., 2011; Hofstede, 2001; House et al., 2004). When building values for multinational or multicultural teams, explicitly test every anchor: *does this translate? Does it create unintended exclusion?*

In high power-distance cultures, the participatory format may require anonymous input or external facilitation. However, safeguarding obligations remain strictly non-negotiable across all cultural contexts (International Safeguarding Children in Sport Working Group, 2016; Mountjoy et al., 2016).

4.2.5 Whose Conflicts Get Excavated

Conflict archaeology is only as honest as the room doing the digging.

In most professional sport organizations, the conflicts that surface are those experienced by people with the most voice: senior coaches, executives, and established athletes (Morrison, 2014). Conversely, the conflicts experienced by international players, women in male-dominated structures, or minority athletes are far less likely to surface unless the facilitator purposefully creates space for them.

This is not speculation; it is a documented structural reality. For example, Lapchick (2023) consistently reports that while Black athletes make up over 70% of player rosters in major leagues such as the NBA and NFL, they occupy less than 15% of executive leadership and coaching roles. When the room defining the values lacks representation, it creates a dangerous blind spot. Broader organizational data shows that Black employees receive disproportionately more formal discipline—often at rates up to double that of their white counterparts—despite comparable rates of alleged misconduct (Walter et al., 2021; Cunningham, 2010).

If your decision tree is built on anchors excavated from a homogeneous room, it will encode the very bias it was designed to prevent—resulting in the "false objectivity" failure mode (see Table 4.4).

4.3 Decision Architecture Under Pressure

Principle: Intuition breaks under stress. Build pathways that keep values in frame when threat spikes.

Conflict archaeology gives you a diagnosis: the values hierarchy your organization actually operates by, translated into behavioral anchors concrete enough to pass the fly-on-the-wall test. That is necessary—but insufficient. A clear-eyed map of who you are does not, by itself, prevent the next status exception, the next quiet reclassification, or the next "football decision" that routes a welfare concern away from the people hired to catch it. Sian (Box 4.1) had the diagnosis. She mapped the pattern, named the inconsistency, and sent it up the chain. The system had no architecture to receive it.

This section builds what was missing. It takes the behavioral anchors and values hierarchy produced by conflict archaeology and converts them into repeatable decision pathways—structural mechanisms that keep values in frame when pressure spikes, status intervenes, or timelines compress. The core components are a safeguarding gate that hard-wires welfare checks before any team-level process begins, a classification system that forces comparable incidents into the same category regardless of who is involved, a values filter that makes status-based exceptions visible in real time, and documentation standards that create the institutional memory most sport organizations lack.

Before introducing the tools, Section 4.3.1 explains *why* architecture rather than judgment: the neurological, psychological, and institutional forces that predictably degrade decision-making under threat. Section 4.3.2 provides the primary practitioner tool—a fully worked discipline decision tree with an integrated safeguarding gate, including structural variants for selection and return-to-play pathways. Section 4.3.3 maps the failure modes—over-rigidity, gaming, weaponization, and false objectivity—because architecture that cannot be questioned becomes another instrument of control.

4.3.1 Why Architecture, Not Intuition

Under threat, stress impairs the prefrontal cortex capacities that flexible judgment requires (Arnsten, 2009). At the organizational level, the same dynamic plays out: threat triggers rigidity, constricting information processing and defaulting groups to well-learned, dominant responses (Staw et al., 1981). Put those together in a high-stakes sport environment and the pattern is predictable. When pressure spikes, decisions revert to habit, hierarchy, and status protection.

This reversion has a name: **institutional decoupling** (Meyer & Rowan, 1977)—where the formal rules on the wall are entirely separated from the actual behaviors rewarded on the floor.

A cognitive failure compounds the structural one: **ethical fading** (Tenbrunsel & Messick, 2004). Under pressure, the brain stops seeing a dilemma as a "values" decision and recodes it as a "business," "competitive," or "tactical" necessity. This psychological sleight-of-hand lets otherwise good people make values-inconsistent choices without feeling like hypocrites.

BOX 4.3 TIMEOUT — THE INCONSISTENCY IS NOT A CHARACTER PROBLEM

When a coach applies different consequences to the same behavior depending on who did it, the instinct is to call it hypocrisy. It is not. It is ethical fading under pressure—the brain recoding a values decision as a tactical one (Tenbrunsel & Messick, 2004). The coach is not lying about their values. They have stopped seeing the decision as a values question at all. That is why motivation talks fail and architecture works. A better speech will not fix a structural problem.

Decision architecture structures the choice environment so values stay in frame when pressure spikes (Thaler & Sunstein, 2008; Kahneman et al., 2021). High-reliability organizations—aviation, medicine, and nuclear power—sustain performance under pressure not through heroic individual judgment but through structural mechanisms that anticipate failure (Weick & Sutcliffe, 2015).

Elite sport tells the same story. Cruickshank and Collins (2012) argued that effective culture change in elite sport requires more than motivational appeals. Their subsequent grounded theory studies of professional sport performance teams identified structural mechanisms—environmental management, role clarity, and regulated power dynamics—as central to sustained change across leadership transitions and competitive pressure (Cruickshank et al., 2013, 2014, 2015). The implication is direct: if culture change depends on structural mechanisms, then decision architecture is the operational form those mechanisms take.

4.3.1.1 The Structural Test

Decision architecture is orientation-dependent. Every mechanism in this chapter assumes the organizational orientation established earlier in this book—that the institution exists to develop and protect people, not to extract from them. Reverse that orientation—make the operating assumption "you're lucky to be here"—and every process becomes an extraction instrument with better documentation.

A discipline tree can enforce compliance *or* protect fairness. The safeguarding gate is the structural test. If it can be overridden by competitive pressure, reputational concern, or status—if the board chair can collapse the safeguarding timeline to manage a news cycle—the architecture is serving the institution's convenience, not the people inside it. The question is not whether you have a decision architecture. It is *whom* the architecture is built to protect.

4.3.2 Discipline Decision Tree: Fully Worked Example

Status: Theoretically grounded. Adapts Just Culture principles from healthcare and aviation (Dekker, 2012; Reason, 1997) and procedural justice research (Colquitt, 2001; Lind & Tyler, 1988). Sport-specific pathway not formally validated.

This section provides the chapter's primary practitioner tool: a five-step discipline decision tree with an integrated safeguarding gate (Figure 4.5). The tool operationalizes everything built so far—behavioral anchors from conflict archaeology, the values hierarchy, and the fly-on-the-wall standard—into a single, repeatable pathway that any decision-maker in the organization can follow.

The pathway is designed around the conditions that make discipline in sport structurally different from other organizational contexts: compressed timelines that reward speed over process, public visibility that creates reputational pressure to act (or not act) before the facts are clear, and power gradients between high-status athletes and the staff responsible for enforcing standards. A discipline pathway prevents exception drift—the gradual normalization of deviance (Vaughan, 1996)—and protects safeguarding by hard-wiring a gate before "team discipline" begins. The pathway adapts Just Culture principles (Dekker, 2012; Reason, 1997) for these sport-specific pressures.

The tree runs in five steps: a non-negotiable safeguarding gate (Step 0), incident classification by category and severity (Step 1), values filter application (Step 2), response selection matched to severity using the Discipline Response Matrix in Table 4.3 (Step 3), and communication and documentation protocols (Steps 4 and 5). A worked documentation example follows.

Step 0: Safeguarding Gate (Non-Negotiable)

Before you treat anything as "team discipline," ask: *is this a safeguarding issue or credible risk of serious harm (abuse, harassment, boundary violations, retaliation, coercion, safety threats)?*

- If **yes**, stop. Trigger the independent safeguarding pathway. This is a welfare and governance obligation (International Safeguarding Children in Sport Working Group, 2016; Mountjoy et al., 2016).
- *Note:* In youth/academy contexts, the safeguarding gate operates at a lower threshold. When in doubt, route through the independent pathway first. The cost of over-triggering is a brief process delay; the cost of under-triggering is a child left unprotected.

Step 1: Incident Classification

- **Category:** Conduct (violates team standards), Performance (repeated standard failures), Legal/Ethical (potential breach of law, policy, or public trust), and Safety (endangers self or others).
- **Severity:** Minor (first occurrence; limited harm), Moderate (repeated pattern or broader impact), Major (high-profile or serious harm; clear policy breach), and Severe (potential criminality, victim involved, or safeguarding concerns).

Step 2: Values Filter Application

Run the incident through your operational values (Table 4.2). Keep the questions few and explicit:

- **Consistency:** Would we use the same process and similar consequences if a lower-status person did this?
- **Development:** What response teaches and restores standards, not just punishes?
- **Trust:** What precedent does this set for the group?
- *Crucially:* If the filter reveals that severity was assigned inconsistently (e.g., a behavior was classified "minor" for a star player but "moderate" for a rookie), return to Step 1 and reclassify before proceeding.

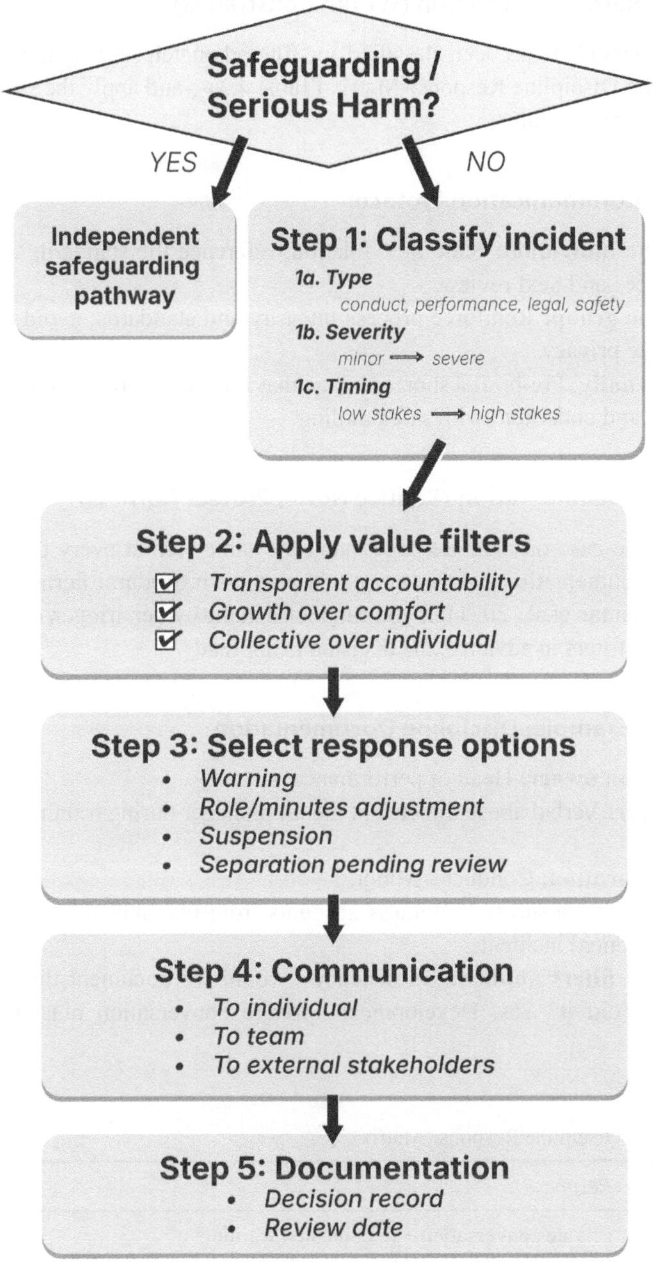

FIGURE 4.5 Discipline Decision Tree With Integrated Safeguarding Gate.

A discipline pathway with a non-negotiable safeguarding gate at Step 0. If the safeguarding gate can be overridden by competitive pressure, reputational concern, or status, the architecture is serving the institution's convenience, not the people inside it.

Step 3: Response Selection (Within Constraints)

Once the incident has been classified and filtered, match severity to response using the Discipline Response Matrix (Table 4.3)—and apply the same process regardless of status.

Step 4: Communication Protocol

- **To the individual:** State the violation; reference the standard; state consequences and next review.
- **To the group:** Reinforce process integrity and standards; avoid details that violate privacy.
- **Externally:** Pre-brief a short message that is truthful, bounded by confidentiality, and consistent with safeguarding.

Step 5: Documentation (Reduce Noise; Protect Fairness)

Record the case on a single page using the same format every time. Consistent documentation reduces noise and protects procedural fairness over time (Kahneman et al., 2021). If you cannot fill in the owner, trigger, evidence, and values filters in advance, the decision is not ready.

Worked Example: Discipline Documentation

- **Decision owner:** Head of performance.
- **Trigger:** Verbal abuse directed at the kit manager during training (Incident 1 of 3).
- **Classification:** Conduct—Minor.
- **Evidence considered:** Witness accounts from two staff members; no prior documented incidents.
- **Values filters applied:** Consistency—would we document this if a junior player did it? Yes. Development—private conversation plus documented

TABLE 4.3 Discipline Response Matrix

Severity	*Response*
Minor	Private conversation + documented warning
Moderate	Formal warning + restitution/repair plan + performance plan
Major	Suspension/removal from selection + formal review + conditions for return
Severe	Immediate removal from environment + external investigation/safeguarding route

warning teaches the standard. Trust—undocumented "conversations" set a precedent that standards are informal.

- **Response selected:** Private conversation + documented warning.
- **Communications:** Individual notified of standard, consequence, and review date. Group: no announcement required for minor first occurrence.
- **Review date:** 30 days.

Fly-on-the-wall check: Run your last three discipline incidents through this tree. Would a stranger observing all three conclude that standards apply equally? If the pathway would have changed based on status, fix the architecture now.

Sian's briefing note (Box 4.1) did this work manually—she put three incidents side by side, and the inconsistency was immediate. The discipline tree makes that comparison structural rather than dependent on one person's diligence. The architecture does not guarantee the right outcome. It guarantees that the inconsistency cannot hide.

Structural Variants

The architecture is not discipline-specific. The same *gate → classify → filter → decide → document* pattern applies to selection, hiring, and return-to-play decisions with adapted inputs.

- **Selection Decisions:** Step 0 remains unchanged. Step 1 substitutes incident classification with capability assessment and person–organization fit (Kristof-Brown et al., 2005). Step 2 asks: *would we apply these criteria identically regardless of the candidate's market value or public profile?*
- **Return-to-Play Decisions:** Step 0 screens for duty-of-care concerns. Step 1 maps clinical readiness against the competitive context. Step 2 asks: *would the return timeline be identical for a player with lower tactical importance?*

BOX 4.4 SKEPTIC'S CORNER — WE'RE A SPORT TEAM, NOT A HOSPITAL

"We're a sport team, not a hospital. We don't need flowcharts."

The pushback: Decision trees, documentation, and safeguarding gates—this is corporate bureaucracy dressed up in sports language. Good coaches make fast decisions based on experience. Adding process slows everything down and dismisses the experience of people who have been doing this for decades. Coaching judgment cannot be reduced to a flowchart.

The answer: Aviation's most experienced pilots still use checklists. Not because they lack judgment—because the operating environment is too complex and too high-stakes to rely on memory under pressure. The checklist does not replace expertise. It protects expertise from the conditions that degrade it (Gawande, 2009).

The decision architecture in this chapter works the same way. It does not tell you *what* to decide. It tells you who owns the decision, who must be consulted, what questions to ask, and what to document. It slows the decision by 90 seconds—long enough to run the values filter, short enough to act before the media cycle forces your hand.

The real question is not whether the architecture slows you down. It is whether the alternative—ad hoc decisions made under threat, influenced by status, undocumented, and inconsistent—is actually faster. Ask any organization that has had to explain a discipline inconsistency to a grievance panel or a media inquiry. The "fast" decision without process creates months of cleanup. The "slow" decision with documentation creates 30 seconds of protection that lasts years. And if the real concern is that the flowchart will reveal inconsistency—that is not an argument against the flowchart. That is the flowchart doing its job.

4.3.3 Boundary Conditions: When Decision Architecture Backfires

Decision architecture is a guardrail, not a replacement for judgment. Practical wisdom—knowing when and how to apply rules, and when the rules do not fit the situation—remains essential (Schwartz & Sharpe, 2010). Treated as a mechanistic rulebook, architecture fails in predictable ways.

TABLE 4.4 Decision Architecture Failure Modes—Recognize and Fix

Failure Mode	*What It Looks Like*	*The Fix*
Over-rigidity	Staff follow the tree even when the situation contains information that the tree does not capture. People say: *"The process says . . ."* when judgment is needed.	Allow a documented override: *"We deviated from the pathway because [X], and we will review this exception on [date]."*
Gaming	People learn to manipulate categories—"make it look minor," delay reporting until stakes change, or re-classify to avoid escalation.	Audit patterns: repeat incidents, timing clusters, who gets exceptions. Treat trends as escalation triggers.

(*Continued*)

TABLE 4.4 (Continued)

Failure Mode	*What It Looks Like*	*The Fix*
Weaponization	Frameworks become tools for punishment or retaliation against low-status people who speak up (a characteristic of pathological cultures; Westrum, 2004).	Build voice protections and independent safeguarding lanes into the architecture. Monitor retaliation signals explicitly.
False objectivity	Rubrics launder bias (*"the score says . . ."*), especially when the criteria are vague. Apparent fairness masks systematic disadvantage.	Keep anchors behavioral. Run calibration sessions and review for adverse impact across demographic groups and power gradients.
Hyper-conformity	"Values alignment" is weaponized to demand absolute agreement and suppress legitimate diversity of thought (Chatman & O'Reilly, 2016).	Explicitly separate values alignment from demographic or cognitive similarity. Protect constructive dissent.

The test is simple: does the architecture increase fairness, Speed of Truth, and consistent standards—or does it become another way to protect status?

4.4 Stress-Testing Values Against Decisions

Principle: If values do not survive contact with real decisions, they are theater. Audit the gap before building the systems that enforce them.

Even well-constructed decision architecture requires testing. An organization can audit the gap between its stated values and its values-in-use by reviewing 5–10 recent, high-stakes decisions—discipline calls, budget reallocations, selection criteria, or crisis responses made under pressure over the last year.

For each past decision, leadership should score how well the outcome aligned with the organization's stated values on a simple scale: *did the decision strongly protect the value, partially honor it while trading it for another, weakly align by sacrificing it, or actively contradict the value entirely?*

Who does this scoring matters immensely to? The same motivated reasoning that produces values drift in real time (Kunda, 1990) can easily inflate alignment scores after the fact. To reduce self-serving bias, include scorers who experienced the *consequences* of the decision, not merely those who made the call.

When you average these scores across several decisions, a distinct pattern will emerge. The values that consistently score low are your *decorative values*—the ones on paper that do not survive contact with cost. This behavioral integrity gap predicts the erosion of trust, commitment, and performance (Simons, 2002;

Simons et al., 2015). Once you identify a decorative value, the fix is not a cultural initiative; it is a structural one. If "athlete development" consistently loses to "short-term results," you must design a system rule—such as requiring board approval for any budget cut to development categories—that makes the value non-negotiable in the future.

Beyond auditing the past, organizations must stress-test their architecture against future pressure scenarios. Take the scenario where the architecture is most likely to bend—signing a high-performing player at the trade deadline who carries credible reports of boundary violations, or facing intense media pressure to release a statement before a safeguarding process concludes. Replay these scenarios through the decision tree. If a board chair or a head coach can override the timeline to manage a news cycle or a win–loss record, the architecture has a load-bearing failure at the exact point it matters most.

4.5 When Values Collide

Principle: When two legitimate values collide, you cannot fully honor both. The architecture's job is to make the trade-off explicit, documented, and reviewable—not to pretend the collision did not happen.

Even a perfectly audited decision architecture will eventually face a scenario where two non-negotiables compete. Excellence versus well-being, loyalty versus fairness, truth versus reputation—Kidder (1995) calls these "right versus right" dilemmas, and they are different from clear ethical violations. The architecture's job is not to miraculously resolve the tension, but to force leadership to navigate it transparently.

The first step in any collision is to separate true value dilemmas from legal hierarchies. Safety, safeguarding, and legal obligations always sit above performance and reputation. If a safeguarding obligation conflicts with a competitive interest, safeguarding wins. That is not a values collision; it is a preset hierarchy.

When a true collision occurs, the tension must be named out loud: *"We can protect X or Y right now; we cannot do both fully."* Naming the trade-off prevents drift into self-justification. Left unnamed, motivated reasoning allows decision-makers to quietly convince themselves that the collision doesn't exist (Kunda, 1990). Predecisional accountability counteracts this bias by forcing deliberative processing before a commitment is made (Lerner & Tetlock, 1999). If leadership cannot state the collision in a single sentence, they have not successfully diagnosed it yet.

Once the collision is named, rely on the values hierarchy excavated during conflict archaeology. Choose the priority, document the logic as transparently as privacy allows, and—most crucially—mitigate the damage to the sacrificed value. A collision does not erase the losing value. Organizations must accept a temporary cost and build a documented plan to restore what was lost. Without that mitigation plan, "temporary" sacrifices inevitably become permanent.

4.5.1 Chapter Synthesis

Value statements fail not because organizations lack conviction, but because they lack architecture. That is the argument of this chapter—and it has operational consequences.

Conflict archaeology diagnoses what the organization actually protects under pressure. Safeguarding gates hard-wire non-negotiables. Decision trees make status-based exceptions visible. None of these tools replace judgment—they protect it from the conditions that degrade it.

Treat values inconsistency as a motivation or character problem, and you will prescribe the wrong intervention. Procedural justice and decision consistency are not bureaucratic additions to high-performance culture. They are load-bearing infrastructure. The operating implication is that value consistency is maintained by an architecture that makes inconsistency visible, documentable, and correctable before it compounds into the systemic trust erosion the composite case study illustrated.

Key Chapter Takeaways

1. **Your real values live in your decisions under pressure, not on your walls.** Conflict archaeology extracts the actual values hierarchy from an organization's decision history—revealing which values consistently win and which are decorative.
2. **Generic values justify any behavior; behavioral anchors constrain it.** Convert every stated value into a fly-on-the-wall observable standard specific enough that a stranger could verify it in a week of observation.
3. **Decision architecture prevents the predictable reversion to status, convenience, and hierarchy under threat.** Safeguarding gates and decision trees do not replace judgment—they protect judgment from the conditions that degrade it.
4. **The safeguarding gate is structural, not aspirational.** Every discipline and selection pathway must route through an independent welfare check before team-level processes begin—and the gate must be immune to competitive or reputational override.
5. **Stress-test before you need it.** Run recent high-stakes decisions through a values-alignment audit and pressure scenarios through the decision trees—identifying architecture failures when the cost of discovery is a conversation, not a crisis.

Discussion Questions

1. Conduct a conflict archaeology of your organization's last three high-stakes decisions. What values hierarchy does the pattern reveal—and where does it diverge from the stated values?

2. Design a safeguarding gate for a decision pathway in your context. What structural features would make it genuinely independent of the coaching and performance hierarchy, rather than nominally so?
3. Evaluate the trade-off between decision architecture and practical wisdom: at what point does procedural consistency become over-rigidity, and how would you design a system that distinguishes legitimate exceptions from status-based ones?
4. Your organization's values-alignment audit reveals that "athlete development" scores 1.2 out of 3 across 10 recent decisions. Justify a single structural change—not a cultural initiative—that would protect this value in the next collision.

References

Argyris, C., & Schön, D. A. (1974). *Theory in practice: Increasing professional effectiveness*. Jossey-Bass.

Arnsten, A. F. T. (2009). Stress signalling pathways that impair prefrontal cortex structure and function. *Nature Reviews Neuroscience, 10*(6), 410–422. https://doi.org/10.1038/nrn2648

Bandura, A. (1977). *Social learning theory*. Prentice Hall.

Chatman, J. A., & O'Reilly, C. A. (2016). Paradigm lost: Reinvigorating the study of organizational culture. *Research in Organizational Behavior, 36*, 199–224. https://doi.org/10.1016/j.riob.2016.11.004

Collins, J. C., & Porras, J. I. (1994). *Built to last: Successful habits of visionary companies*. HarperBusiness.

Colquitt, J. A. (2001). On the dimensionality of organizational justice: A construct validation of a measure. *Journal of Applied Psychology, 86*(3), 386–400. https://doi.org/10.1037/0021-9010.86.3.386

Cruickshank, A., & Collins, D. (2012). Culture change in elite sport performance teams: Examining and advancing effectiveness in the new era. *Journal of Applied Sport Psychology, 24*(3), 338–355. https://doi.org/10.1080/10413200.2011.650819

Cruickshank, A., Collins, D., & Minten, S. (2013). Culture change in a professional sports team: Shaping environmental contexts and regulating power. *International Journal of Sports Science & Coaching, 8*(2), 271–290. https://doi.org/10.1260/1747-9541.8.2.271

Cruickshank, A., Collins, D., & Minten, S. (2014). Driving and sustaining culture change in Olympic sport performance teams: A first exploration and grounded theory. *Journal of Sport & Exercise Psychology, 36*(1), 107–120. https://doi.org/10.1123/jsep.2013-0133

Cruickshank, A., Collins, D., & Minten, S. (2015). Driving and sustaining culture change in professional sport performance teams: A grounded theory. *Psychology of Sport and Exercise, 20*, 40–50. https://doi.org/10.1016/j.psychsport.2015.04.007

Cunningham, G. B. (2010). Understanding the under-representation of African American coaches: A multilevel perspective. *Sport Management Review, 13*(4), 395–406. https://doi.org/10.1016/j.smr.2009.07.006

David, F. R. (1989). How companies define their mission. *Long Range Planning, 22*(1), 90–97. https://doi.org/10.1016/0024-6301(89)90055-1

Davis, A. L., & Rothstein, H. R. (2006). The effects of the perceived behavioral integrity of managers on employee attitudes: A meta-analysis. *Journal of Business Ethics, 67*(4), 407–419. https://doi.org/10.1007/s10551-006-9034-4

Dekker, S. W. A. (2012). *Just culture: Balancing safety and accountability* (2nd ed.). Ashgate. https://doi.org/10.4324/9781315251271

Edmondson, A. C. (1999). Psychological safety and learning behavior in work teams. *Administrative Science Quarterly*, *44*(2), 350–383. https://doi.org/10.2307/2666999

Gawande, A. (2009). *The checklist manifesto: How to get things right*. Metropolitan Books.

Gelfand, M. J., Raver, J. L., Nishii, L., Leslie, L. M., Lun, J., Lim, B. C., Duan, L., Almaliach, A., Ang, S., Arnadottir, J., Aycan, Z., Boehnke, K., Boski, P., Cabecinhas, R., Chan, D., Chhokar, J., D'Amato, A., Ferrer, M., Fischlmayr, I. C., . . . & Yamaguchi, S. (2011). Differences between tight and loose cultures: A 33-nation study. *Science*, *332*(6033), 1100–1104. https://doi.org/10.1126/science.1197754

Hofstede, G. (2001). *Culture's consequences: Comparing values, behaviors, institutions, and organizations across nations* (2nd ed.). Sage.

House, R. J., Hanges, P. J., Javidan, M., Dorfman, P. W., & Gupta, V. (Eds.). (2004). *Culture, leadership, and organizations: The GLOBE study of 62 societies*. Sage.

International Safeguarding Children in Sport Working Group. (2016). *International safeguards for children in sport* [Report]. Sport England. https://safeinsport.org/wp-content/uploads/2021/11/International-Safeguards-for-Children-in-Sport-English.pdf

Kahneman, D., Sibony, O., & Sunstein, C. R. (2021). *Noise: A flaw in human judgment*. Little, Brown Spark.

Kidder, R. M. (1995). *How good people make tough choices: Resolving the dilemmas of ethical living*. William Morrow.

Kristof-Brown, A. L., Zimmerman, R. D., & Johnson, E. C. (2005). Consequences of individuals' fit at work: A meta-analysis of person–job, person–organization, person–group, and person–supervisor fit. *Personnel Psychology*, *58*(2), 281–342. https://doi.org/10.1111/j.1744-6570.2005.00672.x

Kunda, Z. (1990). The case for motivated reasoning. *Psychological Bulletin*, *108*(3), 480–498. https://doi.org/10.1037/0033-2909.108.3.480

Lapchick, R. E. (2023). *2022 racial and gender report card: A comprehensive analysis of the hiring practices of Major League Baseball, the National Basketball Association, the Women's National Basketball Association, the National Football League, Major League Soccer and college sport* [Report]. The Institute for Diversity and Ethics in Sport, University of Central Florida. https://www.tidesport.org/_files/ugd/ac4087_31b60a6a51574cbe9b552831c0fcbd3f.pdf

Lerner, J. S., & Tetlock, P. E. (1999). Accounting for the effects of accountability. *Psychological Bulletin*, *125*(2), 255–275. https://doi.org/10.1037/0033-2909.125.2.255

Lind, E. A., & Tyler, T. R. (1988). *The social psychology of procedural justice*. Plenum Press.

Meyer, J. W., & Rowan, B. (1977). Institutionalized organizations: Formal structure as myth and ceremony. *American Journal of Sociology*, *83*(2), 340–363. https://doi.org/10.1086/226550

Morrison, E. W. (2014). Employee voice and silence. *Annual Review of Organizational Psychology and Organizational Behavior*, *1*(1), 173–197. https://doi.org/10.1146/annurev-orgpsych-031413-091328

Mountjoy, M., Brackenridge, C., Arrington, M., Blauwet, C., Carska-Sheppard, A., Fasting, K., Kirby, S., Leahy, T., Marks, S., Martin, K., Starr, K., Tiivas, A., & Budgett, R. (2016). International Olympic Committee consensus statement: Harassment and abuse (non-accidental violence) in sport. *British Journal of Sports Medicine*, *50*(17), 1019–1029. https://doi.org/10.1136/bjsports-2016-096121

Reason, J. (1997). *Managing the risks of organizational accidents*. Ashgate. https://doi.org/10.4324/9781315543543

Schein, E. H. (2010). *Organizational culture and leadership* (4th ed.). Jossey-Bass.

Schwartz, B., & Sharpe, K. (2010). *Practical wisdom: The right way to do the right thing*. Riverhead Books.

Simons, T. (2002). Behavioral integrity: The perceived alignment between managers' words and deeds as a research focus. *Organization Science*, *13*(1), 18–35. https://doi.org/10.1287/orsc.13.1.18.543

Simons, T., Leroy, H., Collewaert, V., & Masschelein, S. (2015). How leader alignment of words and deeds affects followers: A meta-analysis of behavioral integrity research. *Journal of Business Ethics*, *132*(4), 831–844. https://doi.org/10.1007/s10551-014-2332-3

Skinner, B. F. (1953). *Science and human behavior*. Macmillan.

Smith, P. C., & Kendall, L. M. (1963). Retranslation of expectations: An approach to the construction of unambiguous anchors for rating scales. *Journal of Applied Psychology*, *47*(2), 149–155. https://doi.org/10.1037/h0047060

Staw, B. M., Sandelands, L. E., & Dutton, J. E. (1981). Threat-rigidity effects in organizational behavior: A multilevel analysis. *Administrative Science Quarterly*, *26*(4), 501–524. https://doi.org/10.2307/2392337

Tenbrunsel, A. E., & Messick, D. M. (2004). Ethical fading: The role of self-deception in unethical behavior. *Social Justice Research*, *17*(2), 223–236. https://doi.org/10.1023/B:SORE.0000027411.35832.53

Thaler, R. H., & Sunstein, C. R. (2008). *Nudge: Improving decisions about health, wealth, and happiness*. Yale University Press.

Vaughan, D. (1996). *The Challenger launch decision: Risky technology, culture, and deviance at NASA*. University of Chicago Press. https://doi.org/10.7208/chicago/9780226851785.001.0001

Walter, S. L., Gonzalez-Mulé, E., Guarana, C. L., O'Boyle, E. H., Jr., Berry, C. M., & Baldwin, T. T. (2021). The race discipline gap: A cautionary note on archival measures of behavioral misconduct. *Organizational Behavior and Human Decision Processes*, *166*, 166–178. https://doi.org/10.1016/j.obhdp.2020.03.010

Weaver, G. R., Treviño, L. K., & Cochran, P. L. (1999). Corporate ethics programs as control systems: Influences of executive commitment and environmental factors. *Academy of Management Journal*, *42*(1), 41–57. https://doi.org/10.2307/256873

Weick, K. E., & Sutcliffe, K. M. (2015). *Managing the unexpected: Sustained performance in a complex world* (3rd ed.). Wiley.

Westrum, R. (2004). A typology of organisational cultures. *Quality & Safety in Health Care*, *13*(Suppl 2), ii22–ii27. https://doi.org/10.1136/qshc.2003.009522

5

THE TRANSFORMATIONAL LEADER—SKILLS FOR HIGH-STAKES ENVIRONMENTS

Learning Objectives

By the end of this chapter, the reader will be able to:

1. Evaluate leader disclosure decisions using the Open, Filtered, and Restricted disclosure zones framework to distinguish strategic vulnerability from manipulation.
2. Apply the game-day regulation protocol to regulate emotional responses before, during, and after high-pressure events.
3. Design high-stakes conversations using performance safety zones that separate learning contexts from accountability contexts.
4. Construct selection and deselection conversations grounded in procedural justice principles and culturally adaptive feedback delivery.
5. Analyze the decision-making degradation pathway during losing streaks and apply structured protocols to protect decision quality.

BOX 5.1 CASE STUDY — THE ROOM WENT QUIET

Connor was a good coach. Not just results—process. He'd built his reputation on debriefs where people actually spoke, on saying "I got that wrong" in front of the group when he had. His assistants described him the same way: intense, demanding, but safe to disagree with.

Then the club lost five in a row.

DOI: 10.4324/9781003631217-6

After the fourth loss, the board shifted their language: "results need to improve quickly," and "the supporters are losing patience." Connor didn't sleep that night.

The next morning, an analyst presented a report suggesting the midfield pressing structure—Connor's design—was leaving the back line exposed. Before the losing run, he would have pulled the thread. This time: "We're not scrapping the press. We need better execution, not a different system." Voice flat. Arms crossed.

He didn't yell. But the room registered the shift instantly.

The analyst adjusted his next report to focus on execution errors rather than structural problems. The assistant coach stopped challenging tactical assumptions in Monday meetings. The goalkeeper coach, about to raise a concern about set-piece vulnerability, decided it could wait.

Connor didn't notice. He was managing his own stress by narrowing his attention—a neurobiological response he would have recognized in his athletes but couldn't see in himself. From the outside, he looked composed. From inside the staff room, he had become someone people managed rather than informed.

The pressing structure collapsed in the sixth match. Three goals from transition play—the same corridor the analyst had flagged. Connor asked his assistant the next morning: "Why didn't anyone say something about the press?"

The assistant paused. "We did, Connor. Three weeks ago."

That gap—between what a leader believes they are doing and what the room actually experiences—is where the vulnerability–authority paradox lives.

5.1 Transformational Leadership Under Pressure

Leadership under pressure fails not because leaders lack character but because organizations lack systems. This chapter installs the leadership infrastructure: behavioral protocols that hold under load, transfer across transitions, and convert individual competence into institutional capacity (see Figure 5.1).

The vulnerability–authority paradox operates in every high-stakes environment, but elite sport makes it visible. The room needs leaders who make decisions athletes can follow immediately—while also telling the leader what those decisions missed. Leaders need to appear confident enough that the room stays calm while remaining open enough that problems surface before they metastasize.

Resolve the paradox wrong—all authority, no vulnerability—and the result is compliance theater. Athletes nod in meetings and hide information in hallways.

CHAPTER 5: LEADERSHIP

DIAGNOSTIC QUESTION

When pressure rises, do your behaviors stabilize the system—or become the volatility?

KEY INSIGHT

The leader's worst day becomes everyone's baseline.

FIGURE 5.1 You Are Here—Operating System.

The HPCOS seven-layer architecture with Layer 4 (Operating System) highlighted. This chapter continues to answer Question 4—how do we decide when it matters?—by addressing leader nervous-system regulation, emotional contagion, disclosure boundaries, and high-stakes conversation scripts under load.

Resolve it the other way—all vulnerability, no authority—and the result is committees that cannot execute under pressure. Get it right and something rare emerges: a high-standards environment where people speak early, execute precisely, and trust the leader to make the final call.

Transformational leadership—the conversion of values into behavior through modeling, meaning-making, intellectual challenge, and individualized attention (Bass, 1985)—works differently under competitive compression. Corporate transformational leadership unfolds over quarters and fiscal years. In sport, leaders have minutes to model the standard, seconds to invite challenge, and no time for process theater. The mechanisms stay the same. The execution compresses. Idealized influence becomes pre-game preparation that the room can see. Inspirational motivation compresses into identity cues—"People like us do this" works; "We need to dig deep" does not—connecting today's pain to a group identity athletes already carry (Haslam et al., 2020). Intellectual stimulation becomes tactical invitations: "What are you seeing?" not "Does anyone disagree?" The first is specific and safe. The second forces public dissent—a high-cost behavior in environments where athletes hold implicit theories about when speaking up is safe and when it threatens standing (Detert & Edmondson, 2011). Individualized consideration means knowing which athletes need detail and which need autonomy—and adapting in real time. Generational dynamics sharpen this—younger athletes increasingly expect dialogue, transparent rationales, and explicit attention to identity and mental health, recalibrating practices that worked with prior cohorts (McDougall & Saarinen, 2024).

Meta-analytic evidence links these mechanisms to performance outcomes, follower satisfaction, and organizational commitment (Judge & Piccolo, 2004). In sport specifically, transformational coaching predicts athlete well-being, motivation, and team cohesion across competitive levels, from youth (Vella et al., 2013) to elite (Arthur et al., 2016; Stenling & Tafvelin, 2014). But athletes audit the gap between what leaders say and what leaders reward. One punished truth teaches more than 10 speeches about honesty (Baumeister et al., 2001). That is behavioral integrity (Simons, 2002)—either present or a performance that lasts until the first real test.

The systems in this chapter exist because athletes and staff deserve leadership architecture that does not export dysfunction onto them. The organization recruited these people into a high-pressure environment and asked them to stake their careers, their health, and their identity on its outcomes. Every protocol that follows—disclosure zones, regulation sequences, conversation scripts, and losing streak architecture—is built on a structural premise: the organization is lucky to have these people, and its leadership systems should reflect that. The first structural challenge those systems must solve is the tension at the center of every leadership interaction under pressure.

5.1.1 The Vulnerability–Authority Paradox

The paradox is structural, not personal. Edmondson (2018) describes the core challenge as leaders needing to simultaneously set high standards and lower interpersonal risk. Elite sport compresses that tension—the time horizon is seconds, not quarters, and execution consequences are immediate.

Elite sport selects for leaders who project certainty. Athletes follow people who look like they know where they are going. But certainty suppresses information. The empirical pattern is consistent: leader behaviors that flatten status—soliciting input, acknowledging fallibility, inviting disagreement—predict psychological safety with effects strongest where status differences are largest (Nembhard & Edmondson, 2006). Elite sport stress-tests the finding. If the leader always sounds sure, the athlete with the niggling doubt doesn't raise it. The resolution is not less authority. It is strategic vulnerability: calibrated disclosure that invites information without undermining decision control.

Examples of open-zone disclosure in practice—adapted to the leader's natural register:

> "I am not seeing this clearly yet. What are you seeing?"
>
> "We have three options. Here is what I know and what I don't. Talk me through the trade-offs."
>
> "I made a call last week that cost us. Here is what I learned."

The disclosure needs to serve the team's learning, not the leader's need to be seen as human. Mainstream vulnerability discourse (Brown, 2012) correctly identifies vulnerability as a precursor to courage, but elite sport requires a more bounded application: disclosure filtered through the team's operational needs. Research on transparent leadership confirms that calibration determines everything—what is shared, with whom, and when separates vulnerability that builds trust from vulnerability that erodes it (Simons, 2002; Vogelgesang et al., 2013). The disclosure zones in Section 5.1.2 make that calibration concrete.

BOX 5.2 PSYCHOLOGY SIDELINES WITH DR. MCB — THE DOUBLE BIND ISN'T HYPOTHETICAL

The vulnerability–authority paradox is gendered. Women in leadership face credibility challenges that make vulnerability disclosure higher risk (Brescoll, 2016). In sport specifically, female coaches operating in male-dominated environments navigate a double bind: authority is questioned by default, making strategic vulnerability a move with structurally different costs.

Consider the same disclosure—"I'm not seeing this clearly yet. What are you seeing?"—delivered by two leaders. The first is a male head coach whose authority the room has never questioned. For him, this is open-zone disclosure: it signals confidence, invites input, and builds psychological safety. The second is a female head coach in her first season leading a men's program. For her, the identical words carry a different cost. The room may read uncertainty as confirmation of a pre-existing doubt about her competence—not because the athletes are hostile, but because implicit credibility assumptions operate before anyone consciously evaluates the statement.

In practice, female leaders in male-dominated sport environments may need to lean more heavily on problem-focused disclosure—sharing uncertainty about the tactical situation rather than emotional disclosure—because the latter carries higher credibility risk when authority is already under scrutiny. A third scenario sharpens the point: the same female coach says, "I made a call last week that cost us. Here's what I learned." In an environment where her authority is assumed, this is filtered disclosure that models accountability. In an environment where her authority is contested, it may be heard as evidence for the case against her.

The disclosure zone framework applies across gender. The cost–benefit calculus of each zone does not. Organizations that claim to value vulnerability without addressing the structural conditions that make vulnerability differentially costly are exporting the problem onto the leaders who can least afford it.

FIGURE 5.2 Leader Security and Insecurity Pathways Under Pressure.

Two cascading pathways are triggered by the leader response under pressure. The security pathway proceeds from openness through psychological safety, voice, and shared ownership to organizational resilience. The insecurity pathway proceeds from threat perception through control, blame, and error hiding to organizational fragility.

How the paradox resolves determines the system's trajectory. Figure 5.2 maps the two cascading pathways.

When a leader under pressure resolves toward security—holding openness alongside authority—the adaptive cascade follows: psychological safety, curiosity, voice, information flow, repair after error, shared ownership, and learning under pressure. The nature of that safety varies by context—Section 5.4 distinguishes psychological safety in learning environments from performance safety in accountability environments—but the cascade's logic holds: leader security enables the conditions under which truth flows. The endpoint is organizational resilience.

When the resolution tilts toward insecurity, the protective cascade takes over: threat perception, control, blame, silence, risk avoidance, defensive routines, and error hiding. This pathway aligns with established models of destructive leadership (Padilla et al., 2007), fostering vulnerable followers, a conducive environment of silence, and a leader prioritizing self-preservation over team function. The endpoint is fragility—the pathway Connor's story in the opening vignette illustrates.

The protocols in this chapter are designed to keep leaders on the security side of that diagram.

BOX 5.3 TIMEOUT — THE FORK HAPPENS BEFORE THE ROOM KNOWS IT

The security–insecurity split is not a deliberate choice. It is a nervous system response that sets the cascade before the leader is consciously aware of it. By the time a leader notices they have closed down, the room has already adjusted. Connor's staff stopped challenging three weeks before he noticed the silence.

The intervention point is not the moment of the bad decision–it is the regulation that prevents the fork from tilting toward insecurity in the first place. That is why every protocol in this chapter targets regulation upstream of behavior.

5.1.2 Calibrating Disclosure: Open, Filtered, and Restricted Zones

Status: Practitioner heuristic. Derived from transparent leadership research (Vogelgesang et al., 2013), behavioral integrity theory (Simons, 2002), and clinical observation of leader disclosure in elite sport. Not a validated instrument.

Not all disclosure is strategic. Some is reckless. The strategic vulnerability introduced above—disclosure that serves the team's learning while preserving decision authority—maps onto three zones (see Table 5.1).

TABLE 5.1 Disclosure Zone Classification

Zone	*What to Disclose*	*Audience*	*Function*	*Risk If Misused*
Open disclosure	Uncertainty about the problem. Tactical gaps. Strategic options. Process errors.	Share widely—full team, staff meetings	Invites voice. Protects decision quality.	Minimal. Under-disclosing in this zone suppresses information flow.
Filtered disclosure	Emotional honesty that models regulation. Regulated discomfort.	Share selectively—with intention and timing	Models that discomfort does not require panic. Teaches emotional regulation.	Sharing before regulation is complete converts filtered to restricted.
Restricted disclosure	Personal doubt about competence. Job security anxiety. Unprocessed distress.	Supervision only—clinical supervisor, peer consultant, therapist	Protects the leader's processing space and the team's stability.	Delivered to the wrong audience destroys trust faster than any tactical mistake.

The error that most leaders make is treating all vulnerability as equally valuable. It is not. Open disclosure builds psychological safety. Filtered disclosure models emotional regulation. Restricted disclosure, delivered to the wrong audience, destroys trust.

Applying the zones in real time requires three questions before speaking:

Does this disclosure serve the team's learning or the leader's need to be seen as authentic? If it serves the leader's need, do not share it with the team.

Is the uncertainty about the problem or about the self? Uncertainty about the problem is open disclosure—share widely. Uncertainty about the self moves to the third question.

Has the emotion already been regulated, or is it being processed in real time? Already regulated is filtered disclosure—share selectively, with intention. Still processing is restricted disclosure—supervision only, never the team.

5.1.3 When Vulnerability Becomes Manipulation

Vulnerability that serves the leader's image rather than the team's function is manipulation. Athletes sense the difference immediately.

Signs that disclosure has crossed from strategic to manipulative:

Emotional dumping: "I don't know if I am cut out for this."

Competence signaling disguised as honesty: "I considered seventeen variables you would not understand."

Sharing doubt to deflect accountability: "I was not sure about that call, but . . ."

Oversharing to create intimacy that bypasses earned trust.

Using emotional disclosure as a shield against feedback: "I am being vulnerable here" as defense rather than invitation.

When vulnerability becomes a pattern of emotional manipulation, it extends into the territory of emotional abuse in coaching relationships. While foundational research on emotional abuse primarily focuses on overt behaviors like belittling or threatening (Stirling & Kerr, 2013), the weaponization of a leader's vulnerability functions as a more covert extension of this spectrum, carrying similar documented downstream effects on athlete well-being and trust.

The diagnostic is simple: does the disclosure make it easier or harder for the athlete to tell the truth next time? If easier, it was strategic. If harder, it was performance.

BOX 5.4 PSYCHOLOGY SIDELINES WITH DR. MCB — WHEN AUTHENTICITY BECOMES DISRUPTIVE

Sometimes leaders undermine psychological safety by over-disclosing unprocessed personal distress in the name of "being real." When disclosure shifts the emotional load onto athletes or staff, it reverses the duty of care: the room becomes responsible for managing the leader's state.

The fix is not "never be human." It is calibrated disclosure: share uncertainty about the *problem* to invite input, and process uncertainty about *self* in supervision/peer support—not in the team room.

This is usually what happens: the coach shares something deeply personal—childhood trauma, marriage struggles, and competence anxiety—and frames it as modeling vulnerability. The room goes quiet. Not because they are moved. Because they have just been handed responsibility for their leader's emotional regulation.

Athletes are not your therapists. Staff are not your support group. Authenticity is not the goal. The goal is to build an environment where people can do hard things together. If your disclosure makes that harder, it was not vulnerability. It was a boundary violation.

The test: After you share, does the room feel safer to speak or more careful around you? If they are walking on eggshells, you disclosed in the wrong zone. Vulnerability serves the team's function, or it serves your image. There is no third option.

BOX 5.5 TIMEOUT — THE ROOM READS YOU BEFORE YOU SPEAK

Emotional contagion does not wait for words. Athletes read the leader's physiology—posture, breathing rate, and facial tension—before the first tactical instruction. A dysregulated leader walking into a room is a threat cue.

The room downregulates to survival mode before anything is said. Regulation is not preparation for leadership. Regulation is leadership. The six seconds it takes to run three breaths is not lost time. It is the difference between a room that executes and a room that braces.

The contagion dynamic Box 5.5 describes—the room reading the leader's nervous system before a word is spoken—is why disclosure calibration alone is insufficient. Knowing what to share is one competency. Regulating the physiology that the room reads before the sharing even begins is another. The next section installs the regulation architecture.

5.2 Emotion Regulation for Leaders

Principle: Leaders do not suppress emotion. They regulate it early enough that decisions stay clean.

Emotion is not the problem. Dysregulated emotion in making decisions is the problem. Coaches' emotional intelligence—the capacity to perceive, use, understand, and regulate emotion (Mayer & Salovey, 1997)—has consequences that show up on the field. Coaches' regulation skills shape athlete outcomes and team climate (Tamminen et al., 2024), and their EI predicts behavioral reactivity under match pressure, with coach efficacy beliefs mediating the relationship (Teques et al., 2019). Leaders who recognize and regulate their emotions make better decisions under pressure. When leaders fail to regulate, they export their dysregulation onto the room, and athletes spend cognitive resources managing the leader's mood instead of executing.

5.2.1 Regulation in Real Time: The Stoplight Check

Status: Practitioner heuristic. Component of the Game-Day Regulation Protocol (Section 5.3). Synthesized from emotion regulation research (Gross, 2015) and aviation crew resource management (Helmreich et al., 1999). Not a validated instrument.

Game-day regulation requires a system that runs while the game is happening. The stoplight check is a rapid, real-time self-assessment.

Green (regulated): Multiple variables held in mind. Decisions feel grounded. Voice is steady. Athletes look over and settle. Intervention: No intervention needed. Proceed.

Yellow (dysregulating): Attention narrows. Irritability spikes. Solving for the wrong problem or solving too fast. This is where the most costly game-day decisions get made. Intervention: Name the state internally. Three full breaths. One clarifying question before deciding. No need to announce—just do it.

Red (dysregulated): Tunnel vision. Reactivity. Decisions are not being made—the nervous system is defending itself. Intervention: Call a process time-out if possible. If not, defer the decision to someone briefed before the game to provide accountability at red.

Aviation uses checklists because pilots' judgment degrades under pressure (Helmreich et al., 1999), and the same logic drove their adoption in surgery, where a structured safety checklist reduced complications and mortality across diverse hospital settings (Haynes et al., 2009). The same design problem applies to coaching. The full game-day regulation protocol (Section 5.3) integrates the stoplight check with pre-event routines and a post-event emotional hygiene reset.

5.2.2 Contagion: The Leader's Mood Is the Room's Weather

Emotional contagion is the primary mechanism through which leader dysregulation becomes team climate. Emotional states transfer through observation and mimicry, with negative contagion increasing conflict and degrading cooperation (Barsade, 2002; Hatfield et al., 1994). Power differentials amplify the effect: followers attend more closely to the leader's emotional signals (Sy et al., 2005; Tamminen et al., 2024). Regulate before entering the space, or the space regulates on its own—and groups rarely regulate upward (Barsade, 2002; Sy et al., 2005). The leader's job is not to absorb every upstream anxiety and pass it downstream. The job is to filter it, regulate it, and deliver only the signal the room needs.

5.2.3 Long-Game Regulation: Leader Sustainability

Short-term regulation gets through the game. Long-term regulation keeps leaders in the job. Coach burnout is real and measurable. Chronic stress, emotional exhaustion, and depersonalization are the predictable outcomes of sustained high-pressure environments without recovery systems (Olusoga & Bentzen, 2019). The specific emotion regulation strategies that coaches deploy matter—adaptive strategies buffer well-being, while maladaptive strategies accelerate the damage (Santi et al., 2021).

The pattern is consistent: leaders enter with high commitment, absorb every stressor as personal responsibility, sacrifice sleep and relationships for marginal performance gains, and dysregulate slowly enough that no one notices until the breakdown is public. The solution is not resilience training. It is structural: protected recovery windows, peer consultation, and supervision as organizational policy, not personal discipline. Organizations that demand sustained high performance from leaders without protecting recovery are engineering the burnout they later diagnose as individual failure (Olusoga & Bentzen, 2019).

Six markers function as a leader sustainability self-check, mapped across functional, drifting, and compromised zones. The drifting zone is the intervention point, where most leaders are deteriorating before anyone notices.

These are rough markers, not diagnostic cut-offs, but they serve as the early-warning system that structural recovery requires. The corrective action they flag often requires organizational response. When dysregulation compromises the capacity to lead well, the most responsible move is stepping back to regulate. The room does not need heroism. It needs steadiness.

5.3 Game-Day Regulation Protocol

Status: Practitioner-derived. Synthesized from emotion regulation research (Gross, 2015), aviation crew resource management (Helmreich et al., 1999), and surgical safety checklist design (Haynes et al., 2009). Not a validated instrument.

This protocol integrates the stoplight check as its real-time assessment mechanism and adds pre-event routines and a post-event emotional hygiene reset into a single sequence for use before, during, and after high-pressure events.

TABLE 5.2 Leader Sustainability Self-Check

Marker	*Functional*	*Drifting*	*Compromised*
Sleep	Consistent and restorative	Disrupted; racing thoughts at bedtime	Chronic insomnia or using substances to sleep
Irritability	Proportional to triggers	Snapping at low-stakes interactions	Baseline hostility; people avoid you
Rumination	Reviews and then moves on	Replaying decisions; difficulty disengaging	Intrusive loops dominating off-hours
Connection	Engaged with family, friends, and interests	Withdrawing; relationships feel effortful	Isolated; work is the only identity
Recovery capacity	Bounces back after hard weeks	Recovery takes longer; weekends feel insufficient	No recovery between cycles; running on fumes
Coping drift	Healthy habits maintained	Relying on caffeine, alcohol, or screen numbing	Coping mechanisms are the problem; denial of decline

TABLE 5.3 Game-Day Regulation Protocol

Phase	*Timing*	*Actions*
Pre-event	2 hours before	Run the pre-game routine. Same every time. Routine frees cognitive resources for novel problems (Klein, 1998).
Pre-event	30 minutes before	Run the stoplight check. Green/Yellow/Red? If yellow, regulate now. If red, delegate or postpone.
Pre-event	10 minutes before	Three-breath reset. Name the intention: "I am here to protect truth and execute the plan."
During event	Every stoppage (timeout, quarter break, and halftime)	Three-second internal check. Green/Yellow/Red? At yellow: ask one clarifying question before the next decision. At red: take a process timeout if possible; if not, execute the pre-briefed backup plan. No new decisions from red.
Post-event	Immediately after	Run the emotional hygiene reset (5 minutes): name the emotion without judgment. Locate it in the body. Three full breaths—controlled breathing activates the parasympathetic nervous system (Gross, 2015). Ask: "Is this emotion information or dysregulation?" If dysregulation, wait 30 minutes before deciding.
Post-event	30 minutes after	No decisions. No media comments, roster discussions, or strategic pivots. Dysregulation makes bad decisions feel urgent.
Post-event	Before leaving	One question: "What decision am I about to make that I will regret tomorrow?" If the answer is not "none," it can wait.

Emotional hygiene is performance hygiene—the same operational logic surgeons use between procedures.

BOX 5.6 SKEPTIC'S CORNER — "I DON'T HAVE TIME FOR BREATHING EXERCISES DURING A GAME"

The objection: This emotional regulation stuff is fine for therapy, but in a game, calls need to happen in seconds. There is no time to check the nervous system.

The answer: The nervous system is already being checked. The question is whether it is being checked consciously or whether it is making decisions on its own. Every high-pressure decision runs through the autonomic nervous system first. When dysregulated, the threat response narrows options before they are consciously evaluated. What feels like a tactical decision is often a survival reflex.

The three-breath reset takes six seconds. It is not adding time. It is recovering the prefrontal capacity needed to see all the options instead of the two that the amygdala flagged as safe.

What to try anyway: This week, pick one moment where a fast decision under pressure is typical—a substitution, a tactical adjustment, a media comment. Before deciding, take three full breaths and ask one clarifying question. Track whether the decision quality changes.

5.4 High-Stakes Conversations

Sections 5.1–5.3 installed the internal architecture—what leaders disclose, how they regulate, and the protocols that keep both calibrated under pressure. That architecture exists to serve what comes next: the conversations where trust is built or destroyed. Regulation is the prerequisite. Without it, even well-structured conversations degrade under the leader's unmanaged nervous system. With it, leaders can hold the process that follows.

Principle: The hardest conversations require the clearest process. The Performance Safety Zone framework separates learning from selection from evaluation.

Selection and deselection. Conflict. Performance feedback. These are the conversations where trust gets built or destroyed, and most leaders handle them badly—not because they lack skill, but because they lack structure. A common pattern in high-stakes sport environments: leaders avoid difficult conversations until avoidance costs more than honesty. By then, the conversation is contaminated by months of unexpressed tension. The intervention: structured honesty, delivered early, with procedural clarity.

5.4.1 Performance Safety Zones: Learning, Selection, and Accountability

Status: Theoretically grounded. Adapts the performance safety framework (Taylor et al., 2026) and Edmondson's (1999) learning—execution distinction. Zone-naming protocol is author-operationalized. Not a validated instrument.

Not every environment needs the same kind of safety. Performance safety (Taylor et al., 2026) distinguishes safety to learn from safety to execute under evaluation—complementing broader models linking psychologically safe sport environments to athlete mental health (Walton et al., 2024) and building on Edmondson's (1999) learning–execution distinction.

In a learning zone, errors are data. Feedback is descriptive. The goal is improvement. Psychological safety is high because mistakes do not carry immediate consequences.

In an accountability zone, performance is evaluated. Standards are enforced. Consequences follow. Performance safety exists—honesty about the task is protected, but standards are not negotiable—and the frame is distinct from the learning zone's psychological safety.

A third zone—selection—sits between learning and accountability, where performance is evaluated against known criteria but the conversation remains forward-facing. Elite sport operates across all three zones simultaneously. The training session is a learning zone until it becomes a selection session. The game is an accountability zone, but the film review afterward is a learning zone—unless someone makes it punitive. And that happens more often than most organizations want to admit.

The leader's job is to name which zone is active before the conversation starts. The room needs to know whether this is "help me get better" or "here is where you stand." Pause on what the athlete is doing in each zone. In the learning zone, the athlete is voluntarily exposing weakness—showing where skills break down, experimenting with moves that might fail, and reporting errors instead of hiding them. In the accountability zone, the athlete is submitting to evaluation by people who control playing time, contract status, and career trajectory. Neither of these is passive. Both require trust that the system will not weaponize honesty or punish vulnerability. Zone-naming is a leader tool, but the athlete's willingness to be honest inside each zone is structural courage the organization should recognize—not cheerleading, but reinforcement that the system rewards the behavior it claims to value.

Conflate the two, and the result is athletes who hide errors in training (because they learned that training is really evaluation) and freeze in games (because they learned that games are learning zones where failure is okay—which it is not).

Each zone carries a different mistake meaning, a different leader feedback rhythm, and a different consequence logic. When leaders fail to declare which zone is active, athletes default to the highest-threat interpretation.

BOX 5.7 TIMEOUT — NAME THE ZONE OR THE ROOM WILL GUESS

When leaders fail to declare whether a conversation is learning or accountability, athletes default to the higher-threat assumption. Every ambiguous film review becomes a selection meeting. Every unclear check-in becomes a performance review.

The cost is not just anxiety—it is information loss. Athletes stop experimenting in training, stop reporting errors, and start managing impressions instead of developing skills. Five words fix this: "This is a learning zone." Say them first. Say them every time.

5.4.2 Selection and Deselection Scripts

Selection conversations occupy the middle zone—where performance is evaluated against known criteria, but the orientation is still forward-facing. Athletes experience them as accountability because consequences follow, but the leader's stance is developmental: the conversation exists to clarify the gap and the path back. Deselection conversations are pure accountability: the standard is not being met. Here is what happens next.

Self-Determination Theory (Deci & Ryan, 2000) explains why these scripts require procedural care: deselection threatens competence (ability judged insufficient) and relatedness (belonging severed). The psychological stakes are existential. Because the stakes are that high, both selection and deselection require strict procedural justice: consistency, transparency, voice, and respect (Colquitt et al., 2001; Slade et al., 2024). Sport-specific research confirms that athletes' perceptions of selection fairness are driven more by procedural clarity—transparency, consistency, and voice—than by the outcome itself (Slade et al., 2024).

Before any high-stakes conversation, five questions set the architecture.

With that architecture in place, the conversation follows zone-specific scripts. Table 5.5 presents both scripts side by side for quick reference.

TABLE 5.4 High-Stakes Conversation Pre-Flight Checklist

#	*Question*	*Decision Rule*
1	What zone is this—learning or accountability?	Name it explicitly at the start.
2	What is non-negotiable?	Write down the one thing that cannot change by the end of this conversation.
3	What does procedural justice require?	Consistency: would the same call be made for a different athlete? Transparency: can the rationale be explained clearly? Voice: will the athlete have a chance to be heard? Respect: is their dignity protected?
4	What happens if they get emotional?	Pre-decide. Do not improvise. The job is to stay regulated and hold the process.
5	What happens after this conversation?	Write down the next step so the athlete leaves with clarity, not ambiguity.

TABLE 5.5 Selection and Deselection Conversation Scripts

Step	*Selection Script (Learning Zone)*	*Deselection Script (Accountability Zone)*
1. Open	Name the standard: "Here is what earns starting minutes."	Name the decision: "You are not in the starting lineup this week."
2. Locate	Describe current performance against the standard: "Here is where you are now."	Name the reason: "Here is the standard. Here is where the gap showed up."
3. Bridge	Identify the gap: "Here is what closes the distance."	Clarify the path back (if one exists): "Here is what changes the decision."
4. Invite	Invite input: "What is your read on this? What support do you need?"	Separate the decision from the person: "This is about performance right now, not your value to this team."
5. Close	Set the timeline: "We review progress in two weeks."	Listen without relitigating: "Tell me what you need from me to move forward."

The deselection script is not negotiation. The decision is made. The conversation is about dignity and clarity.

What tends to go wrong:

- Softening the message so much that the athlete misses the decision. "You are not starting this week, but you are so valuable" sounds like "Maybe you will start if you ask again."
- Inviting debate about the decision. The athlete's perspective matters. Reopening the call mid-conversation does not.
- Delivering personal bad news in public. Feedback that targets the person—their character, their effort, and their value—is humiliation dressed as coaching. Public accountability for behaviors the group has collectively agreed to is a different mechanism, and one some teams use effectively. The distinction: "We agreed to communicate switches, and we didn't" is public accountability. "You let us down" is public shaming.

5.4.3 Feedback That Changes Behavior

Feedback only works if it lands in the learning zone. Punitive feedback teaches silence; vague feedback teaches confusion; public feedback teaches impression management.

The formula is simple: "When you [specific behavior], here is what happened [observable consequence]. Next time, here is what I need [actionable adjustment]." Example: ineffective: "You need to communicate better." Effective: "When you did not call the switch on that last play, the rotation collapsed. Next time, I need you to signal verbally before you move."

The feedback needs to be:

Specific (behavior, not character).
Timely (within 24 hours while the context is still vivid).
Private (one-on-one unless the whole team made the same error).
Actionable (clear next step, not a referendum on worth).
Feedback research is consistent: feedback that targets task and process improves performance. Feedback that targets the person damages it (Hattie & Timperley, 2007).

BOX 5.8 TIMEOUT — FEEDBACK SCRIPTS ARE CULTURALLY SHAPED

What reads as "direct and honest" in a low-context culture can read as humiliating in a high-context culture (Hall, 1976; Hofstede, 1980; Schinke et al., 2016). The standard holds; the delivery adapts. Consider the same feedback—"You did not call the switch on that last play, and the rotation collapsed"—delivered in two cultural contexts. In a low-context environment, delivering this directly and immediately after the session is expected and received as professional. In a high-context environment, the same message may land better delivered privately, framed relationally ("I want to help you get this right"), and with the correction embedded in a forward-looking conversation rather than an isolated critique. The expectation ("You must call switches") stays firm. The delivery adapts. Meyer's (2014) culture map offers a practitioner-accessible framework for navigating these dimensions; Section 6.3.2 in Chapter 6 provides the full operational framework for culturally adaptive feedback systems.

5.4.4 Conflict Conversations

Status: Practitioner heuristic. Synthesizes structural conflict resolution principles and organizational voice research (Morrison & Milliken, 2000). Not a validated instrument.

Selection and feedback conversations are vertical—leader to athlete, and authority to report. Conflict conversations are often lateral: coach to coach, athlete to athlete, and department to department. The power dynamics differ, and so does the architecture.

Most conflict in high-performance environments is structural: competing priorities that the organization has not reconciled. The head coach wants more training load; the medical staff wants recovery. Two athletes want the same role.

These are design conflicts, not personality clashes, and treating them as interpersonal problems misdiagnoses the issue.

This translates into a four-step protocol:

Name the structural tension: Identify the conflict as a system design problem, not a personality clash. "This is a resource conflict, not a relationship problem. You both want something the system cannot give simultaneously."

Separate the decision from the relationship: Make the call. Explain the rationale. Make clear that disagreement with the decision does not damage standing. "I have decided X because [rationale]. You can disagree with this and still be in good standing."

Close the loop: After the decision, check whether the losing side can still operate with full commitment. If not, address it directly. "Can you execute this fully? If something is still unresolved, say it now—not in the corridor later."

Follow up: Within 48 hours, check in privately with the party whose position was not adopted. "How is this landing? Is there anything the decision missed that I need to know?"

What goes wrong: Leaders avoid the conversation until it metastasizes, or treat every disagreement as requiring consensus. Conflict needs a decision, a rationale, and a check-in. Not a workshop.

Conflict conversations also operate vertically—upward. Losing streaks and organizational pressure produce bad ideas from boards and owners that the leader must resist, what the voice literature calls upward voice (Detert & Edmondson, 2011). The architecture is the same as lateral conflict: frame the alternative ("Here is what I am doing instead and why it addresses the actual problem"), name the cost of the proposed action ("If we do X, here is what we lose"), and offer a decision timeline ("I will review this in seven days. If the situation has not changed, we revisit"). Upward courage is not defiance. It is protecting the organization from panic dressed as strategy.

5.5 Leading Through Losing Streaks

Principle: Losing streaks are decision-making disasters waiting to happen. The work is protecting relationships and preventing panic-driven decisions.

Three straight losses and the narrative forms. Five losses and the pressure becomes existential. Seven losses and even rational leaders start making calls they'll regret. Losing streaks compress every leadership challenge into one week: emotional dysregulation, public scrutiny, upstream panic, roster doubt, and media narrative. Without a protocol before the streak starts, improvisation happens under the worst conditions.

Losing streak leadership operates across three phases—preparation, navigation, and recovery—distinguishing what should stay constant (identity, relationships, and process standards) from what can change (tactical adjustments, role assignments, and communication frequency). The protocol that follows operationalizes the navigation phase day by day.

5.5.1 What Losing Does to Decision-Making

Sustained losses do three things:

Time horizons collapse. Thinking shifts from seasons to games. Then quarters. Then plays. Cognitive tunneling narrows the decision window until the problem being solved is "stop the bleeding" instead of "what does this team actually need?"

Reactive decisions feel urgent. The threat system flags every decision as high-stakes. Roster changes, strategy pivots, public criticism—they all feel like the intervention that will turn the season. Most are noise. This is the threat-rigidity effect: under perceived threat, groups restrict information processing and constrict control, narrowing to familiar responses (Staw et al., 1981; Weick, 1993).

Relationships fracture. Athletes stop trusting the process. Staff stop trusting each other. Owners stop trusting the leader. The coordination infrastructure built during wins disappears—precisely when it is most needed.

Research on losing streaks in elite sport is sparse but consistent: coaches report decision-making degradation and the pull toward short-term fixes that create long-term damage (Gibson & O'Connor, 2023). The protocols that follow extrapolate from this evidence base, supplemented by threat-rigidity theory (Staw et al., 1981) and organizational silence research (Morrison & Milliken, 2000), and should be treated as practitioner-derived protocols, not independently validated instruments.

5.5.2 Managing the First 72 Hours

Status: Practitioner heuristic. Derived from threat-rigidity theory (Staw et al., 1981), implementation intentions research (Gollwitzer, 1999), and organizational silence literature (Morrison & Milliken, 2000). Not a validated instrument.

The core principle: no major decisions within 72 hours of a loss.

The specific timeframe is a practitioner guideline, not an empirically validated threshold, but the underlying principle—that decisions made under acute stress disproportionately reflect threat-response narrowing (Staw et al., 1981)—is well established. Major decisions include roster moves, strategy overhauls, public criticism of players, and firing or reassigning staff.

The exception: decisions that were already planned and documented before the loss. If the pre-decision was "If X happens, we do Y," execution is clean. This operationalizes what cognitive psychologists refer to as implementation intentions (Gollwitzer, 1999)—pre-committing to a specific course of action when a predefined trigger occurs, thereby bypassing the compromised decision-making of the acute threat response.

If the decision is being made in the 72-hour window because the loss made it feel urgent, it can wait. The 72-hour rule does not mean ignoring problems. It means naming the problem, documenting it, and reviewing it when regulation has returned—when solutions are visible instead of just the scoreboard. The following protocol translates that principle into a daily sequence.

BOX 5.9 TIMEOUT — THE 72-HOUR SEQUENCE

72-Hour Post-Loss Protocol: Daily Sequence

Day 1: Loss Day

Immediately after the game, initiate the emotional hygiene reset. This process should take no more than five minutes and must not be skipped under any circumstances. On this day, refrain from making any decisions—no matter how minor they may seem. To ensure accountability, communicate to a trusted individual: "Hold me to the 72-hour rule."

Day 2: 24 Hours Post-Loss

Conduct a team film review, clearly framing the session as a learning opportunity rather than a punitive measure. The primary focus should be on identifying what broke down, determining necessary adjustments, and recognizing what strategies remain effective. In addition, hold private check-ins with team captains and staff, asking: "What is the room feeling that I am not seeing?" As decisions or solutions begin to feel tempting, write them down for future consideration, but do not act on them yet—documentation only at this stage.

Day 3: 48 Hours Post-Loss

Review the list of decisions documented the previous day. Critically assess each idea by asking: "Is this addressing the actual problem, or is it simply a reaction to emotional dysregulation?" Consult with a peer or supervisor, sharing your thought process: "Here is what I am thinking. What am I missing?" This collaborative check helps safeguard against impulsive or narrow decision-making.

Day 4: 72 Hours Post-Loss

After three days have passed, reassess each documented decision. If, upon review, the decision still appears sound and necessary, it is now appropriate to take action. The passage of time increases the likelihood that the decision is thoughtful and clear, rather than reactive.

Ongoing: If the Streak Continues

Hold a weekly debrief with staff to evaluate decision quality, asking: "Are we reacting or are we diagnosing?" During these meetings, revisit identity cues as outlined in Section 5.6.1 to reinforce team cohesion and clarity. It is important to remember that losing streaks can erode a sense of collective identity. Deliberate efforts must be made to rebuild and strengthen the team's unity and shared purpose.

When losses compound—a second loss arriving before the first 72-hour window closes—the protocol does not reset. Decisions documented during the first cycle that still appear sound after the second loss are likely clean. Decisions born from accumulated panic enter their own 72-hour hold.

5.5.3 Protecting Voice During Adversity

Losing streaks silence the room—the insecurity pathway from Figure 5.2 in real time. Athletes learn that honesty gets punished when results are bad; staff learn that dissent gets interpreted as disloyalty (Morrison & Milliken, 2000; Van Puyenbroeck et al., 2019). The intervention maps directly onto the disclosure zones and security pathway established in Section 5.1: name the silence explicitly ("I need to hear what is breaking"), reward the first person who speaks with visible action, and separate learning contexts from accountability contexts. Three operational signals mark whether voice is functioning or degrading: unsolicited problem reports (healthy: staff raise issues without being asked; degrading: problems surface only through formal channels), Speed of Truth (healthy: hours between problem identification and leader awareness; degrading: leaders learn from external sources), and contradiction frequency (healthy: someone disagrees with the leader's framing at least once per week; degrading: meetings produce unanimous agreement on the first pass). These are operational rules of thumb derived from organizational silence research (Morrison & Milliken, 2000) and voice behavior literature (Detert & Edmondson, 2011; Van Puyenbroeck et al., 2019), not validated metrics—but they give the leader a concrete way to assess whether the system is producing voice or performing consensus.

The losing streak literature is almost entirely coach-facing. It asks how leaders survive adversity. It rarely asks what athletes are owed during it. Athletes enduring a losing streak absorb organizational failure, while their market value, mental health, and public reputation take damage they did not design. They need information (the actual diagnosis, not spin), agency (what they can control), and consistency (leader behavior that does not change with the scoreboard). When athletes report that a coach "lost the room," they typically describe the moment the leader's behavior became outcome-dependent—steady during wins, volatile during losses (Gibson & O'Connor, 2023). Consistency under adversity is the behavioral test of everything this chapter describes.

5.6 Identity Leadership and Meaning-Making

Principle: People endure hardship for a team they belong to. Build identity before it is needed.

5.6.1 Building and Sustaining "Us"

Identity leadership creates a shared sense of "us" that makes sacrifice meaningful and standards collective (Haslam et al., 2020). Four mechanisms drive it: being one of us (the leader is perceived as a group member, not above it), doing it for us (actions advance group interests), crafting a sense of us (actively shaping what the group stands for), and making us matter (elevating the group's significance). These four dimensions were operationalized and validated through the Identity Leadership Inventory (ILI; Steffens et al., 2014). Identity leadership predicts higher team identification, collective efficacy, and perceived leadership effectiveness (Fransen et al., 2014; Slater & Barker, 2019; Hoult et al., 2024). Identity leadership is complicated when the leader and team do not share demographic backgrounds—the "us" must be deliberately constructed, not assumed. Chapter 6 provides the full operational framework for building and sustaining identity leadership as cultural infrastructure.

BOX 5.10 PSYCHOLOGY SIDELINES WITH DR. MCB — THE USE OF THE WORD FAMILY

"We are a family" is identity leadership when it means "We protect each other, we tell the truth, and we hold the standard together." It becomes manipulation when it means "Do not challenge me, do not leave, and do not prioritize your actual family over this team."

Athletes have heard "family" used to guilt them into playing injured, silence dissent, and justify exploitation. The word is not the problem. The behavior underneath it is.

If you use "family" language, audit it: does it increase voice or suppress it? Does it protect boundaries or violate them? Family metaphors work when they create belonging. They fail when they create an obligation that bypasses consent.

5.6.2 Meaning-Making During Hardship

Most teams face defeat more often than victory. Leadership that is only effective during winning streaks is fundamentally incomplete. The process of meaning-making transforms setbacks into opportunities for growth by reframing loss as informative data, adversity as a test of identity, and difficulty as a challenge that "people like us" endure together (Morgan et al., 2015).

Three scripts are used to operationalize this approach:

- **Data reframe:** "This loss tells us what we need to work on. We are not broken. We have a gap. We close it."
- **Identity reframe:** "People like us do not quit when it is hard. This is the work."
- **Process reframe:** "We do not control outcomes. We control preparation. We stay on process."

Research on resilience at both team (Morgan et al., 2015) and organizational (Fasey et al., 2021) levels supports this pattern: meaning-making acts as a buffer against demoralization and disengagement.

5.7 Leadership as System, Not Personality

The protocols in this chapter—disclosure zones, regulation sequences, conversation scripts, and losing streak architecture—are individual leader tools. Converting them into institutional capacity requires a structural shift: from leadership as personality to leadership as system. Systems survive turnover. Charisma does not.

That shift has three components. Distributed leadership spreads influence across formal and informal leaders who fill complementary roles—task, motivational, social, and external (Fransen et al., 2020). Leadership development replaces leadership selection: structured observation, scenario-based rehearsal of high-stakes protocols, and regular feedback on leadership behaviors

(Lara-Bercial & Mallett, 2016). And succession planning treats leadership transitions as predictable events requiring transferable documentation—the same logic as the 72-hour rule, applied at an institutional scale.

Chapter 6 operationalizes this shift in full, treating distributed leadership as structural redundancy for culture and providing the frameworks for culture continuity documents, transition management, and leadership development pipelines. The question this chapter leaves the practitioner with is direct: is the current leadership approach a system that survives the leader, or a single-point-of-failure dependency?

5.7.1 Chapter Synthesis

Leadership under pressure fails not because leaders lack character but because organizations lack systems. That is the structural argument running through every section of this chapter. The vulnerability–authority paradox, emotional contagion, high-stakes conversation breakdowns, and losing streak decision degradation—they all come back to the same root: improvisation where repeatable protocol should operate.

Three core instruments anchor the chapter's architecture: the game-day regulation protocol, performance safety zones, and the disclosure zone classification—the first targeting emotional regulation, the second structuring conversation contexts, and the third calibrating what leaders share, with whom, and when. These anchor a broader architecture that includes selection scripts and losing streak management, reframing leader development as system design. The shift for practitioners is direct: stop selecting for leadership personality and start installing behavioral infrastructure that holds under load, transfers across transitions, and converts individual competence into institutional capacity. Chapter 6 operationalizes that shift at the organizational level.

Key Chapter Takeaways

1. Strategic vulnerability is calibrated, not spontaneous. Run the three-question filter before every high-stakes disclosure—does it serve the team's learning, is the uncertainty about the problem or the self, and has the emotion already been regulated?
2. Open disclosures build psychological safety; restricted disclosures destabilize it.
3. Regulate before entering the room. Emotional contagion transmits the leader's state to the group before a word is spoken. The game-day regulation protocol—pre-event baseline, real-time stoplight checks, and post-event emotional hygiene reset—is performance infrastructure, not therapy.
4. Name the zone before the conversation starts. When leaders fail to declare whether an interaction is learning, selection, or accountability, athletes

default to the highest-threat interpretation and withhold the information the leader most needs.

5. Impose the 72-hour rule after losses. Decisions made under acute threat responses disproportionately reflect dysregulation, not strategy. Document the impulse, defer the action, and decide only after deliberative processing returns.
6. Build leadership systems that survive the leader. Distributed roles, structured development pipelines, and succession documentation convert individual skill into institutional capacity—because charisma does not transfer and protocols do. Chapter 6 provides the full operational framework.

Discussion Questions

1. Apply the disclosure zone framework to a leader interaction you have witnessed. Would reclassifying the disclosure from one zone to another have changed the room's willingness to speak?
2. Design a realistic implementation plan for introducing the game-day regulation protocol to a coaching staff that views emotional regulation as incompatible with competitive intensity.
3. The 72-hour decision moratorium assumes delay is possible. Identify a specific organizational scenario where legitimate urgency conflicts with this rule and justify how you would resolve the tension without abandoning the protocol's logic.
4. Evaluate your organization's leadership structure against the distributed leadership model: is it a system or a single-point-of-failure dependency, and what is the first structural change required?

References

Arthur, C. A., Wagstaff, C. R. D., & Hardy, L. (2016). Leadership in sport organizations. In C. R. D. Wagstaff (Ed.), *The organizational psychology of sport: Key issues and practical applications* (pp. 153–175). Routledge. https://doi.org/10.4324/9781315666532-19

Barsade, S. G. (2002). The ripple effect: Emotional contagion and its influence on group behavior. *Administrative Science Quarterly, 47*(4), 644–675. https://doi.org/10.2307/3094912

Bass, B. M. (1985). *Leadership and performance beyond expectations*. Free Press.

Baumeister, R. F., Bratslavsky, E., Finkenauer, C., & Vohs, K. D. (2001). Bad is stronger than good. *Review of General Psychology, 5*(4), 323–370. https://doi.org/10.1037/1089-2680.5.4.323

Brescoll, V. L. (2016). Leading with their hearts? How gender stereotypes of emotion lead to biased evaluations of female leaders. *The Leadership Quarterly, 27*(3), 415–428. https://doi.org/10.1016/j.leaqua.2016.02.005

Brown, B. (2012). *Daring greatly: How the courage to be vulnerable transforms the way we live, love, parent, and lead*. Gotham Books.

Colquitt, J. A., Conlon, D. E., Wesson, M. J., Porter, C. O. L. H., & Ng, K. Y. (2001). Justice at the millennium: A meta-analytic review of 25 years of organizational

justice research. *Journal of Applied Psychology*, *86*(3), 425–445. https://doi.org/10.1037/0021-9010.86.3.425
Deci, E. L., & Ryan, R. M. (2000). The "what" and "why" of goal pursuits: Human needs and the self-determination of behavior. *Psychological Inquiry*, *11*(4), 227–268. https://doi.org/10.1207/S15327965PLI1104_01
Detert, J. R., & Edmondson, A. C. (2011). Implicit voice theories: Taken-for-granted rules of self-censorship at work. *Academy of Management Journal*, *54*(3), 461–488. https://doi.org/10.5465/amj.2011.61967925
Edmondson, A. C. (1999). Psychological safety and learning behavior in work teams. *Administrative Science Quarterly*, *44*(2), 350–383. https://doi.org/10.2307/2666999
Edmondson, A. C. (2018). *The fearless organization: Creating psychological safety in the workplace for learning, innovation, and growth*. Wiley.
Fasey, K. J., Sarkar, M., Wagstaff, C. R. D., & Johnston, J. (2021). Defining and characterizing organizational resilience in elite sport. *Psychology of Sport and Exercise*, *52*, Article 101834. https://doi.org/10.1016/j.psychsport.2020.101834
Fransen, K., Mertens, N., Cotterill, S. T., Vande Broek, G., & Boen, F. (2020). From autocracy to empowerment: Teams with shared leadership perceive their coaches to be better leaders. *Journal of Applied Sport Psychology*, *32*(1), 5–27. https://doi.org/10.1080/10413200.2019.1617370
Fransen, K., Vanbeselaere, N., De Cuyper, B., Coffee, P., Slater, M. J., & Boen, F. (2014). The impact of athlete leaders on team members' team outcome confidence: A test of mediation by team identification and collective efficacy. *The Sport Psychologist*, *28*(4), 347–360. https://doi.org/10.1123/tsp.2013-0141
Gibson, D., & O'Connor, D. (2023). Leading while losing: Elite coaches' perspectives of losing streaks. *International Sport Coaching Journal*, *10*(1), 42–53. https://doi.org/10.1123/iscj.2021-0054
Gollwitzer, P. M. (1999). Implementation intentions: Strong effects of simple plans. *American Psychologist*, *54*(7), 493–503. https://doi.org/10.1037/0003-066X.54.7.493
Gross, J. J. (2015). Emotion regulation: Current status and future prospects. *Psychological Inquiry*, *26*(1), 1–26. https://doi.org/10.1080/1047840X.2014.940781
Hall, E. T. (1976). *Beyond culture*. Anchor Press/Doubleday.
Haslam, S. A., Reicher, S. D., & Platow, M. J. (2020). *The new psychology of leadership: Identity, influence and power* (2nd ed.). Routledge. https://doi.org/10.4324/9781351108232
Hatfield, E., Cacioppo, J. T., & Rapson, R. L. (1994). *Emotional contagion*. Cambridge University Press.
Hattie, J., & Timperley, H. (2007). The power of feedback. *Review of Educational Research*, *77*(1), 81–112. https://doi.org/10.3102/003465430298487
Haynes, A. B., Weiser, T. G., Berry, W. R., Lipsitz, S. R., Breizat, A.-H. S., Dellinger, E. P., Herbosa, T., Joseph, S., Kibatala, P. L., Lapitan, M. C. M., Merry, A. F., Moorthy, K., Reznick, R. K., Taylor, B., & Gawande, A. A. (2009). A surgical safety checklist to reduce morbidity and mortality in a global population. *The New England Journal of Medicine*, *360*(5), 491–499. https://doi.org/10.1056/NEJMsa0810119
Helmreich, R. L., Merritt, A. C., & Wilhelm, J. A. (1999). The evolution of Crew Resource Management training in commercial aviation. *The International Journal of Aviation Psychology*, *9*(1), 19–32. https://doi.org/10.1207/s15327108ijap0901_2
Hofstede, G. (1980). *Culture's consequences: International differences in work-related values*. Sage.
Hoult, A., Mansell, P., & Slater, M. J. (2024). The influence of a reflective identity leadership intervention on perceived identity leadership, social identity, and psychological safety in cricket. *Behavioral Sciences*, *14*(8), Article 655. https://doi.org/10.3390/bs14080655

Judge, T. A., & Piccolo, R. F. (2004). Transformational and transactional leadership: A meta-analytic test of their relative validity. *Journal of Applied Psychology*, *89*(5), 755–768. https://doi.org/10.1037/0021-9010.89.5.755

Klein, G. A. (1998). *Sources of power: How people make decisions*. MIT Press.

Lara-Bercial, S., & Mallett, C. J. (2016). The practices and developmental pathways of professional and Olympic serial winning coaches. *International Sport Coaching Journal*, *3*(3), 221–239. https://doi.org/10.1123/iscj.2016-0083

Mayer, J. D., & Salovey, P. (1997). What is emotional intelligence? In P. Salovey & D. J. Sluyter (Eds.), *Emotional development and emotional intelligence: Educational implications* (pp. 3–31). Basic Books.

McDougall, M., & Saarinen, M. (2024). Coaching generation Z: Practice from a different perspective and base. *Journal of Applied Sport Psychology*, *36*(3), 429–439. https://doi.org/10.1080/10413200.2024.2329537

Meyer, E. (2014). *The culture map: Breaking through the invisible boundaries of global business*. PublicAffairs.

Morgan, P. B. C., Fletcher, D., & Sarkar, M. (2015). Understanding team resilience in the world's best athletes: A case study of a rugby union World Cup winning team. *Psychology of Sport and Exercise*, *16*, 91–100. https://doi.org/10.1016/j.psychsport.2014.08.007

Morrison, E. W., & Milliken, F. J. (2000). Organizational silence: A barrier to change and development in a pluralistic world. *Academy of Management Review*, *25*(4), 706–725. https://doi.org/10.5465/amr.2000.3707697

Olusoga, P., & Bentzen, M. (2019). Coach burnout: A scoping review. *International Sport Coaching Journal*, *6*(1), 42–62. https://doi.org/10.1123/iscj.2017-0094

Padilla, A., Hogan, R., & Kaiser, R. B. (2007). The toxic triangle: Destructive leaders, susceptible followers, and conducive environments. *The Leadership Quarterly*, *18*(3), 176–194. https://doi.org/10.1016/j.leaqua.2007.03.001

Santi, G., Quartiroli, A., Costa, S., Di Fronso, S., Montesano, C., & Bertollo, M. (2021). The impact of emotion regulation strategies on coaches' well-being. *Journal of Sports Sciences*, *39*(8), 870–879. https://doi.org/10.1080/02640414.2020.1848117

Schinke, R. J., Blodgett, A. T., McGannon, K. R., & Ge, Y. (2016). Finding one's footing on foreign soil: A composite vignette of elite athlete acculturation. *Psychology of Sport and Exercise*, *25*, 36–43. https://doi.org/10.1016/j.psychsport.2016.04.001

Simons, T. (2002). Behavioral integrity: The perceived alignment between managers' words and deeds as a research focus. *Organization Science*, *13*(1), 18–35. https://doi.org/10.1287/orsc.13.1.18.543

Slade, K., Jowett, S., & Rhind, D. (2024). Developing guidelines for selection-deselection in high-performance sport for athletes, coaches, and organisations: A Delphi study. *Journal of Sports Sciences*, *42*(13), 1209–1223. https://doi.org/10.1080/02640414.2024.2387968

Slater, M. J., & Barker, J. B. (2019). Doing social identity leadership: Exploring the efficacy of an identity leadership intervention on perceived leadership and mobilization in elite disability soccer. *Journal of Applied Sport Psychology*, *31*(1), 65–86. https://doi.org/10.1080/10413200.2017.1410255

Staw, B. M., Sandelands, L. E., & Dutton, J. E. (1981). Threat-rigidity effects in organizational behavior: A multilevel analysis. *Administrative Science Quarterly*, *26*(4), 501–524. https://doi.org/10.2307/2392337

Steffens, N. K., Haslam, S. A., Reicher, S. D., Platow, M. J., Fransen, K., Yang, J., Ryan, M. K., Jetten, J., Peters, K., & Boen, F. (2014). Leadership as social identity management: Introducing the Identity Leadership Inventory (ILI) to assess and validate a four-dimensional model. *The Leadership Quarterly*, *25*(5), 1001–1024. https://doi.org/10.1016/j.leaqua.2014.05.002

Stenling, A., & Tafvelin, S. (2014). Transformational leadership and well-being in sports: The mediating role of need satisfaction. *Journal of Applied Sport Psychology*, *26*(2), 182–196. https://doi.org/10.1080/10413200.2013.819392

Stirling, A. E., & Kerr, G. A. (2013). The perceived effects of elite athletes' experiences of emotional abuse in the coach–athlete relationship. *International Journal of Sport and Exercise Psychology*, *11*(1), 87–100. https://doi.org/10.1080/1612197X.2013.752173

Sy, T., Côté, S., & Saavedra, R. (2005). The contagious leader: Impact of the leader's mood on the mood of group members, group affective tone, and group processes. *Journal of Applied Psychology*, *90*(2), 295–305. https://doi.org/10.1037/0021-9010.90.2.295

Tamminen, K. A., Wolf, S. A., Dunn, R., & Bissett, J. E. (2024). A review of the interpersonal experience, expression, and regulation of emotions in sport. *International Review of Sport and Exercise Psychology*, *17*(2), 1132–1169. https://doi.org/10.1080/1750984X.2022.2132526

Taylor, J., Gretton, T. W., & Sweeney, L. (2026). Performance safety: conceptualising psychological safety when errors have consequences. *Journal of Applied Sport Psychology*, *38*(1), 1–15. https://doi.org/10.1080/10413200.2025.2521261

Teques, P., Duarte, D., & Viana, J. (2019). Coaches' emotional intelligence and reactive behaviors in soccer matches: Mediating effects of coach efficacy beliefs. *Frontiers in Psychology*, *10*, Article 1629. https://doi.org/10.3389/fpsyg.2019.01629

Van Puyenbroeck, S., Stouten, J., & Vande Broek, G. (2019). Can losing teams cope with destructive voice behaviour? The role of game results and athletes' perceived motivational climate. *Journal of Sports Sciences*, *37*(7), 819–826. https://doi.org/10.1080/02640414.2018.1528656

Vella, S. A., Oades, L. G., & Crowe, T. P. (2013). The relationship between coach leadership, the coach–athlete relationship, team success, and the positive developmental experiences of adolescent soccer players. *Physical Education and Sport Pedagogy*, *18*(5), 549–561. https://doi.org/10.1080/17408989.2012.726976

Vogelgesang, G. R., Leroy, H., & Avolio, B. J. (2013). The mediating effects of leader integrity with transparency in communication and work engagement/performance. *The Leadership Quarterly*, *24*(3), 405–413. https://doi.org/10.1016/j.leaqua.2013.01.004

Walton, C. C., Purcell, R., Pilkington, V., Hall, K., Kenttä, G., Vella, S. A., & Rice, S. M. (2024). Psychological safety for mental health in elite sport: A theoretically informed model. *Sports Medicine*, *54*(3), 557–564. https://doi.org/10.1007/s40279-023-01912-2

Weick, K. E. (1993). The collapse of sensemaking in organizations: The Mann Gulch disaster. *Administrative Science Quarterly*, *38*(4), 628–652. https://doi.org/10.2307/2393339

6

BUILDING CHAMPIONSHIP CULTURE—HOW TO DIAGNOSE, BUILD, AND SUSTAIN IT

How do we decide when it matters?—completed. This time, the question is aimed at the system itself: what is it actually reinforcing?

Culture is built by consequences, not declarations—it is diagnosed, then redesigned by changing what gets reinforced rather than what gets messaged. Every unaddressed exemption, every ignored disclosure, every inconsistent standard is building culture whether anyone intends it or not. This chapter defines culture as a reinforcement system—the consequence architecture that drives behavior under competitive pressure. It outlines a four-phase sequence: diagnose current reinforcement loops by mapping cue–behavior–consequence sequences, build a season-aware change architecture that sequences interventions around competitive demands, embed standards in systems that survive results volatility (including the wobble moment—the 48-hour window after a pressure spike that reveals whether standards hold or revert), and succession-proof the culture against leadership turnover through continuity documentation and distributed ownership. Not what culture do we want, but what culture are our consequences currently producing—and does that answer survive the next coaching change?

Learning Objectives

By the end of this chapter, the reader will be able to:

1. Diagnose the reinforcement loops operating in a high-performance environment by mapping the cue–behavior–consequence sequences that maintain current culture patterns.

DOI: 10.4324/9781003631217-7

2. Evaluate the gap between an organization's stated culture and its enacted culture using multiple data sources, and differentiate between interventions that alter reinforcement and those that constitute performance theater.
3. Design a season-aware culture change architecture that sequences interventions around competitive demands and targets consequences rather than messaging.
4. Maintain culture integrity during performance crises by naming the wobble moment, holding scheduled processes, and debriefing the reversion pull.
5. Document non-negotiable standards, decision rights, voice channels, and known vulnerabilities in a transferable continuity document that survives leadership turnover.

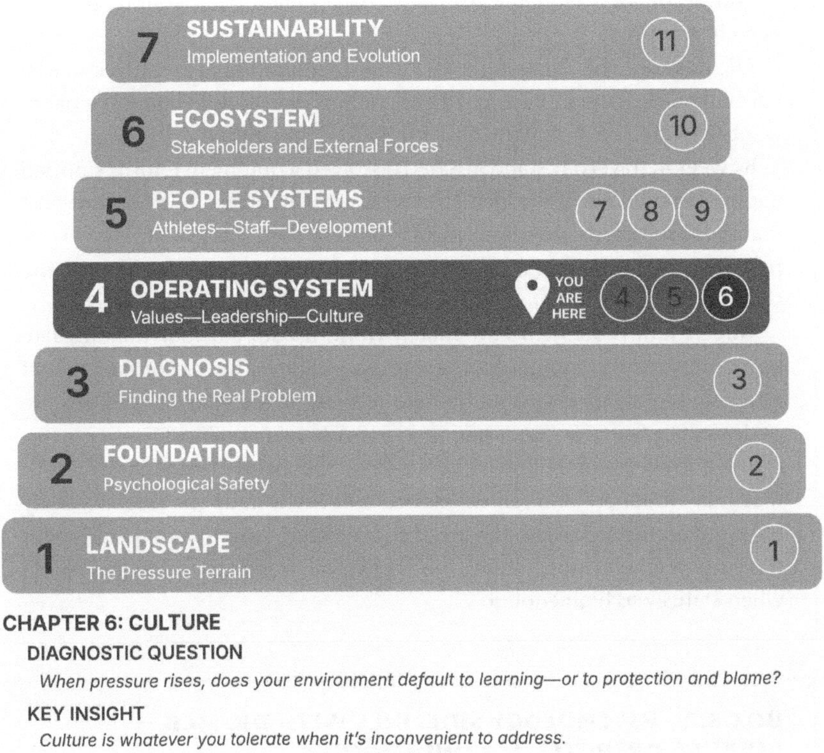

FIGURE 6.1 You Are Here—Operating System.

The HPCOS seven-layer architecture with Layer 4 (Operating System) highlighted. This chapter answers Question 4—How do we decide when it matters?—by designing culture architecture: the reinforcement loops, standards, rituals, and consequence pathways that teach the organization what is real.

BOX 6.1 CASE STUDY — THE EQUIPMENT MANAGER WHO STOPPED ENFORCING

Composite vignette. Details changed to protect privacy.

Ade had managed matchday operations for six years. He ran logistics, but everyone knew he was also the culture thermometer. He enforced the small things—punctuality at the team bus, dress code on travel days, and returning borrowed equipment—because the previous head coach had been explicit: "Standards live in the details. If the details slip, the big things follow."

The new head coach arrived mid-season. Week 1, the star striker showed up to the team bus 14 minutes late, wearing tracksuit bottoms instead of the travel suit. Ade flagged it. The new coach smiled. "Pick your battles. We need him happy."

Ade noted it. The following week, two other senior players arrived in casual clothes. He flagged it again. The operations director told him: "The gaffer wants a relaxed environment. Ease off on the dress code."

By week 4, travel day standards had dissolved. Equipment returns stopped happening on time. The under-21 players—who had been told for two years that these standards were non-negotiable—watched the senior players walk past every rule without consequence. One of them said to a teammate in the changing room: "So that was all just for us, then."

Three months later, the pre-match warm-up started four minutes late because players were still in the dressing room. The performance staff scrambled to compress the activation protocol. The head coach blamed the performance team for "poor preparation." Ade said nothing.

The end-of-season culture review noted "inconsistent engagement with matchday routines" and recommended a new warm-up protocol. Nobody traced the timeline back to the bus, the tracksuit bottoms, and the moment the reinforcement loop taught the room that standards were negotiable when status was high enough.

BOX 6.2 PSYCHOLOGY SIDELINES WITH DR. MCB — CULTURE OPERATES AS CONDITIONING

Culture operates as conditioning, even when it feels like something else. Under pressure, people default to the behavior that has paid off before. That's reinforcement at work.

A young athletic therapist raises a legitimate concern in a staff meeting? The head coach doesn't yell. He just moves on—quickly, visibly, without acknowledgment. The room registers it instantly. Next week, she has nothing to report. The week after, nobody did.

That's a reinforcement loop in action. The cue was the meeting. The behavior was speaking up. The consequence was being ignored. The learning? "What I say doesn't really matter here."

Reinforcement and social learning research has shown for decades that behavior follows consequences more reliably than stated intentions—and that people learn the rules not just from their own experience but from watching what happens to the person who speaks up (Bandura, 1977; Skinner, 1953). You can put "We Value Honesty" on every wall. If the person who tells the truth gets ignored or excluded, the nervous system learns the real rule.

The fix is simple. Change the consequence—publicly—so honesty is rewarded. Next time someone raises an uncomfortable truth, stop the room. Say: "Thank you. That's exactly the kind of information we need." Then act on it. One visible moment of reinforcement often teaches more than a year of values workshops.

6.1 Diagnose the Culture You Actually Have

Principle: Culture is the behaviors your environment repeatedly rewards, punishes, or tolerates under pressure.

This chapter assumes the trust and communication infrastructure from Layer 3 is in place—that people can speak without immediate punishment. If that infrastructure is absent, the diagnostic tools here will surface it, but the fix belongs in Layer 3 before Layer 4 can operate.

Every organization already has a culture. The question is whether leadership has named it accurately (see Figure 6.1). Most have not—not out of negligence, but because the reinforcement loops that sustain culture operate below the level of deliberate attention. The diagnosis is often the intervention. Making those implicit loops explicit—naming aloud what gets rewarded and what gets punished—changes the calculus. Once a leadership group maps the cue–behavior–consequence sequence sustaining a problem, it becomes actionable (Argyris, 1990; Edmondson, 1999). Even the naming changes the consequence structure.

This is where culture work moves beyond culture messaging. Kotter (1995) found that transformation breaks down when leaders communicate vision without altering structures. Beer and Nohria (2000) argued that soft cultural appeals without structural realignment produce superficial results. Under pressure, people do what has kept them safe and selected. The reinforcement loop, not the values deck, determines what persists. Diagnose the loop before prescribing the change.

The reinforcement system also determines how fast truth moves. When honesty is reinforced, Speed of Truth shrinks. When silence is reinforced, it expands. The three leading indicators—Speed of Truth, Voice Normalization, and decision clarity—are observable outputs of whatever reinforcement loops are actually running. Diagnosing those loops is the first step toward changing the outputs.

Before the diagnostic tools: the reinforcement loop does not just shape behavior—it communicates worth. When standards apply consistently across status levels, the message is clear: everyone here matters, and the organization invests in them accordingly. Culture architecture that operates from a "we're lucky to have you" orientation—treating people as investments to develop—creates the conditions under which diagnostic tools function as intended. Where that orientation is absent, the same tools risk functioning as control mechanisms rather than genuine culture-building instruments. Name that distinction before the work begins.

You can run a clean culture diagnosis without building a new department. You need a shared language, a causal hypothesis, and a baseline.

6.1.1 Culture Is a Reinforcement Loop (Not a Mission Statement)

Culture lives downstream of the values deck. It's what happens after someone tells the truth, makes a mistake, challenges a coach, or violates a standard. Working definition: culture is the consequence architecture—the reinforcement loops, information pathways, and decision structures—that determines which behaviors persist. The cue → behavior → consequence loop is the mechanism that makes values observable or hollow, and here, the same loop becomes a diagnostic tool (see Figure 6.2). To understand what a culture actually is, look beyond the mission statement to what gets rewarded, punished, and conspicuously ignored when pressure arrives.

6.1.2 Culture Is an Information System (Voice, Silence, and Speed)

High-performance environments win partly on learning speed: how quickly you surface problems, test adjustments, and update plans (Levitt & March, 1988). Culture is the system that decides which information travels—and which gets trapped.

Under pressure, "generative" cultures seek information; "pathological" cultures penalize the messenger (Westrum, 2004). When a high-performance culture turns pathological, it often shows up as abusive supervision (Tepper, 2000)—public belittling, withholding information, and explosive outbursts. Whatever label they carry, these are diagnostic markers of a dysfunctional reinforcement loop, and they erode learning speed. In sport, "voice" is tied directly

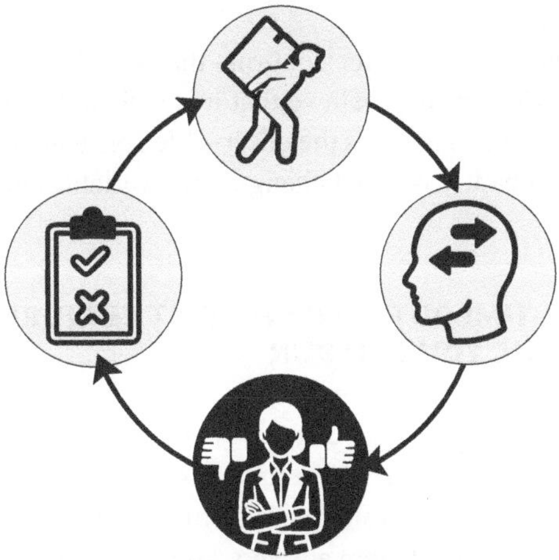

FIGURE 6.2 The Reinforcement Loop as a Diagnostic Tool.

A four-element culture feedback loop: Cues/Pressure → Norms/Values-in-Use → Consequences/ Leader Response → Behavior, cycling back to Cues. The question it answers: what consequences are currently running in your environment, and which behaviors are those consequences reinforcing?

to performance safety: the clarity and fairness of performance consequences (selection, deselection, minutes, and contracts) and whether mistakes are treated as learning signals or career threats.

Speed of Truth describes the lag between a problem occurring and leadership learning about it accurately enough to act.

You can track it simply. Pick three information pathways: injury reporting (how long between an athlete noticing a niggle and the medical team knowing about it?), performance feedback (how long between a tactical problem appearing on video and the coaching staff discussing it?), and interpersonal conflict (how long between a relational issue emerging and leadership being informed?). Estimate the current lag in hours or days. That's your baseline.

In environments with strong psychological safety, the lag tends to narrow—bad news travels nearly as fast as good news because the consequences of disclosure do not include punishment (Edmondson, 1999). In environments characterized by fear, the lag stretches to weeks—or the information never arrives at all. The athlete hides the niggle. The assistant hides the conflict. A narrowing Speed of Truth across the season signals that voice and safety may be improving. A widening one—especially after losses or leadership changes—is an early warning of cultural drift.

Research in voice behavior confirms that whether people speak up depends primarily on whether they believe that it is safe and worthwhile to do so (Morrison, 2011). Speed of Truth is the observable consequence of that calculus—and the rest of this chapter is about changing the variables that drive it.

BOX 6.3 TIMEOUT — THE FASTEST CULTURE DIAGNOSTIC YOU CAN RUN

You don't need a survey to diagnose culture. You need one question asked across three status levels: "What happens here when someone tells the truth about a problem?" Ask a star player, a fringe player, and a junior staff member. If you get three different answers, you don't have one culture–you have a hierarchy of realities. The size of that gap predicts how slowly truth travels upward–the greater the divergence across status levels, the longer the lag before leadership hears accurate information. Use it as your qualitative Speed of Truth baseline. Close the gap, and the lag shrinks. Widen it, and no amount of values messaging will matter.

6.1.3 Decision Clarity Under Pressure

Where Speed of Truth measures how fast information moves and Voice Normalization measures who contributes it, decision clarity measures what the organization does with information once it arrives.

Decision clarity is the observable output of whether the decision-rights structure is actually running under pressure. When decision clarity is high, the right people decide, with the best available information, within a known authority structure, and the rationale can be articulated after the fact. When it degrades, three patterns appear: authority ambiguity (nobody knows who is deciding), rationale opacity (decisions happen but nobody can explain why), and political capture (decisions serve relationships rather than performance). Decision rights (Section 6.2.1) are the structure; decision clarity is what you observe when that structure holds or fails.

Track it the same way you track Speed of Truth—pick three recent consequential decisions and ask: who decided, on what basis, and can they explain it without hedging? If the answers are clean, the structure is holding. If the answers involve qualifications, deflections, or "it was a collective decision" without anyone able to name who held the final call, decision clarity has degraded—and the reinforcement loop is teaching the room that ambiguity is safer than ownership.

6.1.4 Use a Shared Language for Culture Types

You can't change what you can't describe. The Competing Values Framework (CVF) gives you a shared language for this—it avoids "good/bad" labels and instead describes trade-offs (Cameron & Quinn, 2011).

CVF maps cultures across two fundamental tensions: flexibility versus stability, and internal focus versus external focus. These intersect to produce four common patterns. Clan cultures emphasize loyalty, belonging, and development. Adhocracy cultures prioritize innovation, experimentation, and speed. Market cultures center on results, accountability, and winning. Hierarchy cultures value structure, clarity, and risk management.

None of these are inherently wrong. The risk is over-dominance—when one pattern gets so strong it crowds out the others. And in elite sport, that happens fast. Feddersen et al. (2020) documented how quickly a high-performance focus can turn into a "destructive culture" of fear and silence if not actively regulated.

To make this usable in the locker room, translate the academic framework into a language that athletes and staff actually recognize. Table 6.1 maps the four academic archetypes to "Locker Room" equivalents and adds the Shadow—what I've seen happen under pressure when each archetype's virtues become vices. The shadow states are not part of the original CVF; they reflect patterns repeatedly observed across high-performance environments.

TABLE 6.1 Locker-Room Culture Matrix (CVF Archetypes and Shadow States)

CVF Mode	*Locker-Room Translation*	*Reinforces When Useful*	*Shadow Under Pressure*
Clan (collaborate)	Connection, loyalty, "family"	Belonging, care, developmental feedback	Harmony becomes avoidance; standards soften to keep peace
Adhocracy (create)	Experimentation, initiative	Innovation, adaptive problem-solving, speed	Chaos; constant change; role confusion
Market (compete)	Results, accountability	High standards, urgency, "win" focus	Fear and burnout; short-termism; blame
Hierarchy (control)	Structure, clarity	Process discipline, risk management, consistency	Rigidity; bureaucracy; suppressed voice

Quadrant framework adapted from Cameron & Quinn (2011). Shadow states are practitioner-derived.

These observations closely align with the "Dark Side" personality traits of leadership (Hogan & Hogan, 2001). Under acute pressure, organizational strengths can flip—high accountability turns into fear, and a desire for harmony turns into conflict avoidance.

A common failure mode is to treat a quadrant as a badge ("we're a Clan team") instead of naming trade-offs. These shadow states map directly onto Edmondson's Safety/Accountability Matrix (see Chapter 2): Clan shadows produce Comfort Zones, Market shadows produce Anxiety Zones, and the Learning Zone requires both high safety and high accountability simultaneously.

Once you can name the pattern, measure it. You don't need a 60-item survey battery, but you do need something beyond gut feeling. Three constructs matter most: cohesion (Carron et al., 1985), psychological safety (Sport Psychological Safety Inventory, Rice et al., 2022), and voice—whether athletes and staff raise issues early and constructively (Jowett et al., 2023). The key is not the instrument. It's the signal: are people speaking early, with detail, without fear?

6.1.5 The Culture Hypothesis (and Whose Reality It Captures)

Before building the hypothesis, ask: whose experience is informing this diagnosis? Most culture conversations default to the leadership's version of reality. If your data comes only from coaches and senior players, you're diagnosing the culture experienced by the people with the most power—which is rarely where the problems live.

Include junior athletes, support staff, and anyone whose voice carries the least weight in selection decisions. Their answers to "what gets rewarded here?" will look different—and that difference is diagnostic. A culture that feels fair to the starting lineup and unsafe to the fringe player is better understood as a stratified reinforcement system—and the stratification is the problem. If the Speed of Truth baseline from Section 6.1.2 varies significantly across status levels, that variation is telling you whose reality the culture currently serves.

Demographic and identity factors also enter the diagnosis here. Gender, race, disability status, sexuality, and cultural background all shape how people experience the same consequence structure. A "direct feedback" culture may feel empowering to those whose communication norms match the dominant group and punishing to those whose norms don't. The diagnostic question is not whether diverse perspectives are "represented" but whether the reinforcement loop operates equitably across identity lines—and the only way to answer that is to ask people at every level and from every background.

Once you've broadened the data, build the hypothesis.

Most culture conversations stall at the level of complaint: "We don't have accountability." "Communication is broken." "People don't speak up." These statements describe symptoms, not mechanisms. They tell you something is wrong without telling you what is maintaining it—which means any intervention is a guess.

The culture hypothesis moves the conversation from symptom to mechanism. It asks a leadership group to do one thing: name the reinforcement loop. That means identifying the cue that triggers the behavior, the behavior itself, and the consequence that reinforces it. A group that says "we need more accountability" has not yet identified anything actionable. A group that says "when senior players miss recovery sessions, no one addresses it because the coaching staff avoids conflict with high-status athletes" has identified a cue, a behavior, and a consequence—and now has a concrete target for intervention.

The process synthesizes reinforcement theory (Skinner, 1953) and organizational learning frameworks (Argyris, 1990) into a practical sequence. Start with the diagnostic from Section 6.1.1—"In this environment, you get ahead by ______." Name the behavior you want to change. Identify what reinforces it. Then write what you will change. The output is a one-sentence hypothesis in the format: "In this environment, [behavior] happens because [consequence reinforces it]. We will change [specific consequence]."

Once the hypothesis is written, it becomes a testable prediction framed in the language of the three leading indicators: "If we change this consequence, voice will normalize in this domain within this timeframe." Without a testable prediction, culture change is aspiration. With one, it becomes measurable. If the reinforcement mechanism is difficult to articulate, the problem may not yet be understood well enough to intervene effectively—and the default is often messaging fixes that leave the consequence structure intact.

A hypothesis built on leadership's experience alone will miss the loops that operate below the power line. A hypothesis informed by the full range of voices in the system—especially those with the least protection—will surface the reinforcement patterns that matter most and are hardest to see from the top. Figure 6.3 maps the full diagnostic sequence as a six-step flowchart—from observation to action and back.

6.1.6 Organizational Defenses That Block Change

High-pressure systems develop predictable defenses against uncomfortable truth. You don't need a clinical degree to spot them—you need pattern recognition.

Common organizational defenses in elite sport: denial ("That's not happening here"), projection ("The athletes are the problem"), rationalization ("That's just elite sport"), splitting ("Those people are toxic" instead of addressing systems), and performative agreement—saying yes in meetings while quietly undermining the change.

These defenses are contagious. One leader's anxiety or avoidance can shift the affective tone of an entire group within minutes (Barsade, 2002). This makes the

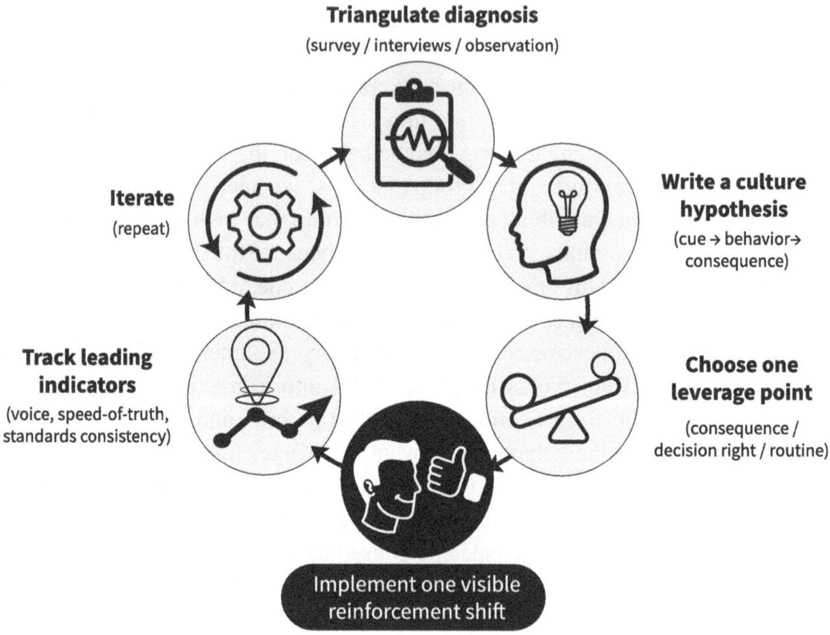

FIGURE 6.3 Culture Diagnostic Flowchart—From Observation to Action.

Six-step cycle: triangulate diagnosis (survey/interviews/observation) → write a culture hypothesis (cue → behavior → consequence) → choose one leverage point (consequence/decision right/routine) → implement one visible reinforcement shift → track leading indicators (voice, speed-of-truth, standards consistency) → iterate. The cycle repeats because the diagnosis is ongoing.

leader's visible emotional regulation a culture variable—and one of the reasons the Wobble Protocol (Section 6.2.7) prioritizes naming the pressure moment publicly rather than allowing anxiety to spread through unmanaged contagion. Leaders who model regulated response under pressure teach the room a different consequence: stress does not automatically produce reversion.

Defenses are not moral failures; they're threat responses. Treat them as data: where is the system feeling unsafe? When a specific defense is identified, the diagnostic follow-up is: what consequence makes this defense rational?

Denial persists when acknowledging a problem threatens someone's position. Projection persists when the system lacks mechanisms for shared accountability. Rationalization persists when the alternative—admitting the standard is wrong—would require structural change nobody has the authority to initiate. Once you map a defense to its reinforcing consequence, it converts from a frustrating interpersonal pattern into a solvable system-design problem—the same cue–behavior–consequence logic the Culture Hypothesis applies to any other behavior. Argyris (1990) called these defensive routines; they persist because people hold competing commitments—hidden goals that make the old behavior feel necessary even when the person consciously wants to change (Kegan & Lahey, 2009). That gap between intention and action is where most culture interventions stall.

Boundary condition (safeguarding): If your diagnosis indicates coercion, bullying, discrimination, or other safeguarding concerns, treat this as a welfare/safeguarding issue—not a "culture alignment" problem. Culture tools can help you surface risk, but they're not a substitute for formal reporting pathways, independent oversight, and clinical/safeguarding support (Mountjoy et al., 2016).

6.2 Build the Change Architecture

Now that the reinforcement loops have been diagnosed, the organization must build a season-aware architecture to change them.

Principle: Culture change typically requires a season-aware sequence that stabilizes truth and decision-making before it demands new behaviors.

Diagnosis tells you what you have. The harder question is how to shift it without breaking what's already working. A common failure point comes before any change is launched: the diagnosis itself gets rejected. The organizational defenses from Section 6.1.6—denial, rationalization, and projection—frequently activate not after the change begins, but after the diagnosis is shared. A leadership group that commissions a culture review and then dismisses its findings is exactly displaying the defensive routines the review identified. Anticipate this: present findings in behavioral language tied to observable consequences, ground them in the organization's own data, and frame the diagnosis as a hypothesis to test rather than a verdict to accept.

Aviation's Crew Resource Management is the clearest parallel: it changed cockpit culture not by talking about teamwork, but by making it procedurally expected for junior crew to challenge senior crew when they detected a problem (Helmreich et al., 1999). The culture followed the consequence change, not the other way around.

Culture change competes with match results, media scrutiny, contracts, selection pressure, stakeholder politics, and staff fatigue. Your architecture needs to be season-aware and pressure-tested.

6.2.1 Align Upward Before You Launch

Culture change often stalls at the top before it stalls anywhere else. Coaches may work to shift culture in the locker room while the board and executive tier inadvertently reinforce competing behaviors: short-termism, blame, secrecy, and political survival. If leaders react to losses with panic, the system learns that truth carries risk and image management carries reward.

Before you launch any culture program, align upward on three non-negotiables: what behaviors are required and from whom—distinguishing between non-negotiable behavioral standards, which apply universally, and operational accommodations, which may vary by individual need—who decides what (selection, discipline, spending, and hiring), and what happens when standards are violated, even by high performers (consequences, kept proportional via a Just Culture lens; Dekker, 2012).

Ask the executive tier four questions and record the answers:

1. Which behaviors are you willing to confront even if the person is valuable?
2. Where are you currently sending mixed messages between stated values and actual incentives?
3. What decision rights are unclear—and who benefits from that ambiguity?
4. If results dip, what will you protect—learning or political survival?

If leaders find it difficult to answer these cleanly, it's worth pausing to ask why—the culture program may be building on an unstable foundation.

6.2.2 Sequence the Change Across a Season (Kotter in Sport)

Kotter's (1995) eight-stage change model provides a useful sequencing structure. The following adaptation groups Kotter's stages into a four-phase sport-specific roadmap (Figure 6.4), integrating pressures identified by Cruickshank and Collins (2012) and Cruickshank et al. (2014), who documented how elite sport performance teams navigate culture change within competitive cycles.

The key: you're not "communicating values." You're changing consequences. Table 6.2 maps the sequence.

6.2.3 Build a Guiding Coalition

A guiding coalition is not a committee. It's a small group with credibility, cross-role reach, and the authority to model the change (Phase 2 of Kotter's sequence). At minimum: the head coach or performance lead, one respected veteran athlete, one emerging athlete leader, one "truth teller" staff member (often medical or performance side), and one executive sponsor with decision authority. The test: if this group behaves differently, will the rest of the organization notice and copy it?

Identity matters. Durable culture change is identity change: "I do the extra rep because people like us don't cut corners" beats "I do the extra rep because the coach is watching" (Haslam et al., 2011).

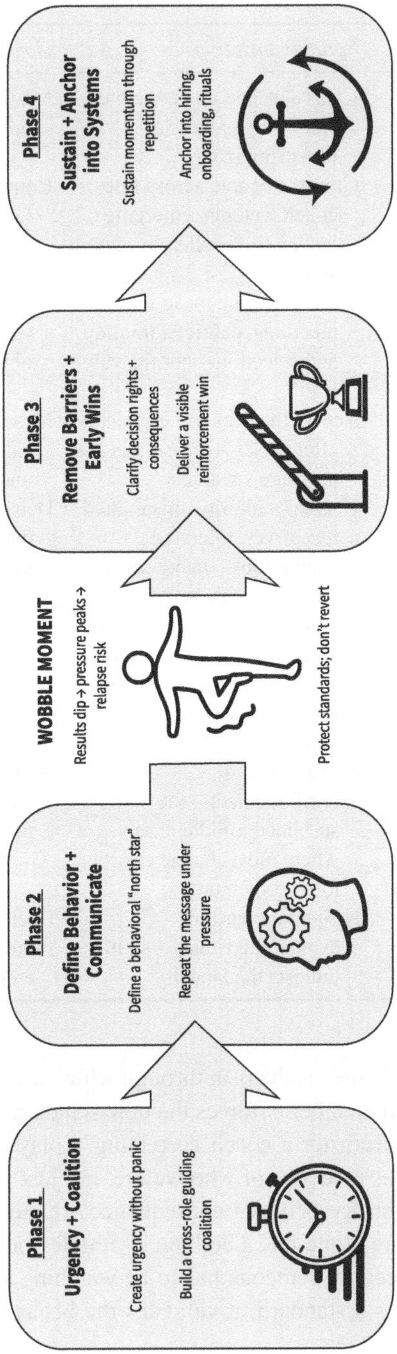

FIGURE 6.4 The Four Phases of Culture Change.

The operational sequence for surviving a competitive season, highlighting the "Wobble Moment" in Phase 2. Adapted from Kotter (1995).

TABLE 6.2 Season-Aware Culture Change Sequence. Adapted From Kotter (1995)

Phase	*Kotter Stage*	*Sport Translation*	*Common Failure Mode*
1	Create urgency	Clear data and one concrete story—no panic, no catastrophizing	Manufactured crisis that erodes trust
2	Form a guiding coalition	Credible people across roles: coach, veteran, emerging leader, truth-teller, executive sponsor	Committee of positional leaders without informal credibility
3	Define the behavior change	What the value looks like in meetings, debriefs, training, and selection—not the value itself	Announcing a value shift without specifying observable behavior
4	Communicate under stress	Repeat the standard especially after losses—pressure is the message's real test	Messaging only during calm periods; silence under pressure
5	Remove barriers	Unclear authority, misaligned incentives, tolerated exemptions—name them and change them	Debating philosophy publicly while the old incentives stay in place
6	Generate short-term wins	Visible process improvements: a debrief rhythm that holds, a standard enforced on a star, a concern acted on quickly	Wins that look good externally but reinforce the old loop internally
7	Sustain momentum	Repetition and reinforcement—the sustained middle phase where most change efforts lose momentum	Abandoning the work after the first performance dip
8	Anchor in systems	Hiring, onboarding, evaluation, rituals—so it outlasts the launch	Declaring victory after the launch without embedding in systems

The guiding coalition is the mechanism through which identity shift becomes visible. When a coalition member enforces the new standard at personal cost—a veteran correcting a peer, not a coach correcting a player—the rest of the group reads that action as evidence of who we are, not just what you must do. This is the operational bridge between consequence architecture and identity. Consequence architecture alone has a ceiling; if athletes only meet standards because they fear deselection, someone has to be watching all the time. When a veteran player enforces a standard, it validates the behavior as identity, not compliance.

6.2.4 Communicate the Change in Behavioral Language

Values are not wrong. They're incomplete. A culture message that travels is specific enough that athletes and staff can audit behavior against it. "We value respect" stays on the wall. "We challenge ideas directly and protect people" travels into behavior. Pick three behaviors and repeat them until they become boring—then prove them in decisions. Behavior is the message.

6.2.5 Handling Resistance and Cynicism

Resistance is information, and dealing with it is how you remove barriers to change (Phase 5 of Kotter's sequence). Most of it reflects fear: fear of incompetence ("I don't know how to do this"), loss of status ("this costs me power"), or change fatigue ("not another initiative") (Kegan & Lahey, 2009). When fear is treated as defiance, the threat state escalates, and opposition hardens.

Response sequence:

1. Name the behavior without moralizing. Focus on what you observed, not what you inferred.
2. Ask what's at stake. Is it competence, status, workload, or identity? The answer determines the intervention.
3. Restate the non-negotiable. The standard is not up for debate. The path to meeting it is.
4. Offer support and assign a role. Ownership reduces threat.
5. Follow through. Mixed consequences teach people that the change is optional.

Cynicism is a specific variant: people have been promised change before and watched nothing shift. Trying to talk cynics out of their skepticism rarely works. What works is changing reinforcement until belief follows behavior. Give skeptics a defined role ("tell us when we're faking it") and protect them when they use it constructively.

6.2.6 Design Early Wins That Change Reinforcement

Culture change needs momentum, and momentum comes from visible wins (Phase 6 of Kotter's sequence). The trap is choosing wins that look good externally but teach the wrong internal lesson. An early win should change reinforcement—you should be able to point to a specific behavior shift and say: "That's the new rule."

Examples of culture-aligned early wins: a consistent debrief rhythm after wins and losses demonstrates that learning is non-negotiable. A clear decision-rights statement reduces politics. A first "standard enforced on a star" moment—consequence ladder pre-agreed, applied with zero drama—sends the most powerful signal a culture change can send. And a "concern raised early and acted on quickly" story teaches the room that voice has consequences worth taking.

6.2.7 The Wobble Moment: Holding the System Under Pressure

Once the change is launched, communicated, and securing early wins, the system will inevitably be tested. This is the climax of the Build Phase.

BOX 6.4 TIMEOUT — THE WOBBLE PROTOCOL

The following is a practitioner-developed tool based on crisis management principles (Reason, 1997) and change management research (Kotter, 1995). The 48-hour timeframe reflects applied observation, not validated thresholds. Not a validated instrument.

Definition: The Wobble Moment is the first point in a culture change process where external pressure creates sufficient threat to trigger reversion to pre-change behaviors. It's not a failure of the change–it's the change's first real test.

Wobble Moments are when the three leading indicators regress. Speed of Truth slows as people wait to see what leadership will do. Voice contracts as the room reads the emotional temperature. Decisions get muddier as leaders revert to expedience. Predictable triggers include consecutive losses, key player injuries, coaching changes, media scrutiny, or board-level panic. The trigger matters less than whether the system holds.

The 48-Hour Protocol

(Timeframes are approximate–adapt to your competitive calendar and organizational rhythm. The structure matters more than the clock.)

- **Step 1: Name it (within hours).** Tell the leadership group: "This is the Wobble Moment. It was always going to come. The question is what we do next."
- **Step 2: Hold the process (first day).** Run the next scheduled debrief, review, or feedback meeting exactly as designed. Same agenda, same standards. Do not cancel, shorten, or soften.
- **Step 3: Reinforce the coalition (first day).** Brief your guiding coalition privately. Align on messaging: "The system is not the problem. The system is how we solve the problem."

- **Step 4: Go public with the hold (Day 2).** Let the room see that the process survived pressure. A system that holds under load teaches more than any amount of messaging in calm conditions.
- **Step 5: Debrief the wobble (once acute pressure passes).** After-action review (AAR): what triggered it? Where did the pull to revert come from? What do we protect next time?

The rule: You don't earn culture in the good weeks. You earn it in the wobble.

6.3 Embed Culture in Systems (So It Survives the Season)

A new culture architecture will only survive the friction of a long season if it is embedded into daily systems.

Principle: If you want culture to endure, embed it in systems—what Schein (2010) calls primary embedding mechanisms: what leaders pay attention to, how they react to crises, how they allocate resources, and what they reward and punish.

The hard part is not the launch. It's the Tuesday three months later when you're tired, injured, and trying to win. Under load, people drift to shortcuts and status exceptions—a form of normalization of deviance (Vaughan, 1996). High-reliability organizations manage this by building defenses in depth: multiple independent barriers so no single failure point produces a catastrophic outcome (Reason, 1997). In sport, those barriers are the systems this section builds: hiring, selection, feedback, rituals, and environment design.

6.3.1 Hiring as a Culture-Level Intervention

A single misaligned hire can undermine a season of culture work. Felps et al. (2006) modeled how negative behaviors—interpersonal deviance, withholding effort, and persistent negativity—asymmetrically depress group outcomes. Addressing a disruptive member may improve functioning more than adding a high performer. Values alignment in hiring is not a soft extra; it is a culture-level intervention.

Use "values alignment" rather than "cultural fit," which often functions as a proxy for demographic similarity and risks creating groupthink (Rivera, 2012). Screen for a "culture add" instead—someone who shares the core behavioral standards but brings something the room is currently missing. Structured behavioral interviews outperform unstructured formats in predicting performance and reducing bias (Campion et al., 1997; Levashina et al., 2014).

A useful hiring rubric tests four dimensions: role competence, values alignment, coachability, and culture add. Role competence is straightforward—can this person perform at the required standard? But the interview question matters more than the credentials. Ask a candidate to walk you through their last major technical failure and how they fixed it. The person who owns the gap and explains the repair in granular detail is showing you a method. The person who attributes the failure entirely to others is showing you a different pattern.

Values alignment requires behavioral evidence, not stated intentions. Ask about a time the candidate disagreed with a head coach or boss. You are listening for someone who disagreed directly but respectfully and kept the team goal in view. A signal worth noting is the candidate who stayed silent in the room but complained to peers afterward—the "shadow chat" pattern that erodes trust from below.

Coachability may be the most underweighted dimension in hiring. Ask what the hardest piece of feedback was that the candidate received recently. A coachable person can quote the feedback verbatim and describe the behavior change that followed. "I don't really get bad feedback" is worth noting as a concern rather than a strength. The standards in these four dimensions hold across cultures, but the behavioral expression varies—calibrate to the candidate's cultural background (Meyer, 2014). Red flag behaviors often reflect rational adaptation to previous environments, not fixed character traits, which is precisely why coachability matters as much as current alignment.

Finally, test for culture add: what does this person see the team doing that they would do differently? You want a constructive, fresh perspective rooted in experience that the room does not yet have. Wholesale validation can signal groupthink more than genuine alignment. Criticism without context offers little to work with.

The highest-risk hiring profile is high competence with low values alignment—sometimes called the "Mercenary." This person delivers results early but can gradually erode the environment over time. Person–organization fit often predicts retention and satisfaction more strongly than skill alone (Kristof-Brown et al., 2005). The New Zealand All Blacks codified this principle: they prioritize character alignment alongside ability, even when it means passing on talented players (Kerr, 2013).

Structure the process to protect it from bias. Before the interview, assign one rubric dimension to each panel member and write one behavioral question and one disqualifier probe per dimension. Score candidates independently on a 1–5 scale, and then compare scores before anyone discusses "fit." Document the decision rationale, so the reasoning is transparent and auditable.

Once a hire is made, front-load the operating rules. Day 1: decision rights and escalation triggers. Week 1: conflict rules. Week 2: standards and consequences. Week 3: voice channels. The alternative is that new arrivals learn the real rules through trial and error—a costly gap that culture work cannot afford.

6.3.2 Selection and Feedback Are Culture Decisions

Selection and feedback are the two mechanisms through which athletes learn what the culture actually rewards. When either feels opaque or inconsistent, people default to impression management (Colquitt et al., 2001). Feedback functions as a reinforcement mechanism—it changes behavior when it targets specific observable actions rather than character, and when consequences are predictable (Hattie & Timperley, 2007; Deci et al., 1999). Table 6.3 illustrates the shift from character-based to behavior-based feedback scripts; see Section 5.4.3 in Chapter 5 for the full feedback protocol.

After any selection, discipline, or role-change decision, apply four procedural justice checks: consistency, neutrality, voice, and transparency (Colquitt et al., 2001; Leventhal, 1980; Ben-Ari et al., 2006). The no-surprises rule: give the same feedback in training that you will later use to justify the decision. In high-context cultures, keep the standard firm but adapt delivery to preserve dignity (Meyer, 2014).

6.3.3 Handling Superstars: The "Exemption Tax"

Every culture book insists on treating everyone identically, but this conflates two different things. Non-negotiable behavioral standards must be enforced equally, regardless of status. Operational accommodations—loading, travel, and scheduling—can and should be adapted to individual needs. A 10-year veteran with chronic knee issues requires different loading than a rookie. If the organization treats them as identical, the room will notice the inconsistency.

The goal is equity, not equality, but equity requires a tax. Social psychologists call the mechanism "idiosyncrasy credits" (Hollander, 1958): high performers

TABLE 6.3 Feedback Scripts—Character Versus Behavior

Instead of (Character)	*Say This (Task/Process)*	*Why It Works*
"You were lazy on that play."	"You were 2 yards behind on the cover—watch the video at 34:12. What adjustment will you make?"	Targets a specific, correctable action; invites the athlete into problem-solving rather than defense.
"You need to be a leader out there."	"When the press broke down in the third quarter, the back line needed someone to reset the shape. That's your job. Let's walk through the call."	Names the moment, the behavior, and the role expectation. "Be a leader" is too vague to act on.
"Your attitude has been terrible."	"You've been late to two of the last three film sessions, and you were on your phone during the set-piece review. What's going on?"	Describes observable behavior and opens a door. "Attitude" is a judgment; lateness is a fact.

earn the right to deviate from norms, but only while they continue delivering group success. The practical question is how to grant accommodations without corroding the standards that hold everything else together.

Any exemption must meet three conditions. It must be performance-based—"he does this because it maximizes his Sunday output," not "he does this because he is famous." It must be transparent—explained to the group by leadership, not discovered through gossip. And it must be taxed—the privilege carries a reciprocal cost, such as extra video work, mentoring duties, or rehab strictness. Privilege without a corresponding responsibility tends to erode the environment over time.

The deeper diagnostic is what the exemption communicates to everyone who does not receive one. An unexplained accommodation tells the room that their investment in the standard does not matter. A transparent, taxed exemption tells the room the system is intelligent. When these conditions are met, accommodation strengthens culture. When they are not, it erodes it.

6.3.4 Environment Design (The Building Teaches People)

Your environment is a silent coach. Physical proximity remains one of the strongest predictors of communication frequency (Allen, 1977), and workspace design directly shapes collaboration patterns (Bernstein & Turban, 2018). You don't need a new facility to use this.

Four design levers: create collision points—places where staff and athletes naturally interact. Build in privacy—spaces for difficult conversations so problems aren't handled in corridors. Signal learning—put learning artifacts where people see them: whiteboards, written standards, and question prompts. And don't underestimate seating charts. If cliques are undermining cohesion, assign seats for meals and meetings and rotate monthly. Zero cost, immediate effect.

6.3.5 Leading From the Middle: The "Sanctuary" Concept

Not everyone reading this is the Head Coach. If you're a Physio, a Strength Coach, or an Assistant, you might feel powerless to fix a broken wider culture. Don't wait for the Head Coach. You can build a Cultural Sanctuary—a bounded space operating by your standards, even if the rest of the building is chaotic.

BOX 6.5 TIMEOUT — THE CULTURAL SANCTUARY CONCEPT

Psychological safety varies at the team level (Edmondson, 1999). That means you can build it locally, even if the rest of the organization is a mess.

Subcultures form around repeated interaction and shared problem-solving (Schein, 2010)—a sanctuary just accelerates that process on purpose.

Two examples:

- **The Medical Room Rule:** "In here, we tell the truth about pain, no matter what the Coach says outside."
- **The Weight Room Rule:** "In here, nobody is too famous to rack their weights."

Players notice. If they find a pocket of sanity in your department, they gravitate toward it.

How to Build One

1. **Define non-negotiables.** Three max. Write them down, post them, say them out loud to everyone who walks in.
2. **Reinforce early.** Acknowledge the first person who follows the standard—especially if it costs them something. Correct the first violation. Both signals matter equally.
3. **Protect your people.** If an athlete discloses an injury and that information gets used against them in selection without consent, the sanctuary loses its credibility—and that trust is very difficult to rebuild.
4. **Align upward—don't rebel.** A sanctuary isn't a resistance cell. If your standards bump up against organizational direction, raise it formally: "I'm running the same standards you set—I'm just running them consistently."

A note on safeguarding: In youth sport especially, mandatory reporting obligations apply, and duty of care supersedes organizational politics (Mountjoy et al., 2016). If leadership punishes the disclosures your sanctuary protects, escalate through formal governance pathways.

6.3.6 Rituals, Symbols, and What Gets Celebrated

Rituals teach people what matters. Not speeches—repetition. Structured debriefs and AARs can improve team learning and performance (Keiser & Arthur, 2021; Tannenbaum & Cerasoli, 2013).

Design rituals that run regardless of results (Table 6.4).

Example: "Sweep the Sheds" (New Zealand All Blacks). Senior players clean the locker room after every match—the ritual works because it's visible, non-negotiable, and applies to the highest-status members first (J. Kerr, 2013).

Audit any ritual with three questions: what behavior does it reinforce? Who benefits from it, and who avoids cost? And does it create learning—or performance theater?

6.3.7 Culture Levers That Cost Nothing

You can change culture without new spending by changing three things already under your control—the same primary embedding mechanisms introduced at the top of this section (Schein, 2010): time (what gets airtime—what you meet about, review, and repeat), attention (what leaders notice and comment on), and consequences (what leaders tolerate or correct). The fastest culture move is not adding a new initiative. It's stopping the reinforcement of the old one.

6.3.8 Leading Indicators (How to Know Culture Is Shifting)

Culture change doesn't show up first on the scoreboard. It shows up in behavior. The goal of measuring culture is not precision; it's to gather a directional signal that allows you to detect drift before it compounds.

TABLE 6.4 Rituals That Earn Their Keep

Ritual	*Format*	*What It Reinforces*
AAR	Three questions after every significant event: what happened? Why? What do we change?	Learning is non-negotiable—win or lose, the debrief runs
Standards spotlight	Publicly praise one specific behavior each week	Makes "good" visible—reinforces the standard, not the person
Truth moment	One hard thing said respectfully in every staff meeting	Candor is process, not courage—normalizes discomfort as routine

BOX 6.6 TIMEOUT — THE DIFFERENCE BETWEEN A CULTURE PROGRAM AND A CULTURE CHANGE

A culture program adds something–workshops, posters, offsites, and consultants. A culture change removes a reinforcement that was protecting the old behavior. Every culture problem is sustained by a consequence that makes the problem rational. Find that consequence. Remove it or replace it. If the consequence stays, the behavior stays–regardless of how many programs you layer on top.

BOX 6.7 TIMEOUT — CULTURE HEALTH DASHBOARD (LEADING INDICATORS)

There are a few things worth tracking when we are looking at cultural health. Table 6.5 reminds us of those.

TABLE 6.5 Culture Health Dashboard

Indicator	*What to Track*	*Improving*	*Drifting*
Early issue reporting	Concerns raised proactively per month (a simple shared log works)	Issues surface before crisis; frequency increases	Issues only emerge as crises; reporting drops after losses
Quality of disagreement	Are disagreements targeting decisions or people? (Code live with a tally)	People challenge ideas, not each other	Disagreements get personal; silence replaces challenge
Speed of learning loops	Time between a problem flagged in review and adjusted behavior in the next session	Adjustments visible within one to two sessions	Same problems recur across multiple sessions
Standards enforcement	Do standards apply equally across status levels? (Use Exemption Tax audit criteria)	Consequences applied regardless of status	High-status exceptions increase; junior staff stop flagging
Retention and discretionary effort	Exit interviews and informal pulse checks	Voluntary retention stable; people invest beyond the minimum	Key staff leave; effort drops to contractual minimum

What matters: If these improve and performance doesn't, you still have something valuable—a healthier system that keeps adapting. If performance improves but these worsen, you may be winning unsustainably.

6.4 Succession-Proof the Culture

Culture durability is the test most organizations fail. The most common point of failure isn't resistance or resources—it's turnover. When the leader who carries the culture leaves, the informal norms leave with them. Unless those norms live in systems that run independently of any single person, the culture walks out the door.

This happens constantly. Coaching changes are among the most frequent disruptions in professional sport, and their impact depends on whether the culture was person-dependent or system-embedded before the transition (Galdino et al., 2021; Gómez et al., 2021). When culture belongs to the leader rather than the system, the gap between coaches becomes a period of unmonitored drift.

Succession-proofing addresses this by building redundancy: codified behaviors, documented decision rights, protected voice channels, and distributed leadership that doesn't depend on a single point of authority.

The "Boot Room" Versus the "Genius." Liverpool FC (1970s–1980s) dominated English football by promoting managers from within a small circle of coaches—the "Boot Room"—ensuring institutional knowledge survived transitions (Kelly, 2012). The culture lived in documented routines and shared decision norms, not in any single leader. The alternative model—culture built around a transformational figure—produces spectacular results while the figure is present and predictable regression when they leave. If the head coach leaves tomorrow, what survives?

6.4.1 Making Culture Transferable

Most culture knowledge lives in one person's head. When that person leaves, the next leader walks in blind and spends months guessing at rules everyone else already knows. The following tool eliminates that guessing.

BOX 6.8 TIMEOUT — THE CULTURE CONTINUITY DOCUMENT

Status: Practitioner heuristic drawing on succession planning and organizational learning frameworks (Levitt & March, 1988; Schein, 2010). Not a validated instrument.

What it is: A two- to three-page document that makes implicit culture standards explicit so they survive leadership transitions. A new coach, interim leader, or incoming staff member should be able to read it in 15 minutes and operate from it immediately.

When to build it: Before any coaching change, leadership transition, or major roster turnover. Ideally during a stable period—not a crisis. Update quarterly.

What feeds into it: Your culture hypothesis (Section 6.1), decision-rights documentation, behavioral standards, and reinforcement architecture.

The Four Sections

1. Non-Negotiable Behaviors (Five Max)

Write these as observable actions—things a fly on the wall would see, not values they'd have to infer. "Debriefs run after every match, win or loss, same agenda, same tone" passes the test. "We value accountability" doesn't—it's an abstraction that means different things to different people and gives an incoming leader nothing to enforce. If you can't describe what it looks like when it's happening, it's not a behavioral standard yet.

2. Decision Rights

Who decides what—selection, discipline, playing time, medical clearance, and spending. Clear enough that a new leader can operate immediately without guessing.

3. Voice Channels

How do concerns reach leadership? Which channels exist, who monitors them, and what protection is guaranteed? Include the Speed of Truth baseline so the incoming leader knows what "normal" looks like and can spot when something shifts.

4. Known Vulnerabilities

Where the culture is most likely to drift under pressure. Which exemptions exist and why. Where the reinforcement loop is weakest. This is the honest version—the information a successor needs that won't be captured in formal value statements.

Governance: Assign ownership to a role, not a person, so the document survives coaching changes. Review quarterly, tied to an existing calendar event (international break, midseason review). Each review asks one question: does this document still describe what actually happens? If the answer is no, the gap between the document and reality is your current culture drift.

6.4.2 *Distributed Leadership as Structural Redundancy*

A culture that depends on one leader has a single point of failure. Distributed leadership mitigates this by spreading standards enforcement and voice across multiple people, so that the departure of any one person does not collapse the system. Teams with multiple individuals occupying leadership functions demonstrate higher collective efficacy and greater resilience to disruption (Fransen et al., 2014; Leo et al., 2019), and the distribution pattern matters as much as the presence of leadership itself (Chamberlin et al., 2024).

Fransen et al.'s (2014) taxonomy provides a useful audit: the Task Leader drives performance standards, the Social Leader manages relational health, the External Leader interfaces with coaching staff and management, and the Motivational Leader sustains effort under adversity. Most teams over-invest in the first function and under-invest in the second—which means when the Task Leader departs, there is no relational infrastructure to absorb the shock.

Distribution requires more than nomination. It requires decision rights, protection, and clarity. Naming someone a "leader" without giving them the authority to enforce standards amounts to a symbolic gesture that rarely changes behavior. It must also account for informal influence. The veteran who holds no captaincy but sets the locker room temperature matters more than most people with titles. Succession-proofing means identifying those informal hubs and aligning them with the consequence structure before a transition hits.

6.4.3 *Managing Transitions: Coaching Changes and Performance Volatility*

The continuity document is the primary mechanism for surviving leadership transitions. Three additional practices strengthen the system during the vulnerable period between coaches.

First, identify and brief culture carriers—the two to three athletes and staff whose behavior the rest of the group watches for cues. They are not always the formal leaders. Brief them explicitly: here are the non-negotiables, and here is what we need you to hold. Second, protect voice channels. The interregnum is when athletes are most likely to suppress concerns; maintaining existing feedback mechanisms signals that voice will not be punished retroactively. Third, schedule a culture realignment meeting within the first two weeks of new leadership—not to impose the old culture, but to make the existing architecture visible so the new leader decides what to keep, modify, or replace from an informed position rather than from the impression the room gives in the first 48 hours.

Cultures should evolve—the goal is not immunity to change. It's preventing the transition gap from becoming unmonitored drift, where the loudest voices fill the vacuum and reinforcement loops quietly revert.

6.5 Context Adaptations

The principles in this chapter—reinforcement architecture, information flow, and decision rights—travel across sport contexts. The delivery mechanisms change; the logic does not. Table 6.6 maps the key adjustments.

Of the aforementioned adaptations, para-sport contexts are worth singling out. Classification–disclosure tension and access–equity audits across disability categories add structural diagnostic dimensions that mainstream frameworks often overlook, and where formal research on reinforcement architecture remains

TABLE 6.6 Context Adaptations—Key Adjustments by Setting

Context	*Primary Challenge*	*Culture Lever Adaptation*	*Diagnostic Priority*
National teams	Compression: short camps, limited contact time (Cruickshank & Collins 2012)	Portable constitution (one page); fixed debrief rhythm; decision rights documented before the squad assembles	Speed of Truth under time pressure
Individual sports	No team infrastructure; isolated athlete–coach dyads	Focus on information flow (injury disclosure, training feedback honesty) and return-to-play decision-rights clarity	Who holds final authority when medical judgment and competitive pressure collide?
Para-sport	Classification disputes affect opportunity; access varies across disability categories; visibility gap shapes resources	Add two diagnostic lines to the Culture Hypothesis: (1) classification–disclosure tension and (2) access–equity audit across disability categories	What reinforcement loop operates around the willingness to report changes in functional capacity?
Youth sport	Developmental identity; heightened power asymmetry; mandatory reporting thresholds	Sanctuary concept carries legal weight (Mountjoy et al., 2016); duty of care supersedes organizational politics; safeguarding obligations are non-negotiable	Is the system reinforcing identity breadth or identity foreclosure?
Cross-cultural	Structural differences in employment relationships, player power, and feedback norms	Adapt voice channel design and feedback delivery to cultural communication norms while maintaining non-negotiable behavioral standards	Where does the feedback loop break across cultural expectations?

limited. Practitioners working in these settings should document adaptations and outcomes systematically to contribute to an evidence base that does not yet exist.

6.5.1 *Chapter Synthesis*

Culture is built by consequences, not declarations—it is diagnosed and then redesigned by changing what gets reinforced rather than what gets messaged. Every unaddressed exemption, every ignored disclosure, and every inconsistent standard is building culture whether anyone intends it or not. The operating question for practitioners is not what culture do we want, but what culture are our consequences currently producing—and whether that answer survives the next leadership change. The standards and decision architecture embedded here become the inputs for Layer 5 (People Systems), where the organization translates stable culture into adaptive strategy under competitive pressure.

Key Chapter Takeaways

1. Culture is the consequence architecture currently running, not necessarily the one leadership intends. Diagnose it by mapping cue–behavior–consequence loops and tracking Speed of Truth across status levels before prescribing any intervention.
2. Culture change requires altering reinforcement, not just communicating values. Sequence change around seasonal demands, target consequences rather than attitudes, and use the wobble moment sequence to hold standards when pressure arrives.
3. Standards that exempt high-status individuals erode faster than standards that were never set. Apply the Exemption Tax: any deviation must be performance-based, transparent, and carry a reciprocal cost.
4. Culture survives leadership transitions only when it lives in systems, not in a single leader. Build structural redundancy through distributed leadership, codified decision rights, and a continuity document that makes the operating system transferable.
5. Leading indicators of culture shift are behavioral, not outcome-based. Track early issue reporting frequency, disagreement quality, and standards enforcement consistency—these precede performance results and detect drift before it compounds.

Discussion Questions

1. Map one reinforcement loop in your current environment using the cue–behavior–consequence framework. What consequence would you need to change, and what resistance would that change provoke from people who benefit from the current loop?

2. Design a wobble moment response for a specific pressure scenario in your context. What makes the 48-hour window after the trigger more diagnostic than the trigger itself?
3. If your head coach left tomorrow, what would survive and what would collapse? Use this to identify the single highest-priority item for a continuity document.

References

Allen, T. J. (1977). *Managing the flow of technology: Technology transfer and the dissemination of technological information within the R&D organization.* MIT Press.

Argyris, C. (1990). *Overcoming organizational defenses: Facilitating organizational learning.* Allyn & Bacon.

Bandura, A. (1977). *Social learning theory.* Prentice Hall.

Barsade, S. G. (2002). The ripple effect: Emotional contagion and its influence on group behavior. *Administrative Science Quarterly*, *47*(4), 644–675. https://doi.org/10.2307/3094912

Beer, M., & Nohria, N. (2000, May–June). Cracking the code of change. *Harvard Business Review*, *78*(3), 133–141. https://hbr.org/2000/05/cracking-the-code-of-change

Ben-Ari, R., Tsur, Y., & Har-Even, D. (2006). Procedural justice, stress appraisal, and athletes' attitudes. *International Journal of Stress Management*, *13*(1), 23–44. https://doi.org/10.1037/1072-5245.13.1.23

Bernstein, E. S., & Turban, S. (2018). The impact of the "open" workspace on human collaboration. *Philosophical Transactions of the Royal Society B: Biological Sciences*, *373*(1753), 20170239. https://doi.org/10.1098/rstb.2017.0239

Cameron, K. S., & Quinn, R. E. (2011). *Diagnosing and changing organizational culture: Based on the Competing Values Framework* (3rd ed.). Jossey-Bass.

Campion, M. A., Palmer, D. K., & Campion, J. E. (1997). A review of structure in the selection interview. *Personnel Psychology*, *50*(3), 655–702. https://doi.org/10.1111/j.1744-6570.1997.tb00709.x

Carron, A. V., Widmeyer, W. N., & Brawley, L. R. (1985). The development of an instrument to assess cohesion in sport teams: The Group Environment Questionnaire. *Journal of Sport Psychology*, *7*(3), 244–266. https://doi.org/10.1123/jsp.7.3.244

Chamberlin, M., Nahrgang, J. D., Sessions, H., & de Jong, B. (2024). An examination of shared leadership configurations and their effectiveness in teams. *Journal of Organizational Behavior*, *45*(4), 595–619. https://doi.org/10.1002/job.2774

Colquitt, J. A., Conlon, D. E., Wesson, M. J., Porter, C. O. L. H., & Ng, K. Y. (2001). Justice at the millennium: A meta-analytic review of 25 years of organizational justice research. *Journal of Applied Psychology*, *86*(3), 425–445. https://doi.org/10.1037/0021-9010.86.3.425

Cruickshank, A., & Collins, D. (2012). Culture change in elite sport performance teams: Examining and advancing effectiveness in the new era. *Journal of Applied Sport Psychology*, *24*(3), 338–355. https://doi.org/10.1080/10413200.2011.650819

Cruickshank, A., Collins, D., & Minten, S. (2014). Driving and sustaining culture change in Olympic sport performance teams: A first exploration and grounded theory. *Journal of Sport and Exercise Psychology*, *36*(1), 107–120. https://doi.org/10.1123/jsep.2013-0133

Deci, E. L., Koestner, R., & Ryan, R. M. (1999). A meta-analytic review of experiments examining the effects of extrinsic rewards on intrinsic motivation. *Psychological Bulletin*, *125*(6), 627–668. https://doi.org/10.1037/0033-2909.125.6.627

Dekker, S. W. A. (2012). *Just culture: Balancing safety and accountability* (2nd ed.). CRC Press. https://doi.org/10.4324/9781315251271

Edmondson, A. C. (1999). Psychological safety and learning behavior in work teams. *Administrative Science Quarterly*, *44*(2), 350–383. https://doi.org/10.2307/2666999

Feddersen, N. B., Morris, R., Littlewood, M., & Richardson, D. (2020). The emergence and perpetuation of a destructive culture in an elite sport in the United Kingdom. *Sport in Society*, *23*(6), 1004–1022. https://doi.org/10.1080/17430437.2019.1680639

Felps, W., Mitchell, T. R., & Byington, E. (2006). How, when, and why bad apples spoil the barrel: Negative group members and dysfunctional groups. *Research in Organizational Behavior*, *27*, 175–222. https://doi.org/10.1016/S0191-3085(06)27005-9

Fransen, K., Vanbeselaere, N., De Cuyper, B., Vande Broek, G., & Boen, F. (2014). The myth of the team captain as principal leader: Extending the athlete leadership classification within sport teams. *Journal of Sports Sciences*, *32*(14), 1389–1397. https://doi.org/10.1080/02640414.2014.891291

Galdino, M., Wicker, P., & Soebbing, B. P. (2021). Gambling with leadership succession in Brazilian football: Head coach turnovers and team performance. *Sport, Business and Management: An International Journal*, *11*(3), 245–264. https://doi.org/10.1108/SBM-06-2020-0059

Gómez, M. A., Lago-Peñas, C., Gómez, M.-T., Jiménez, S., & Leicht, A. S. (2021). Impact of elite soccer coaching change on team performance according to coach- and club-related variables. *Biology of Sport*, *38*(4), 603–608. https://doi.org/10.5114/biolsport.2021.101600

Haslam, S. A., Reicher, S. D., & Platow, M. J. (2011). *The new psychology of leadership: Identity, influence and power.* Psychology Press. https://doi.org/10.4324/9780203833896

Hattie, J., & Timperley, H. (2007). The power of feedback. *Review of Educational Research*, *77*(1), 81–112. https://doi.org/10.3102/003465430298487

Helmreich, R. L., Merritt, A. C., & Wilhelm, J. A. (1999). The evolution of crew resource management training in commercial aviation. *International Journal of Aviation Psychology*, *9*(1), 19–32. https://doi.org/10.1207/s15327108ijap0901_2

Hogan, R., & Hogan, J. (2001). Assessing leadership: A view from the dark side. *International Journal of Selection and Assessment*, *9*(1–2), 40–51. https://doi.org/10.1111/1468-2389.00162

Hollander, E. P. (1958). Conformity, status, and idiosyncrasy credit. *Psychological Review*, *65*(2), 117–127. https://doi.org/10.1037/h0042501

Jowett, S., Nascimento-Júnior, J. R. A. D., Zhao, C., & Gosai, J. (2023). Creating the conditions for psychological safety and its impact on quality coach-athlete relationships. *Psychology of Sport and Exercise*, *65*, 102363. https://doi.org/10.1016/j.psychsport.2022.102363

Kegan, R., & Lahey, L. L. (2009). *Immunity to change: How to overcome it and unlock the potential in yourself and your organization.* Harvard Business Press.

Keiser, N. L., & Arthur, W., Jr. (2021). A meta-analysis of the effectiveness of the after-action review (or debrief) and factors that influence its effectiveness. *Journal of Applied Psychology*, *106*(7), 1007–1032. https://doi.org/10.1037/apl0000821

Kelly, S. F. (2012). *The boot room boys: The unseen story of Anfield's Boot Room.* HarperSport.

Kerr, J. (2013). *Legacy: What the All Blacks can teach us about the business of life.* Constable.

Kotter, J. P. (1995, March–April). Leading change: Why transformation efforts fail. *Harvard Business Review*, *73*(2), 59–67. https://hbr.org/1995/05/leading-change-why-transformation-efforts-fail-2

Kristof-Brown, A. L., Zimmerman, R. D., & Johnson, E. C. (2005). Consequences of individuals' fit at work: A meta-analysis of person–job, person–organization, person–group, and person–supervisor fit. *Personnel Psychology*, *58*(2), 281–342. https://doi.org/10.1111/j.1744-6570.2005.00672.x

Leo, F. M., García-Calvo, T., González-Ponce, I., Pulido, J. J., & Fransen, K. (2019). How many leaders does it take to lead a sports team? The relationship between the number of leaders and the effectiveness of professional sports teams. *PLOS ONE, 14*(6), e0218167. https://doi.org/10.1371/journal.pone.0218167

Levashina, J., Hartwell, C. J., Morgeson, F. P., & Campion, M. A. (2014). The structured employment interview: Narrative and quantitative review of the research literature. *Personnel Psychology, 67*(1), 241–293. https://doi.org/10.1111/peps.12052

Leventhal, G. S. (1980). What should be done with equity theory? New approaches to the study of fairness in social relationships. In K. J. Gergen, M. S. Greenberg, & R. H. Willis (Eds.), *Social exchange: Advances in theory and research* (pp. 27–55). Plenum Press. https://doi.org/10.1007/978-1-4613-3087-5_2

Levitt, B., & March, J. G. (1988). Organizational learning. *Annual Review of Sociology, 14*, 319–340. https://doi.org/10.1146/annurev.so.14.080188.001535

Meyer, E. (2014). *The culture map: Breaking through the invisible boundaries of global business.* PublicAffairs.

Morrison, E. W. (2011). Employee voice behavior: Integration and directions for future research. *Academy of Management Annals, 5*(1), 373–412. https://doi.org/10.1080/19416520.2011.574506

Mountjoy, M., Brackenridge, C., Arrington, M., Blauwet, C., Carska-Sheppard, A., Fasting, K., Kirby, S., Leahy, T., Marks, S., Martin, K., Starr, K., Tiivas, A., & Budgett, R. (2016). International Olympic Committee consensus statement: Harassment and abuse (non-accidental violence) in sport. *British Journal of Sports Medicine, 50*(17), 1019–1029. https://doi.org/10.1136/bjsports-2016-096121

Nembhard, I. M., & Edmondson, A. C. (2006). Making it safe: The effects of leader inclusiveness and professional status on psychological safety and improvement efforts in health care teams. *Journal of Organizational Behavior, 27*(7), 941–966. https://doi.org/10.1002/job.413

Reason, J. (1997). *Managing the risks of organizational accidents.* Ashgate. https://doi.org/10.4324/9781315543543

Rice, S., Walton, C. C., Pilkington, V., Gwyther, K., Olive, L. S., Lloyd, M., Kountouris, A., Butterworth, M., Clements, M., & Purcell, R. (2022). Psychological safety in elite sport settings: A psychometric study of the Sport Psychological Safety Inventory. *BMJ Open Sport & Exercise Medicine, 8*(2), e001251. https://doi.org/10.1136/bmjsem-2021-001251

Rivera, L. A. (2012). Hiring as cultural matching: The case of elite professional service firms. *American Sociological Review, 77*(6), 999–1022. https://doi.org/10.1177/0003122412463213

Schein, E. H. (2010). *Organizational culture and leadership* (4th ed.). Jossey-Bass.

Skinner, B. F. (1953). *Science and human behavior.* Macmillan.

Tannenbaum, S. I., & Cerasoli, C. P. (2013). Do team and individual debriefs enhance performance? A meta-analysis. *Human Factors, 55*(1), 231–245. https://doi.org/10.1177/0018720812448394

Tepper, B. J. (2000). Consequences of abusive supervision. *Academy of Management Journal, 43*(2), 178–190. https://doi.org/10.2307/1556375

Vaughan, D. (1996). *The Challenger launch decision: Risky technology, culture, and deviance at NASA.* University of Chicago Press. https://doi.org/10.7208/chicago/9780226851785.001.0001

Westrum, R. (2004). A typology of organizational cultures. *Quality and Safety in Health Care, 13*(Suppl 2), ii22–ii27. https://doi.org/10.1136/qshc.2003.009522

7

TRANSITIONS—SUPPORTING ATHLETES THROUGH CAREER-DEFINING MOMENTS

Learning Objectives

By the end of this chapter, the reader will be able to:

1. Evaluate an organization's transition readiness across five diagnostic domains—awareness, resources, protocols, culture, and integration—using the Transition Support Audit framework.
2. Apply Schlossberg's 4 S's model to diagnose which factor is weakest for a specific athlete in transition and direct intervention accordingly.
3. Distinguish between threat appraisal and challenge appraisal in rookie integration and design onboarding protocols that shift the balance toward challenge.
4. Analyze how the contribution paradox and identity foreclosure interact to produce veteran disengagement, and design role-change interventions that make mentorship measurable.

BOX 7.1 CASE STUDY

The Player Liaison Who Stopped Checking In

Composite vignette. Details changed to protect privacy.

Deepa was the player liaison officer—hired specifically to manage transitions. She ran the 30/60/90-day check-ins. She knew which new signings

DOI: 10.4324/9781003631217-8

were eating alone, which returning players were avoiding the gym, and which veterans had gone quiet after losing their starting spot.

When Marcus, a 10-year veteran, was told his role would change from starter to rotation player, Deepa flagged the transition risk immediately and scheduled a check-in. The coaching staff canceled it. "He's a professional. He'll handle it." She rescheduled. Canceled again. "We can't be seen coddling a senior player."

Marcus handled it the way athletes handle most things when no one asks: alone. He trained hard. Said the right things in the press. Stopped speaking in team meetings. Stopped mentoring the two younger players who had looked to him all season. One asked Deepa privately: "Is Marcus okay? He won't even look at us." The response: "He's adjusting. Give him space."

Eight weeks later, Marcus confronted the head coach publicly after being left out of a cup squad. The exchange was overheard by players and a member of the media team. By evening, a reporter had the story. Marcus was fined and suspended. Two young players who had watched the sequence—flagging concern got you ignored, emotion got you punished—went silent for the rest of the season.

The end-of-season review cited "poor leadership from senior players" and recommended a new captain structure. Nobody examined why the system designed to catch role transitions had been overridden three times. Nobody asked about Deepa.

7.1 The Transition Framework

Principle: Transitions become crises not because of the event itself, but because the system lacks the resources to meet the demand. This chapter sits within the People Systems layer of the HPCOS architecture (Figure 7.1), answering Question 5: are we listening—and using what we hear?

Every transition in this chapter—rookie arrival, veteran role change, injury, and mental health crisis—activates the silence calculus. The rookie is calculating whether to ask a question. The veteran is deciding whether to name frustration. The injured athlete is weighing whether to disclose fear. They are all running the same cost–benefit analysis: is honesty safe here? Transitions are when this calculus runs hottest, because the athlete's position in the system is actively uncertain.

Schlossberg's (1981) model of human adaptation to transition provides the diagnostic scaffold. It identifies four factors—the "4 S's"—that shape how well a person copes (Table 7.1).

FIGURE 7.1 You Are Here—People Systems.

The HPCOS seven-layer architecture with Layer 5 (People Systems) highlighted. This chapter starts to answer Question 5—are we listening, and using what we hear?—by designing athlete-facing systems for high-risk transitions: onboarding, role change, deselection, injury, mental health escalation, and post-exit support.

The weakest S is where intervention should focus first. For a rookie, that is often Support—no mentor, no one translating the unwritten rules. For a veteran, it may be Situation—the role change has not been named. We return to the 4 S's in the chapter-closing transition audit (Section 7.6).

Transitions in total institutions have long been recognized as periods of acute psychological vulnerability (Goffman, 1961). Structured transition support is standard in other high-stakes industries—the U.S. military's Transition Assistance Program (Kamarck, 2024), aviation's crew resource management protocols (Helmreich et al., 1999)—because transition moments are when failures produce the most damage.

Elite sport has been slower to build comparable infrastructure (Stambulova et al., 2009; Voorheis et al., 2023). The willpower is often there. The architecture usually is not.

TABLE 7.1 Schlossberg's 4 S's—Diagnostic Definitions

Factor	*Core Question*	*What to Assess*
Situation	What is happening, and what is outside the athlete's control?	Expected or sudden? Voluntary or imposed? Timing, trigger, duration, and prior experience with similar transitions.
Self	What identity resources and risks does the athlete carry?	Does the athlete's sense of self depend entirely on playing, or is there breadth? Psychological flexibility, coping history, and identity foreclosure risk.
Support	Who is safe, present, and available?	Access to mentors, welfare leads, trusted peers, and external resources. Quality of relationships, not just existence.
Strategies	What coping routines and skills are currently working?	Does the athlete have ways to manage uncertainty, or are they improvising under pressure? Active coping versus avoidance.

7.2 Rookie Integration

Every rookie remembers the same thing about their first week: not the drills, not the playbook, but the social map. Who made eye contact? Who explained jargon without being asked? Who looked through them? The hardest part of the jump to professional sport is rarely tactical. It is the weight of interpreting normal struggle as evidence of not belonging—and that failure belongs to the organization, not the athlete.

Principle: The system's first impression determines whether a new athlete learns to use voice or learns to self-protect. The burden of proof sits with the organization. The move is not removing rookie pressure—it is increasing perceived resources (role clarity, mentorship, psychological safety, and predictable feedback) until the athlete's appraisal flips from threat to challenge.

7.2.1 Mechanism: Threat Versus Challenge

Rookie integration is a threat appraisal problem disguised as onboarding. In week 1, a rookie runs two playbooks: the tactical one the staff teaches, and the social one nobody says out loud. Every correction, joke, and eye-roll becomes data about consequences. When the first public mistake earns humiliation, the system gets silence—and silence costs learning time (Edmondson, 1999; Newman et al., 2017).

The line practitioners hear most often: "I just don't want to be the problem." It sounds humble, but it is a threat signal. The athlete is already optimizing for not being noticed—fewer risks, fewer questions, and small issues hidden until they become big ones.

BOX 7.2 TIMEOUT

"I Don't Want to be the Problem" Is the Problem

When a rookie says this, they are not being humble—they are reporting threat. The system has already taught them that visibility is dangerous, so they are optimizing for invisibility: fewer questions, smaller risks, and hidden struggles. If the first thing an organization hears from a new athlete is compliance dressed as modesty, the integration protocol has already failed its first test. Humility is not the goal. Approach behavior is.

Stress is not binary. What matters is the athlete's appraisal of demands versus resources (Blascovich & Tomaka, 1996; Jones et al., 2009). When demands feel bigger, the system shifts toward threat—more self-protection, less learning. When resources feel sufficient, the same pressure becomes a challenge.

Psychological safety (Edmondson, 1999) determines whether rookies use voice or default to silence. The test is concrete: will asking for clarification cost playing time? Standard workplace psychological safety measures were not designed for elite sport's unique pressures; recent psychometric work has begun developing sport-specific alternatives (Lundqvist et al., 2025). Figure 7.2 maps this feedback loop.

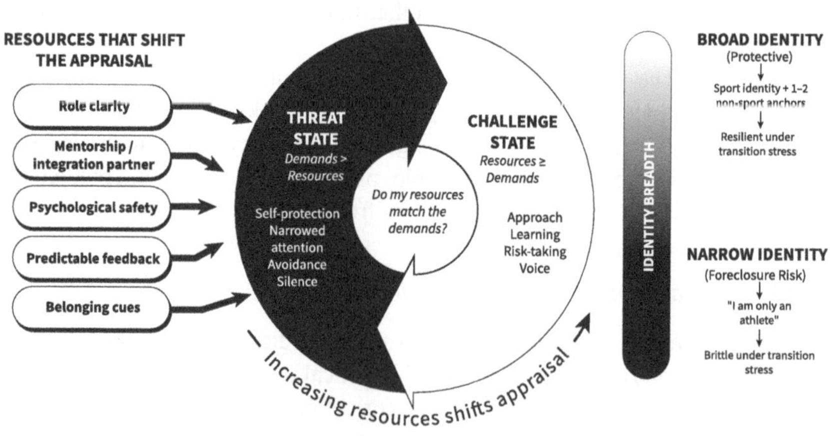

FIGURE 7.2 Rookie Integration Loop: From Threat to Challenge.

How a rookie's appraisal shifts from threat (self-protection) to challenge (approach behavior) as the system provides belonging cues, predictable feedback, and identity breadth. Based on challenge–threat appraisal theory (Blascovich & Tomaka, 1996).

Threat compounds for athletes navigating multiple identity pressures. The impostor phenomenon—the persistent internal experience of fraudulence despite objective evidence of competence (Clance & Imes, 1978)—is common in high-achieving populations (Bravata et al., 2020) and intensifies under compound threat. A rookie who is one of the few athletes of color on a roster faces performance scrutiny plus identity scrutiny, and the perceived cost of mistakes rises when the athlete believes errors will be attributed to group membership rather than individual learning (Steele & Aronson, 1995; Beamon, 2012). Organizations that rely on "culture" to do the work of belonging without examining whose culture is being reproduced will under-serve athletes at these intersections. Belonging cues are not identity-neutral—the micro-moments that signal inclusion for a majority-group athlete may not register the same way for an athlete monitoring for bias.

7.2.2 Identity Breadth as a Resilience Mechanism

One hidden risk—and one of the most consequential—is athletic identity foreclosure: commitment without exploration (Marcia, 1966). Foreclosure drives short-term performance but makes transitions brittle. Injury, deselection, or role change becomes identity collapse rather than a performance problem (Brewer et al., 1993; Edison et al., 2021). The protective move is building a diversified identity on purpose—one or two non-sport anchors that still exist when training is removed. The predictable objection: identity breadth sounds like distraction. Athletes with diversified identity handle setbacks as performance problems rather than existential crises (Brewer et al., 1993) and show better post-career adjustment (Barth et al., 2021). This mechanism recurs across every transition type in this chapter; it is introduced here because the window to build identity breadth opens widest at entry.

7.2.3 Whose Transition Is It?

Partners and families are also undergoing a transition—relocation, social disruption, and role uncertainty—and their adjustment shapes the athlete's coping capacity. Integration protocols should include partner orientation where feasible: one named point of contact, practical settlement information, and a check-in at 30 days. The 30/60/90-day framework (Table 7.2) can accommodate this without significant additional resources.

Cultural transitions add another layer. International athletes face performance pressure plus cultural adaptation, and practical settlement support often determines whether the first 30 days are spent adapting to the performance environment or managing survival needs (Hirose & Meijen, 2022).

7.2.4 Protocol and Markers

Markers to track: days to first unsolicited question in a team setting; 30-day self-ratings on role clarity and belonging; integration partner check-in completion; and early disclosure of confusion or struggle—approach behavior, not compliance. Table 7.2 consolidates these into a 30/60/90-day check-in structure.

7.3 Veteran Transitions: Role Evolution and the Contribution Paradox

Principle: The system's promises get tested when an athlete's value changes. Veterans built the culture that current athletes benefit from—the organization carries a debt for that contribution. How the organization treats declining value teaches every athlete on the roster what "we value you" actually means.

TABLE 7.2 Rookie Integration Protocol—30/60/90-Day Quick Reference

Checkpoint	*Prompts*	*Markers to Track*	*Red Flag*
Day 30	Role clarity: "Can you describe your role and what's expected this week?" Belonging: "Who would you go to if something felt off?" Identity: "What's one thing outside sport that still has your attention?"	Self-ratings on role clarity and belonging; integration partner check-in completed; at least one unsolicited question in a team setting.	Athlete cannot name one safe person; has not asked a question publicly; reports confusion about role.
Day 60	Progress: "What's making more sense now than it did a month ago?" Voice: "Have you raised a concern or asked for help—and how did it land?" Connection: "How are things outside training?"	Shift from compliance to approach behavior; help-seeking instances; partner/family settling indicators (if applicable).	Athlete still optimizing for invisibility; no evidence of voice; non-sport life unaddressed.
Day 90	Integration: "Do you feel like you belong here—and what would make that more true?" Development: "What do you need from us that you're not getting?"	Belonging self-report stabilized; early disclosure of struggle occurring without prompting; performance trajectory consistent with learning curve, not threat suppression.	Persistent "I don't want to be the problem" framing; avoidance of feedback settings; identity narrowing rather than broadening.

BOX 7.3 SKEPTIC'S CORNER

"We Don't Have Time for a 90-Day Onboarding Program"

The objection: "We are in a compressed season. We don't have time for onboarding hand-holding." The answer: This is not a 90-day program. It is three structured conversations and one named person—approximately two hours of staff time over three months. The alternative—an unintegrated athlete who self-protects, hides mistakes, and delays development—costs significantly more.

What to try anyway: Pair one incoming athlete with an integration partner this week. Schedule a 30-day check-in with three prompts: role clarity, belonging, and one non-sport anchor. Track whether the athlete asks a question in a meeting before day 30.

BOX 7.4 TIMEOUT

Adapting for Youth Athletes

These protocols were developed for adult professional athletes. Youth contexts require substantive adaptation, not just scaling down: identity foreclosure is developmentally normative in mid-adolescence (Marcia, 1966), power asymmetry between a 16-year-old and adult coaches is substantially greater, and mandatory reporting thresholds change the confidentiality calculus. When in doubt, default to safeguarding.

7.3.1 The Pattern

Veteran transitions are when the organization proves whether "we are so lucky to have you" survives peak performance. When the change goes unnamed and dignity goes unprotected, athletes fill the silence with shame—and the whole roster notices.

At its core, this is status grief—non-finite loss triggered by ongoing changes in role, capacity, or standing (Bruce & Schultz, 2001). In sport, this manifests as rank collapse: the athlete experiences role reduction as a public verdict on declining worth. Left unspoken, the pattern shows up as defensiveness, withdrawal, or passive resistance.

The psychological sequence is predictable: first doubts, seeking alternatives, turning points, creating an ex-role (Ebaugh, 1988). When the demands of the transition exceed available resources, a normative process becomes a crisis (Stambulova et al., 2009). Athletes with identity breadth (see Section 7.2.2) and a concrete plan recover faster (Barth et al., 2021; Lavallee, 2005). Barth et al. analyzed over 2,000 retired professional soccer players across 17 studies—predominantly male—and found that around half reported involuntary retirement, with forced or unplanned exits producing worse outcomes.

This pattern also produces the contribution paradox: the organization asks the veteran to mentor the next wave, but without defining, protecting, training, or rewarding that work. The term is a practitioner-derived label for a pattern documented across knowledge management (DeLong, 2004), mentoring research (Kram, 1985), and developmental psychology (Erikson, 1950). What makes it distinct in sport is the public visibility of the replacement—the veteran watches their successor take the field while being asked to accelerate the process. The emotional core is legacy anxiety—what am I if I am not starting?—which intensifies when the only identity the system has rewarded is "starter."

In Schlossberg's terms, the Situation is ambiguous, and the Strategies are untested. Marcus, in the opening case study, illustrates the full sequence: the role change was visible to everyone, named by no one, and the system designed to catch it was overridden three times.

Without a legacy pathway, the veteran cannot find meaning in declining physical output, and the result is stagnation, withdrawal, or passive resistance. The organization's obligation is proportional to what it extracted: protected time, training, role clarity, and a clear future pathway keep mentorship from feeling like supervised obsolescence (DeLong, 2004; Kram, 1985; Voorheis et al., 2023).

7.3.2 Managing Veteran Role Changes

Most of the damage in veteran transitions happens in the gap between what the organization knows is coming and what it says out loud. Silence forces the veteran to interpret the change alone, usually in the worst possible light. The following protocol is derived from role exit theory (Ebaugh, 1988), career transition research (Stambulova et al., 2009), and knowledge management literature (DeLong, 2004). The sequence matters.

Step 1. Name the change. Have a private conversation before the athlete has to guess. This is a planning conversation, not a verdict. Framing that tends to land well: "Your value here is bigger than minutes. I want to plan how we use your strengths now and prepare for what is next." That works when genuine co-design comes next. *Signal it is working:* the athlete can articulate the new role and timeline without filling in the blanks themselves.

Step 2. Protect the public narrative. Script how the transition is communicated to the team. Define the veteran's value in the new role publicly. *Signal it is working:* the veteran is not learning the organization's messaging in real time.

Step 3. Offer agency. Co-design the new role—leadership responsibilities, specialist minutes, mentorship, and transition planning. The athlete chooses the direction. *Signal it is working:* the role feels like contribution, not assignment.

Step 4. Make mentorship measurable. Document metrics: mentee milestones, knowledge-transfer goals, and developmental benchmarks. This is where most organizations lose credibility. Mentorship gets announced with enthusiasm and tracked with nothing. If the system rewards performance metrics and ignores developmental ones, the veteran reads the incentive structure accurately. When the role is invisible, veterans read it as demotion. *Signal it is working:* mentorship is tracked with the same rigor as performance data.

Step 5. Build mentorship conditions. Protected time, mentorship training, and a clear understanding of the veteran's own future pathway. *Signal it is working:* the veteran is not doing two jobs with resources for neither.

Step 6. Reduce competing demands. When mentorship responsibilities are added, other expectations decrease. *Signal it is working:* evaluation criteria reflect the actual role, not the old one.

Step 7. Design the exit role. Coaching pathway, ambassador role, education, and second-career support—planned with the same rigor as succession. *Signal it is working:* a post-role pathway exists on paper and is revisited on a set cadence.

Markers to track: veteran engagement in meetings, mentor–mentee satisfaction, reduction in passive resistance behaviors, and clarity ratings on role definition. A minimum-viable entry point: identify one veteran whose role is shifting this month, schedule a private conversation, write a one-page role definition, and attach one measurable contribution metric.

7.3.3 Planned Retirement

When retirement is anticipated, the emotional terrain differs from managed role change. The dominant experience is anticipatory grief—the athlete mourns a loss that has not occurred while still performing. Staff who misread this as "distraction" miss the complexity: the athlete is simultaneously playing for legacy and processing loss (Stambulova, 2003; Barth et al., 2021).

Start early—well before the final season—and treat career development as a performance-support function, not an exit problem (Voorheis et al., 2023).

7.3.4 Deselection and Involuntary Exit

Not every veteran transition is gradual. Deselection—being cut, waived, and not re-signed—is among the most psychologically acute transitions in professional sport and the one organizations are least likely to have a protocol for.

The appraisal dynamics differ from managed role change. A deselected athlete loses organizational membership, daily structure, and purpose at once. In

Schlossberg's terms, all four S's can collapse simultaneously. Social exclusion is not only psychologically painful—it measurably impairs self-regulation, persistence, and impulse control (Baumeister et al., 2005). The athlete's capacity to make sound decisions in the hours after the news is diminished by the news itself, which is part of why the 48-hour welfare contact (Table 7.3) is structural rather than pastoral. The triage question shifts from which factor is weakest to which can be restored fastest—usually support: a named welfare contact and a scheduled follow-up call.

Athletes who perceive the process as procedurally fair report less distress than those who experience deselection as arbitrary (Colquitt, 2001; Stambulova, 2003). Athletes can accept "you are not in our plans" far more readily than discovering the news through a press release or silence.

BOX 7.5 TIMEOUT

Exits Are Auditions The Organization Doesn't Know It's Giving

Every athlete on the roster is watching when someone gets cut. The question they are answering is not "Was that fair?"–it is "What happens to me when my value drops?" If the answer is ghosting, leaked decisions, and no follow-up, the roster learns that voice is a liability and self-protection is rational. Deselection protocols are not charity for departing athletes. They are trust infrastructure for the athletes who remain.

The goal is not to make deselection painless—it is to ensure that it is delivered with dignity, practical support, and follow-up (Table 7.3).

7.4 Injury Rehabilitation

Principle: When the system loses control of an athlete's trajectory, the default is erasure. Treat rehabilitation as dual-track: physical recovery and identity recovery.

7.4.1 Mechanism

Injury is a transition imposed, not chosen. It removes routine, status, and the daily proof of competence—sometimes overnight. Athletes frequently describe injury as "being erased" from the performance narrative. That description is more literal than metaphorical: social exclusion activates the same neural

TABLE 7.3 Deselection Protocol—Quick Reference

Step	*Action*	*Signal It Is Working*
1. Deliver the news directly	In person, privately, before it becomes public. Be specific about what drove the decision: roster construction, salary dynamics, performance trajectory. "We're going in a different direction" without specifics reads as disrespect.	The athlete heard the decision from leadership first—not from media, teammates, or a revised roster sheet.
2. Plan the 48 hours after	Script in advance: who communicates what to the team, when facility access changes, who checks in, and what practical transition support is available—career counseling, agent access, and mental health referral.	First 48 hours are managed, not improvised. The athlete is not navigating logistics alone.
3. Offer a clean goodbye	Some athletes want to address teammates; others want to leave quietly. Ask, and honor the answer.	Departure happens on the athlete's terms within organizational constraints.
4. Follow up at two and four weeks	Deselection is a known risk period for mental health deterioration (Grove et al., 1997), and the athletes most at risk are often the least likely to reach out.	Welfare contact confirms connection at both check-ins; athlete knows the door is still open.

circuitry as physical pain (Eisenberger et al., 2003), which is why isolation from team rhythms during rehab is itself a clinical variable, not a peripheral concern.

What practitioners observe is grief plus uncertainty, compounding in real time. The dual-process model (Stroebe & Schut, 1999)—oscillation between processing loss and rebuilding daily life—maps the territory better than stage models: the athlete is simultaneously grieving and recovering. When injury ends a career, the grief shifts from oscillatory to non-finite (Bruce & Schultz, 2001)—and the intervention must shift with it.

Self-determination theory explains much of what practitioners observe. When injury strips autonomy, competence, and relatedness, motivation drops, and mental health risk climbs (Ryan & Deci, 2000, 2017). The integrated model of psychological response to sport injury (Wiese-Bjornstal et al., 1998) confirms that identical injuries produce very different psychological trajectories—the injury is the same; the meaning is not (Golub & Steinfeldt, 2025). A rehab plan that restores control, mastery, and connection is doing mental health work whether anyone calls it that or not.

Injury is where identity foreclosure (see Section 7.2.2) becomes expensive. When an athlete's identity is exclusively tied to performance, injury is not "time out"—it is something closer to identity collapse. Even a single stable non-sport anchor can reduce the sense that injury equals erasure (Brewer et al., 1993; Beamon, 2012).

7.4.2 Four-Phase Psychological Rehabilitation Protocol

Use this when an athlete experiences a moderate-to-severe injury (or any injury that threatens identity, role, or selection status).

Goal: Provide a predictable psychological structure alongside the physical plan, so the athlete stays connected, in control, and supported. The protocol is derived from the integrated model of psychological response to sport injury (Wiese-Bjornstal et al., 1998), self-determination theory (Ryan & Deci, 2000, 2017), and return-to-sport readiness research (Ardern et al., 2013, 2016). In individual sports, rehabilitation support may need external coordination; treat it as a framework for clinical reasoning, not a rigid sequence. Table 7.4 maps the four phases.

Leader behaviors: Name the dual-track reality explicitly: "We rehab the body and the mind. Both are expected." Preserve relatedness—keep the athlete inside team routines. Build micro-mastery by replacing "I can't" with near-term controllables. Protect autonomy by offering choices wherever possible. Escalate early when risk markers appear: severe hopelessness, self-harm cues, disordered eating, substance misuse, or inability to function requires clinical escalation.

Metrics/markers: Check-in completion at phase transitions; athlete self-report of connection, control, and confidence; help-seeking and early disclosure of fear or frustration; and return-to-play confidence calibration (appropriate caution, not avoidance or recklessness).

7.4.3 Return to Play and Reintegration

Return-to-play readiness is not only physical. Psychological readiness shapes return-to-sport behavior independently of tissue healing (Ardern et al., 2013, 2016; Podlog & Eklund, 2006). Coach check-in prompts: "What movement are you most worried about?" and "Who will you go to if fear spikes?" Reintegration is its own transition—clarify role, normalize early errors, and debrief after first competitive exposure.

A minimum-viable entry point for any injured athlete: add one scheduled psychological check-in to the rehab plan. Ask: "What feels hardest right now—control, confidence, or connection?" Adjust the support plan accordingly.

TABLE 7.4 Four-Phase Psychological Rehabilitation Protocol

Phase	*Physical Focus*	*Psychological Interventions (Minimum Viable)*
Phase 1: Acute response	Diagnosis, pain control, and immediate stabilization	Validate emotions; clarify the plan; establish communication cadence; preserve dignity (privacy, information boundaries).
Phase 2: Rehab grind	Strength, mobility, conditioning, and skill reintroduction	Build micro-goals; track progress; address threat narratives using defusion techniques—naming the thought as a thought rather than a fact (Gardner & Moore, 2007; Hayes et al., 2012); maintain team connection; develop identity breadth. With athlete consent, orient partner, or family: expected timeline, emotional patterns, and one point of contact.
Phase 3: Return to play	Sport-specific load, exposure, controlled competition	Graded exposure to feared movements; confidence calibration; ACT-based acceptance when fear produces avoidance (Gardner & Moore, 2007); re-script setbacks as information; clear return criteria to reduce uncertainty.
Phase 4: Reintegration	Full training load, role reintegration	Rebuild role clarity; address "I am behind" narratives; restore competitive identity without over-functioning; monitor mental health for delayed reactions.

7.4.4 Career-Ending Injury

When an injury ends a career, the transition becomes identity reconstruction. Leader actions (minimum viable): coordinate the message across medical, coaching, and welfare. Create a transition meeting to plan the next two weeks. Offer closure options and protect practical stability—contracts, benefits, education, and career development. A career-ending injury should not become organizational disappearance.

7.5 Mental Health Systems: Athlete Voice and Duty of Care

Principle: The hardest transition is the one the athlete must choose to reveal. Athletes disclose when they believe they will be helped and not punished. "Voice" requires infrastructure—clear roles, safe channels, confidentiality boundaries, and a rehearsed duty-of-care response—and structural power: the ability to shape the systems that affect them, not just permission to speak.

7.5.1 *Why Athletes Don't Speak*

Mental health advocacy is a system design problem under pressure: when an athlete is afraid, ashamed, or trapped, will the organization make it rational to speak? The barriers are well-documented: stigma, lack of mental health literacy, and negative past experiences with providers (Confectioner et al., 2021; Gulliver et al., 2012).

Help-seeking barriers are not identity-neutral. LGBTQ+ athletes face a double-disclosure problem: seeking support may require revealing both psychological distress and stigmatized aspects of identity (Symons et al., 2017). Athletes from cultural backgrounds where mental health is more heavily stigmatized face additional barriers (Reardon et al., 2019; Schinke et al., 2018). In men's professional sport, masculine norms around stoicism and self-reliance are frequently identified as help-seeking barriers (Gulliver et al., 2012; Rice et al., 2016). Build reporting channels that offer diversity in providers, not only in access points.

The IOC consensus statement calls for clear identification, referral, and care pathways (Reardon et al., 2019), and Purcell et al. (2019) call for early intervention frameworks—but screening without a clear referral pathway increases disclosure without increasing safety.

The core tension is confidentiality versus duty of care. Athletes will not disclose if they believe information will travel to selectors; leaders still have non-negotiable duties when there is risk to life or safety. Set clear role boundaries and explicit escalation criteria before the first disclosure moment—not after.

Confidentiality infrastructure addresses the procedural dimension, but athletes are employees in precarious roles where the people they must disclose to often control playing time and contracts. A reporting channel that runs through an organization where athletes have no grievance process, no union representation, and no independent advocate operates at reduced trust, regardless of design quality. The Transition Support Audit (Section 7.6) can surface this gap even when the organization cannot close it immediately.

BOX 7.6 PSYCHOLOGY SIDELINES WITH DR. MCB — THE FIRST DISCLOSURE IS ALWAYS A TEST

The first time an athlete discloses a mental health concern, they are not asking for help. They are running an experiment.

The hypothesis: *If I say something, will it be used against me?* The athlete has already mapped the room—who talks to the coach, who keeps confidences, and who treats vulnerability as weakness. They have watched what happened to the last person who said something honest. The disclosure is not the beginning of the process. It is the result of weeks or months of surveillance.

What I see clinically is that the window is narrow and non-repeating. If the first response is a referral that moves at the speed of bureaucracy, or a well-meaning "let me talk to the coach," the experiment has produced its result. The athlete does not come back angry. They come back managed—saying the right things, performing wellness, and routing their distress somewhere the system cannot see it.

The intervention that matters most is not the treatment plan. It is the first 60 seconds. The person who receives the disclosure does not need clinical training. They need one skill: the ability to stay in role without overreaching. Acknowledge. Do not diagnose. Connect to the right person the same day—not next week, not when there is an opening. Same day. The athlete is watching the clock, and every hour of silence confirms the hypothesis they were already testing.

Organizations build disclosure pathways on paper. Athletes test them in practice. The two versions rarely match.

7.5.2 How a Disclosure Moves Through the System

To make role boundaries concrete, consider how a single disclosure travels. A midfielder tells a strength coach after a session: "I've been having panic attacks before games. I don't want anyone to know."

What should happen: The strength coach stays in role—no diagnosing, no probing for clinical detail, and no promises they can't guarantee: "I'm glad you told me. I'm going to connect you with our welfare lead today—they'll keep this as private as possible. This won't go to the coaching staff unless there's a safety concern."

The welfare lead meets with the athlete the same day and explains the confidentiality boundary: "What you share stays between us and the clinician unless there is risk to your safety or someone else's. Coaching staff will only be told what they need to manage your availability—not the reason."

If referred, the clinician assesses and treats. Functional recommendations stay functional: "Player X needs a modified schedule this week" is sufficient. "Player X has panic disorder" is not.

What should not happen: The strength coach tells the head coach at dinner, who pulls the athlete aside. The athlete concludes that disclosure travels instantly and stops talking. Table 7.5 maps each role's correct action against the most common failure.

TABLE 7.5 Disclosure Pathway—Role Boundaries

Role	*Correct Action*	*Common Failure*	*Why It Matters*
First contact (e.g., strength coach, teammate, and analyst)	Acknowledge, do not diagnose or probe. Connect to welfare lead the same day. Make no confidentiality promises you can't keep.	Tells head coach informally; probes for clinical detail; promises total secrecy, then can't deliver.	The first response teaches the athlete—and every future observer—whether disclosure is safe.
Welfare lead	Meet the same day. Explain the confidentiality boundary and its limits. Coordinate referral if needed. Share only functional information with coaching staff.	Delays contact; shares clinical detail with selectors; treats the disclosure as a performance management issue.	The welfare lead is the trust bottleneck. If this role leaks, the entire channel shuts down.
Clinician	Assess and treat. Provide functional recommendations only ("modified schedule this week"), not diagnostic labels.	Shares diagnosis with coaching staff; frames recommendations in clinical language that identify the condition.	"Player X has panic disorder" travels differently than "Player X needs a modified schedule." The distinction protects the athlete's future disclosure willingness.
Coaching staff	Receive functional availability information only. Do not seek the underlying reason. Adjust plans accordingly.	Pulls the athlete aside to "check in" based on leaked information; treats modified availability as evidence of weakness.	When coaches know more than they should, athletes learn that disclosure has selection consequences—and stop talking.

7.5.3 Reporting Infrastructure

Six operational priorities anchor the reporting infrastructure. Table 7.6 provides an implementation checklist with minimum viable versions for each.

Minimum-viable channel: An anonymous web form or hotline, owned by the welfare lead (independent of selection), with a 24–48 hour response commitment, a published confidentiality statement ("We will keep this as private as possible. We will escalate only if there is risk to safety, safeguarding concerns, or legal obligations"), and safeguarding-triggered escalation for any credible risk to self or others.

TABLE 7.6 Reporting Infrastructure—Implementation Checklist

Priority	*Implementation Action*	*Minimum Viable Version*
1. Make role boundaries visible	Include role boundary definitions in athlete and staff onboarding materials.	One-page handout: who does what when someone discloses.
2. Create multiple reporting channels	At least two channels—one bypassing the head coach and selectors entirely.	Anonymous web form or hotline plus one named welfare contact independent of selection.
3. Publish confidentiality limits	Plain-language statement of what stays private, what gets escalated, and under what conditions.	Posted in onboarding pack and treatment rooms; reviewed verbally at intake.
4. Guarantee non-retaliation	Explicit organizational commitment that disclosure will not affect selection. Close the loop: "You said, we did."	Written policy; one documented example of follow-through shared (anonymized) with the squad.
5. Train staff for the first disclosure	Scripts and rehearsal for the first moment an athlete says, "I'm struggling."	One 60-minute scenario rehearsal per season: "An athlete tells you they are struggling. What do you say, who do you call, and what do you not do?"
6. Track trust metrics	Time-to-first-response and a simple trust pulse.	Two-item check: "I know where to go" and "I believe I will be treated fairly." Administered quarterly.

BOX 7.7 SKEPTIC'S CORNER

"This Turns the Training Ground Into a Therapy Clinic"

The objection: "We are a sport organization, not a mental health service. This is over-medicalization." The answer: It is the opposite. Clear role boundaries exist so that coaches stay coaches, welfare leads manage pathways, and clinicians treat. Without boundaries, everyone improvises, and athletes get inconsistent responses that train silence. Structure is not over-medicalization. It is the alternative to it.

What to try anyway: Can an athlete reach help without going through the head coach? If not, add a second pathway this month. Rehearse one disclosure scenario with staff: "An athlete tells you they are struggling. What do you say, who do you call, and what do you not do?"

Even with strong infrastructure, the hardest cases to catch are athletes who appear to be coping well. Watch for rigidity: over-functioning, values–behavior gaps (talking recovery while training through pain), and compulsive information-seeking. When you see rigidity, you are seeing threat, regardless of what the athlete says (Hayes et al., 2012; Kashdan & Rottenberg, 2010).

7.6 Putting It Together: The Transition Support Audit

Transitions are predictable. Whether the operating system has built enough structure to support them often is not. That gap between knowing a transition is coming and being ready for it is exactly what the audit addresses.

7.6.1 Minimum-Viable Audit: Five Domains

The first step in supporting a transition is ensuring that leaders recognize it before it occurs. *Awareness* asks whether those responsible for guiding the team understand the impending change and its potential impact. Without that recognition, every downstream effort is reactive rather than preventive.

Once leaders see the transition coming, the next question is whether they can act on it. *Resources* examine who owns the transition and what support can be deployed. Clarifying ownership early prevents the diffusion of responsibility that leaves athletes unsupported at the moment it matters most.

Knowing who is responsible, however, means little without a plan. *Protocols* determine whether established, repeatable procedures exist to guide the process or whether the response will be improvised. Improvisation produces unpredictable outcomes; consistent pathways maintain stability.

Even the best protocol fails if people are afraid to use it. *Culture* assesses whether the organizational environment encourages open communication—whether it is safe for individuals to speak up, ask questions, or express difficulty. A culture that supports vulnerability enables athletes and staff to navigate transitions honestly rather than in silence.

Finally, none of the previous domains endure unless the transition is woven into daily operations. *Integration* asks how the change connects to everyday routines and decision-making processes, particularly when schedules tighten and decision rights shift. A transition plan that lives outside the workflow is a plan that gets forgotten.

Score each domain green (protocol exists and has been tested), amber (protocol exists on paper but has not been activated), or red (no protocol). Two or more red domains indicate systemic transition risk requiring intervention before the next predictable transition.

7.6.2 Staff Turnover as a Transition

When coaching staff changes, every athlete on the roster re-enters threat appraisal—a new head coach disrupts the psychological safety baseline, and trust norms reset until new patterns are proven. Practitioners can apply the five-domain audit to the coaching change itself and run the 4 S's for the highest-risk athletes. The minimum viable intervention is naming the reset: "New staff means new rules, and it is normal to feel uncertain about what is safe."

Staff turnover is included in Table 7.7 as a transition type because it activates the same threat-appraisal dynamics described throughout this chapter. It does not receive a dedicated section because the organizational-level interventions—leadership succession, onboarding of new staff, culture-reset protocols—operate at a different layer of the HPCOS architecture. Here, the focus is on the athlete-facing implications.

7.6.3 Transition Types at a Glance

Athlete-level check-in using the 4 S's (see Section 7.1): score each factor as green, amber, or red. The weakest S is where action should focus.

7.6.4 Diagnostic Questions

After completing the transition audit, three questions can help interpret the pattern:

Where does the system break first? Which of the five domains scored weakest—and is it the same domain across different transition types? The opening case study illustrates this: the end-of-season review cited "poor leadership from senior players" while never examining why the transition support system had been overridden three times.

Who is most vulnerable in the next 90 days? Identify athletes currently in transition or approaching one. Run the 4 S's for each. The athlete with the weakest profile and the fewest organizational resources is the highest-priority intervention.

If a new welfare lead started tomorrow, what would they not be able to see? The unnamed role changes, the unacknowledged grief, and the unreported struggles—those are the transitions most likely to produce silent crises.

7.6.4.1 Chapter Synthesis

Athlete transitions—onboarding, role change, injury, mental health crisis, and exit—are not unpredictable disruptions. They are recurring structural events

TABLE 7.7 Transition Types Mapped to Theoretical Frameworks, Mechanisms, and Primary Interventions

Transition Type	*Primary Framework*	*Key Mechanism*	*Weakest S (Typical)*	*Primary Intervention Focus*
Rookie integration (7.2)	Challenge–threat appraisal (Blascovich & Tomaka, 1996)	Threat appraisal; impostor phenomenon; identity foreclosure	Support	Integration partner, role clarity, belonging cues, 30/60/90 check-ins
Veteran role change (7.3)	Role exit theory (Ebaugh, 1988)	Status grief; contribution paradox; legacy anxiety	Situation	Name the change; protect dignity; make mentorship measurable
Deselection (7.3)	Organizational justice (Colquitt, 2001; Schlossberg, 1981)	Simultaneous collapse of all four S's; procedural fairness shapes distress	All four	Procedural fairness; dignified delivery; practical support; welfare follow-up
Planned retirement (7.3)	Career transition (Stambulova, 2003); identity breadth	Anticipatory grief; identity reconstruction	Self	Pre-retirement identity planning; non-sport development; ex-role pathway
Injury (7.4)	Self-determination theory (Ryan & Deci, 2000); integrated injury model (Wiese-Bjornstal et al., 1998)	Loss of autonomy, competence, relatedness; fear of reinjury	Strategies	Dual-track rehab; micro-mastery; preserve connection; graded exposure
Mental health disclosure (7.5)	Psychological safety; help-seeking barriers (Gulliver et al., 2012)	Stigma; confidentiality uncertainty; power asymmetry	Support	Role boundaries; multiple channels; rehearsed response; structural independence
Coach/staff turnover (7.6)	Challenge–threat appraisal; psychological safety reset	Roster re-enters threat appraisal; rules reset	Situation	Name the reset; apply transition audit; accelerate norm clarification

where the operating system either delivers on its promises or exposes its limits. When organizations lack transition protocols, athletes default to silence and self-protection—converting manageable stress points into avoidable crises. Schlossberg's 4 S's identifies which resource is weakest for which athlete at which moment, making intervention targeted rather than generic. Transition infrastructure is not pastoral care bolted onto the performance system. It is the performance system—tested at its most consequential pressure points.

Key Chapter Takeaways

1. **Transitions become crises when the system lacks structure, not when the event is severe.** The silence calculus runs hottest when an athlete's position is uncertain; protocols that lower the cost of voice during these windows prevent escalation.
2. **Diagnose the weakest S before intervening.** Applying Schlossberg's 4 S's identifies whether the gap is Situation (unnamed change), Self (identity foreclosure), Support (no safe person), or Strategies (no coping routines)—directing resources accordingly.
3. **Deselection protocols are a trust infrastructure for the athletes who remain.** Every roster member recalibrates their silence calculus by watching how departures are handled; dignified exits protect the psychological safety system-wide.
4. **Mental health disclosure requires structural independence, not just procedural safety.** Reporting channels that route through selectors train silence regardless of policy; separating clinical care from selection power is the minimum viable architecture.
5. **Identity breadth is protective across every transition type.** Athletes with even one non-sport anchor handle role change, injury, and exit as performance problems rather than identity collapse—a developmental investment, not a distraction.

Discussion Questions

1. Using the five-domain transition audit, evaluate your organization's readiness for the next predictable transition. Which domain would fail first, and what structural feature produces that gap?
2. When an organization asks a veteran to mentor their replacement without protected time, measurable outcomes, or a future pathway, what behavioral adaptation should practitioners expect—and how would you design the role differently?
3. A star athlete discloses panic attacks to a strength coach. Map the disclosure through your current reporting infrastructure: where does the system hold, and where does information leak?
4. Distinguish between procedural voice (permission to speak within existing channels) and structural voice (power to shape the systems). Which does your organization actually provide—and what would closing the gap require?

References

Ardern, C. L., Glasgow, P., Schneiders, A., Witvrouw, E., Clarsen, B., Cools, A., Gojanovic, B., Griffin, S., Khan, K. M., Moksnes, H., Mutch, S. A., Phillips, N., Reurink, G., Sadler, R., Silbernagel, K. G., Thorborg, K., Wangensteen, A., Wilk, K. E., & Bizzini, M. (2016). 2016 consensus statement on return to sport from the First World Congress in Sports Physical Therapy, Bern. *British Journal of Sports Medicine, 50*(14), 853–864. https://doi.org/10.1136/bjsports-2016-096278

Ardern, C. L., Taylor, N. F., Feller, J. A., Whitehead, T. S., & Webster, K. E. (2013). Psychological responses matter in returning to preinjury level of sport after anterior cruciate ligament reconstruction surgery. *The American Journal of Sports Medicine, 41*(7), 1549–1558. https://doi.org/10.1177/0363546513489284

Barth, M., Güllich, A., Forstinger, C., Schlesinger, T., Schröder, F., & Emrich, E. (2021). Retirement of professional soccer players: A systematic review from social sciences perspectives. *Journal of Sports Sciences, 39*(8), 903–914. https://doi.org/10.1080/02640414.2020.1851449

Baumeister, R. F., DeWall, C. N., Ciarocco, N. J., & Twenge, J. M. (2005). Social exclusion impairs self-regulation. *Journal of Personality and Social Psychology, 88*(4), 589–604. https://doi.org/10.1037/0022-3514.88.4.589

Beamon, K. K. (2012). "I'm a baller": Athletic identity foreclosure among African-American former student-athletes. *Journal of African American Studies, 16*(2), 195–208. https://doi.org/10.1007/s12111-012-9211-8

Blascovich, J., & Tomaka, J. (1996). The biopsychosocial model of arousal regulation. In M. P. Zanna (Ed.), *Advances in experimental social psychology* (Vol. 28, pp. 1–51). Academic Press. https://doi.org/10.1016/S0065-2601(08)60235-X

Bravata, D. M., Watts, S. A., Keefer, A. L., Madhusudhan, D. K., Taylor, K. T., Clark, D. M., Nelson, R. S., Cokley, K. O., & Hagg, H. K. (2020). Prevalence, predictors, and treatment of impostor syndrome: A systematic review. *Journal of General Internal Medicine, 35*(4), 1252–1275. https://doi.org/10.1007/s11606-019-05364-1

Brewer, B. W., Van Raalte, J. L., & Linder, D. E. (1993). Athletic identity: Hercules' muscles or Achilles heel? *International Journal of Sport Psychology, 24*(2), 237–254.

Bruce, E. J., & Schultz, C. L. (2001). *Nonfinite loss and grief: A psychoeducational approach.* Paul H. Brookes Publishing Co.

Clance, P. R., & Imes, S. A. (1978). The imposter phenomenon in high achieving women: Dynamics and therapeutic intervention. *Psychotherapy: Theory, Research & Practice, 15*(3), 241–247. https://doi.org/10.1037/h0086006

Colquitt, J. A. (2001). On the dimensionality of organizational justice: A construct validation of a measure. *Journal of Applied Psychology, 86*(3), 386–400. https://doi.org/10.1037/0021-9010.86.3.386

Confectioner, K., Currie, A., Gabana, N., van Gerven, N., Kerkhoffs, G. M. M. J., & Gouttebarge, V. (2021). Help-seeking behaviours related to mental health symptoms in professional football. *BMJ Open Sport & Exercise Medicine, 7*(2), e001070. https://doi.org/10.1136/bmjsem-2021-001070

DeLong, D. W. (2004). *Lost knowledge: Confronting the threat of an aging workforce.* Oxford University Press.

Ebaugh, H. R. F. (1988). *Becoming an ex: The process of role exit.* University of Chicago Press.

Edison, B. R., Christino, M. A., & Rizzone, K. H. (2021). Athletic identity in youth athletes: A systematic review of the literature. *International Journal of Environmental Research and Public Health, 18*(14), 7331. https://doi.org/10.3390/ijerph18147331

Edmondson, A. (1999). Psychological safety and learning behavior in work teams. *Administrative Science Quarterly, 44*(2), 350–383. https://doi.org/10.2307/2666999

Eisenberger, N. I., Lieberman, M. D., & Williams, K. D. (2003). Does rejection hurt? An fMRI study of social exclusion. *Science*, *302*(5643), 290–292. https://doi.org/10.1126/science.1089134

Erikson, E. H. (1950). *Childhood and society*. Norton.

Gardner, F. L., & Moore, Z. E. (2007). *The psychology of enhancing human performance: The mindfulness-acceptance-commitment (MAC) approach*. Springer Publishing Company.

Goffman, E. (1961). *Asylums: Essays on the social situation of mental patients and other inmates*. Anchor Books.

Golub, N. A., & Steinfeldt, J. A. (2025). High school football player experiences with multiple injuries: A qualitative biopsychosocial model application. *Frontiers in Sports and Active Living*, *7*, 1583467. https://doi.org/10.3389/fspor.2025.1583467

Grove, J. R., Lavallee, D., & Gordon, S. (1997). Coping with retirement from sport: The influence of athletic identity. *Journal of Applied Sport Psychology*, *9*(2), 191–203. https://doi.org/10.1080/10413209708406481

Gulliver, A., Griffiths, K. M., & Christensen, H. (2012). Perceived barriers and facilitators to mental health help-seeking in elite athletes. *BMC Psychiatry*, *12*, 157. https://doi.org/10.1186/1471-244X-12-157

Hayes, S. C., Strosahl, K. D., & Wilson, K. G. (2012). *Acceptance and commitment therapy: The process and practice of mindful change* (2nd ed.). Guilford Press.

Helmreich, R. L., Merritt, A. C., & Wilhelm, J. A. (1999). The evolution of crew resource management training in commercial aviation. *International Journal of Aviation Psychology*, *9*(1), 19–32. https://doi.org/10.1207/s15327108ijap0901_2

Hirose, K., & Meijen, C. (2022). An exploration of elite Japanese female footballers' acute cultural transition experiences in Europe. *Science and Medicine in Football*, *6*(5), 660–667. https://doi.org/10.1080/24733938.2022.2133161

Jones, M., Meijen, C., McCarthy, P. J., & Sheffield, D. (2009). A theory of challenge and threat states in athletes. *International Review of Sport and Exercise Psychology*, *2*(2), 161–180. https://doi.org/10.1080/17509840902829331

Kamarck, K. N. (2024, June 27). *Military Transition Assistance Program (TAP): Background and issues for Congress* (CRS Report No. R48114). Congressional Research Service. https://www.congress.gov/crs-product/R48114

Kashdan, T. B., & Rottenberg, J. (2010). Psychological flexibility as a fundamental aspect of health. *Clinical Psychology Review*, *30*(7), 865–878. https://doi.org/10.1016/j.cpr.2010.03.001

Kram, K. E. (1985). *Mentoring at work: Developmental relationships in organizational life*. Scott, Foresman and Company.

Lavallee, D. (2005). The effect of a life development intervention on sports career transition adjustment. *The Sport Psychologist*, *19*(2), 193–202. https://doi.org/10.1123/tsp.19.2.193

Lundqvist, C., Bermon, S., & Timpka, T. (2025). A psychometric study of the team psychological safety scale and sport psychological safety inventory in Swedish elite sports. *Scientific Reports*, *15*, 20227. https://doi.org/10.1038/s41598-025-06963-1

Marcia, J. E. (1966). Development and validation of ego-identity status. *Journal of Personality and Social Psychology*, *3*(5), 551–558. https://doi.org/10.1037/h0023281

Newman, A., Donohue, R., & Eva, N. (2017). Psychological safety: A systematic review of the literature. *Human Resource Management Review*, *27*(3), 521–535. https://doi.org/10.1016/j.hrmr.2017.01.001

Podlog, L., & Eklund, R. C. (2006). A longitudinal investigation of competitive athletes' return to sport following serious injury. *Journal of Applied Sport Psychology*, *18*(1), 44–68. https://doi.org/10.1080/10413200500471319

Purcell, R., Gwyther, K., & Rice, S. M. (2019). Mental health in elite athletes: Increased awareness requires an early intervention framework to respond to athlete needs. *Sports Medicine—Open*, *5*(1), 46. https://doi.org/10.1186/s40798-019-0220-1

Reardon, C. L., Hainline, B., Aron, C. M., Baron, D., Baum, A. L., Bindra, A., Budgett, R., Campriani, N., Castaldelli-Maia, J. M., Currie, A., Derevensky, J. L., Glick, I. D., Gorczynski, P., Gouttebarge, V., Grandner, M. A., Han, D. H., McDuff, D., Mountjoy, M., Polat, A., . . . Engebretsen, L. (2019). Mental health in elite athletes: International Olympic Committee consensus statement (2019). *British Journal of Sports Medicine*, *53*(11), 667–699. https://doi.org/10.1136/bjsports-2019-100715

Rice, S. M., Purcell, R., De Silva, S., Mawren, D., McGorry, P. D., & Parker, A. G. (2016). The mental health of elite athletes: A narrative systematic review. *Sports Medicine*, *46*(9), 1333–1353. https://doi.org/10.1007/s40279-016-0492-2

Ryan, R. M., & Deci, E. L. (2000). The "what" and "why" of goal pursuits: Human needs and the self-determination of behavior. *Psychological Inquiry*, *11*(4), 227–268. https://doi.org/10.1207/S15327965PLI1104_01

Ryan, R. M., & Deci, E. L. (2017). *Self-determination theory: Basic psychological needs in motivation, development, and wellness*. Guilford Press.

Schinke, R. J., Stambulova, N. B., Si, G., & Moore, Z. (2018). International Society of Sport Psychology position stand: Athletes' mental health, performance, and development. *International Journal of Sport and Exercise Psychology*, *16*(6), 622–639. https://doi.org/10.1080/1612197X.2017.1295557

Schlossberg, N. K. (1981). A model for analyzing human adaptation to transition. *The Counseling Psychologist*, *9*(2), 2–18. https://doi.org/10.1177/001100008100900202

Stambulova, N. B. (2003). Symptoms of a crisis-transition: A grounded theory study. In N. Hassmén (Ed.), *SIPF Yearbook 2003* (pp. 97–109). Örebro University Press.

Stambulova, N. B., Alfermann, D., Statler, T., & Côté, J. (2009). ISSP position stand: Career development and transitions of athletes. *International Journal of Sport and Exercise Psychology*, *7*(4), 395–412. https://doi.org/10.1080/1612197X.2009.9671916

Steele, C. M., & Aronson, J. (1995). Stereotype threat and the intellectual test performance of African Americans. *Journal of Personality and Social Psychology*, *69*(5), 797–811. https://doi.org/10.1037/0022-3514.69.5.797

Stroebe, M., & Schut, H. (1999). The dual process model of coping with bereavement: Rationale and description. *Death Studies*, *23*(3), 197–224. https://doi.org/10.1080/074811899201046

Symons, C., O'Sullivan, G., Borkoles, E., Andersen, M. B., & Polman, R. C. J. (2017). The impact of homophobic bullying during sport and physical education participation on same-sex-attracted and gender-diverse young Australians' depression and anxiety levels. *Journal of Sport & Social Issues*, *41*(3), 204–215. https://doi.org/10.1177/0193723517699443

Voorheis, P., Silver, M., & Consonni, J. (2023). Adaptation to life after sport for retired athletes: A scoping review of existing reviews and programs. *PLOS ONE*, *18*(9), e0291683. https://doi.org/10.1371/journal.pone.0291683

Wiese-Bjornstal, D. M., Smith, A. M., Shaffer, S. M., & Morrey, M. A. (1998). An integrated model of response to sport injury: Psychological and sociological dynamics. *Journal of Applied Sport Psychology*, *10*(1), 46–69. https://doi.org/10.1080/10413209808406377

8

THE INVISIBLE ARCHITECTURE—STAFF SYSTEMS AS PERFORMANCE INFRASTRUCTURE

Learning Objectives

By the end of this chapter, the reader will be able to:

1. Analyze how structural features of elite sport organizations produce rational silence among support staff.
2. Evaluate the difference between burnout and moral injury in sport support staff and determine appropriate intervention targets.
3. Apply the Fix/Skill/Fit framework to distinguish system-induced underperformance from individual competence gaps.
4. Apply the RACI framework (Responsible, Accountable, Consulted, Informed) to clarify decision rights and escalation rules for recurring high-stakes decisions in a performance support environment.
5. Critique hiring practices for homophily bias and evaluate structural alternatives to informal selection processes.
6. Evaluate the structural conditions that produce staff system failure and identify where failures cluster within an organization.

8.1 The Double Bind—Same Pressures, Fewer Protections

A note on scope. *This chapter focuses on support staff in major professional team sports—the environment where role ambiguity, political hiring, and power asymmetry are most structurally entrenched. The burnout–moral injury distinction draws on healthcare and military psychology and is applied to sport by structural analogy; dedicated sport-specific empirical study remains a priority.*

DOI: 10.4324/9781003631217-9

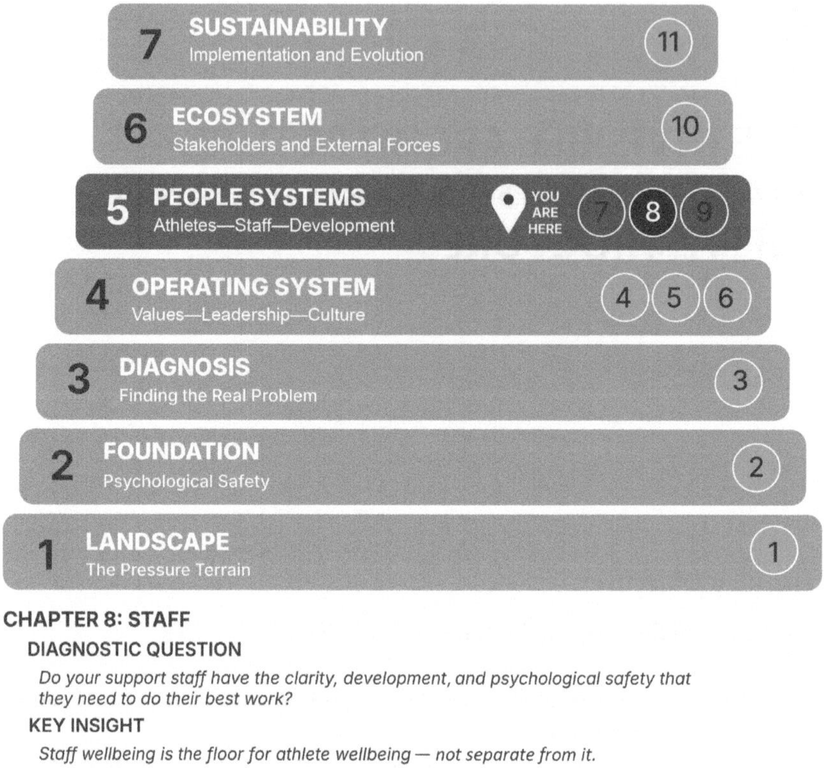

FIGURE 8.1 You Are Here—People Systems.

The HPCOS seven-layer architecture with Layer 5 (People Systems) highlighted. This chapter continues to answer Question 5—are we listening, and using what we hear?—by designing staff infrastructure: role clarity, decision rights, workload protection, and coordination routines that convert specialist input into action.

BOX 8.1 CASE STUDY — THE ANALYST WHO STOPPED FLAGGING

Composite vignette. Details changed to protect privacy.

The analyst spotted it on a Tuesday. The midfielder's load data showed a clear trend of cumulative fatigue markers rising across three weeks, soft-tissue risk climbing past every threshold the department had set. He drafted the flag for the performance meeting.

Then he remembered last time.

Three months earlier, he had flagged a similar pattern for a different player. The head coach listened, nodded, and then started the player anyway. After the match, the coach pulled him aside: "I need people who help me solve problems, not people who create them."

The analyst deleted the draft. He filed the data in the shared drive where it would technically be accessible. He told himself someone else would notice.

The physio noticed. She checked the same dashboard but said nothing as she had watched the analyst get shut down and drawn her own conclusions. The strength coach saw both of them go quiet and adjusted his own reporting. Within a month, three qualified practitioners were holding information that the system could not act on because none of them believed that the system wanted it.

The midfielder tore his hamstring in week 6. The post-incident review identified "gaps in interdisciplinary communication." The performance director recommended a new data-sharing platform. Nobody asked why three people who had the data chose not to share it.

The frameworks require adaptation across individual sport, collegiate and national organization settings, non-Anglo cultural structures, and professional role disaggregation.

The analyst spotted a fatigue trend, drafted the flag for the performance meeting—then remembered what happened last time and deleted it. That pattern—rational silence—is the structural problem this chapter diagnoses. Staff systems are load-bearing performance infrastructure: when they fail, athlete outcomes degrade, not because individuals are incompetent but because the systems surrounding them are underspecified. The chapter maps staff vulnerability relative to athletes (fewer protections, more political exposure, and less bargaining power) and introduces the differential diagnosis between burnout and moral injury—two conditions that look similar but require fundamentally different interventions.

As Figure 8.1 indicates, this chapter answers HPCOS Question 5: *are we listening, and using what we hear?* The answer lives in infrastructure most organizations never build: role clarity, decision rights, workload protection, and coordination routines that convert specialist input into action.

Staff are the early warning system for the three HPCOS leading indicators: Speed of Truth (elapsed time between someone knowing something and the organization acting on it), Voice (whether people with knowledge speak up), and Decision Clarity (whether decision rights are specified and honored). When staff stop flagging, Speed of Truth collapses upstream, where data originates. When staff filter reports to match what leadership wants to hear, Voice has already failed. When load decisions are made without the people who hold the data,

Decision Clarity is theater. These signals degrade at the staff level before the athlete level—which is why staff system health is a leading indicator of the leading indicators. Table 8.1 maps how staff silence degrades each.

8.1.1 *Why Staff Are More Exposed*

Staff face the same structural pressures as athletes. The difference is what they lack.

Power gradients shape every interaction. A physio who disagrees with a head coach's timeline risks their job. An analyst whose data contradicts the manager's preference learns to present selectively. Staff who stay quiet keep their contracts; staff who speak up risk termination. Transience compounds the problem: short-term contracts, regime changes, and "new broom" appointments mean institutional knowledge walks out the door within a single coaching cycle.

The critical difference is structural protection. Athletes have unions, guaranteed contracts, agents, and public visibility. A physio on a one-year contract has less protection than a rookie on a guaranteed deal. That asymmetry shapes every decision staff make about what to say and how much risk to absorb. Table 8.2 compares these structural protections across the two populations.

The job insecurity research confirms the pattern. Sverke et al. (2002) found consistent associations between perceived job insecurity and reduced well-being,

TABLE 8.1 How Staff Silence Degrades the Three Leading Indicators

Leading Indicator	*How Staff Silence Degrades It*	*Observable Signal*
Speed of Truth	Staff withhold or delay critical information because raising concerns carries career risk. Data originates at the staff level; when it stalls there, it never reaches decision-makers.	The time between a practitioner identifying a concern and a decision-maker hearing it increases. Concerns arrive as crises rather than early flags.
Voice	Staff filter reports to match what leadership wants to hear. Dissent moves to back channels or disappears entirely.	Fewer questions in performance meetings. Disagreements surface only in private. Staff describe "picking battles" rather than reporting data.
Decision Clarity	Decisions are made without the people who hold the relevant data. Accountability becomes diffuse because no one with expertise was in the room.	Load, return-to-play, or selection decisions made without input from the practitioners responsible for the data those decisions depend on.

TABLE 8.2 Staff Versus Athlete Structural Protections

Structural Feature	*Athletes*	*Staff*
Power gradients	Subject to the coaching authority over playing time and selection	Subject to coaching authority over employment, contract renewal, and career trajectory
Contract security	Union-negotiated contracts; guaranteed money common in major leagues; agents negotiate protections	Short-term contracts common; minimal negotiating leverage; "at-will" or fixed-term employment standard
Formal protections	Players' unions, CBAs, agents, and grievance procedures	Typically none. No union, no collective agreement, no formal grievance pathway in most settings
Public visibility	High—media scrutiny creates informal accountability; mistreatment carries reputational cost for the organization	Low—staff departures rarely attract attention; mistreatment is invisible to external stakeholders
Silence calculus	Staying quiet risks playing time and role; speaking up risks the coach relationship, but the athlete retains structural protections	Staying quiet preserves contract; speaking up risks termination with no structural recourse. Silence is the rational default.

Note: Structural protections reduce the employment consequences of speaking up for athletes relative to staff—they do not eliminate the psychological cost. Athletes still suppress information in psychologically unsafe environments. The asymmetry described here is about structural exposure, not about whether silence harms athlete outcomes.

lower job satisfaction, and increased turnover intentions across 72 studies. De Witte et al. (2016) extended this with 30 years of longitudinal evidence showing that job insecurity predicts health deterioration over time. Haluch et al. (2025) documented precarious and vulnerable work conditions specifically among applied sport psychologists—the people organizations hire to protect athlete welfare.

The downstream effect is predictable. Staff who feel unprotected withhold critical information, soften bad news, and prioritize self-preservation over athlete outcomes. This is not a character flaw. It is a rational response to a system that punishes honesty. Edmondson (1999) demonstrated that psychological safety predicts learning behavior and error reporting. When staff lack structural protection, psychological safety collapses at the staff level first.

This is a Speed of Truth problem. Speed of Truth is the signature metric of a functioning information system. High-Reliability Organizations treat the suppression of bad news as a critical systemic failure, optimizing for "deference to expertise" regardless of rank (Weick & Sutcliffe, 2001). When staff systems in sport are under-specified, they fail this fundamental test.

Measuring Speed of Truth at the staff level—how long does it take for a concern raised by a support staff member to reach a decision-maker with authority to act?—is one of the most direct indicators of whether the invisible architecture is functioning or failing.

BOX 8.2 TIMEOUT — ROLE-THREAT, NOT PERSONALITY

When roles are unclear, people do not just feel confused—they feel exposed. Under pressure, that threat response looks like defensiveness, territorialism, and lane policing: authority fights ("who owns load?"), backchannel workarounds, and conflict mislabeled as "communication problems." Every time I see the same interpersonal conflict recurring, I check the system before I check the people. If the structure is under-specified, the behavior is adaptation, not dysfunction.

Evidence note: Role ambiguity and role conflict are associated with lower job satisfaction and poorer performance, with higher turnover intentions (Gilboa et al., 2008; Tubre & Collins, 2000).

8.1.2 Job Insecurity and the Three-Year Cycle

Coaching tenures are short: Bridgewater (2010) estimated average tenures of 1.5–3 years in English professional football, and similar patterns have been documented in other major leagues (Lago-Peñas, 2011). While formal cross-sport meta-analytic data are limited, short coaching cycles are widely recognized as a structural feature of elite team sport.

For support staff, this creates a recurring cycle: hire, establish relationships, and lose them when the regime changes. Why build systems that will be dismantled? Job insecurity stops being an occasional stressor and becomes a structural feature of the work.

Conservation of resources theory explains the downstream effect: individuals facing resource threat shift toward defensive, risk-averse behavior, reducing innovation and knowledge sharing (Hobfoll, 1989). In sport, organizational stressors predict burnout and turnover in both athletes and support staff (Arnold & Fletcher, 2012; Bentzen et al., 2016; Larner et al., 2017). Wagstaff et al. (2018)

found that psychological resilience moderates this relationship, but resilience is a personal resource, not a structural fix.

Middle managers absorb pressure from above and below while creating psychological safety for direct reports (Floyd & Wooldridge, 1997; Huy, 2002). When they feel unsupported, their capacity to protect voice diminishes (Detert & Burris, 2007).

8.1.3 The Informal Versus Formal Systems Gap

In elite sport, decisions rarely follow the org chart. A strength coach designs a program; the physiotherapist overrules it; the head coach overrules the physiotherapist; the high-earning player overrules everyone by refusing to participate. Whose decision was it?

That is role ambiguity—uncertainty about tasks, responsibilities, and evaluation criteria (Kahn et al., 1964; Rizzo et al., 1970). Meta-analytic evidence shows a moderate negative association between role ambiguity and job performance (Tubre & Collins, 2000), with stronger negative relationships when stressor dimensions are disaggregated (Gilboa et al., 2008). Role ambiguity is also associated with lower satisfaction and higher turnover (Abramis, 1994; Jackson & Schuler, 1985) and triggers a breach of the psychological contract (Rousseau, 1989). When a practitioner is hired to "lead" but discovers that they have no authority, they feel betrayed.

The RACI matrix offers a practical fix (Friedman, 2008): for any recurring decision, specify who is Responsible (does the work), Accountable (owns the outcome), Consulted (input before decisions), and Informed (told after). Aviation's Crew Resource Management protocols solved a version of this decades ago (Helmreich et al., 1999).

Status: Practitioner heuristic. Derived from the RACI responsibility assignment framework (Friedman, 2008) and Crew Resource Management principles (Helmreich et al., 1999). Not a validated instrument. Table 8.3 provides a minimum viable RACI for four common performance support decisions.

Replace titles to fit the context, but keep the logic: medical and safeguarding decisions have stop authority; performance decisions have one accountable owner.

Minimum viable disagreement rules:

1. No hallway veto. Disagreements get resolved in the designated forum.
2. Timebox decisions. If unresolved in 24 hours, escalate. Safety concerns escalate immediately.
3. Safety overrides performance. If a clinician says "no," the answer is no.
4. Document dissent. Capture evidence and "what would change our mind?"
5. One message to the athlete. Disagreement is handled internally.

TABLE 8.3 Minimum Viable RACI for Common Performance Support Decisions

Decision	*Responsible (R)*	*Accountable (A)*	*Consulted (C)*	*Informed (I)*	*Escalation Rule*
Training load plan (weekly microcycle)	S&C lead + sport science	Performance director	Medical lead, athlete, analyst, head coach	Head coach, welfare lead	If the coach and performance staff disagree, timebox a same-day alignment meeting; the performance director resolves. Default: protect availability.
Injury return (clearance + graduated return-to-play plan)	Medical lead (physio/ physician)	Medical lead for clearance; head coach for selection once cleared	S&C, sport science, athlete, head coach	Performance director	Medical clearance is non-negotiable. Escalate to the performance director for resource/calendar trade-offs, not for overriding clearance.
Selection decision (match roster/ tournament)	Coaching staff	Head coach	Analyst, performance director, medical lead (availability only)	Staff team	The head coach makes the call within medical/safeguarding constraints. Capture dissent in a decision record, communicate one message.
Mental health referral activation	Welfare lead	Welfare lead	Licensed clinician, athlete, coach (support role)	Head coach (functional impacts only)	When in doubt, refer. Safeguarding/ mandatory reporting overrides preferences. Coaches informed only about training adjustments, not clinical details.

The logic is portable: replace titles to fit the context, but preserve the principle that medical and safeguarding decisions carry stop authority. Resistance to completing this matrix is often diagnostic.

BOX 8.3 SKEPTIC'S CORNER — WE'RE TOO SMALL FOR FORMAL ROLE CLARITY

Small staffs are exactly where informal power runs unchecked. Resistance to mapping decision rights is diagnostic: it means someone benefits from keeping authority ambiguous.

What to try anyway: Map decision rights for your three most recurring conflicts this week. If it takes fewer than 30 minutes, the objection does not hold. If it takes longer, you have discovered how much ambiguity you were carrying.

8.1.4 Proximity and the Political Skill Tax

Formal authority and actual power rarely align in sport. Expert and referent power override legitimate authority (French & Raven, 1959): a beloved veteran coach's informal influence can exceed a director's formal power. Cruickshank and Collins (2012, 2015) describe how informal influence shapes "what gets done" in elite performance teams. New staff are particularly exposed; without the social capital that provides access to information and influence, they find themselves outside the information flow that makes their roles effective (Burt, 1992). When proximity determines influence, clinical decisions get made by network position rather than clinical competence—and athletes experience inconsistent, fragmented care.

Organizations claim to hire for competence. Then they require political skill to survive. The physio has to know when to push back on the coach's timeline and when to let it go. The analyst has to know which data to present and which to hold. The psychologist has to manage the athlete's trust, the coach's suspicion, and the organization's legal exposure simultaneously. None of this appears in a job description. All of it determines who survives.

This is not "soft skills." It is a structural tax on technical expertise. We use the term *political skill tax* to reframe what the organizational literature treats as an individual competency as a structural cost borne unevenly. Ferris et al. (2005) found that political skill predicted effectiveness in organizationally charged environments. The cost falls disproportionately on those with the least structural power: Ibarra (1993) showed that women and minorities face higher costs to build the informal networks that political survival requires, and Kanter (1977) described how "tokens" face heightened scrutiny and reduced access to protective networks.

The result is selective attrition that operates invisibly. Competent but politically naive staff leave. Politically skilled but technically mediocre staff stay.

TABLE 8.4 Reducing the Political Skill Tax—Structural Interventions

Domain	*How the Tax Operates*	*Structural Reduction*
Selection	Informal hiring rewards candidates with network access and political fluency over technical competence	Structured interviews with standardized, behaviorally anchored questions remove political filtering from the selection process
Role clarity	Staff spend energy negotiating jurisdiction, managing upward, and reading political signals instead of doing technical work	RACI matrices replace political negotiation with documented decision rights—reducing the need for political navigation
Career advancement	Advancement depends on visibility, relationships, and proximity to power rather than demonstrated competence	Transparent career pathways with documented criteria make progression visible rather than requiring network navigation

Over time, the talent pool is shaped not by the quality the organization claims to value but by the political demands it actually rewards. The political skill tax is a diagnostic lens, not a standalone tool. Its operational implications are embedded in the hiring and retention structures that follow. Table 8.4 maps how the tax operates across three domains and identifies structural interventions to reduce it.

BOX 8.4 TIMEOUT — THE STRUCTURAL BURDEN OF BOUNDARY SPANNING

Support staff are classic "boundary spanners" (Aldrich & Herker, 1977)—translating information across silos, converting medical data into coaching timelines, and biomechanical analysis into strength programming. When an organization lacks formal integration systems, the entire burden of boundary spanning falls on the individual practitioner's political skill. The exhaustion staff feel is not just from their technical job; it is the hidden cost of manually bridging organizational gaps that the system failed to engineer.

8.2 Values-Based Hiring, the Homophily Trap, and the Access Gap

Principle: Organizations say that they hire for values. In practice, they often hire for comfort. The result: demographic homogeneity, intellectual stagnation, and a team that cannot detect its own blind spots.

8.2.1 Why Sport Organizations Are Bad at Hiring

Sport organizations hire under time pressure, with unclear role definitions, and without formal HR infrastructure (Fletcher & Wagstaff, 2009). The incentive structure says: *hire someone who can start tomorrow and will not cause problems.*

The result is predictable. Homophily is not a bias overcome with awareness training. It is a rational response to uncertainty and time pressure (Rivera, 2012). When the role is poorly defined, the default is someone who "feels right"—and "feels right" means familiar.

Dobbin and Kalev (2016) reviewed three decades of diversity initiatives and found that the most common approaches—mandatory training and grievance procedures—often fail because they trigger resistance without changing the structural conditions that produce homogeneity. The pattern is not that organizations do not value diversity. It is the structural trap that defeats it.

8.2.2 Hired but Not Included—The Access Gap

Hiring qualified women is not the same as giving them access. Some elite sport organizations hire female practitioners—sport psychologists, physicians, psychiatrists, nutritionists, and performance scientists—into roles supporting men's teams and then restrict the informal access that makes those roles effective. The credential box gets checked. The access does not follow.

The pattern is familiar. A female clinician holds the highest relevant qualification on staff, but she is never invited to travel. She hears about critical incidents days later, filtered through male colleagues. A male "athlete mentor" with no clinical training has a seat on every road trip. When asked, leadership offers familiar explanations: logistics, optics, and tradition.

Two forces drive the exclusion. The first is straightforward: women are systematically kept outside informal settings where trust is built and influence is negotiated (Bruening & Dixon, 2008; Ibarra, 1992, 1993; Kanter, 1977; LaVoi, 2016; Walker & Sartore-Baldwin, 2013; see also Cunningham, 2019). The second is subtler: male leaders report discomfort being alone with female colleagues and respond by limiting proximity (Atwater et al., 2019; Tan & Porzecanski, 2018). Social Identity Theory explains the mechanism: entrenched in-groups reflexively distance out-groups under stress (Tajfel & Turner, 1979). "Risk management" becomes a justification for maintaining homosocial boundaries (Cunningham, 2019; LaVoi, 2016).

In practice, when a male head coach debriefs the male S&C coach over a post-match meal but only meets the female psychologist in a glass-walled office during business hours, she does not experience "caution." She experiences access deprivation. Without informal access, her clinical work operates at reduced capacity, which the organization will interpret as a performance problem rather than an access problem.

What drives it: Homosocial reproduction—the tendency to hire, mentor, and promote people who resemble current power holders (Kanter, 1977; Rivera, 2012). When access flows through informal relationships, "culture fit" becomes a filter for demographic similarity (Ibarra, 1992, 1993). The athlete cost is fragmented care; the system cost is a signal that credentials matter less than fitting in. The structural failure is treating access as an individual risk-management decision rather than an organizational design problem.

When exclusion operates through informal mechanisms—"optics," comfort, and tradition—the fix must be structural. Table 8.5 maps six common access barriers to specific organizational design responses.

Equity note: This section focuses on gender because the exclusion pattern is well-documented and pervasive in men's professional sport. The same access audit applies to practitioners from other underrepresented groups.

8.2.3 Assessing Values Fit Without Clone Stamping

The question is not whether to hire for values. It is how to assess values without selecting for similarity. Structured interviews—where questions are standardized, behaviorally anchored, and consistently scored—improve reliability and validity across virtually every review of the evidence (Campion et al., 1997). The operational principle is straightforward: ask candidates to describe past

TABLE 8.5 Gendered Access Barriers and System Fixes

Problem	*System Fix*
"Optics" concerns exclude women from travel	Tie travel to role requirements; make inclusion the default
Male leaders limit proximity to avoid accusation risk	Institutional conduct policies, transparent meeting norms, structured mentoring with accountability
Female practitioners excluded from informal gatherings	Audit who has informal access; normalize mixed-gender professional settings
Information flows through channels women cannot access	Build formal information-sharing structures that do not depend on "being in the room"
Underqualified insiders hired over credentialed outsiders	Require structured interviews, external panel members, and credential verification
Access policies designed without input from affected women	Include women in decisions about travel, access, and safeguarding protocols

TABLE 8.6 The Performance-Values Matrix

	High Values	*Low Values*
High performance	Invest, protect, and develop leadership capacity. These are the culture carriers.	Do not build the culture around them. Set clear boundaries. If value violations continue, escalate to termination—the cost of the exception exceeds its benefit.
Low performance	Coach and develop. Often role-fit issues, not ability issues. Consider role redesign or reassignment.	Exit cleanly and quickly. Neither performance nor values are in place. Speed of Truth and psychological safety erode daily.

behavior under pressure—moments where values cost them something, where they disagreed upward, where they owned errors, and where they protected confidentiality boundaries. Score for behavioral evidence of clarity, boundaries, accountability, and escalation discipline rather than for narrative polish or cultural familiarity. A strong answer names decision rights, protects confidentiality, and shows repair after errors. Once hired, staff performance decisions benefit from a classification framework. Table 8.6 provides a two-by-two matrix that maps staff across performance and values alignment.

Status: Practitioner heuristic. Derived from common management classification frameworks applied to sport staff decisions. Not a validated instrument.

The matrix is only credible if applied consistently; a single "star exception" teaches the system what is actually rewarded.

8.3 Retention—Why the Competent Leave

Principle: Retention is not an engagement problem. It is a systems problem. Fix the environment before building career pathways—otherwise, the pathways lead through the same broken terrain.

8.3.1 The Retention Formula

Staff turnover costs are substantial and routinely underestimated. To the best of the authors' knowledge, no published study has systematically quantified replacement costs for performance staff in elite sport settings, though the broader organizational literature consistently estimates professional-level replacement costs at 50–200% of annual salary when accounting for separation, recruitment, selection, onboarding, and productivity loss during ramp-up (Cascio & Boudreau,

2011). The absence of data is itself a structural feature: it allows decision-makers to treat staff as interchangeable without confronting the actual price.

The general estimate almost certainly *understates* the cost in elite sport contexts, because it does not capture relational capital. The physiotherapist who has treated an athlete through two injuries holds knowledge no onboarding process can transfer. When that person leaves, the replacement arrives at zero—and the rebuild takes seasons, not weeks.

8.3.2 Why Development Pathways Stay Opaque

Employees perceiving clear advancement pathways show higher commitment and lower turnover intentions (Kraimer et al., 2011). Self-Determination Theory explains why: opaque pathways thwart the basic psychological needs for competence, autonomy, and relatedness that sustained engagement requires (Deci & Ryan, 2000). When these needs are chronically frustrated, the result is compliance without commitment.

Pathways stay opaque because making them explicit would expose how advancement actually works. Keeping criteria informal protects the existing power structure and guarantees that staff focused on technical excellence rather than political positioning never find advancement.

Transparent pathways require four elements: what positions exist above current roles, what competencies advancement requires, what timeline advancement typically follows, and what developmental support the organization provides. For example, a minimum viable pathway document for a sport science department might state: *current role: Sport Scientist (Level 1). Next role: Senior Sport Scientist (Level 2). Required competencies: independent match-day reporting, athlete load programming, and interdisciplinary case leadership. Typical timeline: two to three seasons with documented progression. Development support: assigned mentor at Level 2+, annual external conference attendance funded, and quarterly case review with the performance director.* The document does not need to be elaborate. It needs to exist, be communicated at hiring, and be referenced in performance conversations.

Low-resource adaptation: Small clubs may not have vertical ladders. Career lattices offer an alternative: horizontal growth (new responsibilities, project leadership, specialist tracks) that still increases competence, status, and meaning. Job crafting—allowing staff to redesign parts of their role to align with strengths and interests—expands horizontal responsibilities that feed autonomy (Wrzesniewski & Dutton, 2001).

8.3.3 Mentorship and Sponsorship

Mentorship and sponsorship are not the same thing. Meta-analytic work shows mentors report higher job satisfaction and lower turnover intention (Ghosh &

Reio, 2013), and protégés experience career benefits, including higher compensation and more promotions (Allen et al., 2004). Table 8.7 distinguishes the two across key dimensions.

Junior staff, particularly women and minorities, receive plenty of advice, but no one is willing to spend capital on their advancement (Ibarra, 1993). Dobbin and Kalev (2016) found that mentorship programs work best when people opt in and leadership backs the time cost.

Try this: Can anyone name one person who has actively spent political capital to advance a junior staff member in the last year?

A candid caveat: Everything in this section assumes that the systems survive leadership transitions. In many elite sport contexts, they do not. When a new head coach arrives with their own staff preferences, transparent pathways and mentorship investments can be dismantled overnight. This does not make the investment pointless—it makes it a design challenge. Organizations that embed retention structures at the institutional level (performance director, board policy, and contractual protections) rather than at the head-coach level give those structures a chance to survive the three-year cycle discussed in the next section. Organizations that build retention around a single leader's preferences are building on sand.

TABLE 8.7 Mentorship Versus Sponsorship

Dimension	*Mentorship*	*Sponsorship*
Core action	Gives advice, feedback, and guidance	Spends political capital on the person's behalf
Relationship to power	Can operate without positional authority	Requires the sponsor to hold and deploy organizational influence
Career mechanism	Develops the individual's capability	Advances the individual's visibility and opportunity
What it sounds like	"Here is how I would handle that situation"	"I am putting your name forward for this role"
Who typically receives it	Broadly distributed; relatively low-cost to provide	Concentrated among those who already resemble power holders Ibarra (1993)
Organizational risk	Low—advice carries no political exposure	High—the sponsor's reputation is tied to the outcome
Retention impact	Moderate—improves satisfaction but does not change structural position	High—changes career trajectory and signals organizational investment

8.4 Staff Well-Being as Load-Bearing Infrastructure

Principle: Staff instability fragments the athlete experience. Burnout, moral injury, and turnover are not personal failures—they are system failures with measurable performance costs.

8.4.1 The Performance Case for Staff Well-Being

Staff well-being has intrinsic value regardless of its performance impact. The instrumental argument that follows is strategic, not reductive: it meets leaders where their incentives sit.

It comes down to relational continuity. A sport scientist who has learned which metrics actually predict a particular athlete's performance holds knowledge that no handover document can transfer. A nutritionist who has navigated an athlete's disordered eating over two seasons has earned trust that a replacement will need months to approximate. When that staff member leaves, the athlete loses institutional memory and relational safety simultaneously.

The downstream costs are measurable: late injury reporting because the new physio has not earned trust, suppressed mental health concerns because the athlete does not want to start the story over, and fragmented preparation because the new analyst has no context. Treating specialized staff as interchangeable ignores both replacement costs (Cascio & Boudreau, 2011) and the performance degradation that occurs while institutional knowledge and athlete trust are rebuilt.

8.4.2 Burnout Versus Moral Injury

These are not the same thing, and confusing them leads to the wrong intervention.

Burnout is a state of chronic workplace stress characterized by emotional exhaustion, depersonalization, and a reduced sense of personal accomplishment (Maslach et al., 2001). In support staff, the early signals typically appear weeks before formal performance problems (Schaufeli & Enzmann, 1998): compression (people stop raising concerns), hardening (increased cynicism), and withdrawal (attendance drift, doing the minimum).

Clinicians have a shorthand for the distinction—the "vacation test." Burnout symptoms tend to lift with sustained rest—the person returns from two weeks off feeling restored. Moral injury does not lift. The person returns, re-encounters the structural conditions that demand complicity, and the distress returns immediately—because the source is institutional, not physiological. This is an observational distinction, not a validated diagnostic criterion; formal differential diagnosis requires clinical assessment. But as a first-pass screen, it reliably separates "I need rest" from "I need the system to change."

Moral injury is different. Jameton (1984) described moral distress as knowing the right action but being unable to take it due to institutional constraints. Litz et al. (2009) defined moral injury as the lasting psychological damage from perpetrating, failing to prevent, or witnessing acts that transgress deeply held moral beliefs. In healthcare, "moral residue" predicts professional identity erosion and exit (Dean et al., 2019; Epstein & Hamric, 2009). In sport, the conditions are parallel: the physio who clears an athlete early because the coach pressured them, the psychologist who cannot share critical risk information, the analyst who watches data get ignored, and the preventable injury occurs.

The moral injury pathway may manifest differently across professional groups. Clinicians with licensure obligations face a specific form: their regulatory duties may directly conflict with organizational pressure, creating moral distress with professional consequences. Non-licensed staff face moral injury without external accountability structures to support refusal.

Burnout says: "I am exhausted." Moral injury says: "I am complicit." The distinction matters for the three signals because the two conditions produce different failure patterns. Burnout slows truth through exhaustion—the staff member does not flag because they do not have the energy. Moral injury stops truth through betrayal—the staff member does not flag because they have learned that flagging produces harm. The intervention for each is structurally different: workload redesign for burnout, institutional repair for moral injury. Table 8.8 contrasts the minimum viable prevention response for each diagnosis.

BOX 8.5 TIMEOUT — THE MISDIAGNOSIS THAT KEEPS THE SYSTEM INTACT

When an organization treats moral injury as burnout, the prescription is rest, resilience training, and wellness programming–interventions that return the person to the same system that broke them. The misdiagnosis is not accidental. Calling it burnout locates the problem in the individual's capacity. Calling it moral injury locates the problem in the institution's conduct. The diagnostic label determines who has to change. Ask which label the organization prefers, and you have your answer about where accountability actually sits.

The diagnostic question matters. If you treat moral injury as burnout, you give people rest and return them to the same system. If you treat burnout as moral injury, you restructure a system that just needed load management.

8.4.3 Emotional Labor as Invisible Work

Emotional labor is a structural feature of support staff work, not an individual coping challenge (Hochschild, 1983). Hings et al. (2018) documented the

TABLE 8.8 Minimum Viable Prevention—Matched to Diagnosis

	Burnout	*Moral Injury*
Core intervention	Load reduction and recovery	Structural change that restores authority to act ethically
Immediate action	Protect recovery time for staff the same way athlete recovery is protected—non-negotiable rest windows, protected off-season	Build a safe escalation route that does not punish truth-telling. When someone flags moral distress, the response is system change, not "resilience coaching"
Systemic fix	Clarify decision rights for recurring conflicts, so staff do not have to navigate politics around every disagreement	Remove institutional constraints that force practitioners to compromise clinical or ethical judgment

emotional labor demands facing sport psychologists, physiotherapists, and S&C coaches, and Larner et al. (2017) confirmed the causal chain: structural pressure, emotional labor, burnout, and exit (see also Hings et al., 2020, on the emotional labor training gap in sport psychology education).

Consider a team psychologist on match day: an athlete distraught after de-selection, a volatile head coach, and a parent calling the front office. The psychologist manages all three emotional states while suppressing their own because professional effectiveness depends on appearing calm and composed. By season's end, the cumulative cost is invisible to everyone except the psychologist.

The organizational failure is treating this labor as a personality trait ("she is good with people") rather than as a structural demand that requires structural support: supervision, peer processing time, and explicit acknowledgment that emotional labor is real work with real costs.

One structural response is peer support—specifically, protected peer processing time among same-level staff. Conservation of resources theory (Hobfoll, 1989) predicts that social support buffers the relationship between workplace stressors and burnout, and meta-analytic evidence confirms consistent negative associations between work-related social support and emotional exhaustion (Halbesleben, 2006). A monthly 90-minute session among same-level staff—no leaders, no direct reports—gives people space to name pressure and problem-solve. The implementation details matter less than the principle: peer support must be protected from the same informal power dynamics that compromise everything else. If the space becomes one where people self-censor because they worry about being quoted to leadership, it is worse than useless.

BOX 8.6 PSYCHOLOGY SIDELINES WITH DR. MCB — WHEN YOU ARE BOTH THE ARCHITECTURE AND THE PERSON INSIDE IT

One of the more recognizable patterns in applied work is the practitioner who has started describing their own workplace using the language they were trained to use for clients. They can name the dynamic precisely—moral distress, compassion fatigue, and role conflict—and that precision does not make them immune to it.

There is a particular tension in working inside a system you are simultaneously trying to improve. The practitioner who teaches athletes emotional regulation still has their own nervous system to manage when a coach undermines them in front of the squad. The welfare lead who builds disclosure pathways for athletes may not have an equivalent pathway of their own. The staff member who screens others for burnout is not automatically protected from it—and the organization may not have a mechanism to notice because noticing would require the system to turn the lens on itself.

The instinct is to recommend supervision, peer support, and self-care. And those matter. But the more useful diagnostic question comes first: *is the system asking you to do something that violates your professional judgment on a regular basis?* If the answer is yes, peer support alone will not resolve what is fundamentally a moral injury. The intervention is not resilience. It is institutional repair—or, when repair is not yet available, an honest conversation about what sustainable practice looks like from here.

Practitioners deserve the same diagnostic precision we bring to athlete care. The same logic applies: diagnose the system before prescribing individual coping.

8.5 Compassionate Accountability—When Someone Has to Go

Principle: Accountability without safety is cruelty. Safety without accountability is negligence. The system needs both.

8.5.1 The Just Culture Frame

The Just Culture framework originated in aviation safety and healthcare, where the same diagnostic question—is this a system failure, a skill gap, or a willful violation?—determines the organizational response (Reason, 1997; Dekker, 2012). Healthcare's adoption of Just Culture similarly required distinguishing system-induced error from individual negligence before determining consequences.

Elite sport faces the same diagnostic challenge but has largely skipped the structural step, defaulting to individual blame.

A necessary caveat: the taxonomy is a diagnostic shortcut, not a bright line. Even in aviation and healthcare, the boundary between system-induced error and individual negligence is frequently contested (Dekker, 2012). The taxonomy's value is not that it produces clean categories. It forces the diagnostic question *before* the accountability decision. Without it, organizations default to blaming the individual, skipping the system audit, and repeating the failure with the next person in the role.

Organizational justice research reinforces why process matters: when staff perceive accountability processes as fair and respectful, they accept even adverse outcomes; when they perceive arbitrary processes, even justified decisions erode trust (Colquitt, 2001). Compassionate accountability is not a softening; it is a design specification.

Feedback often backfires when it triggers threat. Kluger and DeNisi's (1996) meta-analysis found that roughly one-third of feedback interventions decreased performance. The pattern: effectiveness drops as attention moves from task to self. Feedback that threatens self-concept triggers defensiveness and undermines learning.

The takeaway: focus on the work, not the worker.

- "Your program design missed the recovery windows" targets task.
- "You are not strategic enough" targets identity. Same underlying issue; different psychological impact.

Effective task-focused feedback follows a consistent sequence: name the specific behavior or output observed, describe its impact on the athlete, team, or system, state the standard that was needed, and then ask what support would help—whether that means removing an obstacle, building a skill, changing the process, or reassigning a task. The sequence keeps attention on the work rather than the worker's identity.

8.5.2 Fix/Skill/Fit

When someone is underperforming, the diagnostic step comes before the decision. The sequence is deliberate: system audit first, skill investment second, and separation last.

Fix: Is the system preventing good work? Unclear decision rights, political interference, and impossible workload. If the system has not been fixed, the organization has not yet earned the right to evaluate the person.

Skill: Is there a genuine competence gap? Can it be closed with training, mentoring, or supervised practice? If yes, invest. If the person is willing but under-skilled, the organization owes them a development plan before accountability.

Fit: After fixing the system and investing in the skill—if the person still cannot or will not meet the standard—this is a genuine fit issue. Separation is appropriate, handled with dignity and process fairness.

Most organizations skip to Step 3 because it is easier than auditing their own systems.

8.5.3 Exit Interviews as Diagnostic Data, Not PR

Exit interviews routinely fail because departing employees manage impressions even on the way out, motivated by reference dependence and fear of retaliation (Giacalone et al., 1997). The result: sanitized feedback that confirms what leadership already believes.

The structural fix is third-party interviews conducted three to six months post-departure. By then, the person has a new role and less to lose. Two questions produce more diagnostic data than a 20-item survey: (1) what should the organization keep doing? (2) What would you change if you ran the place?

The pattern to watch: if exit interviews consistently blame "fit" or "personal reasons" without naming systems or leadership behavior, the silence extends beyond the organization's walls.

8.6 Assessing Staff System Health

The five structural failures described in this chapter—role ambiguity, hiring distortion, retention collapse, well-being erosion, and accountability failure—do not operate independently. They compound. An organization that lacks role clarity will also struggle with retention, because competent staff leave when decision rights are unspecified. An organization that misdiagnoses moral injury as burnout will lose the people who care most about doing the work right—and the exit interviews will blame "fit."

The question is where to look first. For any given organization, the failures will cluster differently, and the diagnostic starting point matters. Three questions help locate the pattern: Where does the system fail first—and do failures cluster in one domain or distribute across all five? Which professional roles sit at the intersection of multiple system failures, and are those the positions experiencing the highest turnover? And where systems nominally exist, are they structural (written decision rights and formal escalation routes) or aspirational (stated values and verbal commitments that evaporate under pressure)?

Table 8.9 maps each domain across three levels of structural maturity—from no formal structure through paper-only structures to embedded routines that survive leadership transitions. Most elite sport organizations sit in the middle—structures that hold under normal conditions but collapse under pressure, which is precisely when they matter most.

TABLE 8.9 Staff System Health Quick Scan

Domain	*Red (No Structure)*	*Amber (Paper Structure)*	*Green (Embedded Structure)*
Role clarity	Staff cannot describe their decision rights; recurring conflicts about ownership	RACI exists but is not referenced in meetings; defaults to informal power under pressure	Decision rights are documented, referenced in real time, and survive leadership transitions
Hiring integrity	No structured interviews; selection based on network proximity and "fit"	Structured process exists, but exceptions are made for "urgent" hires or senior preferences	Standardized interviews with external panel members; credential verification enforced regardless of the timeline
Retention	No career pathways documented; advancement depends on political positioning	Pathways exist in policy but are not communicated or resourced; mentorship is informal	Transparent pathways with documented competencies, timelines, and institutional (not coach-dependent) backing
Well-Being	No distinction between burnout and moral injury; wellness programming is the only response	Burnout recognized, but moral injury unaddressed; peer support exists informally	Differential diagnosis informs intervention; protected peer processing time; escalation routes for moral distress
Accountability	Underperformance defaults to blame or termination; no system audit precedes decisions	Fix/Skill/Fit logic is understood but inconsistently applied; the process depends on the manager	System audit is the documented first step; feedback is task-focused; exit data is collected by a third party post-departure

The practitioner developed a tool based on Synthesizes role theory (Kahn et al., 1964), Just Culture (Reason, 1997; Dekker, 2012), and organizational justice research (Colquitt, 2001). Not a validated instrument.

Score the organization honestly. If the answer falls between amber and green, it is amber—embedded structures are not ambiguous to the people who work under them.

Note that system failures affect professional groups differently. A physician facing pressure to clear an athlete may have regulatory recourse through their licensure board; an operations coordinator facing the same organizational dynamics has none. Any assessment of staff system health must account for this differential exposure.

A final caveat: organizations rarely audit their systems while they are winning. Winning temporarily suppresses the symptoms of a broken staff system—athletes tolerate poor coordination, staff absorb moral injury, and leaders ignore structural failures because the scoreboard provides a false positive. When the winning stops, the system cracks instantly—not because something new broke, but because the fractures were always there. The assessment is best conducted during periods of stability, not crisis, precisely because success masks the signals it is designed to detect.

8.6.1 Chapter Synthesis

Staff systems are not HR infrastructure. They are performance infrastructure. When role clarity, hiring integrity, retention structures, well-being protections, and accountability processes are absent or broken, the people closest to athletes adapt rationally: they go quiet. The resulting silence degrades every downstream function the performance operation depends on. The choice is not whether to invest in staff systems. It is whether to pay proactively through design or reactively through preventable injuries, talent attrition, and fragmented athlete experience. Ultimately, building load-bearing performance infrastructure requires organizational leaders to recognize five key structural realities:

1. **Staff silence is a system output, not a character trait.** When qualified practitioners stop raising concerns, the diagnostic target is the structure, not the individual.
2. **Burnout and moral injury require different interventions.** Burnout responds to load reduction and recovery; moral injury responds only to structural change that restores practitioners' authority to act on what they know is right.
3. **Role ambiguity is measurable and fixable.** A minimum viable RACI matrix converts political negotiation into operational clarity.
4. **Hiring for "culture fit" without a structured process selects for demographic similarity.** Values-based interview protocols with behaviorally anchored questions and consistent scoring assess alignment without reproducing the existing template.
5. **Accountability must diagnose before it decides.** The Fix/Skill/Fit sequence prevents organizations from blaming individuals for structural failures they created.

Discussion Questions

1. Apply the Fix/Skill/Fit framework to the last staff departure in your organization. Where would the diagnostic sequence have changed the outcome—and what prevented that sequence from occurring?

2. If you mapped decision rights for return-to-play in your current environment, where would formal authority and actual power diverge—and what does that divergence cost the athlete?
3. Evaluate the distinction between burnout and moral injury in a context you know well. How would misdiagnosing one as the other change the intervention—and whose interests does the misdiagnosis serve?
4. Evaluate a staff system during a coaching transition. Which of the five structural failure domains—role clarity, hiring integrity, retention, well-being, or accountability—is most vulnerable during regime change, and what minimum protections would you prioritize?

References

Abramis, D. J. (1994). Work role ambiguity, job satisfaction, and job performance: Meta-analyses and review. *Psychological Reports*, *75*(3), 1411–1433. https://doi.org/10.2466/pr0.1994.75.3f.1411

Aldrich, H., & Herker, D. (1977). Boundary spanning roles and organization structure. *Academy of Management Review*, *2*(2), 217–230. https://doi.org/10.5465/amr.1977.4409044

Allen, T. D., Eby, L. T., Poteet, M. L., Lentz, E., & Lima, L. (2004). Career benefits associated with mentoring for protégés: A meta-analysis. *Journal of Applied Psychology*, *89*(1), 127–136. https://doi.org/10.1037/0021-9010.89.1.127

Arnold, R., & Fletcher, D. (2012). A research synthesis and taxonomic classification of the organizational stressors encountered by sport performers. *Journal of Sport & Exercise Psychology*, *34*(3), 397–429. https://doi.org/10.1123/jsep.34.3.397

Atwater, L. E., Tringale, A. M., Sturm, R. E., Taylor, S. N., & Braddy, P. W. (2019). Looking ahead: How what we know about sexual harassment now informs us of the future. *Organizational Dynamics*, *48*(4), 100677. https://doi.org/10.1016/j.orgdyn.2018.08.008

Bentzen, M., Lemyre, P. N., & Kenttä, G. (2016). Development of exhaustion for high-performance coaches in association with workload and motivation: A person-centered approach. *Psychology of Sport and Exercise*, *22*, 10 19. https://doi.org/10.1016/j.psychsport.2015.06.004

Bridgewater, S. (2010). *Football management*. Palgrave Macmillan.

Bruening, J. E., & Dixon, M. A. (2008). Situating work–family negotiations within a life course perspective: Insights on the gendered experiences of NCAA Division I head coaching mothers. *Sex Roles*, *58*(1–2), 10–23. https://doi.org/10.1007/s11199-007-9350-x

Burt, R. S. (1992). *Structural holes: The social structure of competition*. Harvard University Press.

Campion, M. A., Palmer, D. K., & Campion, J. E. (1997). A review of structure in the selection interview. *Personnel Psychology*, *50*(3), 655–702. https://doi.org/10.1111/j.1744-6570.1997.tb00709.x

Cascio, W. F., & Boudreau, J. W. (2011). *Investing in people: Financial impact of human resource initiatives* (2nd ed.). FT Press.

Colquitt, J. A. (2001). On the dimensionality of organizational justice: A construct validation of a measure. *Journal of Applied Psychology*, *86*(3), 386–400. https://doi.org/10.1037/0021-9010.86.3.386

Cruickshank, A., & Collins, D. (2012). Culture change in elite sport performance teams: Examining and advancing effectiveness in the new era. *Journal of Applied Sport Psychology*, *24*(3), 338–355. https://doi.org/10.1080/10413200.2011.650819

Cruickshank, A., & Collins, D. (2015). Illuminating and applying "the dark side": Insights from elite team leaders. *Journal of Applied Sport Psychology*, *27*(3), 249–267. https://doi.org/10.1080/10413200.2014.982771

Cunningham, G. B. (2019). *Diversity and inclusion in sport organizations: A multilevel perspective* (4th ed.). Routledge. https://doi.org/10.4324/9780429504310.

De Witte, H., Pienaar, J., & De Cuyper, N. (2016). Review of 30 years of longitudinal studies on the association between job insecurity and health and well-being: Is there causal evidence? *Australian Psychologist*, *51*(1), 18–31. https://doi.org/10.1111/ap.12176

Dean, W., Talbot, S., & Dean, A. (2019). Reframing clinician distress: Moral injury not burnout. *Federal Practitioner*, *36*(9), 400–402. https://pmc.ncbi.nlm.nih.gov/articles/PMC6752815/

Deci, E. L., & Ryan, R. M. (2000). The "what" and "why" of goal pursuits: Human needs and the self-determination of behavior. *Psychological Inquiry*, *11*(4), 227–268. https://doi.org/10.1207/S15327965PLI1104_01

Dekker, S. (2012). *Just culture: Balancing safety and accountability* (2nd ed.). CRC Press.

Detert, J. R., & Burris, E. R. (2007). Leadership behavior and employee voice: Is the door really open? *Academy of Management Journal*, *50*(4), 869–884. https://doi.org/10.5465/amj.2007.26279183

Dobbin, F., & Kalev, A. (2016). Why diversity programs fail. *Harvard Business Review*, *94*(7), 52–60. https://hbr.org/2016/07/why-diversity-programs-fail

Edmondson, A. C. (1999). Psychological safety and learning behavior in work teams. *Administrative Science Quarterly*, *44*(2), 350–383. https://doi.org/10.2307/2666999

Epstein, E. G., & Hamric, A. B. (2009). Moral distress, moral residue, and the crescendo effect. *Journal of Clinical Ethics*, *20*(4), 330–342. https://doi.org/10.1086/jce200920406

Ferris, G. R., Treadway, D. C., Kolodinsky, R. W., Hochwarter, W. A., Kacmar, C. J., Douglas, C., & Frink, D. D. (2005). Development and validation of the political skill inventory. *Journal of Management*, *31*(1), 126–152. https://doi.org/10.1177/0149206304271386

Fletcher, D., & Wagstaff, C. R. D. (2009). Organizational psychology in elite sport: Its emergence, application, and future. *Psychology of Sport and Exercise*, *10*(4), 427–434. https://doi.org/10.1016/j.psychsport.2009.03.009

Floyd, S. W., & Wooldridge, B. (1997). Middle management's strategic influence and organizational performance. *Journal of Management Studies*, *34*(3), 465–485. https://doi.org/10.1111/1467-6486.00059

French, J. R. P., & Raven, B. (1959). The bases of social power. In D. Cartwright (Ed.), *Studies in social power* (pp. 150–167). Institute for Social Research.

Friedman, S. (2008, October). Roles, responsibilities, and resources: Best practices in managing people [Paper presentation]. In *PMI Global Congress 2008—North America*, Denver, CO, United States. https://www.pmi.org/learning/library/best-practices-managing-people-quality-management-7012

Ghosh, R., & Reio, T. G. (2013). Career benefits associated with mentoring for mentors: A meta-analysis. *Journal of Vocational Behavior*, *83*(1), 106–116. https://doi.org/10.1016/j.jvb.2013.03.011

Giacalone, R. A., Knouse, S. B., & Montagliani, A. (1997). Motivation for and prevention of honest responding in exit interviews and surveys. *Journal of Psychology*, *131*(4), 438–448. https://doi.org/10.1080/00223989709603528

Gilboa, S., Shirom, A., Fried, Y., & Cooper, C. (2008). A meta-analysis of work demand stressors and job performance: Examining main and moderating effects. *Personnel Psychology*, *61*(2), 227–271. https://doi.org/10.1111/j.1744-6570.2008.00113.x

Halbesleben, J. R. B. (2006). Sources of social support and burnout: A meta-analytic test of the conservation of resources model. *Journal of Applied Psychology*, *91*(5), 1134–1145. https://doi.org/10.1037/0021-9010.91.5.1134

Haluch, P., Rowley, C., Nelson, L., & Radcliffe, J. (2025). Precarious and vulnerable work: The experiences of applied sport psychologists. *Journal of Applied Sport Psychology*, *37*(3), 348–369. https://doi.org/10.1080/10413200.2024.2414022

Helmreich, R. L., Merritt, A. C., & Wilhelm, J. A. (1999). The evolution of Crew Resource Management training in commercial aviation. *International Journal of Aviation Psychology*, *9*(1), 19–32. https://doi.org/10.1207/s15327108ijap0901_2

Hings, R. F., Wagstaff, C. R. D., Anderson, V., Gilmore, S., & Thelwell, R. C. (2018). Professional challenges in elite sports medicine and science: Composite vignettes of practitioner emotional labor. *Psychology of Sport and Exercise*, *35*, 66–73. https://doi.org/10.1016/j.psychsport.2017.11.007

Hings, R. F., Wagstaff, C. R. D., Anderson, V., Gilmore, S., & Thelwell, R. C. (2020). Better preparing sports psychologists for the demands of applied practice: The emotional labor training gap. *Journal of Applied Sport Psychology*, *32*(4), 335–356. https://doi.org/10.1080/10413200.2018.1560373

Hobfoll, S. E. (1989). Conservation of resources: A new attempt at conceptualizing stress. *American Psychologist*, *44*(3), 513–524. https://doi.org/10.1037/0003-066X.44.3.513

Hochschild, A. R. (1983). *The managed heart: Commercialization of human feeling*. University of California Press.

Huy, Q. N. (2002). Emotional balancing of organizational continuity and radical change: The contribution of middle managers. *Administrative Science Quarterly*, *47*(1), 31–69. https://doi.org/10.2307/3094890

Ibarra, H. (1992). Homophily and differential returns: Sex differences in network structure and access in an advertising firm. *Administrative Science Quarterly*, *37*(3), 422–447. https://doi.org/10.2307/2393451

Ibarra, H. (1993). Personal networks of women and minorities in management: A conceptual framework. *Academy of Management Review*, *18*(1), 56–87. https://doi.org/10.5465/amr.1993.3997507

Jackson, S. E., & Schuler, R. S. (1985). A meta-analysis and conceptual critique of research on role ambiguity and role conflict in work settings. *Organizational Behavior and Human Decision Processes*, *36*(1), 16–78. https://doi.org/10.1016/0749-5978(85)90020-2

Jameton, A. (1984). *Nursing practice: The ethical issues*. Prentice-Hall.

Kahn, R. L., Wolfe, D. M., Quinn, R. P., Snoek, J. D., & Rosenthal, R. A. (1964). *Organizational stress: Studies in role conflict and role ambiguity*. Wiley.

Kanter, R. M. (1977). *Men and women of the corporation*. Basic Books.

Kluger, A. N., & DeNisi, A. (1996). The effects of feedback interventions on performance: A historical review, a meta-analysis, and a preliminary feedback intervention theory. *Psychological Bulletin*, *119*(2), 254–284. https://doi.org/10.1037/0033-2909.119.2.254

Kraimer, M. L., Seibert, S. E., Wayne, S. J., Liden, R. C., & Bravo, J. (2011). Antecedents and outcomes of organizational support for development. *Journal of Applied Psychology*, *96*(3), 485–500. https://doi.org/10.1037/a0021452

Lago-Peñas, C. (2011). Coach mid-season replacement and team performance in professional soccer. *Journal of Human Kinetics*, *28*, 115–122. https://doi.org/10.2478/v10078-011-0028-7

Larner, R. J., Wagstaff, C. R. D., Thelwell, R. C., & Corbett, J. (2017). A multistudy examination of organizational stressors, emotional labor, burnout, and turnover in sport organizations. *Scandinavian Journal of Medicine & Science in Sports*, *27*(12), 2103–2115. https://doi.org/10.1111/sms.12833

LaVoi, N. M. (2016). *Women in sports coaching*. Routledge.

Litz, B. T., Stein, N., Delaney, E., Lebowitz, L., Nash, W. P., Silva, C., & Maguen, S. (2009). Moral injury and moral repair in war veterans: A preliminary model and intervention strategy. *Clinical Psychology Review*, *29*(8), 695–706. https://doi.org/10.1016/j.cpr.2009.07.003

Maslach, C., Schaufeli, W. B., & Leiter, M. P. (2001). Job burnout. *Annual Review of Psychology, 52*, 397–422. https://doi.org/10.1146/annurev.psych.52.1.397
Reason, J. (1997). *Managing the risks of organizational accidents*. Ashgate.
Rivera, L. A. (2012). Hiring as cultural matching: The case of elite professional service firms. *American Sociological Review, 77*(6), 999–1022. https://doi.org/10.1177/0003122412463213
Rizzo, J. R., House, R. J., & Lirtzman, S. I. (1970). Role conflict and role ambiguity in complex organizations. *Administrative Science Quarterly, 15*(2), 150–163. https://doi.org/10.2307/2391486
Rousseau, D. M. (1989). Psychological and implied contracts in organizations. *Employee Responsibilities and Rights Journal, 2*(2), 121–139. https://doi.org/10.1007/BF01384942
Schaufeli, W. B., & Enzmann, D. (1998). *The burnout companion to study and practice: A critical analysis*. CRC Press.
Sverke, M., Hellgren, J., & Näswall, K. (2002). No security: A meta-analysis and review of job insecurity and its consequences. *Journal of Occupational Health Psychology, 7*(3), 242–264. https://doi.org/10.1037/1076-8998.7.3.242
Tajfel, H., & Turner, J. C. (1979). An integrative theory of intergroup conflict. In W. G. Austin & S. Worchel (Eds.), *The social psychology of intergroup relations* (pp. 33–47). Brooks/Cole.
Tan, G., & Porzecanski, K. (2018, December 3). Wall Street rule for the #MeToo era: Avoid women at all cost. *Bloomberg*. https://www.bloomberg.com/news/articles/2018-12-03/a-wall-street-rule-for-the-metoo-era-avoid-women-at-all-cost
Tubre, T. C., & Collins, J. M. (2000). Jackson and Schuler (1985) revisited: A meta-analysis of the relationships between role ambiguity, role conflict, and job performance. *Journal of Management, 26*(1), 155–169. https://doi.org/10.1177/014920630002600104
Wagstaff, C. R. D., Hings, R. F., Larner, R. J., & Fletcher, D. (2018). Psychological resilience's moderation of the relationship between the frequency of organizational stressors and burnout in athletes and support staff. *The Sport Psychologist, 32*(3), 178–188. https://doi.org/10.1123/tsp.2017-0094
Walker, N. A., & Sartore-Baldwin, M. L. (2013). Hegemonic masculinity and the institutionalized bias toward women in men's collegiate basketball: What do men think? *Journal of Sport Management, 27*(4), 303–315. https://doi.org/10.1123/jsm.27.4.303
Weick, K. E., & Sutcliffe, K. M. (2001). *Managing the unexpected: Assuring high performance in an age of complexity*. Jossey-Bass.
Wrzesniewski, A., & Dutton, J. E. (2001). Crafting a job: Revisioning employees as active crafters of their work. *Academy of Management Review, 26*(2), 179–201. https://doi.org/10.5465/amr.2001.4378011

9

YOUR PEOPLE—SELECTION, DEVELOPMENT, AND THE ATHLETE LIFECYCLE

Learning Objectives

By the end of this chapter, the reader will be able to:

1. Evaluate selection processes for structural bias—including maturation timing, relative age effects, and demographic access—and design assessment frameworks that capture developmental trajectory rather than current physical state.
2. Apply decision architecture principles to selection and deselection, including documented evidence, required dissent, bias checks, and reversibility protocols.
3. Analyze how the acquisition–extraction cycle operates at each athlete lifecycle transition and identify where the silence calculus drives concealment at each seam.
4. Design development environments that build capacity across physical, psychological, and identity domains, distinguishing system architecture from coaching technique.
5. Evaluate pipeline permeability by mapping entry points, return mechanisms, and transfer pathways, and propose structural corrections where pathways systematically exclude late developers or demographic groups.

This chapter focuses on professional team sports in North America and Europe, where the acquisition–extraction cycle is most evident. Three key boundaries should be noted: NCAA collegiate pathways operate with distinct incentives, such as eligibility, transfer rules, and NIL economics; relative age and maturation biases are strongest in team sports but require adaptation for individual, aesthetic, and para-sports, which have unique transition challenges; and issues of race, socioeconomic

DOI: 10.4324/9781003631217-10

FIGURE 9.1 You Are Here—People Systems.

The HPCOS seven-layer architecture (see Chapter 2) with Layer 5 (People Systems) highlighted. This chapter extends the guiding question to talent identification, development pathways, and pipeline architecture—asking what the system built or failed to build before the athlete arrived.

status, gender, and maturation in selection demand further study. In youth development, the parent–child–coach relationship affects whether mastery climate principles extend beyond program control.

BOX 9.1 CASE STUDY — THE PROSPECT WHO STOPPED ASKING

Composite vignette. Details changed to protect privacy.

Kaleb arrived at preseason with a guaranteed roster spot and no idea what came next. He was 19, signed six weeks earlier, and relocated from a city where he had been the best player anyone had seen. The organization sent a housing packet, a playbook, and a media-training schedule. Nobody mentioned that the first three months would be the hardest of his life.

He struggled immediately. The speed was different. The veterans communicated in shorthand that he could not decode. In the first week, a tactical error drew a public correction from the assistant coach. That night, he called his mother. He did not call the team psychologist–he had met her once, in a hallway, and she reported to the same coaching staff who evaluated him.

Kaleb stopped asking questions in film sessions. When the strength coach asked how his body was recovering, he said "good" regardless. When the nutritionist flagged his weight loss, he said he was adjusting to the schedule.

By midseason, the coaching staff described him as "physically talented but mentally fragile." The development report noted "attitude concerns." The organization discussed whether they had made a selection error.

Nobody discussed what the system had built for him between the signing and the first whistle. The answer was nothing.

9.1 Selection: Where Acquisition Begins

Every selection decision encodes what the system actually values—and the encoding is visible to everyone watching, especially the people who weren't selected.

The athlete lifecycle is where the book's three leading indicators (introduced in Chapter 1)—decision clarity, voice, and Speed of Truth (the latency between an event occurring and leadership learning about it)—become visible to the people inside the system. Athletes watch how selection decisions are made, whether transition concerns are acted on, and how fast the organization responds when something goes wrong. Every lifecycle transition is a test of those indicators—and everyone is watching.

The guiding question—are we listening, and using what we hear?—frames this chapter. Listening means attending to transition signals: distress at entry, silence during injury, disengagement at exit. Using what you hear means building structural responses—onboarding architecture, lane discipline, and transition planning—rather than treating each signal as an individual case. Figure 9.1 locates the People Systems layer within the HPCOS architecture.

Walk into most scouting meetings, and the vocabulary is familiar: size, speed, strength, and measurables. Traditional scouting works best when the signal is clear and stable. Youth development rarely cooperates. Growth is non-linear, contexts are unequal, and senior-level traits emerge slowly. Under selection pressure, "current advantage" gets mistaken for "future potential."

The underlying logic is emergence: elite performance develops through nonlinear interactions among biology, psychology, skill, environment, and opportunity over time (Den Hartigh et al., 2018). A single-point assessment of a 14–17-year-old is not a forecast. It is one data point in a moving system. What follows is a way to broaden assessment, structure decisions, and make the values embedded in selection visible.

9.1.1 What Snapshot Scouting Gets Wrong

Physical metrics at a single time point capture current state, not trajectory—and on their own, they are insufficient predictors of long-term elite success (Johnston et al., 2018; Rees et al., 2016).

Youth dominance often reflects timing advantages that compress later: relative age (being older within a selection year), biological maturation (early puberty), and unequal access to coaching and resources (Cobley et al., 2009; Johnston et al., 2018). These distortions become self-reinforcing because early selection creates better coaching, more attention, and more opportunity—driven by a classic Pygmalion Effect (Rosenthal & Jacobson, 1968) and the sociological "Matthew Effect" (Merton, 1968), where initial timing advantages convert into cumulative developmental advantages. And the system "proves itself" by feeding the athletes it already prefers.

Physical testing is one input with clear limits—it explains only a portion of variance in who becomes elite (Rees et al., 2016). One longitudinal analysis of German national squad athletes found that developmental patterns leading to adolescent success and senior world-class performance were inconsistent—and in some aspects, contradictory. Early specialization favored short-term results but not long-term elite outcomes (Güllich & Emrich, 2014).

In some contexts, later-born athletes who survive early selection develop compensatory skills (Gibbs et al., 2012), and demographic starting points like community size heavily influence long-term elite emergence (Côté et al., 2006). Early selection often manufactures an advantage that gets misread as talent.

Early selection is a probabilistic bet that requires repeated reassessment—not a confident forecast. If the system cannot distinguish between "we identified talent" and "we created advantage through resource allocation," its scouting process is confirmatory, not diagnostic.

BOX 9.2 TIMEOUT — SELECTION BIAS AUDIT (FIVE STEPS)

Status: Practitioner heuristic. Derived from developmental talent identification research (Johnston et al., 2018; Cobley et al., 2009) and maturation science (Mirwald et al., 2002). Not a validated instrument.

Use this audit to surface where the assessment battery over-indexes on current state and under-indexes on developmental trajectory.

- Audit the current assessment battery. For each metric, ask: does this measure the current state or the developmental trajectory? If 80% is physical testing, that's a gap.

- Add a maturation estimate (e.g., Mirwald et al., 2002; Khamis & Roche, 1994). When a "dominant" 14-year-old shows up, check: are they 14, or biologically 16?
- Track birth quarters (Cobley et al., 2009; Smith et al., 2018). What percentage of selected athletes are born in Q1 versus Q4? If the skew exceeds 10 percentage points, force a bias review.
- Build in reassessment windows. Every six months for youth, annually for senior athletes–selection is a hypothesis, not a verdict.
- Separate "ready now" from "will be ready." Two conversations: who can contribute this season, and who has the trajectory to contribute in two to three years? The first tends to crowd out the second.

Common failure mode: Running the audit once and filing it. The value is in the cadence–quarterly for youth pathways, annually for senior programs.

Boundary note: Relative age and maturation effects vary by sport, competition structure, and sex/gender. Run a pathway audit before redesigning the system (Cobley et al., 2009; Smith et al., 2018). Any pathway that ties evaluation to body composition or leanness needs explicit Relative Energy Deficiency in Sport (RED-S) safeguards (Mountjoy et al., 2018; Bergeron et al., 2015).

9.1.2 Broadening the Assessment Lens

Broadening assessment means measuring what physical metrics miss: psychological development, identity structure, and behavioral evidence of character (MacNamara & Collins, 2011; Stambulova et al., 2009).

As environments become faster, harsher, and more evaluative, psychological skills become load-bearing. MacNamara and Collins frame psychological skills as developmental prerequisites, not "nice-to-have" add-ons (MacNamara & Collins, 2011).

Application: Add at least one psychological indicator to scouting. A simple starting point: *How does this athlete respond to correction?* Document behavior, not interpretation. "Stopped, asked a clarifying question, adjusted technique on next rep" is data. "Good attitude" is not. Observing response to failure—not just performance—shifts what the system sees.

Tools like the PCDEQ2 (Hill et al., 2019) work as development input, not a selection filter. As development input, scores inform the IDP—identifying areas for structured support. As a selection filter, the same scores become gatekeeping criteria that trigger deselection rather than development planning. The safeguard is governance: who sees the scores, and what decisions they inform. The lane

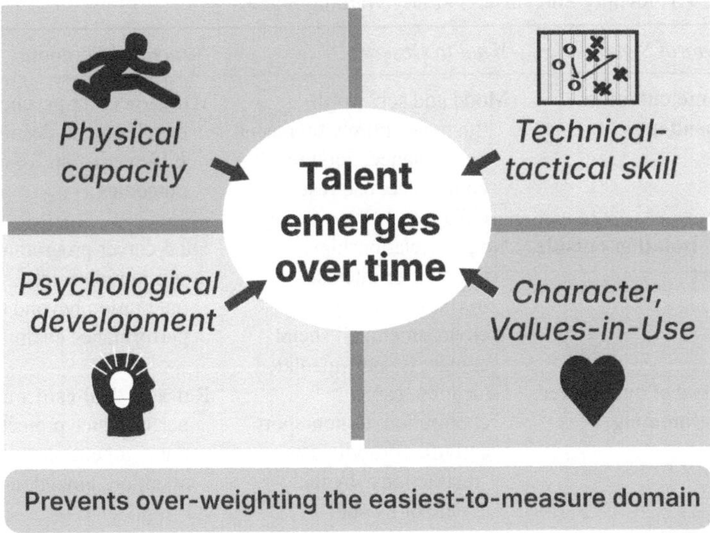

FIGURE 9.2 Multi-Domain Talent Model.

Assessment broadened beyond physical metrics to include psychological development, identity structure, and behavioral evidence of character—domains increasingly linked to transition resilience that physical metrics alone do not capture. A low score at 14 is a development need, not a deselection sentence.

discipline principles in Table 9.5 apply—psychological assessment data sits with the clinician or sport psychologist, not in the selection meeting.

Identity foreclosure—where early, exclusive commitment to the athlete role narrows other identity development and leaves no psychological fallback (Brewer & Petitpas, 2017; originating in the identity status framework of Marcia, 1966, and applied to sport by Brewer et al., 1993)—begins at selection.

Here's how: early selection funnels the athlete into environments where the athlete's role becomes the primary source of status, social connection, and daily structure—precisely the conditions Marcia (1966) identified as promoting premature identity commitment.

The behavioral signals are observable but easy to miss without systematic observation. The structural intervention is the IDP. Table 9.1 lists the early warning signals.

Assessing character and coachability. Character is difficult to measure because high-stakes contexts invite impression management. Self-report tools can be gamed; interviews reward rehearsed narratives. A more reliable approach prioritizes samples over signs: repeated behavioral evidence across ordinary contexts.

Character sampling straddles selection and development—the tool is the same, but the decision context differs. At selection, it replaces single-impression

TABLE 9.1 Identity Foreclosure—Early Warning Signals

Behavioral Signal	*What to Observe*	*Structural Response*
Extreme outcome dependency	Mood and self-worth fluctuate entirely on recent performance; good result = confidence, bad result = collapse	IDP targets for psychological development; decouple self-evaluation from single outcomes
Social isolation outside sport	No peer relationships, hobbies, or interests beyond the team environment; all social contact is sport-mediated	Dual-career programming; structured social integration beyond the performance chain
Dismissal of dual-career programming	Education, career exploration, or non-sport activities described as "distractions" by the athlete or by staff	Reframe dual-career as performance protection, not competition for attention; embed in IDP
Catastrophizing minor setbacks	Routine injury, temporary demotion, or a single poor performance triggers disproportionate distress	Normalize non-linear development; assign mentor who has navigated similar transitions
Mirroring	Athlete expresses only opinions and goals they believe coaches want to hear; avoids independent positions	Create low-stakes opportunities for independent voice; track whether the athlete initiates or only responds

TABLE 9.2 Character Sampling Record

Behavior to Sample	*Context (When)*	*What We Observed (Facts)*	*Pattern Emerging?*	*Next Coaching Move*

judgments with structured behavioral evidence; in development, it feeds the IDP. Table 9.2 provides a recording template for tracking samples across contexts.

Common failure modes: Treating one emotional moment as a character verdict; selective sampling (excusing favorites and scrutinizing outsiders); and confusing impression management with actual coachability. Where multiple staff sample the same athlete, compare notes before converging on a pattern—uncalibrated observers tend to confirm each other's priors rather than triangulate.

9.1.3 *Decision Architecture for Selection*

Selection decisions are where bias concentrates. They happen under time pressure, involve ambiguous data, and carry high emotional stakes. The structural fix is not "better instincts." It is a decision architecture: documented criteria, required dissent, reversibility, and bias checks. These principles draw on decision hygiene research showing that structured protocols reduce noise in complex judgments (Kahneman et al., 2021) and on procedural justice research demonstrating that perceived fairness of process shapes trust independently of outcomes (Colquitt, 2001; see also Thibaut & Walker, 1975).

Surgical training offers a useful contrast. Under the Accreditation Council for Graduate Medical Education (ACGME) competency-based framework, trainees are evaluated at defined milestones with multi-reviewer input, decisions are documented, and "not yet ready" is a system output that triggers additional development—not permanent exclusion (Nasca et al., 2012). Many sport selection systems, by contrast, assume one evaluation window is sufficient.

One structural note: The silence calculus (Chapter 1) operates in selection meetings with particular force. If no one in the room has the structural position to disagree with the head coach about a favored prospect, the decision architecture has a voice problem that no record template will fix. The record captures dissent only if the system makes dissent survivable.

9.1.4 The Demographic Lens

Selection bias also operates along demographic lines—often invisibly. Relative age and maturation effects interact with socioeconomic access: athletes from lower-resourced backgrounds may have fewer opportunities for early coaching and competition, compounding the selection disadvantage. Racial and ethnic biases are well-documented in adjacent domains—coaching opportunity structures (Duru, 2011) and media representation (Eagleman, 2011)—and there is reason to expect similar biases operate in scouting language (such as the racialized "brawn versus brains" narratives documented by Rada and Wulfemeyer (2005)) and selection evaluation, though direct research on selection-room dynamics remains limited.

The structural diagnosis: map who has access to the pipeline, who gets selected, who gets second chances, and who disappears from the system. If those patterns are non-random along demographic lines, the system is doing something—whether or not anyone intended it.

One concrete starting point: selection panels should conduct a post-decision demographic audit—a simple frequency count of who was retained, released, and loaned, disaggregated by race, gender, and age—not as a compliance exercise but as a data mirror that surfaces patterns invisible in real-time decision-making. Run it annually, present results alongside the Selection Decision Record data, and track trends over three-year windows. The audit does not prescribe quotas; it makes the system's outputs visible to the people making the inputs.

Selection is the first structural choice in the athlete lifecycle—and what happens next reveals whether the system was designed for the person or just the pick.

9.2 The Athlete Lifecycle: Where Extraction Becomes Visible

Transitions are the seams of the athlete lifecycle—and most systems fail there because no one designed for them.

We use the term acquisition–extraction cycle to describe a structural pattern: organizations invest heavily in acquiring talent, extract performance during the athlete's useful window, and treat everything else—development, transitions, and exit—as someone else's problem. The pattern echoes March's (1991) distinction between exploitation and exploration: when exploitation dominates—the competency trap (Levinthal & March, 1993)—short-term performance optimization crowds out the development that sustains long-term capacity.

The cycle is not driven by cruelty. It is driven by misaligned time horizons. The organization's clock runs by season; the athlete's career spans a decade or more. When those clocks conflict, the season wins. Table 9.3 maps this investment pattern across the lifecycle.

TABLE 9.3 The Acquisition–Extraction Cycle—Where Organizations Invest and Where They Don't

Lifecycle Stage	*Investment Level*	*What Gets Built*	*What Gets Missed*
Selection/acquisition	**HIGH**	Assessment infrastructure, talent identification pipelines	Developmental trajectory; who the system systematically excludes
Entry	**LOW**	Administrative onboarding (housing, playbook, and media training)	Identity shift, threat appraisal, social integration, and evaluation ramp
Development	**MEDIUM** (physical); **LOW** (psychological/identity)	Physical capacity, sport-specific skill; crisis response when problems surface	Psychological development, dual-career identity, mastery climate architecture, identity foreclosure prevention, and help-seeking pathways
Within-career transitions (injury, deselection, and role change)	**LOW**	Damage control after the fact	Lane discipline, decision records, structured re-entry, and communication protocols
Exit	**MINIMAL**	A gesture (farewell event, maybe a counselor referral)	Identity reconstruction support, post-exit contact structure, transition planning, and reputational signal management

Investment concentrates where the return is immediate and visible, and thins where it is structural and delayed. The rest of this section traces the major transition points—entry, within-career transitions, and exit—through that structural lens.

BOX 9.3 TIMEOUT — TWO CLOCKS, ONE SYSTEM

The organization's clock runs by season. The athlete's career spans a decade. When those clocks conflict, the season always wins—and every lifecycle failure in this chapter traces back to that mismatch. Entry is rushed because the preseason is short. Development is compressed because results are due now. Exit is improvised because next season's roster is the priority. Designing for the athlete's clock is not generosity. It is the only way the organization's clock keeps producing talent.

9.2.1 Entry: The Transition Nobody Thinks Is a Transition

The assumption is that a drafted or signed athlete is "ready"—the selection process has already validated them. The psychological reality is different. Threat appraisal, impostor phenomenon, identity foreclosure, and the silence calculus start operating before the athlete has unpacked. What belongs here is the structural architecture most onboarding systems miss.

Schlossberg's (1981) transition model identifies four factors shaping how individuals cope: Situation, Self, Support, and Strategies. Two frameworks extend this for sport. Wylleman's Holistic Athletic Career model (Wylleman, 2019; Wylleman et al., 2013) maps six interrelated layers—athletic, psychological, psychosocial, academic-vocational, financial, and legal—that shift simultaneously at every transition. Stambulova's Athletic Career Transition Model (Stambulova, 2003) distinguishes normative transitions (expected milestones) from non-normative ones (unexpected injuries and sudden deselection), noting that unresolved transitions escalate into crises.

Both reinforce the structural argument: transitions are predictable, multidimensional events that the system can design for—or leave them to chance. Table 9.4 translates these principles into structural design specifications for entry.

Return to Kaleb: his entry was logistics. Nobody mapped the identity shift. Nobody noticed the silence. By the time the development gaps were visible, the system had interpreted them as character flaws rather than its own failures. This pattern—the silence calculus in action—is well-documented in athlete help-seeking research (Gulliver et al., 2012; Park et al., 2013).

TABLE 9.4 Structural Design for Entry

Design Principle	*What It Looks Like*	*Common Failure Mode*
Map the identity shift explicitly	Built into onboarding—not a therapy session. Name what changes and normalize the difficulty: "Most athletes in your position describe the first three months as harder than expected. Here is what we have in place for that."	Identity shift unacknowledged; athlete expected to adapt silently; distress interpreted as weakness
Assign a structured connection	A veteran mentor, a designated staff contact outside the performance chain, a check-in cadence that doesn't require the athlete to ask for help	Connection left to chance; new athlete expected to self-integrate; only coaching staff assigned as contacts
Extend the evaluation ramp	First 90 days framed as "development period with structured benchmarks"—athlete can afford to be honest about what they need	First 90 days framed as "prove yourself or get cut"; athlete optimizes for impression management, not learning

9.2.2 Within-Career Transitions: Injury, Deselection, and Role Change

Three within-career transitions deserve structural design because they occur frequently, carry high identity stakes, and are handled poorly—not from malice, but from lack of design.

9.2.2.1 Injury

Injury disrupts identity, triggers grief, and forces a dual-track recovery—physical and psychological. This chapter adds a structural question: *who manages the boundary between clinical data and selection decisions?*

The silence calculus operates acutely during injury return: advocating for more recovery time risks being seen as replaceable, so athletes rationally return early (Podlog & Eklund, 2006)—even when clinical frameworks counsel otherwise (Ardern et al., 2016).

Structural design for injury transitions: separate the medical return-to-play process from the identity and role reintegration process. Build a check-in with someone outside the performance chain at defined intervals—48 hours post-injury, weekly during rehab, and at each return-to-play milestone. Make it explicit that reporting pain or readiness concerns will not affect selection status. Then back that statement with visible evidence that it's true.

Maintaining that boundary requires lane discipline—clear rules about who sees what data and for what purpose. During injury rehab, clinical data is most likely to leak into selection conversations. Table 9.5 defines the structural separation.

9.2.2.2 Deselection

The human side of deselection—the delivery conversation, the explanation of evidence, practical support, and structured follow-up—is a design challenge in its own right. The structural contribution here is the decision architecture behind that conversation.

The Selection Decision Record (Section 9.1.3) provides the documentation framework. Applied to deselection, it ensures that four structural elements are in place before the conversation: (1) evidence reviewed and documented—not recalled from memory, but written, multi-context, and dated; (2) the dissenting view captured—what the minority of staff saw, preserved in the record; (3) re-entry rules defined—clear conditions under which the decision is reversible, not rhetorical; and (4) a support path assigned—welfare check-in within 48 hours, with escalation routes for crisis risk.

Escalation triggers—self-harm risk, safeguarding concerns, discrimination allegations, or split-message risk among staff—define when the conversation stops being coach-owned.

9.2.2.3 Role Change and Trade

The veteran asked to accept a reduced role. The prospect told they're "not ready yet." The trade call comes on a Tuesday through an agent. Each is a micro-transition where the same cost–benefit math around speaking up suppresses honest response—challenging the decision risks, confirming a "not a team player" label.

TABLE 9.5 Monitoring Responsibilities—Lane Discipline

Lane	*Owner*	*What They Do*	*What They Do Not Do*
Training load data	Sport science/S&C	Collect, interpret, and recommend adjustments	Use data as discipline/ punishment
Welfare signals	Welfare lead	Triage support and coordinate referrals	Share private clinical details
Clinical assessment	Licensed clinician	Assess/diagnose/treat	Provide selection input
Safeguarding	Safeguarding lead	Triage/report/ investigate as required	Delegate investigations to coaches

Structural design here means honest, timely communication from the decision-maker—not discovered through media or agent channels—clear rationale tied to observable evidence, and a defined path forward. The Selection Decision Record provides the architecture.

9.2.2.4 Pregnancy, Maternity, and Return to Sport

These are lifecycle transitions that most systems have no architecture for—often because those systems were designed around male athletes' careers. Recent policy developments (e.g., Fédération Internationale de Football Association [FIFA], 2020; International Olympic Committee [IOC], 2021) have begun establishing minimum structural standards, but implementation varies widely across sports and levels. The structural questions are the same: who communicates what, when? What support is triggered? What does re-entry look like—including physical reconditioning, role reintegration, and childcare logistics? Operationally, this means a designated transition contact from the moment of disclosure, a staged return-to-sport protocol equivalent to return-to-play after injury (with physical reconditioning benchmarks, role reintegration milestones, and explicit roster protection during the transition), and logistical infrastructure—childcare access, schedule flexibility, lactation accommodations—treated as system requirements, not individual accommodations. The structural minimum mirrors Table 9.6: communication protocol, defined support trigger, staged re-entry pathway, and data governance. That most systems lack even this minimum reveals which athletes' lifecycles the system was designed around.

9.2.3 Exit: What the System Does When It's Done With You

This is where the acquisition–extraction cycle is most visible—and most harmful. The psychological dimensions of exit—anticipatory grief, identity reconstruction, and loss of structure—operate alongside the structural question: what should the system have built before exit became the agenda?

The severity of exit disruption is not evenly distributed. Two mechanisms compound. First, identity foreclosure hits hardest when sport has been the primary identity domain—a pattern more likely when the athlete entered a single-sport pipeline early and had limited access to dual-career programming. Second, financial precarity amplifies every dimension of the transition—identity loss, network disruption, and the urgency of finding post-career income—especially when the athlete has no financial cushion (Torregrossa et al., 2015). These mechanisms interact: athletes from lower-income backgrounds and racialized communities are disproportionately funneled into narrow sport-identity pipelines and lack the financial buffer that extends transition timelines (Beamon, 2012). Exit support must address both identity reconstruction and economic transition.

The same internal arithmetic operates at exit with particular force: articulating "I think I'm near the end" risks accelerating the process, so athletes stay silent, protect remaining contract time, and defer identity work until crisis.

Return to Kaleb one more time. Imagine he survives the entry. He adapts, performs, and gives the organization four productive seasons. Then his body slows, or the system drafts his replacement, or both. The organization that built nothing for his arrival builds nothing for his departure. The same structural absence that made his first three months the hardest of his life makes his last three months invisible. Exit without architecture is entry without architecture—repeated at higher stakes, with less time to recover.

BOX 9.4 TIMEOUT — THE EXIT YOU DESIGN IS THE ENTRY EVERYONE WATCHES

How an organization treats departing athletes is not a private matter. Every current athlete, every incoming recruit, and every agent is watching. The veteran who leaves describing abandonment changes the silence calculus for everyone still inside, operating as a form of vicarious organizational injustice where observing unfairness toward others destroys the observer's trust in the system (Greenberg, 1990). Your exit process is not the end of the lifecycle—it is the beginning of the next recruitment cycle.

In our experience, the organizations that handle exit well share three structural features. First, transition planning starts before exit—career-transition conversations, financial literacy, and identity development beyond sport are built into the development system from mid-career onward, not activated only after the exit decision. Second, the exit process is designed, not improvised: a defined communication sequence, a transition support plan naming who owns what, and post-exit check-ins at 30, 90, and 180 days—because the hardest period is often months after departure. Third, the organization acknowledges its obligation. The system benefited from the athlete's labor, risk, and identity investment; exit support is the minimum structural response to that asymmetry, not charity.

The U.S. military's Transition Assistance Program—beginning 12 months before separation—demonstrates that exit design is feasible at scale, though persistent reintegration difficulties underscore that architecture is necessary but not sufficient (Zogas, 2017).

BOX 9.5 PSYCHOLOGY SIDELINES WITH DR. MCB – WHEN THE SYSTEM IS DONE WITH YOU

In my clinical work with athletes in transition, the pattern I see most often is not sadness. It's disorientation. The athlete who retires or is released doesn't just lose a career–they lose the structure that organized their entire existence. Wake-up time, training schedule, social group, performance goals, travel rhythm, and public identity–all of it disappears simultaneously.

I want to be direct: most organizations I've worked with have no transition architecture at all. The athlete gets a farewell dinner, a gift, maybe a referral to a counselor. The exit is treated as an event, not a process.

The 48-hour rule I recommend to organizations: within 48 hours of any exit decision (release, retirement, and career-ending diagnosis), a designated transition contact–not the person who made the decision–reaches out. Not to counsel. To connect. To make sure that the person isn't sitting alone with a disrupted identity and no structure around them. It's a small structural intervention. It changes whether the athlete's last experience of the organization is abandonment or care.

Table 9.6 maps the structural risks, silence calculus mechanisms, and design minimums for each transition type.

Each transition type triggers the silence calculus through a distinct mechanism, but the design minimums in Table 9.6 are the structural floor. Without them, the acquisition–extraction cycle runs unchecked.

At every seam, the cycle is either operating by default or being interrupted by design. What does that design look like in the daily environment where athletes actually develop?

9.3 The Development Environment: Building Capacity, Not Extracting Performance

The development environment either builds the capacity athletes need to navigate pressure and transitions—or it extracts performance until the person is used up. The default is extraction. This section examines what building looks like as daily structural practice.

9.3.1 Individualized Development as System Architecture

A one-size-fits-all pathway fits no one well. Athletes differ in maturation timing, recovery capacity, psychological readiness, and life context. Bio-banding—

TABLE 9.6 Transition Architecture—Structural Risks and Design Minimums

Transition Type	*Primary Structural Risk*	*Silence Calculus Mechanism*	*Design Minimum*
Entry	System assumes "selected = ready"; no identity transition design	Admitting struggle feels like admitting you don't belong—disclosure threatens competitive standing	Map the identity shift explicitly; assign structured connection outside the performance chain; extend the evaluation ramp beyond "prove yourself"
Injury	Clinical data leaks into selection decisions; return timeline driven by roster need, not recovery	Reporting pain or readiness concerns risks being seen as replaceable—athletes return early as a rational response to incentive structure	Separate medical return-to-play from identity reintegration; lane discipline on data access; check-ins outside the performance chain at defined intervals
Deselection/ role change	Decision treated as transactional roster management; no documented evidence, dissent, or re-entry path	Challenging the decision risks confirming "not a team player" label—silence protects remaining standing	Selection Decision Record with captured dissent and defined re-entry rules; 48-hour welfare contact; communication script with evidence and forward path
Exit	No transition architecture; exit treated as an event, not a process; identity reconstruction left to the individual	Articulating "I think I'm near the end" risks accelerating the process—the athlete defers identity work until crisis	Transition planning from mid-career; designed exit process (communication sequence, support plan, post-exit check-ins at 30/90/180 days); organizational acknowledgment of obligation

grouping athletes by maturation rather than chronological age—reduces maturation bias and creates more appropriate challenge (Cumming et al., 2017; Cumming et al., 2018).

The IDP is the structural tool that links role demands to development priorities with a clear review cadence.

Status: Practitioner heuristic; not a validated instrument.

The essential version fits on one page: role demands (technical, tactical, physical, psychological), top one to two priorities for the next four to six weeks, weekly practice behaviors, program support commitments, and evidence markers for review.

The IDP is also the structural mechanism that counteracts identity foreclosure. When it includes psychological and identity-development targets alongside technical ones—dual-career programming, life skills, interests outside sport—it builds the multi-domain identity that protects athletes at every transition point.

Dual-career pathways are not a Plan B—they are transition protection. A second identity domain buffers selection pressure, supports recovery, and helps athletes take the learning risks development requires (Stambulova & Wylleman, 2014; Stambulova et al., 2009). Research confirms better transition outcomes for athletes who invest in academic-vocational development alongside sport, with emerging evidence of performance neutrality (Stambulova & Wylleman, 2019; European Commission, 2012)—though the evidence base is stronger for transition benefits. That is a system design choice.

Two upgrades sharpen development decision quality: (1) tracking life load alongside training load—well-being and stress measures inform risk and recovery (Duignan et al., 2020); and (2) linking numbers to actions—if an athlete flags high stress, there needs to be a defined support response, not just a data point.

Any monitoring system the IDP draws on requires a trust architecture—governance principles that maintain the boundary between support and surveillance (Arnold & Sade, 2017; Karkazis & Fishman, 2017). Without that boundary, the same disclosure-suppression dynamic colonizes the monitoring system: athletes manage the data rather than reporting honestly.

Six governance principles maintain the boundary between support and surveillance. Data should be purpose-limited—every data point serves a named decision and action trigger. Collection should be minimum necessary—the smallest set that works. Separation keeps clinical and welfare notes in clinical lanes, with coaches receiving operational impacts only. Consent and transparency should be the default, with exceptions explained (safety/safeguarding). Organizations should close the loop—"You said/we did"—with a quarterly review of what is collected. And regular audits should review access and use, removing measures that do not change decisions.

Common failure modes: Turning the IDP into a wish list instead of one to three role-linked priorities, skipping the review cadence, or—most corrosive—saying "develop" while selection signals say "avoid mistakes."

9.3.2 Does the Climate Rhetoric Match the Reinforcement Reality?

Motivational climate theory, including the foundational Achievement Goal Theory literature (Nicholls, 1989; Ames, 1992) and self-determination theory

(Deci & Ryan, 2000), provides the framework. The structural audit question connects climate to every transition point in this chapter: *does what the system says it values match what it actually reinforces?*

The test: if the stated value is "learn from mistakes" but the reinforced behavior is "don't make mistakes in front of selectors," the climate is performance-oriented regardless of what the poster on the wall says. The silence calculus draws its power from this misalignment—athletes learn the real rules quickly, concealing injury (Section 9.2.2) and playing safe rather than taking the learning risks development requires (Vitali et al., 2015). The operational question for staff is not "what climate do we intend?" but "what did we actually reinforce this week?" Table 9.7 provides a weekly audit framework. The value is in the discrepancy between what staff believe they did and what athletes experienced—the conversation is the intervention.

Cadence: Weekly during season (5–10 minutes in existing staff meeting). Review trends monthly. The tool fails when it becomes a compliance exercise—if staff cannot name a concrete moment for Question 1, that is the finding.

Common failure modes: Answering in generalities ("we had a good week") instead of specific observable moments, skipping the reflection during winning streaks—precisely when climate drift is hardest to detect, and treating the exercise as self-assessment rather than system audit.

The harder question is who gets in, who stays, and what happens to the people the system decides it no longer needs.

TABLE 9.7 Weekly Climate Audit—Staff Reflection

Audit Question	*This Week's Evidence*	*Gap Identified (Intended vs. Reinforced)*
Name one moment this week where a mistake was treated as information rather than punishment.		
Name one moment this week where effort or process was praised publicly—not just outcomes.		
Could athletes ask "why" without consequence?		
Name one athlete who was actively invited to speak when they otherwise would not have.		
Where did the gap between intended climate and reinforced climate show up this week?		

9.4 Pipeline Design: Where the Cycle Perpetuates or Breaks

If a pathway has no mechanism for a 19-year-old to enter, the standards aren't high—the system is blind to talent that doesn't fit its timeline.

Selection concentrates bias along maturation, timing, and demographic lines. Pipeline architecture determines whether those biases compound or correct over time. Once someone is labeled "out," what does the system actually do? Many pathways operate like elimination tournaments: one decision, one window, and permanent consequences. Once the label sticks, opportunity shrinks and development options narrow—by the time late potential becomes visible, the athlete has lost access to high-quality coaching and competition.

The Developmental Model of Sport Participation (Côté et al., 2007) makes the developmental case for diversified pathways that delay specialization, but pipeline design is also an equity intervention. The demographic lens applies with compound force: if early selection favors better-resourced athletes and the pipeline offers no re-entry, the architecture locks in that advantage permanently. Figure 9.3 illustrates the contrast between these two designs.

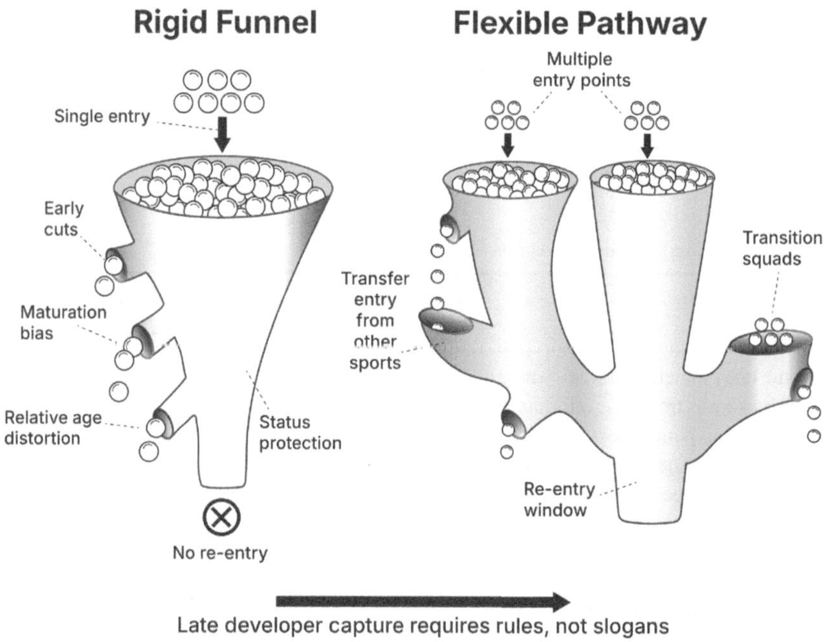

FIGURE 9.3 Rigid Funnel Versus Permeable Pipeline.

Rigid funnels (single entry) shed talent through early cuts, maturation bias, and relative-age distortion—often reinforced by status protection—and typically offer no re-entry. A flexible pathway designs multiple entry points, transfer routes from other sports, transition squads, and re-entry windows to recapture late developers—because late-developer capture requires rules, not slogans.

9.4.1 Designing Permeability: From Ladders to Climbing Walls

The shift is from a ladder—one way up, fall off, and you're done—to a climbing wall: multiple routes, lateral movement, and the ability to come back to a hold you missed. A permeable pipeline does three things structurally:

1. Multiple entry points—including transfer entry from other sports
2. Transition zones—late improvers are not trapped in dead-end teams
3. Return pathways—re-entry is real, not rhetorical

9.4.1.1 Checking Pipeline Permeability

Five questions surface the most common pipeline design gaps (Table 9.8). For each, answer with what the system currently does—not what the handbook says it does.

The last question is often the most diagnostic. If the answer is "we don't track that," that's the blind spot.

An honest caveat: evidence for permeable pathway design is stronger on the problem side than the solution side. Treat these recommendations as structurally reasoned hypotheses—grounded in developmental science rather than controlled trials—and track whether they work.

9.4.2 Talent Transfer (Lateral Entry)

Late development is vertical movement within a sport. Talent transfer is lateral movement—from donor sports into recipient sports—and an efficiency tool, not charity. Transfer athletes often arrive with high training age, strong learning behaviors, and transferable traits. Transfer programs have accelerated entry into

TABLE 9.8 Pipeline Permeability Check

Question	*Current Reality*	*Design Gap?*
Can an athlete enter the pathway after age 16? If so, through what route?		
If an athlete is deselected at one level, is there a defined re-entry mechanism?		
Is there a lateral transfer route from other sports? What does intake look like?		
What percentage of the current senior cohort entered through the "standard" route versus alternative pathways?		
Who in the pathway has never been reviewed for re-entry after an initial "no"?		

sports like skeleton by targeting athletes whose profiles fit new task demands (Bullock et al., 2009; MacNamara & Collins, 2015).

Boundary note (para-sport): Classification systems, equipment access, and variable competition opportunities create additional pathway bias in para-sport contexts. The structural principles apply, but the specific indicators and constraints differ (Dehghansai et al., 2022).

Additional context: Some national systems delay formal ranking in childhood to prioritize broad participation (NIF, 2019)—a structural counterpoint to the urgency-driven selection models common in professional sport.

9.4.3 *Lifecycle Architecture: How Do You Know It's Working?*

The system-level question is whether the lifecycle architecture—taken as a whole—is producing different outcomes than the default. Five observable signals, tracked annually, give a performance director a lifecycle health check without new instrumentation (Table 9.9).

Status: Practitioner heuristic; not a validated instrument.

TABLE 9.9 Lifecycle Architecture Health Check—Five Observable Signals

Signal	*What to Measure*	*How to Track*	*What a Bad Number Tells You*
Pipeline diversity ratio	Percentage of current senior cohort who entered through non-standard routes (late entry, talent transfer, and re-entry after deselection)	Annual cohort audit	If zero: the pipeline is selecting for timing, not talent. The system has no correction mechanism for early selection errors.
Decision documentation rate	Percentage of selection and deselection decisions with a completed Selection Decision Record—including captured dissent and re-entry rules	End-of-cycle audit of records filed versus decisions made	Low rate = decisions are still happening in hallways. Documentation rate is a proxy for decision quality culture.
Transition contact compliance	For every exit, deselection, and major injury: was the 48-hour contact rule met?	Binary log per event (yes/no, with date)	Non-compliance reveals whether structural commitments survive operational pressure. This is the simplest stress test of lifecycle architecture.

(*Continued*)

TABLE 9.9 (Continued)

Signal	*What to Measure*	*How to Track*	*What a Bad Number Tells You*
Athlete-reported decision clarity	Single anonymous item: "I understood the evidence behind the decision that affected me"	End-of-cycle anonymous survey (one item)	The trend matters more than the score. A declining trend is a silence calculus signal—athletes are receiving less explanation, not more.
Exit reputation signal	What recently departed athletes say about the organization's handling of their transition	Brief voluntary post-exit survey at 90 days; attend to unsolicited comments about communication, support, and dignity	The strongest leading indicator of whether lifecycle architecture is functioning or decorative. Negative exit signals change the silence calculus for everyone still inside.

All are observable, auditable, and sensitive to the structural choices this chapter argues matter most. Track them annually. If the numbers don't move, the architecture is policy, not practice.

BOX 9.6 SKEPTIC'S CORNER — "WE CAN'T AFFORD TO WAIT FOR LATE DEVELOPERS"

The Objection: *"We cannot afford to wait for late developers. Our competitors are signing the best talent at 14. If we slow down, we lose."*

The Rebuttal: The choice is not between speed and patience. It is between two selection errors—and only one is visible.

When an organization cuts early, it sees the players it kept. It does not see the ones it lost who would have emerged at 17, 19, or 22. Early performance is a weak predictor of senior success—correlations between youth and senior performance in many sports tend to be modest, meaning that most of the variance in who becomes elite remains unexplained by early selection (Güllich & Emrich, 2014; Johnston et al., 2018). Some evidence suggests that setbacks and adversity—including deselection—can be developmentally productive for athletes who have the support and psychological resources to use them (Collins & MacNamara, 2012).

Competitors who "sign the best at 14" are playing a lottery and calling it scouting. Most of those signings will not convert. Meanwhile, organizations with flexible pathways–transfer entry points, re-entry mechanisms, and mastery-focused development–capture talent that rigid funnels discard.

What to try anyway: Audit one age group in the current pathway. How many athletes entered through the standard route? How many entered late, transferred, or re-entered after deselection? If the second number is zero, the pipeline isn't rigorous–it's rigid.

9.4.3.1 Chapter Synthesis

The athlete lifecycle is not a human resources function. It is the structural test of whether an organization's operating system works under pressure. Selection, entry, development, transition, and exit are seams where the acquisition–extraction cycle either runs unchecked or gets interrupted by design. This chapter demonstrates that the same architectural failures—misaligned time horizons, absent decision records, collapsed lane discipline, and rigid pipelines—produce predictable breakdowns at every seam. The implication: lifecycle architecture is not a resource luxury. It is the minimum structural condition under which psychological safety becomes operational rather than aspirational.

Key Chapter Takeaways

1. **Selection is a hypothesis, not a verdict.** Treat every selection decision as a time-limited bet requiring documented evidence, captured dissent, bias checks, and reassessment windows—not a one-shot forecast validated by the resources poured into it afterward.
2. **The acquisition–extraction cycle is the default, not an aberration.** Organizations over invest in scouting and extraction while under designing entry, transitions, and exit—recognizing this pattern is the first step to interrupting it.
3. **Lane discipline is the structural condition for honest data.** The moment well-being information enters selection conversations, athletes manage the signal rather than reporting it—data governance keeps the silence calculus from colonizing every support system.
4. **Pipeline rigidity converts timing advantages into permanent exclusion.** Permeable pathways—multiple entry points, return mechanisms, and talent transfer intake—are equity interventions that also capture talent rigid funnels discard.
5. **Exit architecture is recruitment architecture.** How the organization treats departing athletes is visible to everyone still inside the system and to everyone considering entering it—dignified exit design is structural self-interest, not generosity.

Discussion Questions

1. Using the acquisition–extraction cycle framework, map one organization you know: which lifecycle seam received the least structural investment, and what was the downstream cost to trust?
2. The Selection Decision Record requires captured dissent. What structural conditions—beyond policy—would make dissent genuinely survivable in a selection meeting you have observed or participated in?
3. Where have you seen the boundary between athlete monitoring-as-support and monitoring-as-surveillance collapse? What would re-establish lane discipline in that context?
4. The chapter argues that permeable pipelines are equity interventions. Under what conditions might a flexibility-oriented pathway introduce new problems—and how would you design against them?

References

Ames, C. (1992). Classrooms: Goals, structures, and student motivation. *Journal of Educational Psychology*, *84*(3), 261–271. https://doi.org/10.1037/0022-0663.84.3.261

Ardern, C. L., Glasgow, P., Schneiders, A., Witvrouw, E., Clarsen, B., Cools, A., Gojanovic, B., Griffin, S., Khan, K. M., Moksnes, H., Mutch, S. A., Phillips, N., Reurink, G., Sadler, R., Silbernagel, K. G., Thorborg, K., Wangensteen, A., Wilk, K. E., & Bizzini, M. (2016). 2016 consensus statement on return to sport from the First World Congress in Sports Physical Therapy, Bern. *British Journal of Sports Medicine*, *50*(14), 853–864. https://doi.org/10.1136/bjsports-2016-096278

Arnold, J. F., & Sade, R. M. (2017). Wearable technologies in collegiate sports: The ethics of collecting biometric data from student-athletes. *American Journal of Bioethics*, *17*(1), 67–70. https://doi.org/10.1080/15265161.2016.1251648

Beamon, K. (2012). "I'm a baller": Athletic identity foreclosure among African-American former student-athletes. *Journal of African American Studies*, *16*(2), 195–208. https://doi.org/10.1007/s12111-012-9211-8

Bergeron, M. F., Mountjoy, M., Armstrong, N., Chia, M., Côté, J., Emery, C. A., Faigenbaum, A., Hall, G., Jr., Kriemler, S., Léglise, M., Malina, R. M., Pensgaard, A. M., Sanchez, A., Soligard, T., Sundgot-Borgen, J., van Mechelen, W., Weissensteiner, J. R., & Engebretsen, L. (2015). International Olympic Committee consensus statement on youth athletic development. *British Journal of Sports Medicine*, *49*(13), 843–851. https://doi.org/10.1136/bjsports-2015-094962

Brewer, B. W., & Petitpas, A. J. (2017). Athletic identity foreclosure. *Current Opinion in Psychology*, *16*, 118–122. https://doi.org/10.1016/j.copsyc.2017.05.004

Brewer, B. W., Van Raalte, J. L., & Linder, D. E. (1993). Athletic identity: Hercules' muscles or Achilles' heel? *International Journal of Sport Psychology, 24*(2), 237–254.

Bullock, N., Gulbin, J. P., Martin, D. T., Ross, A., Holland, T., & Marino, F. (2009). Talent identification and deliberate programming in skeleton: Ice novice to Winter Olympian in 14 months. *Journal of Sports Sciences*, *27*(4), 397–404. https://doi.org/10.1080/02640410802549751

Cobley, S., Baker, J., Wattie, N., & McKenna, J. (2009). Annual age-grouping and athlete development: A meta-analytical review of relative age effects in sport. *Sports Medicine*, *39*(3), 235–256. https://doi.org/10.2165/00007256-200939030-00005

Collins, D., & MacNamara, Á. (2012). The rocky road to the top: Why talent needs trauma. *Sports Medicine*, *42*(11), 907–914. https://doi.org/10.1007/BF03262302

Colquitt, J. A. (2001). On the dimensionality of organizational justice: A construct validation of a measure. *Journal of Applied Psychology*, *86*(3), 386–400. https://doi.org/10.1037/0021-9010.86.3.386

Côté, J., Baker, J., & Abernethy, B. (2007). Practice and play in the development of sport expertise. In G. Tenenbaum & R. C. Eklund (Eds.), *Handbook of sport psychology* (3rd ed., pp. 184–202). Wiley.

Côté, J., Macdonald, D. J., Baker, J., & Abernethy, B. (2006). When "where" is more important than "when": Birthplace and birthdate effects on the achievement of sporting expertise. *Journal of Sports Sciences*, *24*(10), 1065–1073. https://doi.org/10.1080/02640410500432490

Cumming, S. P., Lloyd, R. S., Oliver, J. L., Eisenmann, J. C., & Malina, R. M. (2017). Bio-banding in sport: Applications to competition, talent identification, and strength and conditioning of youth athletes. *Strength & Conditioning Journal*, *39*(2), 34–47. https://doi.org/10.1519/SSC.0000000000000281

Cumming, S. P., Brown, D. J., Mitchell, S., Bunce, J., Hunt, D., Hedges, C., Crane, G., Gross, A., Scott, S., Franklin, E., Breakspear, D., Dennison, L., White, P., Cain, A., Eisenmann, J. C., & Malina, R. M. (2018). Premier League academy soccer players' experiences of competing in a tournament bio-banded for biological maturation. *Journal of Sports Sciences*, *36*(7), 757–765. https://doi.org/10.1080/02640414.2017.1340656

Deci, E. L., & Ryan, R. M. (2000). The "what" and "why" of goal pursuits: Human needs and the self-determination of behavior. *Psychological Inquiry*, *11*(4), 227–268. https://doi.org/10.1207/S15327965PLI1104_01

Dehghansai, N., Pinder, R. A., & Baker, J. (2022). Talent identification and development in Paralympic contexts: Current challenges. *Frontiers in Sports and Active Living*, *4*, Article 926974. https://doi.org/10.3389/fspor.2022.926974

Den Hartigh, R. J. R., Hill, Y., & van Geert, P. L. C. (2018). The development of talent in sports: A dynamic network approach. *Complexity*, *2018*, Article 9280154. https://doi.org/10.1155/2018/9280154

Duignan, C., Doherty, C., Caulfield, B., & Blake, C. (2020). Single-item self-report measures of team-sport athlete well-being and their relationship with training load: A systematic review. *Journal of Athletic Training*, *55*(9), 944–953. https://doi.org/10.4085/1062-6050-0528.19

Duru, N. J. (2011). *Advancing the ball: Race, reformation, and the quest for equal coaching opportunity in the NFL*. Oxford University Press.

Eagleman, A. N. (2011). Stereotypes of race and nationality: A qualitative analysis of sport magazine coverage of MLB players. *Journal of Sport Management*, *25*(2), 156–168. https://doi.org/10.1123/jsm.25.2.156

European Commission. (2012). *EU guidelines on dual careers of athletes: Recommended policy actions in support of dual careers in high-performance sport*. https://ec.europa.eu/assets/eac/sport/library/documents/dual-career-guidelines-final_en.pdf

Fédération Internationale de Football Association. (2020). *Regulations on the status and transfer of players* (amended 2020, maternity provisions). https://www.fifa.com/legal/football-regulatory/regulations-status-transfer-players

Gibbs, B. G., Jarvis, J. A., & Dufur, M. J. (2012). The rise of the underdog? The relative age effect reversal among Canadian-born NHL hockey players: A reply to Nolan and Howell. *International Review for the Sociology of Sport*, *47*(5), 644–649. https://doi.org/10.1177/1012690211414343

Greenberg, J. (1990). Organizational justice: Yesterday, today, and tomorrow. *Journal of Management*, *16*(2), 399–432. https://doi.org/10.1177/014920639001600208

Güllich, A., & Emrich, E. (2014). Considering long-term sustainability in the development of world class success. *European Journal of Sport Science*, *14*(Suppl 1), S383–S397. https://doi.org/10.1080/17461391.2012.706320

Gulliver, A., Griffiths, K. M., & Christensen, H. (2012). Barriers and facilitators to mental health help-seeking for young elite athletes: A qualitative study. *BMC Psychiatry*, *12*, Article 157. https://doi.org/10.1186/1471-244X-12-157

Hill, A., MacNamara, Á., & Collins, D. (2019). Development and initial validation of the Psychological Characteristics of Developing Excellence Questionnaire version 2 (PCDEQ2). *European Journal of Sport Science*, *19*(4), 517–528. https://doi.org/10.1080/17461391.2018.1535627

International Olympic Committee. (2021). *IOC framework on fairness, inclusion and non-discrimination on the basis of gender identity and sex variations*. https://olympics.com/ioc/human-rights/fairness-inclusion-non-discrimination

Johnston, K., Wattie, N., Schorer, J., & Baker, J. (2018). Talent identification in sport: A systematic review. *Sports Medicine*, *48*(1), 97–109. https://doi.org/10.1007/s40279-017-0803-2

Kahneman, D., Sibony, O., & Sunstein, C. R. (2021). *Noise: A flaw in human judgment*. Little, Brown Spark.

Karkazis, K., & Fishman, J. R. (2017). Tracking U.S. professional athletes: The ethics of biometric technologies. *American Journal of Bioethics*, *17*(1), 45–60. https://doi.org/10.1080/15265161.2016.1251633

Khamis, H. J., & Roche, A. F. (1994). Predicting adult stature without using skeletal age: The Khamis-Roche method. *Pediatrics*, *94*(4), 504–507. https://doi.org/10.1542/peds.94.4.504

Levinthal, D. A., & March, J. G. (1993). The myopia of learning. *Strategic Management Journal*, *14*(S2), 95–112. https://doi.org/10.1002/smj.4250141009

MacNamara, Á., & Collins, D. (2011). Development and initial validation of the Psychological Characteristics of Developing Excellence Questionnaire. *Journal of Sports Sciences*, *29*(12), 1273–1286. https://doi.org/10.1080/02640414.2011.589468

MacNamara, Á., & Collins, D. (2015). Second chances: Investigating athletes' experiences of talent transfer. *PLOS ONE*, *10*(11), e0143592. https://doi.org/10.1371/journal.pone.0143592

March, J. G. (1991). Exploration and exploitation in organizational learning. *Organization Science*, *2*(1), 71–87. https://doi.org/10.1287/orsc.2.1.71

Marcia, J. E. (1966). Development and validation of ego-identity status. *Journal of Personality and Social Psychology*, *3*(5), 551–558. https://doi.org/10.1037/h0023281

Merton, R. K. (1968). The Matthew effect in science. *Science*, *159*(3810), 56–63. https://doi.org/10.1126/science.159.3810.56

Mirwald, R. L., Baxter-Jones, A. D. G., Bailey, D. A., & Beunen, G. P. (2002). An assessment of maturity from anthropometric measurements. *Medicine & Science in Sports & Exercise*, *34*(4), 689–694. https://doi.org/10.1097/00005768-200204000-00020

Mountjoy, M., Sundgot-Borgen, J. K., Burke, L. M., Ackerman, K. E., Blauwet, C., Constantini, N., Lebrun, C., Lundy, B., Melin, A. K., Meyer, N. L., Sherman, R. T., Tenforde, A. S., Torstveit, M. K., & Budgett, R. (2018). IOC consensus statement on relative energy deficiency in sport (RED-S): 2018 update. *British Journal of Sports Medicine*, *52*(11), 687–697. https://doi.org/10.1136/bjsports-2018-099193

Nasca, T. J., Philibert, I., Brigham, T., & Flynn, T. C. (2012). The next GME accreditation system—Rationale and benefits. *New England Journal of Medicine*, *366*(11), 1051–1056. https://doi.org/10.1056/NEJMsr1200117

Nicholls, J. G. (1989). *The competitive ethos and democratic education*. Harvard University Press.

Norwegian Olympic and Paralympic Committee and Confederation of Sports (NIF). (2019). *Children's rights in sport and provisions on children's sports* (revised 2019). https://www.idrettsforbundet.no/contentassets/b034b278300846a49afa033e42d8e829/20200320-bestemmelser-og-rettigheter-pa-engelsk.pdf

Park, S., Lavallee, D., & Tod, D. (2013). Athletes' career transition out of sport: A systematic review. *International Review of Sport and Exercise Psychology*, *6*(1), 22–53. https://doi.org/10.1080/1750984X.2012.687053

Podlog, L., & Eklund, R. C. (2006). A longitudinal investigation of competitive athletes' return to sport following serious injury. *Journal of Applied Sport Psychology*, *18*(1), 44–68. https://doi.org/10.1080/10413200500471199

Rada, J. A., & Wulfemeyer, K. T. (2005). Color coded: Racial descriptors in television coverage of intercollegiate sports. *Journal of Broadcasting & Electronic Media*, *49*(1), 65–85. https://doi.org/10.1207/s15506878jobem4901_5

Rees, T., Hardy, L., Güllich, A., Abernethy, B., Côté, J., Woodman, T., Montgomery, H., Laing, S., & Warr, C. (2016). The Great British Medalists Project: A review of current knowledge on the development of the world's best sporting talent. *Sports Medicine*, *46*(8), 1041–1058. https://doi.org/10.1007/s40279-016-0476-2

Rosenthal, R., & Jacobson, L. (1968). *Pygmalion in the classroom: Teacher expectation and pupils' intellectual development*. Holt, Rinehart and Winston.

Schlossberg, N. K. (1981). A model for analyzing human adaptation to transition. *The Counseling Psychologist*, *9*(2), 2–18. https://doi.org/10.1177/001100008100900202

Smith, K. L., Weir, P. L., Till, K., Romann, M., & Cobley, S. (2018). Relative age effects across and within female sport contexts: A systematic review and meta-analysis. *Sports Medicine*, *48*(6), 1451–1478. https://doi.org/10.1007/s40279-018-0890-8

Stambulova, N. B. (2003). Symptoms of a crisis-transition: A grounded theory study. In N. Hassmén (Ed.), *SIPF Yearbook 2003* (pp. 97–109). Örebro University Press.

Stambulova, N. B., Alfermann, D., Statler, T., & Côté, J. (2009). ISSP position stand: Career development and transitions of athletes. *International Journal of Sport and Exercise Psychology*, *7*(4), 395–412. https://doi.org/10.1080/1612197X.2009.9671916

Stambulova, N. B., & Wylleman, P. (2014). Athletes' career development and transitions. In A. G. Papaioannou & D. Hackfort (Eds.), *Routledge companion to sport and exercise psychology: Global perspectives and fundamental concepts* (pp. 605–620). Routledge. https://doi.org/10.4324/9781315880198-46

Stambulova, N. B., & Wylleman, P. (2019). Psychology of athletes' dual careers: A state-of-the-art critical review of the European discourse. *Psychology of Sport and Exercise*, *42*, 74–88. https://doi.org/10.1016/j.psychsport.2018.11.013

Thibaut, J., & Walker, L. (1975). *Procedural justice: A psychological analysis*. Lawrence Erlbaum Associates.

Torregrossa, M., Ramis, Y., Pallarés, S., Azócar, F., & Selva, C. (2015). Olympic athletes back to retirement: A qualitative longitudinal study. *Psychology of Sport and Exercise*, *21*, 50–56. https://doi.org/10.1016/j.psychsport.2015.03.003

Vitali, F., Bortoli, L., Bertinato, L., Robazza, C., & Schena, F. (2015). Motivational climate, resilience, and burnout in youth sport. *Sport Sciences for Health*, *11*(1), 103–108. https://doi.org/10.1007/s11332-014-0214-9

Wylleman, P. (2019). A developmental and holistic perspective on transiting out of elite sport. In M. H. Anshel, T. A. Petrie, & J. A. Steinfeldt (Eds.), *APA handbook of sport and exercise psychology: Sport psychology* (Vol. 1, pp. 201–216). American Psychological Association. https://doi.org/10.1037/0000123-011

Wylleman, P., Reints, A., & De Knop, P. (2013). A developmental and holistic perspective on athletic career development. In P. Sotiaradou & V. De Bosscher (Eds.), *Managing high performance sport* (pp. 159–182). Routledge.

Zogas, A. (2017). *US military veterans' difficult transitions back to civilian life and the VA's response*. Watson Institute for International and Public Affairs, Brown University. https://watson.brown.edu/costsofwar/files/cow/imce/papers/2017/Zogas_Veterans%27%20Transitions_CoW.pdf

10

THE STAKEHOLDER ECOSYSTEM—MANAGING THE UNMANAGEABLE

Learning Objectives

By the end of this chapter, the reader will be able to:

1. Evaluate stakeholder salience using power, legitimacy, urgency, and attitude dimensions to distinguish voice from veto in high-performance sport decisions.
2. Design a crisis communication sequence that maintains values-anchored governance under media velocity, integrating welfare gates and consent protocols across the first 72 hours.
3. Analyze how digital platform mechanics convert fan investment into operational risk, and apply a triage protocol to differentiate volume risk from severity risk in online abuse.
4. Construct boundary systems for agents, families, and sponsors that protect decision architecture while honoring legitimate relationships.

BOX 10.1 CASE STUDY — THE COMMUNICATIONS COORDINATOR WHO STOPPED SAYING NO

Composite vignette. Details changed to protect privacy.

Rena managed the interface between the performance environment and everyone outside it. When a title sponsor requested a behind-the-scenes

DOI: 10.4324/9781003631217-11

documentary crew in the training facility during a difficult run of results, she raised it with the CEO. He said, "They pay the bills. Make it work."

The crew arrived on Monday. By Wednesday, two players had asked the physio to schedule treatment during training—not because they were injured, but because the treatment room had no cameras. The analyst noticed the head coach softening his halftime talk, leaving tactical problems unaddressed. Rena fielded three calls from agents asking why their clients were being filmed without individual consent forms. One parent posted on social media: "My son did not sign up to be content."

She tried to set boundaries—restricted areas, approved filming windows. The sponsor's activation manager called the CEO directly: "We were promised full access." The CEO overruled the restrictions.

Within two weeks, the assistant coaches stopped using the video review room when the crew was present. Tactical conversations moved to car parks and text messages. An athlete welfare concern that should have been raised in the daily meeting was mentioned to a physio in a corridor instead—and was missed.

The end-of-season review noted "communication breakdowns" and "inconsistent adherence to performance protocols." No one mentioned the documentary crew. The recommendation was a team-building retreat.

How do we stay grounded when everyone is screaming?

A sponsor demands behind-the-scenes access during a losing run. Within two weeks, tactical conversations have moved to car parks and text messages. A welfare concern gets mentioned in a corridor instead of a meeting—and is missed. The end-of-season review cites "communication breakdowns." Nobody mentions the documentary crew.

External pressure does not stay external. It enters from the outside and damages everything built on the inside. This chapter argues that managing the external interface is governance work, not communications work, and builds four operational domains: ecosystem mapping that distinguishes voice from veto using stakeholder salience analysis, values-anchored crisis communication with a 72-hour response timeline and welfare gates, digital safety systems that separate volume risk from severity risk so threats are caught early and athletes are not carrying triage alone, and boundary frameworks for agents, families, and sponsors that protect decision architecture while honoring legitimate relationships.

Honor the relationship, protect the architecture. Every unmanaged stakeholder relationship is a structural bypass of everything the previous chapters built.

FIGURE 10.1 You Are Here—Ecosystem.

The HPCOS seven-layer architecture with Layer 6 (Ecosystem) highlighted.

10.1 Seeing the Ecosystem as a System—And as a Relationship

Principle: Stakeholders hold legitimate claims on the organization—fans fund it, families sacrifice for it, sponsors invest in it, and communities host it. Unmanaged, those claims degrade every internal layer of the operating system.

Two patterns lead to trouble: treating the ecosystem as noise or treating every external voice as equally entitled to shape decisions. Between those extremes is the operating position this chapter builds: *honor the relationship, protect the architecture.*

A sponsor's behind-the-scenes demand overrides decision architecture; a media pile-on collapses psychological safety; a fan campaign weaponizes silence—these are structural problems that enter through the ecosystem layer, not PR problems.

10.1.1 Stakeholder Salience and the Voice–Veto Distinction

A stakeholder is anyone who can affect or be affected by the organization's objectives (Freeman, 1984)—a definition so broad it does not actually tell you who can stop you on Tuesday.

Mitchell et al.'s (1997) salience model explains why attention swings. Stakeholders rise in the field of view when they carry power (ability to impose costs), legitimacy (a claim others accept as appropriate), or urgency (time pressure demanding immediate response). In sport, salience is unstable because seasons, events, and injuries re-order what matters (Byun & Leopkey, 2022; Duignan et al., 2023; Parent, 2008). Networked media adds another variable: social reach can raise practical power without formal authority (Naraine et al., 2020).

This is where leaders get trapped. They confuse influence with governance—and end up treating any loud stakeholder as a stakeowner.

A *stakeowner* is a stakeholder with formal decision rights in a defined lane (board governance, league eligibility, safeguarding obligations, or collectively bargained agreements). Everyone else gets voice, not veto—a distinction that collapses under pressure if it has not been stated in advance.

The reason voice still matters is procedural justice. Stakeholders who are heard but overruled still report higher trust than those never consulted (Lind et al., 1990; Tyler, 2006). Voice is a mechanism for reducing friction and preventing surprise campaigns.

10.1.2 Mapping and Engagement

Two linked moves make this operational:

1. **Map the ecosystem with one extra dimension:** Adding attitude (supportive, neutral, and opposed) to a standard power–interest grid turns the map into a prediction tool: the same stakeholder with the same leverage can be either a coalition partner or an active blocker (Demir et al., 2015). Figure 10.2 maps this, and Table 10.1 illustrates how representative stakeholder groups score on each dimension.
2. **Choose an engagement mode that fits the lane:** The IAP2 Spectrum of Public Participation describes five modes—inform, consult, involve, collaborate, and empower (IAP2 International Federation, 2018).

Do not skip mapping the athlete group as a stakeholder in ecosystem decisions—sponsor activations, media access policies, community commitments. That is a governance feature of this layer, not a courtesy.

A default script for setting the voice-without-veto expectation: "We want your voice early. Your input can shape options. The final call sits with the domain owner unless governance rules give you decision authority."

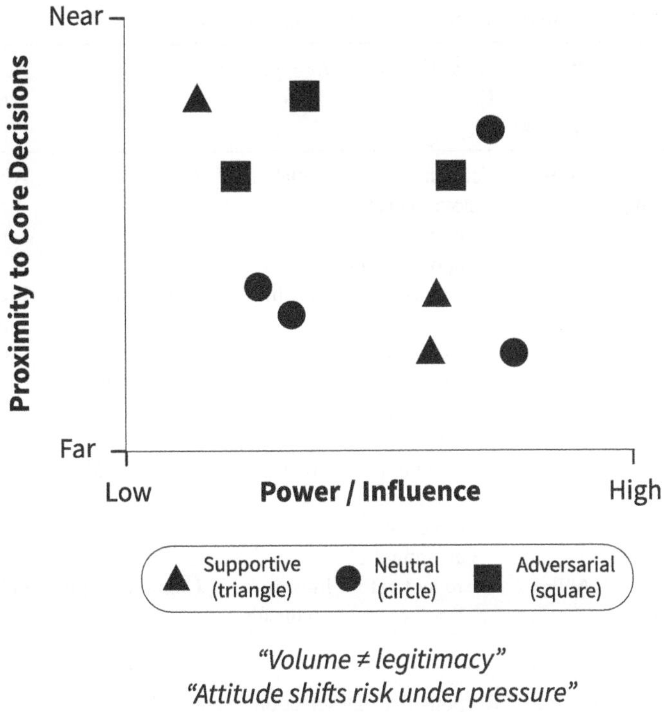

FIGURE 10.2 Stakeholder Mapping Matrix—Power/Influence × Proximity With Attitude Overlay.

Diagnostic map scoring external stakeholders on power, proximity, and attitude.

The check on concentrated decision authority is transparency—closing the loop publicly, genuinely using input, and creating documented escalation avenues. Without those mechanisms, voice-without-veto becomes performative consultation (Tyler, 2006).

10.1.3 When Power Asymmetry Overrides the Framework

A harder truth: when a stakeholder holds existential financial leverage—a title sponsor funding 40% of operations—economic reality confers de facto veto regardless of the framework. Name the dependency explicitly in the map and build contingency plans. Pretending the framework resolves a power asymmetry it cannot resolve undermines its credibility elsewhere (Freeman, 1984).

Example: A coach deselects a starting athlete. Within 24 hours:

The decision lane anchors the entire table: selection is delegated to the head coach, and leadership supports the coach unless safeguarding or eligibility rules are implicated.

TABLE 10.1 Stakeholder Mapping Matrix (Sample Rows)

Stakeholder Group	*Power/ Interest/ Attitude*	*Voice Versus Veto*	*Engagement Mode*	*Owner*	*Next Action (30 Days)*
Board/ ownership	10/9/+2	Veto on governance, budget, appointments	Collaborate	CEO	Align on pressure triggers
Governing body	9/7/0	Veto on rules, eligibility, discipline	Consult	Compliance	Pre-brief on regulatory changes
Athlete leaders/ union	8/10/+4	Voice; veto only where legally bargained	Collaborate	Welfare lead	Confirm reporting channels
Major sponsor	7/8/+5	Voice on brand alignment, not veto on performance	Involve	Commercial	Align values messaging
Fans/ community	6/9/±	Voice, not veto	Inform + consult	Communications	Publish boundary policy

TABLE 10.2 Lane-Based Response to a Deselection Event

Stakeholder	*Without Lane Map (Improvised)*	*With Lane Map (Governed)*
Fans	Flood social media demanding explanations; organization drawn into a public selection debate	Boundary statement published; no public litigation of selection decisions
Athlete's agent	Calls the GM, implies media contacts are ready; organization scrambles	Meeting scheduled; lane held: "Selection remains with the coaching staff"
Sponsor or board member	Emails asking whether the decision aligns with governance; organization over-explains or is caught off guard	Proactive heads-up: "Delegated coaching decision. Process is documented and aligned with duty of care"
Athlete's family	Requests a meeting; organization has no script and negotiates in real time	Meeting offered through boundary protocol; lanes already documented

10.2 Crisis Communication and Media Velocity

Principle: In a high-visibility crisis, communication speed is governance speed. Speed without values produces damage at scale.

Sport crises rarely arrive with clean timing. They land during competition phases, when nervous systems are already loaded. Crisis communication is not only reputational. It is a duty-of-care function (Fiedler et al., 2023), and that changes how the sequence should be designed. Other high-stakes industries have formalized what sport still improvises. Aviation research showed that information flow failures compound organizational accidents (Reason, 1997). Healthcare's disclosure-of-error frameworks separate acknowledging harm from assigning blame (Gallagher et al., 2007)—a distinction sport rarely makes under media velocity.

10.2.1 Crisis Attribution and Sport-Specific Constraints

Crisis attribution determines response intensity: victim crises (low responsibility) need fact clarification, accidental crises need explanation and correction, and preventable crises (misconduct and negligence) require apology, repair, and consequences (Coombs, 2007).

Sport adds four constraints that generic crisis models miss: fan identity makes reactions faster and more emotional than corporate models assume; competitive overlap means leadership cannot stop the season to manage the narrative; celebrity athletes mean an individual incident becomes an organizational crisis instantly; and community symbolism means a roster decision can trigger civic backlash (Simpson et al., 2025).

10.2.2 Communicating Under Legal Constraints

Legal constraints change what gets communicated, not whether to communicate:

TABLE 10.3 What Can and Cannot Be Communicated Under Common Constraints

Constraint	*What Is Typically Restricted*	*What Can Still Be Communicated*
Active investigation	Facts under investigation, witness identities, and evidence details	Investigation exists, its scope, timeline, and who leads it
Medical confidentiality	Diagnosis, treatment, and prognosis without the athlete's consent	Organization is providing support; the athlete's welfare is a priority
Employment/contract law	Terms of employment, disciplinary specifics, and settlement details	Process is underway, follows organizational policy, with update timeline
Safeguarding	Identities of minors, details of allegations during assessment	Concern received, handled by trained personnel, reporting pathway available

Move fast on what is known, mark what is not, and show the work through actions. Two artifacts keep things anchored: one internal fact base (verified facts, open questions, and constraints—everyone pulls from this document, nobody freelances) and one external message spine (what happened, what the organization is doing, and what comes next).

> **BOX 10.2 TIMEOUT — THE FIRST STATEMENT IS A CONTRACT**
>
> Stakeholders tend to tolerate uncertainty better than silence–a pattern consistent with crisis communication research (Coombs, 2007) and procedural justice theory (Tyler, 2006). If the statement says "we will update tomorrow," the update happens tomorrow–even if the update is simply, "The investigation is ongoing and our next update is on Friday." The clock is part of the message. Break it, and stakeholders learn that the organization's words are unreliable. Keep it, and credibility builds while the facts are still emerging.

10.2.3 The 72-Hour Crisis Response Sequence

The first 72 hours stabilize facts, protect people, and hold one message spine:

Yorkshire County Cricket Club's handling of racism allegations raised by Azeem Rafiq illustrates every step failing in sequence (Digital, Culture, Media

TABLE 10.4 72-Hour Crisis Response Timeline

Window	*Focus*	*Key Actions*
Hours 0–2	Stabilize facts + duty of care	Single internal fact base; welfare-and-consent gate (safety, consent, confidentiality); secure records and evidence
Hours 2–6	Align governance	Confirm decision rights; define spokesperson; map legal and HR constraints; choose response strategy (Coombs, 2007)
Hours 6–24	Prevent the vacuum	Publish acknowledgment; state what is known and unknown; name the next update time; direct all staff to one internal message
Hours 24–72	Convert to action	Visible follow-through: investigation steps, support offered, and corrective actions; maintain internal alignment and athlete protection

and Sport Committee, 2021): initial minimization, then partial disclosures perceived as a cover-up, and then sponsor withdrawals and resignations. The deepest damage was internal: staff who had raised concerns privately learned the organization would not protect them. Psychological safety collapsed from the ecosystem layer inward.

If the instinct is "say as little as possible," interrogate the real constraint. Sometimes, facts cannot be disclosed. Process can still be disclosed: acknowledge harm, name an independent process, protect the people involved, and set a clear update cadence.

10.3 Fans, Community, and Digital Safety

Principle: Fans are the financial and emotional foundation of professional sport. Digital platforms have collapsed the distance between investment and access, and when proximity feels like governance, the relationship shifts from support to entitlement.

10.3.1 When Investment Becomes Entitlement

The vast majority of fans are genuine supporters whose passion makes the enterprise possible. The structural challenge emerges from a minority who convert passion into coercion—pseudo-stakeowners who claim governance rights based on attention, emotional investment, or financial exposure rather than formal authority. In Mitchell et al.'s (1997) terms, they carry high urgency and perceived power, but their legitimacy is self-conferred. Confusing the two groups destroys the relationship that funds everything else.

Online abuse is not hypothetical. Monitoring initiatives show that abuse clusters around high-visibility events and women athletes, with gendered patterns that differ qualitatively from abuse directed at male athletes (Kavanagh et al., 2019; Litchfield et al., 2018; World Athletics, 2024). A Premier League study found persistent targeted abuse during the 2021–2022 season (Vidgen et al., 2022). An NCAA pilot study found thousands of verified abusive messages, with a notable portion linked to sports betting and with women athletes receiving higher rates (NCAA, 2024).

Sports betting sharpens the dynamic: users who lose money act as if owed access or punishment. Monitoring reports flag betting-related content as a recurring theme within abusive messages (NCAA, 2024). Include betting-driven abuse as a distinct monitoring category.

10.3.2 Separating Volume Risk From Severity Risk

The triage protocol in Table 10.5 separates volume risk from severity risk rather than treating all high-urgency voices as legitimate claims on governance. The pattern is not limited to fans—agents who threaten media exposure (10.4) and sponsors who condition funding on selection decisions exhibit the same structure.

Separate volume risk from severity risk:

Volume risk is the pile-on: thousands of hostile messages, coordinated quote-tweets, and repeated tagging. It drives overwhelm and withdrawal even when individual messages are not illegal.

Severity risk is a credible threat, doxxing, stalking intent, or attempts to locate family members. It can be low volume and still high danger.

Media-related anxiety is not a character flaw. Athletes can handle physical pressure and confrontational opponents while still experiencing significant distress under public scrutiny—social evaluation activates a distinct stress profile (Dickerson & Kemeny, 2004). Treat it like load management: prepare, dose, recover. If all exposure is removed, avoidance grows. If exposure is flooded, shutdown follows.

BOX 10.3 PSYCHOLOGY SIDELINES WITH DR. MCB — WHY "DON'T LOOK AT IT" DOESN'T WORK

Fans are the reason any of us have jobs. Something I remind athletes of when they are in the thick of it: fans want to love you. They want to adore you. That is the default setting. The issue is narrower than it sounds–a small number of people convert investment into targeted hostility, and when the organization has no system for managing that, the athlete ends up carrying it alone.

The advice they usually get is some version of "don't look at it." That advice misunderstands the nervous system. When someone knows that hostile things are being said about them–accessible in seconds from the device on their nightstand–the threat is already activated. Not reading does not make it disappear. It removes the information about what the threat says, which can increase uncertainty and hypervigilance rather than reducing it.

The organizational design question is whether digital safety is treated as the athlete's private problem or as infrastructure that the system provides. The organizations that build the infrastructure see better outcomes–because the athlete is not carrying the load alone, and because the fan–athlete relationship is protected rather than poisoned by the minority who abuse it.

10.3.3 The Digital Safety Protocol

Online abuse is a stakeholder issue, not only a mental health issue. When harassment is tolerated publicly, it teaches the ecosystem that intimidation works—and athletes learn the organization will not protect them, making them less likely to report internal problems too. The stakes are higher for youth populations: cyber-victimization is linked to stress-related outcomes and suicidal ideation (Kowalski et al., 2014).

Platform algorithms also function as silent stakeholders: engagement-optimizing design can amplify contentious content over supportive content (Gillespie, 2018), and moderation decisions operate independently of the organization's communication strategy. Include algorithmic unpredictability as a scenario variable in tabletop crisis drills.

The digital safety protocol operates in two phases: pre-event setup and in-event triage. Before any high-visibility event: (1) who monitors mentions and tags, and on what schedule, (2) where abusive content is logged and how evidence is preserved, (3) what triggers immediate escalation (threats, doxxing, stalking, or family targeting), (4) what boundary statement is ready to publish if a pile-on starts, and (5) who checks in with the athlete and what support is available.

In-event triage separates three questions: what is the category (criticism, harassment, hate speech, threat, doxxing, or stalking)? What is the target (performance, identity, family, location, or private medical information)? What is the risk level (annoying, destabilizing, or dangerous)?

The protocol: (1) Assign an owner who is not the athlete—athletes cannot monitor their own harassment. (2) Reduce exposure by default—pre-set comment filters, limit direct messages, and use "off periods" around competition. (3) Build an evidence trail—screenshots, URLs, timestamps, and platform identifiers. (4) Set escalation thresholds in advance—what triggers security, family notification, and legal consultation, in writing. (5) Support the athlete in real time—normalize the reaction, adjust media obligations if distress is rising

TABLE 10.5 Digital Abuse Triage

Category	*What It Looks Like*	*Default Response*	*Escalate When*
Performance criticism	"You choked." "You should be benched"	Do not engage; limit exposure; monitor volume	It becomes coordinated harassment or targets identity
Harassment/hate	Sexualized insults, racist language, ableist abuse, and dehumanization	Screenshot, block, report to platform; inform athlete support lead	Persistent patterns, campaign behavior, or credible targeting
Threat/doxxing	Death threats, stalking intent, posting address or school	Immediate security escalation; preserve evidence; consider law enforcement	Any credible threat or private information leak

(Fiedler et al., 2023), and do not penalize boundary-setting. (6) Signal publicly that the organization backs the athlete—one statement plus a boundary reminder. (7) Debrief and update the protocol after any surge.

Williams et al. (2025) confirmed that organizational responses to abuse against sportswomen matter. Without a protocol, the athlete sees it first and carries the fear into the next practice. With a protocol: staff captures evidence, security is notified, the athlete is told what is happening without reviewing it, and media obligations are adjusted.

10.4 Agents, Families, Sponsors, and Boundaries

Principle: Families sacrifice years to support an athlete's development. Agents provide expertise that athletes cannot develop on their own. Sponsors invest resources that fund the enterprise. But without clear lanes, inner-circle and commercial engagement overrides decision architecture, triangulates communication, and turns the athlete into a negotiation surface.

10.4.1 Agents and Incentive Misalignment

The structural risk with agents is incentive misalignment: when the agent's priorities diverge from the athlete's, decisions get distorted (Jensen & Meckling, 1976; Mason & Slack, 2003).

10.4.2 Families and the Triadic System

Families add a second system. As stakes rise across development stages (Côté, 1999), parents can drift from support toward control, especially when they feel powerless. Controlling or pressuring parental behavior predicts worse emotional outcomes in youth sport (Bonavolontà et al., 2021; Harwood & Knight, 2015). The diagnostic question is not "Is the family involved?" but "Is the athlete's development and wellbeing being served by the pattern of involvement?"—a question that requires cultural context, since close family involvement is normative and functional in many non-Western sport cultures (Harwood & Knight, 2015).

Maurice et al. (2021) found that optimal development requires triadic functioning—coach, parent, and athlete as an integrated system—yet most interactions remain dyadic with misaligned expectations.

10.4.3 Sponsors and Boundary Pressure

Sponsors create a third boundary challenge. Sponsor pressure often arrives through "small" activation requests that are actually boundary tests: last-minute appearances, mandatory social posts, or access to training spaces. When it is not possible to say no, the relationship is not a partnership—it is a control relationship. Separate brand alignment from access rights, put access rights in writing, and enforce them.

Boundary pressure clusters at predictable transition points:

10.4.4 Confidentiality, Consent, and the Alignment Meeting

One consent rule cuts most of this noise: treat all medical and mental health information as confidential by default. Unauthorized disclosure to "supportive" family members or agents constitutes a structural breach of the psychological safety layer, regardless of intent. When an athlete learns that personal information moved without consent—even to people who care about them—the lesson suppresses future reporting across every domain. Even when family members are supportive, the athlete owns disclosure. If the athlete wants family involved, document what may be shared and with whom.

Boundaries are easier to hold when a legitimate outlet exists. If an agent, parent, or sponsor has no structured way to raise concerns, they will use informal pressure. A 45-minute alignment meeting at the start of the relationship—or

TABLE 10.6 Boundary-Pressure Transition Points—Proactive Scheduling

Transition Point	*Typical Boundary Pressure*	*Proactive Scheduling Action*
Contract renewals	Agent escalates demands; family anxiety spills into performance conversations	Alignment meeting 30 days before negotiation window; confirm lanes
Selection and deselection	Agent challenges the decision through media; parents contact the coaching staff directly	Pre-brief agent on process; schedule family meeting within 48 hours; restate lanes
Injury and return-to-play	Family demands information; agent pushes accelerated timeline	Confirm confidentiality defaults at injury onset; structured updates with athlete-approved information only
Sponsorship launches	Sponsor requests access conflicting with recovery; agent negotiates side deals	Review activation terms against welfare boundaries; confirm athlete availability through the organization
Public controversy	Agent issues unauthorized statements; family responds on social media	Activate crisis protocol (10.2); restate one-voice principle; debrief with inner circle
Retirement planning	Family anxiety about post-career identity; agent disengages as earning potential declines	Begin transition conversations mid-career; include inner circle in support planning

before any predictable transition point—prevents months of noise. Cover: purpose ("support performance and wellbeing, not renegotiate decision rights"), lanes (time, money, decision rights, and information), communication rhythm and emergency criteria, escalation triggers, and athlete consent. Summarize in writing within 24 hours.

BOX 10.4 TIMEOUT — BOUNDARIES WITHOUT CONSEQUENCES ARE PREFERENCES

If a boundary violation draws no response, no boundary exists. The organization announced a preference. Preferences get tested. Boundaries get respected—but only when the consequence is predictable, proportionate, and consistent. Ask for each boundary in the protocol: what happens when someone crosses it? If the answer is "nothing, but we will be disappointed," revise the protocol or stop calling it a boundary.

When family dynamics become harmful—parents fighting through the athlete, chronic conflict spilling into training—treat it as performance and welfare risk. Re-anchor on consent: the athlete chooses who is in the room. If the pattern persists, refer for specialist support.

When boundary violations occur: respond to the agent ("We can meet to discuss process. Selection remains with the coaching staff"), respond to the parent ("You are welcome in the scheduled meeting. Please do not arrive unannounced"), and close the loop with the athlete in private. Do not make them carry the conflict.

Self-test for any external relationship: (1) Is it in writing what the party can influence and what is out of bounds? (2) Would the organization be proud of this relationship if it became public during a crisis? (3) Was the last commitment delivered on time? (4) Has the party exceeded the agreed lane, and was the boundary held? (5) Are there written exit criteria or escalation protocols? If any answer is "I don't know," that is the first action item.

10.4.4.1 Chapter Synthesis

Every unmanaged stakeholder relationship is a structural bypass of the culture operating system, and the architecture must be built before the pressure arrives.

Key Chapter Takeaways

1. Map stakeholders by salience and attitude, not just influence. Adding attitude converts a static directory into a weekly prediction tool that distinguishes coalition partners from priority risks.

2. Separate voice from veto and enforce the distinction in every lane. Stakeowners hold formal decision rights in defined domains; everyone else gets meaningful consultation, a closed loop, and transparent rationale.
3. Build a crisis communication infrastructure before the crisis. A single fact base, one message spine, a named spokesperson, and a published update clock prevent the vacuum that invites external narrators to write the story.
4. Treat digital abuse as organizational infrastructure, not athlete resilience. Assign monitoring to staff, set escalation thresholds in advance, and separate volume risk from severity risk, so threats are caught early and athletes are not carrying triage alone.
5. Set boundaries in writing before transition points. A 45-minute alignment meeting covering time, money, decision rights, and information prevents months of improvised conflict when pressure arrives.

Discussion Questions

1. Identify a stakeholder in your organization who holds a de facto veto without formal decision rights. What structural conditions sustain that power, and what would converting it to voice require?
2. Design a first 72-hour response for a scenario where an athlete's private medical information is leaked during competition. Where do welfare obligations and communication speed conflict, and how would you sequence the trade-offs?
3. Evaluate where the boundary sits between organizational digital safety infrastructure and overprotection that limits athlete agency. What criteria distinguish protection from control?
4. An agent threatens media exposure, a parent arrives unannounced, and a sponsor requests medical facility access. How does a single boundary framework address all three, and what do they share structurally?

References

Bonavolontà, V., Cataldi, S., Latino, F., Carvutto, R., De Candia, M., Mastrorilli, G., Messina, G., Patti, A., & Fischetti, F. (2021). The role of parental involvement in youth sport experience: Perceived and desired behavior by male soccer players. *International Journal of Environmental Research and Public Health*, *18*(16), 8698. https://doi.org/10.3390/ijerph18168698

Byun, J., & Leopkey, B. (2022). Examining the global spectrum of stakeholders and their salience: A case study of a non-mega sport event. *Sport Management Review*, *25*(5), 898–913. https://doi.org/10.1016/j.smr.2021.12.002

Coombs, W. T. (2007). Protecting organization reputations during a crisis: The development and application of situational crisis communication theory. *Corporate Reputation Review*, *10*(3), 163–176. https://doi.org/10.1057/palgrave.crr.1550049

Côté, J. (1999). The influence of the family in the development of talent in sport. *The Sport Psychologist*, *13*(4), 395–417. https://doi.org/10.1123/tsp.13.4.395

Demir, R., Kaynak, M., & Dalgic, U. (2015). Stakeholder management in sports facilities: A stakeholder mapping approach. *Procedia—Social and Behavioral Sciences, 207*, 609–618. https://doi.org/10.1016/j.sbspro.2015.10.129

Dickerson, S. S., & Kemeny, M. E. (2004). Acute stressors and cortisol responses: A theoretical integration and synthesis of laboratory research. *Psychological Bulletin, 130*(3), 355–391. https://doi.org/10.1037/0033-2909.130.3.355

Digital, Culture, Media and Sport Committee. (2021, November 16). *Azeem Rafiq, former Yorkshire cricketer* [Oral evidence transcript]. UK Parliament. https://committees.parliament.uk/oralevidence/3011/html/

Duignan, M. B., Bichler, B. F., & Peters, M. (2023). A multi-stakeholder perspective on festival and event impacts. *Journal of Sustainable Tourism, 31*(5), 1012–1031. https://doi.org/10.1080/09669582.2021.1906928

Fiedler, R., Heidari, J., Birnkraut, T., & Kellmann, M. (2023). Digital media and mental health in adolescent athletes. *Psychology of Sport and Exercise, 67*, 102421. https://doi.org/10.1016/j.psychsport.2023.102421

Freeman, R. E. (1984). *Strategic management: A stakeholder approach.* Pitman.

Gallagher, T. H., Studdert, D., & Levinson, W. (2007). Disclosing harmful medical errors to patients. *New England Journal of Medicine, 356*(26), 2713–2719. https://doi.org/10.1056/NEJMra070587

Gillespie, T. (2018). *Custodians of the internet: Platforms, content moderation, and the hidden decisions that shape social media.* Yale University Press.

Harwood, C. G., & Knight, C. J. (2015). Parenting in youth sport: A position paper on parenting expertise. *Psychology of Sport and Exercise, 16*, 24–35. https://doi.org/10.1016/j.psychsport.2014.03.001

IAP2 International Federation. (2018). *IAP2 spectrum of public participation.* https://cdn.ymaws.com/www.iap2.org/resource/resmgr/pillars/Spectrum_8.5x11_Print.pdf

Jensen, M. C., & Meckling, W. H. (1976). Theory of the firm: Managerial behavior, agency costs and ownership structure. *Journal of Financial Economics, 3*(4), 305–360. https://doi.org/10.1016/0304-405X(76)90026-X

Kavanagh, E. J., Osborne, J., & Litchfield, C. (2019). Sporting women and social media: Sexualization, misogyny and gender-based violence in online spaces. *International Journal of Sport Communication, 12*(4), 552–572. https://doi.org/10.1123/ijsc.2019-0079

Kowalski, R. M., Giumetti, G. W., Schroeder, A. N., & Lattanner, M. R. (2014). Bullying in the digital age: A critical review and meta-analysis of cyberbullying research among youth. *Psychological Bulletin, 140*(4), 1073–1137. https://doi.org/10.1037/a0035618

Lind, E. A., Kanfer, R., & Earley, P. C. (1990). Voice, control, and procedural justice: Instrumental and noninstrumental concerns in fairness judgments. *Journal of Personality and Social Psychology, 59*(5), 952–959. https://doi.org/10.1037/0022-3514.59.5.952

Litchfield, C., Kavanagh, E., Osborne, J., & Jones, I. (2018). Social media and the politics of gender, race and identity: The case of Serena Williams. *European Journal for Sport and Society, 15*(2), 154–170. https://doi.org/10.1080/16138171.2018.1452870

Mason, D. S., & Slack, T. (2003). Understanding principal-agent relationships in professional hockey: A case study of the National Hockey League's salary arbitration system. *Sport Management Review, 6*(1), 57–79. https://doi.org/10.1016/S1441-3523(03)70038-7

Maurice, J., Devonport, T. J., & Knight, C. J. (2021). Toward improved triadic functioning: Exploring the interactions and adaptations of coaches, parents and athletes in professional academy soccer through the adversity of COVID-19. *Frontiers in Psychology, 12*, 609631. https://doi.org/10.3389/fpsyg.2021.609631

Mitchell, R. K., Agle, B. R., & Wood, D. J. (1997). Toward a theory of stakeholder identification and salience: Defining the principle of who and what really counts. *Academy of Management Review*, *22*(4), 853–886. https://doi.org/10.5465/amr.1997.9711022105

Naraine, M. L., Parent, M. M., Hoye, R., Taks, M., Seguin, B., & Thompson, A. (2020). Examining the interorganizational links between national sport organizations and their stakeholders: A social network analysis. *International Journal of Sport Management*, *21*(3), 239–260

National Collegiate Athletic Association. (2024). *NCAA pilot study 2023–24: Threat Matrix report*. https://ncaaorg.s3.amazonaws.com/ncaa/wagering/NCAAThreatMatrixPilotStudyPublicReport.pdf

Parent, M. M. (2008). Evolution and issue patterns for major-sport-event organizing committees and their stakeholders. *Journal of Sport Management*, *22*(2), 135–164. https://doi.org/10.1123/jsm.22.2.135

Reason, J. (1997). *Managing the risks of organizational accidents*. Ashgate.

Simpson, B., Manoli, A. E., & Skey, M. (2025). A new approach to understanding crisis communication in sport: A news media analysis of the European super league crisis. *European Sport Management Quarterly*, *25*(4), 647–671. https://doi.org/10.1080/16184742.2025.2542354

Tyler, T. R. (2006). *Why people obey the law* (2nd ed.). Princeton University Press.

Vidgen, B., Chung, Y.-L., Johansson, P., Kirk, H. R., Williams, A., Hale, S. A., Margetts, H., Röttger, P., & Sprejer, L. (2022). *Tracking abuse on Twitter against football players in the 2021–22 Premier League season* (Report). The Alan Turing Institute & Ofcom. https://doi.org/10.2139/ssrn.4403913

Williams, A., Fielding-Lloyd, B., Newman, J., & Deller, R. (2025). Sports organisations' responses to social media abuse against professional sportswomen in UK team sports. *Communication & Sport*. Advance online publication. https://doi.org/10.1177/21674795251366402

World Athletics. (2024). *Online abuse in athletics: A four-year analysis and new insights from the Threat Matrix system*. https://assets.aws.worldathletics.org/document/6762bcd37f1b92878441c35f.pdf

11

FUTURE-READY ORGANIZATIONS—SUSTAINABILITY AND EVOLUTION

Learning Objectives

By the end of this chapter, the reader will be able to:

1. **Design** a phased, multi-year transformation sequence that implements psychological safety according to dependency logic and protects core components during scale-up.
2. **Construct** an ownership spine that specifies roles, cadence, decision rights, and escalation triggers to sustain implementation under performance pressure.
3. **Evaluate** measurement systems by distinguishing those that close the feedback loop from those that train silence, and apply the "you said/we did" discipline to maintain credibility.
4. **Analyze** emerging pressures—including AI-driven analytics, wearable biometrics, and mental health instrumentalization—and propose governance responses that protect athlete trust and information flow.
5. **Create** custodianship mechanisms (capture, store, transfer, and audit) that institutionalize psychological safety knowledge beyond individual leader tenures.

BOX 11.1 CASE STUDY: THE SYSTEM THAT WORKED UNTIL IT DIDN'T

Composite vignette. Details changed to protect privacy.

For two years, the culture architecture held. Weekly check-ins between the welfare lead and coaching staff. A quarterly pulse survey with

DOI: 10.4324/9781003631217-12

published response themes and a visible "you said, we did" board. A monthly governance meeting where the head of performance, the welfare lead, and the sporting director reviewed voice channel data together. A culture custodian—Nadira, the head of player development—who had the standing, the relationships, and the protected time to keep the system running.

The first year, the system caught a scheduling conflict that would have sent an under-21 player on an away trip without adequate staff coverage. It caught a drift in debrief quality during a winning streak—coaches had started skipping the "what didn't work" segment because results masked problems. It caught a physio's growing frustration with role ambiguity before it became a resignation letter. Small catches. The kind that never become case studies because they work.

Then three things happened in the same quarter. Nadira was promoted to a regional role. The sporting director who had championed the governance meeting left for another club. And a budget squeeze folded the culture custodian role into "general player development responsibilities."

Nobody cancelled the systems. They just stopped being maintained. The quarterly pulse survey still went out, but nobody published the themes because nobody had been assigned to do it. The governance meeting dropped from monthly to "as needed"—which meant never. The weekly welfare check-in continued, but the new coaching staff treated it as a status update rather than a diagnostic conversation.

Within six months, response rates on the pulse survey dropped from 84% to 41%. The welfare lead raised it with the new sporting director. He said he would look into it. He did not.

A year after Nadira left, a junior analyst noticed the "you said, we did" board still showed actions from nine months ago. He mentioned it to a colleague, who shrugged: "That's from the old regime."

The infrastructure was still physically present—the board, the survey, the meeting placeholder in the calendar. But without a named owner, a protected cadence, and a governance layer that held itself accountable, every component had quietly reverted to theater. The organization had not decided to abandon its culture architecture. It had simply stopped protecting it, and the ordinary weeks did the rest.

As shown in Figure 11.1, Layer 7 answers Question 7—will this survive us?—by turning psychological safety from a program into a sustainable system. Unlike the foundation work in earlier layers, Layer 7 ensures that when leaders change, budgets shift, or pressure spikes, the mechanisms stay alive. The work

CHAPTER 11: IMPLEMENTATION AND EVOLUTION

DIAGNOSTIC QUESTION

How do we make psychological safety and high performance survive turnover—and evolve over time?

KEY INSIGHT

If it leaves when you leave, it was never a system.

FIGURE 11.1 You Are Here—Sustainability.

The HPCOS seven-layer architecture with Layer 7 (Sustainability) highlighted. This final layer answers Question 7—will this survive us?—by ensuring that when leaders change, budgets shift, or pressure spikes, the mechanisms survive.

here is about making what works stick—and preventing the quiet drift back to threat-based defaults.

11.1 Implementation Architecture: The Master Plan

Culture change fails in the ordinary weeks, not the crisis weeks. Under load, people snap back to defaults: meeting rhythms, accountability habits, and familiar power patterns. We call this *default drift*—when time and attention are scarce, the system repeats whatever is easiest. The term is ours; the phenomenon is universal and well-documented as organizational inertia under stress (Lewin, 1947; Schein, 2010).

Sustainability means making psychologically safe behavior the default—embedded in how meetings run, who owns decisions, and what happens when pressure rises. This chapter lays out the architecture: phased sequencing, an ownership spine, readiness assessment, and guidance for managing change fatigue and clearing legacy practices that compete with the new system.

11.1.1 Why Implementation Science Matters

The research-to-practice gap in sport is rarely about ignorance. The infrastructure is what's missing: no owner, no cadence, unclear decision rights, and no mechanism to protect the work when performance pressure rises.

Implementation science bridges "what works" and "what stays" (Donaldson & Finch, 2012; Eccles & Mittman, 2006; Finch, 2011). Three frameworks are directly useful here (Table 11.1):

TABLE 11.1 Implementation Science Frameworks Applied to Sport

Framework	*What It Contributes*	*Diagnostic Question*
RE-AIM Glasgow et al. (1999)	Evaluates whether interventions survive beyond delivery—reach, effectiveness, adoption, implementation, and maintenance	When an effective coach leaves, do the routines persist?
CFIR Damschroder et al. (2009)	Maps whether the inner setting, outer setting, individuals, and process support or block implementation	Do key leaders actually value this—or does it stall regardless of quality?
NPT May & Finch (2009); May et al. (2016)	Assesses whether practices have normalized into routine through coherence, cognitive participation, collective action, and reflexive monitoring	Are athletes calling out learning opportunities themselves, or only when prompted?

All three point to the same conclusion: sustainability has little to do with how good the intervention is. It depends on whether the surrounding system—ownership, routines, decision rights, and learning loops—keeps the work alive when the pressure is on.

Each framework informs a different component of the architecture that follows: RE-AIM maps to the proof signals in the transformation roadmap, CFIR to the Readiness Assessment, and NPT to the measurement-to-action system.

11.1.2 Core Components Versus Adaptable Periphery

Scaling psychological safety work fails in a predictable way. Each unit "tailors" the intervention until the mechanism disappears. The governing rule from implementation fidelity research: protect the core, tailor the delivery (Fixsen et al., 2005). Table 11.2 distinguishes the two categories.

Record the adaptation itself—what changed, why, and what was learned—so the organization accumulates knowledge rather than reinventing the program each season (Stirman et al., 2019). At minimum, an adaptation log entry records four elements: (1) what was changed (specific component), (2) why (the trigger—operational constraint, cultural context, resource limitation), (3) what resulted (observed effect on the proof signals in the transformation roadmap), and (4) whether the change affected a core component or an adaptable periphery element.

A shared document with these four columns, updated at each ownership review, is sufficient. The format matters less than the discipline of recording—because without the log, the organization cannot distinguish intentional adaptation from unintentional drift.

Another trap: Culture programs are routinely judged by activity ("we ran workshops") rather than outcomes. Proctor et al. (2011) identify the distinctions that matter: adoption, fidelity, penetration, and sustainment. If evaluation stays at the level of activity, the program gets funded on visibility rather than function—and becomes the first thing cut when budgets tighten.

11.1.3 Phased Transformation: The Three-Year Model

The three-year model in Table 11.3 adapts Lewin's (1947) and Kotter's (1996) sequencing principles for sport's specific constraints: compressed season

TABLE 11.2 Core Components Versus Adaptable Periphery

Core Components (Protect)	*Adaptable Periphery (Tailor)*
The psychological mechanism being targeted (the threat being reduced and how)	Delivery format (workshops vs. micro-sessions vs. camp blocks)
Confidentiality boundaries (what data is never used for selection/contract decisions)	Language and metaphors (local culture, sport-specific examples)
Leader behaviors under pressure (error response, debrief norms, how voice is handled)	Cadence (weekly rhythm vs. monthly/quarterly in decentralized systems)
The measurement-to-action loop ("you said/we did")	Roles and titles (what "program lead" means locally)
Decision rights and escalation (who owns decisions when performance pressure rises)	Platforms and tools (survey provider, dashboard software, communication channels)

windows, short leadership tenure, and relentless pressure to skip stages. What transfers across contexts is the dependency logic: do not scale before foundations hold, and do not institutionalize before scaling lessons are captured (Fixsen et al., 2005).

The most common failure mode: “We launched, nothing changed, we moved on.” The antidote is explicit sequencing, detailed in Table 11.3. The dependency logic is critical—each year’s work depends on the previous year’s proof signals being met. Skip that step, and you produce cynicism. (For return on investment [ROI] evidence supporting sustained investment in psychological health initiatives, see Deloitte Canada (2019).)

The tenure problem. Leadership tenure in many professional sport contexts is notoriously short. In English football, the League Managers Association (LMA) end-of-season data consistently reports average head coach tenures well below two years, with high within-season dismissal rates (LMA, 2024). Similar compression appears across professional leagues and national programs internationally, though precise figures vary by context. This creates a structural tension: the transformation timeline may outlast the leader who initiated it.

11.1.4 The Ownership Spine

Under pressure, implementation doesn’t fail because the plan is wrong. It fails because ownership disappears when the plan competes with performance priorities. Table 11.4 specifies the minimum roles, decision authority, and escalation triggers.

A structural note on the athlete voice veto: This right functions as a design brake, not a blocking mechanism. In practice, the veto triggers an escalation conversation—the representative raises the concern, the program lead and sponsor must address it explicitly, and the resolution is documented in the adaptation log. The veto does not mean the change cannot proceed; it means that the change cannot proceed without the concern being heard, addressed, and recorded. This is the voice architecture operating at the governance level.

The failure is familiar: program leads “own” implementation without the authority to protect it when performance priorities escalate. Aarons et al. (2014) and Ehrhart et al. (2014) demonstrate that implementation climate—whether the organizational context actively supports and rewards the work—predicts sustainment more reliably than individual commitment. The fix: make decision rights explicit before pressure arrives. That is what makes implementation climate operational.

TABLE 11.3 Three-Year Transformation Roadmap

Year	*Theme*	*What Gets Built (Minimum)*	*Dependencies*	*Proof Signals by Year-End*
Year 1	Foundation	Baseline assessment + confidentiality rules; leadership alignment under pressure; pilot in one receptive unit; ownership spine (roles + cadence + decision rights)	Executive sponsor named; safeguarding and clinical escalation routes clear; staff understand "support data ≠ selection data"	People speak up earlier; fewer surprises; pilot routines run on schedule; decision rights are clearer and less political
Year 2	Scaling and integration	Expand to additional units with adaptation logs; embed routines into season rhythm; train internal capability (reduce reliance on single champion/consultant)	Year 1 pilot lessons documented; measurement owner in place; feedback loops trusted; leaders model non-retaliation	Tools used without prompting; action loops close; transitions coordinated with fewer mixed messages
Year 3	Institution-alization	Convert work into policy, governance, and succession systems; tighten measurement-to-action loops and stakeholder reporting; institutionalize knowledge capture	Stable cadence + ownership; credible reporting to leadership/board; ecosystem engagement rules explicit	System survives turnover; responses under pressure consistent with values; roadmap reviewed and updated annually

TABLE 11.4 Ownership Spine—Minimum Roles

Role	*Primary Responsibility*	*Decision Authority*	*Escalation Trigger*
Executive sponsor	Priority, resources, and protection of non-negotiables when pressure rises	Approves roadmap changes; protects time/budget under performance pressure	Performance drops; concerns about fairness or burnout reach the sponsor
Program lead	Runs roadmap, coordinates units, and protects sequencing	Adaptation decisions within guardrails; escalates core component changes to the sponsor	Initiative falling behind; units drifting from core components

(*Continued*)

TABLE 11.4 (Continued)

Role	*Primary Responsibility*	*Decision Authority*	*Escalation Trigger*
Measurement owner	Instruments, confidentiality rules, analysis, and action loop	Controls data access; decides what is reported and to whom	Safety data declining; confidentiality boundaries breached
Athlete voice representative	Ensures design reflects athlete reality, not only staff intent	Can veto changes that reduce the athlete's voice or safety	Athletes report feeling unheard; changes planned without athlete input
Safeguarding/ integrity lead	Escalation routes, retaliation protections, and boundary violations	Decides escalation threshold and response pathway; owns post-incident debrief	Safeguarding issue occurs; retaliation reported

BOX 11.2 TIMEOUT — OWNERSHIP WITHOUT AUTHORITY IS DECORATION

Naming someone "culture lead" without giving them decision authority and escalation rights is organizational theater. It creates the appearance of ownership while leaving the work vulnerable in resource fights. The test: when performance pressure rises and someone proposes canceling the debrief for video review, does the person who "owns" culture have the authority and backing to say no? If not, the organization does not have an ownership spine. It has a volunteer.

Scaling the spine. The five-role structure is a maximum framework. In smaller organizations, one person may hold multiple roles—but the *functions* still require coverage, and the decision rights still require explicit assignment. The spine scales down to functions, not titles.

11.1.5 Readiness Assessment: Are You Ready to Proceed?

Before launching or expanding psychological safety work, a quick structural readiness check prevents the most common failure mode: scaling before foundations hold. Rate each item in Table 11.5 as 0 (not in place), 1 (partially in place), or 2 (fully in place).

TABLE 11.5 Implementation Readiness Assessment

No.	*Readiness Indicator*	*Score (0–2)*
1	Executive sponsor named and actively engaged	
2	Confidentiality boundaries written and communicated	
3	Safeguarding and clinical escalation routes clear	
4	Decision rights explicit (who decides what under pressure)	
5	Measurement owner identified and structurally separated from selection	
6	Pilot unit identified and willing	
7	Staff understand "support data ≠ selection data"	
8	Minimum cadence (ownership reviews, debriefs) calendared	
9	Adaptation log or documentation system established	
10	Leader capacity assessed (not already at overload)	

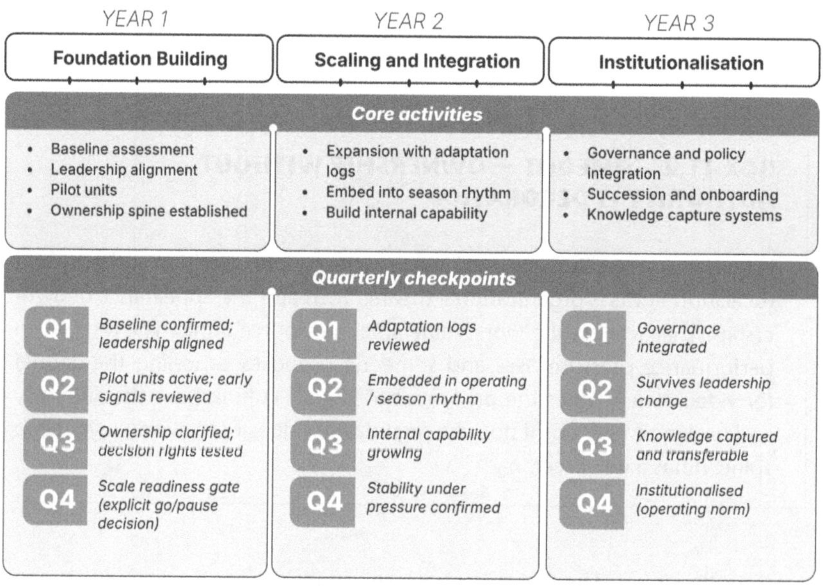

FIGURE 11.2 Culture Signal Response Cycle.

Six-stage operational cycle: Listen → Interpret → Decide → Act → Communicate → Review, then back to Listen. This loop links measurement architecture to leadership behavior—the system that determines whether a signal produces action or silence.

Scoring Guide

- **16–20:** Proceed with implementation or scaling.
- **10–15:** Foundation gaps exist. Address the lowest-scoring items before expanding.

- **Below 10:** Stabilize foundations first. Launching without structural readiness produces the cynicism and fatigue that make future attempts harder.

Its value is forcing an explicit conversation about structural preconditions—rather than assuming readiness because enthusiasm exists.

11.2 Measurement Systems That Close the Loop

Measurement without action trains silence. The credibility of any psychological safety operating system depends less on data quality than on whether people can point to what changed because of their input. When the cost of speaking up—survey data that disappears into a void—exceeds the perceived benefit of visible change, rational actors go quiet (Morrison, 2014). Response rates drop, silence spreads, and the organization has effectively conditioned people to treat voice as theater—undermining the learning behavior that psychological safety exists to protect (Edmondson, 1999, 2019).

The **Measurement-to-Action System** is a single integrated architecture with four components: (1) a three-tier measurement structure with five essential domains, (2) confidentiality protections, (3) the "you said/we did" feedback discipline, and (4) stakeholder reporting boundaries. These are not four separate tools. They are one system, and each component fails without the others.

One honest tension runs through all of this: measurement itself can become performative. When psychological safety scores become key performance indicators (KPIs), organizations learn to optimize the score rather than the culture. As Strathern (1997, p. 308) summarized regarding Goodhart's Law (Goodhart, 1975): "When a measure becomes a target, it ceases to be a good measure."

The safeguard: measure behavior and action loops, not just perceptions. Treat trend direction as a signal rather than chasing absolute benchmarks. And be transparent about purpose, pace, and—critically—when the organization is going to stop asking and start acting.

11.2.1 Essential Metrics

More data does not mean better culture. Measurement burden creates fatigue, and complicated dashboards obscure what actually matters. The objective: find the smallest set of indicators that tells you whether psychological safety is improving, stable, or degrading.

11.2.1.1 Three Tiers of Measurement, Five Essential Domains

Five domains capture the core of what a psychological safety measurement system needs to track: (1) voice frequency—are concerns raised before problems escalate? (2) Response quality—what happens after someone speaks up? (3) Recovery from error—does the system learn or conceal? (4) Action loop closure—can people identify changes resulting from feedback? (5) Trust in confidentiality—do participants believe their data is protected? No single tier covers all five. The three-tier architecture in Table 11.6 distributes them across cadences to match the signal type to the appropriate measurement depth.

Accessibility note. Measurement instruments must be accessible to all athletes in the program. In para-sport contexts, this means reviewing survey formats and response modalities to account for diverse communication needs. The same logic applies across cultural, linguistic, and socio-economic diversity. Athletes from low-resource backgrounds or international athletes operating in a second language may perceive the risks of speaking up differently. A measurement

TABLE 11.6 Three-Tier Measurement Architecture

Tier	*Cadence*	*What It Tracks*	*Domains Covered*	*Infrastructure Required*
Tier 1: Leading indicators	Weekly/ monthly	Behavioral signals observable without surveys	Voice frequency (are concerns raised before problems escalate?); Response quality (what happens after someone speaks up?); Recovery from error (does the system learn or conceal?)	Observation discipline—no survey infrastructure needed
Tier 2: Pulse checks	Quarterly	Trend lines from short, repeatable instruments (5–10 items)	Action loop closure (can people identify changes resulting from feedback?); Trust in confidentiality (do participants believe their data is protected?)	Survey platform; the value is in the direction of change, not absolute score
Tier 3: Deep dives	Annual or after critical events	Root causes across all five domains	All five domains—diagnoses rather than monitors	Focus groups, structured interviews, or longer assessments; prevents survey fatigue while surfacing issues pulse checks miss

system that excludes any population—whether due to physical accessibility, language barriers, or cultural blind spots—is structurally incomplete.

11.2.2 Confidentiality Boundaries and Trust Protection

Measurement fails the moment athletes suspect their data could influence selection decisions, contract renewals, or playing time. The non-negotiable boundary: support data is never used for selection, contract, or disciplinary decisions. This is a core component (see Table 11.2) that cannot be adapted away. Without it, honest information flow is compromised.

Five structural protections maintain this boundary:

1. **Explicit policy.** A written statement—posted visibly and repeated regularly—that data collected through culture surveys, psychological safety assessments, and support team feedback will not be accessed, reviewed, or considered in any selection, contract, or disciplinary decision.
2. **Structural separation.** The measurement owner must not be the person making selection decisions. If the head coach holds both roles, the boundary is already compromised.
3. **Aggregation rules.** Data should never be reported at a level where individuals can be identified. A minimum reporting group size (e.g., five or more) protects anonymity, consistent with privacy and disclosure-risk guidance (Information and Privacy Commissioner of Ontario, 2025).
4. **Access controls.** Explicit definitions of who sees raw data, summaries, and trends. The default: raw data stays with the measurement owner; leaders see aggregated themes.
5. **Breach protocol.** Named consequences for violations. Without visible accountability, the policy is decoration.

The breach that does the most damage is informal: a coach references survey content in a meeting—"I saw that some people think . . ."—and everyone recalculates whether the survey is safe. Governance must protect against casual disclosure, not only formal misuse.

11.2.3 The "You Said/We Did" Discipline

Closing the loop means making action visible. Athletes and staff need to see that their input produced a consequence—even when that consequence is "we heard you, we cannot change this, and here is why."

The discipline operates in four steps:

1. **Acknowledge.** Within two weeks of data collection, communicate the themes—not the raw data. ("Three issues came up repeatedly: transition communication, feedback after losses, and clarity on selection criteria.")

2. **Decide.** Leadership reviews themes and determines what will be acted on, what will not (and why), and what requires further investigation. Decisions are documented.
3. **Act.** Implement changes with named owners and timelines. Visible follow-through builds credibility for the next cycle.
4. **Communicate.** Close the loop publicly—including for items that were not actioned. ("You raised concerns about travel schedules. We reviewed this with the federation and cannot change it this season. Here is why.")

Cadence recommendation: Pulse check → themes communicated within two weeks → decisions within four weeks → actions visible within eight weeks → loop closed with "you said/we did" communication. Consistency matters more than speed.

BOX 11.3 TIMEOUT — THE LOOP IS THE PRODUCT

A measurement system does not produce data. It produces credibility—or erodes it. Every survey sent is a promise: "What you tell us will matter." Every cycle where themes go unacknowledged or actions go invisible is a broken promise. Athletes and staff do not track methodology. They track whether anything changed. One completed loop builds more trust than 10 well-designed instruments.

11.2.4 Stakeholder Reporting Without Surveillance

Boards, funders, and governing bodies want evidence, and reasonably so. The risk: measurement shifts from serving athletes to serving accountability theater. Two legitimate needs pull in opposite directions—stakeholders need enough information to trust that resources are well-spent, and athletes need enough protection to trust that data will not be misused.

Five practices help:

1. **Report trends, not scores.** Boards need to know whether the organization is improving, stable, or declining—not that Team A scored 3.7. Trend lines demonstrate progress while protecting specificity.
2. **Report actions, not just metrics.** "We identified three priority areas, took these actions, and observed these results" demonstrates a functioning system rather than data collection.

3. **Protect unit-level data.** When scores are reported by team, coaches game them—a classic vulnerability to Goodhart's Law where targets corrupt the underlying metric (Strathern, 1997). Aggregate to the level where gaming is difficult and identification is impossible.
4. **Name the boundaries explicitly.** "We do not report data at levels where individuals or small groups could be identified. This protects the integrity of the measurement system." Most boards will respect this framing.
5. **Invite questions, not audits.** Offer to discuss methodology, trends, and actions. Resist requests to access raw data or drill to team level; if a stakeholder insists, escalate to the executive sponsor.

Table 11.7 summarizes the include/exclude boundary for stakeholder reporting.

11.3 Future Pressures and Governance

The environment your culture system operates in is shifting. AI-driven analytics, wearable biometrics, and mental health instrumentalization each create new pressure on psychological safety—and organizations that treat governance as static find their systems eroded by forces they did not anticipate (Staw et al., 1981). Each requires governance if trust is to survive.

11.3.1 AI and Data Systems Governance

Wearable sleep and recovery trackers are standard in many professional programs (Driller et al., 2023), and physiological signal processing—including emotion recognition from biometric data—is advancing rapidly (Shu et al., 2018).

TABLE 11.7 Stakeholder Reporting—Include Versus Exclude

Include	*Exclude*
Overall trend direction (improving/stable/declining)	Individual or team-level scores
Action items identified and percentage closed	Identifiable comments or quotes
Anonymized "you said/we did" examples (1–2)	Data that could inform selection or contract decisions
Systemic barriers requiring board-level support	Comparisons creating internal competition on safety scores
Upcoming measurement activities	

BOX 11.4 TIMEOUT — AI AND DATA SYSTEMS

When analytics platforms collect athlete data, governance is a trust question before it is a compliance question. Worth asking:

- Did athletes consent to *this specific use*—or was it buried in an agreement they had little power to refuse?
- If data were collected for injury prevention, what stops it from surfacing in a contract negotiation? Is that boundary written down?
- Before a predictive model shapes opportunity, has anyone asked what patterns it learned—and from whom? (Barocas & Selbst, 2016; Mehrabi et al., 2021).
- Can athletes see what the system says about them? Can they challenge it?
- When an algorithmic output affects a human outcome, who owns that decision? "The algorithm said so" is not accountability—it is diffusion.
- Consent that starts optional has a way of becoming expected, then mandatory, then coercive. How would you know if yours had shifted?

"We own the data" may be legally accurate and culturally corrosive at the same time. The better question: *Does your data governance build trust, or quietly erode it?*

BOX 11.5 PSYCHOLOGY SIDELINES WITH DR. MCB — WHEN MENTAL HEALTH SUPPORT BECOMES SOMETHING ELSE

Mental health programming can function as genuine support—or it can become a sophisticated form of organizational self-protection. The difference is not always obvious from the inside. I have watched all four of these patterns operate in organizations that believed, sincerely, that they were doing the right thing (Reardon et al., 2019).

Diagnostic creep. An athlete raises a concern about coaching. Rather than investigating the concern, the organization refers the athlete for "mental health support." When a systemic complaint gets rerouted into individual wellness, ask whose problem just got solved—the athlete's or the organization's.

Wellness as surveillance. Mandatory mood tracking or "mental fitness" scores feed into selection decisions. If athletes are managing their reported wellness data the way they manage any other performance metric—strategically, not honestly—the system is not measuring well-being. It is measuring compliance.

Resilience theater. The organization invests in coping skills training while leaving the structural sources of distress untouched. The test: can leadership name the specific stressor the resilience program was designed to address? Or only the program itself?

Conditional support. Mental health resources are available to athletes in good standing and withdrawn upon deselection—precisely when the need is highest. If support disappears the moment someone stops being useful to the organization, it was never really about the person.

These patterns rarely announce themselves. They tend to coexist with genuine good intentions, which is part of what makes them hard to see from the inside. The through-line across all four: is mental health infrastructure structured to protect the athlete's well-being, or to protect the organization from the appearance of neglecting it? Separating support from evaluation, protecting clinical confidentiality, and auditing referral patterns are places to start—but only if leadership is willing to hear what the audit finds.

BOX 11.6 PSYCHOLOGY SIDELINES WITH DR. MCB — WHEN "SUPPORT" BECOMES DEFLECTION

I have seen organizations respond to reports of harmful coaching behavior by defaulting to "support the athlete" without addressing the underlying concern. When an athlete reports mistreatment and the system responds only with therapy or "wellness support," the behavior can continue unchanged—while the athlete becomes framed as "the issue" for raising it. This is not what good support looks like. In clinical ethics, using care pathways in ways that undermine credibility or replace accountability would raise serious concerns. Governance needs explicit safeguards: independent reporting routes, clear investigation thresholds for allegations of harm, and protections against labeling or retaliation when athletes speak up.

11.4 Legacy Building: Systems That Endure

Before turning to custodianship mechanics, the stakes of this work have shifted. Psychological safety is no longer only a performance advantage—in several jurisdictions, it is becoming a legal obligation.

The governance of psychological safety has shifted—from voluntary best practice to legal obligation. In Australia, amendments to the Work Health and Safety Regulations require employers to identify, assess, and manage psychosocial hazards—including poor organizational change management and inadequate support—as workplace health risks (Safe Work Australia, 2022). The European Framework Directive on Safety and Health at Work (Council of the European Communities, 1989) has been interpreted in several member states to encompass psychosocial risk assessment.

Failing to sustain a psychologically safe environment is no longer just a cultural failure. It is a breach of the "duty of care." Boards and executive leaders face increasing liability if they treat culture as a soft metric rather than a governed risk.

By embedding the ownership spine and measurement loops detailed in this chapter, organizations move psychological safety from a well-intentioned HR initiative toward the kind of documented, governed system that regulators increasingly expect. Whether a specific implementation meets legal compliance depends on jurisdiction, organizational context, and legal counsel—but the structural elements here address the core regulatory concern: that psychosocial risks are identified, assessed, and actively managed rather than left to individual coping.

The final test of this operating system is not whether it thrives in a good season with stable leadership. It is whether it survives pressure, turnover, and the slow entropy of "we used to do it that way."

Chapter 6 established why culture must live in systems rather than people, introduced the continuity document, and made the case for distributed leadership as a hedge against single points of failure. Case study evidence reinforces this logic: Henriksen et al. (2010) found that a successful Danish sailing milieu embedded effectiveness in environmental structures rather than individual personalities; Hodge et al. (2014) reached a parallel conclusion studying the All Blacks—sustained success. This section extends those foundations into multi-year custodianship mechanics, knowledge capture loops, and leader sustainability practices.

11.4.1 Cultural Custodianship Mechanisms

The custodianship cycle extends the continuity document into a full-cycle system: season-linked routines that survive turnover, with an audit function that detects drift (Nonaka & Takeuchi, 1995; Senge, 2006).

Five mechanisms do the heavy lifting. Each has a minimum viable version for when resources are tight and time is short.

Ritualized transmission formalizes how cultural knowledge passes to newcomers. At minimum: a structured 90-minute induction covering non-negotiables, decision rules, and how things actually work—delivered by a current custodian, not HR. Run at every new hire or intake and refresh annually. The common failure: delegating to generic onboarding until cultural content is stripped out.

Documentation systems convert tacit knowledge into accessible artifacts. At minimum: one shared, version-controlled document with three sections—non-negotiables, decision rules under pressure, and an onboarding checklist—updated end-of-season and accessible year-round. The common failure: the document exists but is never updated and becomes a historical artifact.

Distributed leadership builds a bench so no single departure resets the system. At minimum: two people who can run the ownership review, deliver the induction, and explain the rationale behind core components. Review bench depth annually. The common failure: a single culture carrier with no succession plan—the Nadira problem from the opening case study.

Alumni engagement uses former athletes and staff as reality checks. At minimum: an annual check-in with two to three recent alumni asking what worked, what did not survive, and what should be protected. Owned by the athlete voice representative. The common failure: treating it as a public relations exercise where feedback is collected but never acted on.

Governance structures ensure that decision rights and accountability survive turnover. At minimum: decision rights documented in writing—not just known verbally—with the ownership spine reviewed at every leadership transition and audited annually. The common failure: decision rights existing in one person's head and disappearing at departure.

Ownership and cadence: Assign a named custodian (or small custodianship group). Attach capture and transfer to season rhythms (end-of-season debrief; preseason onboarding refresh). If the loop is not on the calendar, it will not survive pressure.

These five mechanisms feed into a single repeatable learning cycle (Argote & Miron-Spektor, 2011; Parent et al., 2018).

The Custodianship Cycle: Capture → Store → Transfer → Audit

- **Capture:** AARs, season debriefs, incident learning notes, "what we wish we knew" from athletes/staff.
- **Store:** one accessible home (not personal folders) with version control and named owners.
- **Transfer:** onboarding modules, mentor pairings, and "quick reference" tools at transition points.
- **Audit:** a scheduled check: "What did we learn? What changed? What is drifting back?"

BOX 11.7 SKEPTIC'S CORNER — "WE DO NOT HAVE TIME FOR SUSTAINABILITY PLANNING"

The Objection: "We are in survival mode. We do not have time for 'sustainability planning' or 'implementation architecture.' We need results now."

The Rebuttal: Most organizations in survival mode have tried "results now" before. How did it work?

The recurrence itself is diagnostic. The crisis that feels urgent today is often a recurrence of one that was "solved" two years ago—solved meaning suppressed, worked around, or papered over until the next leadership change reset the clock.

Implementation architecture is not a luxury for stable organizations. In business strategy terms, a sustained HPCOS acts as a Valuable, Rare, Inimitable, and Non-substitutable (VRIN) resource (Barney, 1991). When budgets tighten, this architecture pays for itself—reducing costly staff turnover, mitigating legal risk under duty of care laws, and preventing organizations from repeating the same expensive crises. Without ownership spines, decision rights, and measurement loops, every initiative depends on the leader who started it. When that leader leaves—and they will—the system resets to default. That is renting culture, not building it.

The High Voice, High Standards Test

- **High Standards:** We demand sustainable high performance, not heroic sprints that collapse.
- **High Voice:** We invest in the infrastructure that lets standards survive leadership transitions, losing streaks, and organizational stress.

"Survival mode" is often a symptom, not a cause. The cause is a system that never built the architecture to hold gains. Sustainability planning is the way out.

What to try anyway: Pick one thing from this chapter—the ownership spine, the readiness check, or the "you said/we did" cycle—and install it this week. The whole system does not need to be built at once. But the building needs to start.

11.4.2 Personal Leadership Sustainability

Here is a pattern that recurs across organizations: strong culture architecture gets built, and then the person carrying it burns out. The system collapses—not because it was badly designed, but because it depended on one human operating at capacity indefinitely. If leaders are depleted or burned out, they cannot model the behaviors psychological safety requires. Elite sport accelerates this—public scrutiny, compressed timelines, and emotional labor stacked on operational demand (Lundkvist et al., 2012; Baumann et al., 2024). Leader sustainability is a design requirement, not an afterthought.

Three system moves:

(These apply not only to titled leaders but to anyone carrying culture work—sport psychologists, physiotherapists, performance analysts, and other practitioners who often carry significant relational load without the positional authority to protect their own capacity.)

1. **Distribute load:** Avoid concentrating culture work on one person (build a bench).
2. **Protect recovery:** Schedule recovery and boundaries as non-negotiables, not rewards.
3. **Escalate early:** Treat persistent overload, irritability, sleep disruption, or cynicism as signals to adjust workload and support.

Burnout is typically conceptualized as a syndrome of exhaustion, cynicism, and reduced efficacy that develops in response to chronic workplace stressors (Maslach et al., 2001). The aforementioned time thresholds are an applied rule of thumb, not a diagnostic standard; follow local clinical pathways and safeguarding protocols when risk indicators are present (American Psychiatric Association, 2022). Where formal screening is warranted, validated brief instruments such as the PHQ-9 (Patient Health Questionnaire, Nine-Item) for depression (Kroenke et al., 2001) and the GAD-7 (Generalized Anxiety Disorder Seven-Item Scale) for anxiety (Spitzer et al., 2006) provide clinically anchored starting points.

11.4.3 Change Fatigue: Individual Distress Versus System Overload

Sustained transformation produces predictable fatigue. What matters is diagnosing the source correctly—individual distress and system overload require fundamentally different interventions (Bernerth et al., 2011).

Table 11.8 operationalizes the distinction. The diagnostic question: *is the fatigue concentrated in individuals carrying disproportionate load, or distributed across the system regardless of individual resilience?* If the former, redistribute. If the latter, slow down.

Cynicism deepens. Peters et al. (2017) describe how sustained uncertainty impairs the very decision-making capacity the organization needs to implement well. At the neural level, chronic stress degrades prefrontal function—the

TABLE 11.8 Change Fatigue Differential—Individual Distress Versus System Overload

Dimension	*Individual Distress*	*System Overload*
Signal pattern	Exhaustion, cynicism, or withdrawal concentrated in specific people—often those carrying disproportionate load	Widespread resistance, declining engagement across units, and initiative fatigue regardless of individual resilience
Diagnostic question	Is the fatigue concentrated in individuals carrying disproportionate load?	Is the fatigue distributed across the system regardless of individual resilience?
Correct intervention	Redistribute workload, protect recovery, provide targeted support	Slow down, reduce concurrent changes, sequence more deliberately, protect what is already working
Common misdiagnosis	Treating distributed overload as individual weakness ("they need resilience training")	Treating concentrated burnout as a system problem ("we need to slow everything down") when only one person's load needs adjusting
What makes it worse	Wellness programs applied to a structural distribution problem	Pausing all implementation when only the pacing—not the work—needs to change

executive control systems leaders depend on most (Arnsten, 2009). Pacing is not a luxury. It is a performance variable.

11.4.4 Start Here: Minimum Viable Sustainability

This chapter presents a full sustainability architecture. Not every organization can build it at once. If resources are constrained, the dependency logic still applies—build in this order:

1. **First: the ownership spine.** Without named roles, decision rights, and escalation triggers, nothing else holds. This is the single structural intervention that determines whether work survives the first resource fight.
2. **Second: the "you said/we did" loop.** A functioning feedback cycle builds the credibility that justifies every subsequent investment. One completed loop builds more trust than a year of planning.
3. **Third: the custodianship cycle.** Documentation, distributed leadership, and ritualized transmission are what convert "this leader's project" into "this organization's system." Without custodianship, the first two survive only as long as the people who built them.

Everything else in this chapter—the readiness assessment, the three-year roadmap, the governance checklists, the change fatigue diagnostic—strengthens the architecture. These three components are its foundation.

11.4.4.1 Chapter Synthesis

Sustainability is where the HPCOS thesis meets its strictest test: if psychological safety depends on the leader who built it, it was never structural—it was personal. Sustainability is an engineering problem. Ownership spines, measurement-to-action loops, custodianship cycles, and governance frameworks build safety into structure, so it survives turnover, pressure, budget cuts, and institutional amnesia.

For practitioners in elite sport, the implication is direct: the system you cannot hand off is the system you have not yet built.

Key Chapter Takeaways

1. **Build the ownership spine before launching the work.** Assign named roles with explicit decision rights and escalation triggers; without positional authority, "culture leads" lose every resource fight when performance pressure rises.
2. **Close the measurement loop or stop measuring.** Every unanswered survey teaches people that voice is theater; implement the "you said/we did" discipline within defined timelines so feedback produces visible consequences.
3. **Protect core components during scale-up.** Distinguish non-negotiable mechanisms (confidentiality boundaries, error response norms, measurement-to-action loops) from adaptable delivery features, and log every adaptation so the organization learns rather than drifts.
4. **Diagnose fatigue before intervening.** Individual distress requires workload redistribution and support; system overload requires pacing and sequencing—applying wellness programs to a structural problem deepens cynicism.
5. **Govern data systems for trust, not compliance.** Audit consent drift annually, separate support data from selection decisions structurally, and anticipate that optional monitoring becomes coercive without active governance.

Discussion Questions

1. Evaluate the ownership spine in your own organization: which of the five functions currently has no named owner, and what would break first under performance pressure as a result?
2. A head of performance proposes combining culture survey data with performance analytics to "get a fuller picture." Design the governance argument you would present for or against this integration.

3. Distinguish between diffusion and implementation in a context you have observed—where did the language of psychological safety spread without the underlying mechanisms following?
4. When an organization in "survival mode" resists sustainability planning, how would you justify the investment without dismissing the legitimate urgency leaders feel?

References

Aarons, G. A., Ehrhart, M. G., Farahnak, L. R., & Sklar, M. (2014). The Implementation Leadership Scale (ILS): Development of a brief measure of unit level implementation leadership. *Implementation Science*, *9*, 45. https://doi.org/10.1186/1748-5908-9-45

American Psychiatric Association. (2022). *Diagnostic and statistical manual of mental disorders* (5th ed., text rev.; DSM-5-TR). American Psychiatric Publishing. https://doi.org/10.1176/appi.books.9780890425787

Argote, L., & Miron-Spektor, E. (2011). Organizational learning: From experience to knowledge. *Organization Science*, *22*(5), 1123–1137. https://doi.org/10.1287/orsc.1100.0621

Arnsten, A. F. T. (2009). Stress signaling pathways that impair prefrontal cortex structure and function. *Nature Reviews Neuroscience*, *10*(6), 410–422. https://doi.org/10.1038/nrn2648

Barney, J. (1991). Firm resources and sustained competitive advantage. *Journal of Management*, *17*(1), 99–120. https://doi.org/10.1177/014920639101700108

Barocas, S., & Selbst, A. D. (2016). Big data's disparate impact. *California Law Review*, *104*(3), 671–732.

Baumann, L., Schneeberger, A. R., Currie, A., Iff, S., Seifritz, E., & Claussen, M. C. (2024). Mental health in elite coaches. *Sports Health*, *16*(6), 1050–1057. https://doi.org/10.1177/19417381231223472

Bernerth, J. B., Walker, H. J., & Harris, S. G. (2011). Change fatigue: Development and initial validation of a new measure. *Work & Stress*, *25*(4), 321–337. https://doi.org/10.1080/02678373.2011.634280

Council of the European Communities. (1989). Council Directive 89/391/EEC of 12 June 1989 on the introduction of measures to encourage improvements in the safety and health of workers at work. *Official Journal of the European Communities*, *L 183*, 1–8.

Damschroder, L. J., Aron, D. C., Keith, R. E., Kirsh, S. R., Alexander, J. A., & Lowery, J. C. (2009). Fostering implementation of health services research findings into practice: A consolidated framework for advancing implementation science. *Implementation Science*, *4*, 50. https://doi.org/10.1186/1748-5908-4-50

Deloitte Canada. (2019). *Realizing the positive ROI of supporting employees' mental health*. https://www2.deloitte.com/ca/en/pages/about-deloitte/articles/mental-health-roi.html

Donaldson, A., & Finch, C. F. (2012). Applying implementation science to sports injury prevention. *British Journal of Sports Medicine*, *46*(12), 888–892. https://doi.org/10.1136/bjsports-2011-090602

Driller, M. W., Dunican, I. C., Omond, S. E. T., Boukhris, O., Stevenson, S., Lambing, K., & Bender, A. M. (2023). Pyjamas, polysomnography and professional athletes: The role of sleep tracking technology in sport. *Sports*, *11*(1), 14. https://doi.org/10.3390/sports11010014

Eccles, M. P., & Mittman, B. S. (2006). Welcome to Implementation Science. *Implementation Science*, *1*, 1. https://doi.org/10.1186/1748-5908-1-1

Edmondson, A. C. (1999). Psychological safety and learning behavior in work teams. *Administrative Science Quarterly*, *44*(2), 350–383. https://doi.org/10.2307/2666999
Edmondson, A. C. (2019). *The fearless organization: Creating psychological safety in the workplace for learning, innovation, and growth*. Wiley.
Ehrhart, M. G., Aarons, G. A., & Farahnak, L. R. (2014). Assessing the organizational context for EBP implementation: The development and validity testing of the Implementation Climate Scale (ICS). *Implementation Science*, *9*, 157. https://doi.org/10.1186/s13012-014-0157-1
Finch, C. (2011). No longer lost in translation: The art and science of sports injury prevention implementation research. *British Journal of Sports Medicine*, *45*(16), 1253–1257. https://doi.org/10.1136/bjsports-2011-090230
Fixsen, D. L., Naoom, S. F., Blase, K. A., Friedman, R. M., & Wallace, F. (2005). *Implementation research: A synthesis of the literature* (FMHI Publication #231). University of South Florida, Louis de la Parte Florida Mental Health Institute, National Implementation Research Network.
Glasgow, R. E., Vogt, T. M., & Boles, S. M. (1999). Evaluating the public health impact of health promotion interventions: The RE-AIM framework. *American Journal of Public Health*, *89*(9), 1322–1327. https://doi.org/10.2105/AJPH.89.9.1322
Goodhart, C. A. E. (1975). Problems of monetary management: The UK experience. In *Papers in Monetary Economics* (Vol. 1, pp. 1–20). Reserve Bank of Australia.
Henriksen, K., Stambulova, N., & Roessler, K. K. (2010). Holistic approach to athletic talent development environments: A successful sailing milieu. *Psychology of Sport and Exercise*, *11*(3), 212–222. https://doi.org/10.1016/j.psychsport.2009.10.005
Hodge, K., Henry, G., & Smith, W. (2014). A case study of excellence in elite sport: Motivational climate in a world champion team. *The Sport Psychologist*, *28*(1), 60–74. https://doi.org/10.1123/tsp.2013-0037
Information and Privacy Commissioner of Ontario. (2025). *De-identification guidelines for structured data*. https://www.ipc.on.ca/en/media/5946/download
Kotter, J. P. (1996). *Leading change*. Harvard Business School Press.
Kroenke, K., Spitzer, R. L., & Williams, J. B. W. (2001). The PHQ-9: Validity of a brief depression severity measure. *Journal of General Internal Medicine*, *16*(9), 606–613. https://doi.org/10.1046/j.1525-1497.2001.016009606.x
Lewin, K. (1947). Frontiers in group dynamics: Concept, method and reality in social science; social equilibria and social change. *Human Relations*, *1*(1), 5–41. https://doi.org/10.1177/001872674700100103
LMA (League Managers Association). (2024). *End of season manager statistics*. https://www.leaguemanagers.com
Lundkvist, E., Gustafsson, H., Hjälm, S., & Hassmén, P. (2012). An interpretive phenomenological analysis of burnout and recovery in elite soccer coaches. *Qualitative Research in Sport, Exercise and Health*, *4*(3), 400–419. https://doi.org/10.1080/2159676X.2012.693526
Maslach, C., Schaufeli, W. B., & Leiter, M. P. (2001). Job burnout. *Annual Review of Psychology*, *52*, 397–422. https://doi.org/10.1146/annurev.psych.52.1.397
May, C. R., & Finch, T. (2009). Implementing, embedding, and integrating practices: An outline of normalization process theory. *Sociology*, *43*(3), 535–554. https://doi.org/10.1177/0038038509103208
May, C. R., Johnson, M., & Finch, T. (2016). Implementation, context and complexity. *Implementation Science*, *11*, 141. https://doi.org/10.1186/s13012-016-0506-3
Mehrabi, N., Morstatter, F., Saxena, N., Lerman, K., & Galstyan, A. (2021). A survey on bias and fairness in machine learning. *ACM Computing Surveys*, *54*(6), 1–35. https://doi.org/10.1145/3457607

Morrison, E. W. (2014). Employee voice and silence. *Annual Review of Organizational Psychology and Organizational Behavior*, *1*, 173–197. https://doi.org/10.1146/annurev-orgpsych-031413-091328

Nonaka, I., & Takeuchi, H. (1995). *The knowledge-creating company: How Japanese companies create the dynamics of innovation*. Oxford University Press.

Parent, M. M., Naraine, M. L., & Hoye, R. (2018). A new era for governance structures and processes in Canadian national sport organizations. *Journal of Sport Management*, *32*(6), 555–566. https://doi.org/10.1123/jsm.2018-0037

Peters, A., McEwen, B. S., & Friston, K. (2017). Uncertainty and stress: Why it causes diseases and how it is mastered by the brain. *Progress in Neurobiology*, *156*, 164–188. https://doi.org/10.1016/j.pneurobio.2017.05.004

Proctor, E., Silmere, H., Raghavan, R., Hovmand, P., Aarons, G., Bunger, A., Griffey, R., & Hensley, M. (2011). Outcomes for implementation research: Conceptual distinctions, measurement challenges, and research agenda. *Administration and Policy in Mental Health and Mental Health Services Research*, *38*(2), 65–76. https://doi.org/10.1007/s10488-010-0319-7

Reardon, C. L., Hainline, B., Aron, C. M., Baron, D., Baum, A. L., Bindra, A., Budgett, R., Campriani, N., Castaldelli-Maia, J. M., Currie, A., Derevensky, J. L., Glick, I. D., Gorczynski, P., Gouttebarge, V., Grandner, M. A., Han, D. H., McDuff, D., Mountjoy, M., Polat, A., . . . Engebretsen, L. (2019). Mental health in elite athletes: International Olympic Committee consensus statement (2019). *British Journal of Sports Medicine*, *53*(11), 667–699. https://doi.org/10.1136/bjsports-2019-100715

Safe Work Australia. (2022). *Model code of practice: Managing psychosocial hazards at work*. https://www.safeworkaustralia.gov.au/doc/model-code-practice-managing-psychosocial-hazards-work

Schein, E. H. (2010). *Organizational culture and leadership* (4th ed.). Jossey-Bass.

Senge, P. M. (2006). *The fifth discipline: The art and practice of the learning organization* (Rev. ed.). Doubleday.

Shu, L., Xie, J., Yang, M., Li, Z., Li, Z., Liao, D., Xu, X., & Yang, X. (2018). A review of emotion recognition using physiological signals. *Sensors*, *18*(7), 2074. https://doi.org/10.3390/s18072074

Spitzer, R. L., Kroenke, K., Williams, J. B. W., & Löwe, B. (2006). A brief measure for assessing generalized anxiety disorder: The GAD-7. *Archives of Internal Medicine*, *166*(10), 1092–1097. https://doi.org/10.1001/archinte.166.10.1092

Staw, B. M., Sandelands, L. E., & Dutton, J. E. (1981). Threat rigidity effects in organizational behavior: A multilevel analysis. *Administrative Science Quarterly*, *26*(4), 501–524. https://doi.org/10.2307/2392337

Stirman, S. W., Baumann, A. A., & Miller, C. J. (2019). The FRAME: An expanded framework for reporting adaptations and modifications to evidence-based interventions. *Implementation Science*, *14*, 58. https://doi.org/10.1186/s13012-019-0898-y

Strathern, M. (1997). "Improving ratings": Audit in the British University system. *European Review*, *5*(3), 305–321. https://doi.org/10.1017/S1062798700002660

EPILOGUE

The Structure and the Person Inside It

This book opened with a reframe: the silence, the concealment, and the short-term thinking—these are not breakdowns of character. They are rational responses to structural conditions. Eleven chapters later, that claim lands differently. It is no longer an argument. It is a lens.

What becomes possible when the architecture is in place is surprisingly mundane. A rookie integrates faster because the onboarding system was designed, not improvised. A staff member raises a concern in week two instead of burying it until month 6. A coaching group navigates a losing streak without abandoning the standards they set in preseason. A veteran accepts a role change with dignity because the conversation happened inside a structure that protected it. None of that is dramatic. That is the point. Good architecture makes honesty less expensive—and when honesty is less expensive, people use it.

Elite sport will always be high-stakes, public, and fast. The architecture does not change that. It changes what pressure produces.

The architecture does not guarantee wins. Teams that build it still lose games, still miss playoffs, and still make trades that do not work out. But they lose with better information. They lose without losing the trust that allows them to regroup. They lose a season without losing the people and the culture that give them a chance at the next one. That tension between long-term architecture and short-term results does not resolve. It is managed.

And some of what matters most in this work is not structural at all: the moment a leader chooses vulnerability over self-protection, the conversation where someone finally says the thing everyone was thinking, and the decision to stay in an uncomfortable process long enough for it to produce something real. The

DOI: 10.4324/9781003631217-13

architecture makes those moments more likely. It cannot produce them. People do that part.

If you are a practitioner reading this, you already know that the hardest part of culture work is not the framework. It is the Tuesday morning after the framework has been agreed to, when the first real test arrives and the organization discovers whether it meant what it said. Most of the important work is invisible—the crisis that did not happen, the concern that got caught early, and the athlete who stayed because the environment was worth staying in. Your job in those moments is not to have the answer. It is to hold the structure long enough for the answer to come from the people inside it.

That is what the architecture is for, not to replace judgment, but to protect the conditions under which good judgment becomes possible—and to let the people in these environments do what they came to do.

The question underneath this book has not changed since the Preface: *what does it take to build a high-performance sport organization that works—for everyone in it?*

We do not claim to have answered it completely. We built a structure that makes the question easier to work on and harder to avoid. The rest is yours.

GLOSSARY OF KEY TERMS

This glossary defines key concepts, frameworks, and author-coined terms used throughout the HPCOS. It is intended as a companion to the Glossary of Abbreviations. Entries are arranged alphabetically. Cross-references to related terms appear where relevant.

A

Accountability Zone One of three performance zones (alongside Learning and Selection Zones) in which athletes submit to evaluation against known standards. Consequences follow; performance safety exists—honesty about the task is protected—but standards are non-negotiable. Leaders must name the zone before feedback begins to prevent athletes from misreading evaluation as learning or vice versa.

Acquiescent Silence A form of organizational silence driven by futility rather than fear. People stay quiet because they believe speaking up changes nothing—not because they expect punishment, but because they have lost confidence that the system will respond. Intervention requires demonstrated consequences of voice, not just safety assurances. See also: Quiescent Silence; Prosocial Silence.

C

Cascade Diagnostic (Office-to-Field) A triage framework that determines whether the presenting dysfunction at the coaching tier originates locally or cascades from upstream executive-level instability. Three questions guide the diagnosis: (1) does the dysfunction map to the executive calendar? (2) Does the presenting coach display the same behaviors upward that athletes report experiencing from them? (3) Do multiple coaches in the same system show similar patterns simultaneously? Two or more affirmative answers indicate a systemic origin requiring executive-level intervention.

Conducive Environment The third corner of the Toxic Triangle (Padilla et al., 2007). Environments become conducive to toxicity through absent oversight, cultural values that excuse harm (e.g., "toughness"), organizational instability, and weak institutional memory (see: Normalization of Deviance). Removing a destructive leader without addressing the conducive environment corner typically installs a successor into the same enabling conditions.

Conflict Archaeology A diagnostic method for excavating values-in-use from how an organization has historically resolved real conflicts between competing priorities. By mapping past decisions—especially decisions made under pressure—practitioners can identify what the organization actually values, as distinct from what it states on its values poster.

Consequence Architecture The system of reinforcement loops, information pathways, and decision structures that determines which behaviors persist in an organization. Culture, in this framework, is not a poster or a values statement—it is the consequence architecture operating beneath stated values. The cue → behavior → consequence loop is the mechanism that makes values either observable or hollow. See also: Culture Hypothesis; Reinforcement Loop.

Culture Hypothesis A testable, behaviorally framed prediction about what will change if a specific consequence changes: "If we change this consequence, this behavior will change in this domain within this timeframe." The Culture Hypothesis converts culture from an abstraction into something an organization can design, test, and track. It is the diagnostic expression of the reinforcement logic underlying the HPCOS.

Custodianship Cycle A four-phase mechanism for ensuring that cultural knowledge survives leadership turnover: Capture (AARs, season debriefs, incident learning), Store (one accessible, version-controlled repository), Transfer (onboarding modules, mentor pairings, transition tools), and Audit (a scheduled check on what was learned, what changed, and what is drifting). Part of the HPCOS sustainability layer. See also: Ownership Spine.

D

Decision Clarity The third leading indicator of HPCOS function. Decision clarity is the observable output of whether the decision-rights structure is actually operating under pressure. High decision clarity means the right people decide with the best available information, within a known authority structure, and the rationale can be articulated afterward. Degradation appears as authority ambiguity, rationale opacity, or political capture. See also: Speed of Truth and Voice Normalization.

Decision Rights Explicit specifications of who decides what—selection, discipline, playing time, medical clearance, and spending—and on what basis. Decision rights must be documented, not merely understood verbally, and must survive leadership transition. Without documented decision rights, authority ambiguity defaults to the highest-status person in the room, regardless of role.

Default Drift The tendency of organizations to revert to pre-intervention threat-based defaults when systems are not actively maintained. Default drift is accelerated by leadership turnover, budget pressure, and institutional amnesia. It is the primary sustainability threat addressed by the HPCOS Layer 7 architecture. Countermeasures include the ownership spine, the custodianship cycle, and measurement-to-action feedback loops.

Demanding Versus Damaging Environment A diagnostic distinction between high-performance environments that sharpen people (demanding) and those that silence or harm them (damaging). Demanding environments feature high standards and direct feedback applied consistently; damaging environments feature arbitrary standards, public humiliation, and selective consequences. The diagnostic line is whether feedback targets behavior or identity, and whether the emotional regulation burden falls on the leader or the athlete.

Destructive Leadership Leadership characterized by charisma without integrity, malignant personality traits (narcissism, psychopathy, and Machiavellianism), abusive or controlling behaviors applied selectively, and self-interest driving decisions at the expense of follower and organizational well-being (Einarsen et al., 2007). Destructive leadership is durable when follower susceptibility and conducive environmental conditions reinforce it. See also: Toxic Triangle.

E

Espoused Values Versus Values-in-Use A distinction from Argyris and Schön (1974). Espoused values are what an organization states it stands for; values-in-use are the rules that actually govern decisions, excavated through conflict archaeology and behavioral observation. Culture work fails when it targets espoused values without changing the consequence architecture that sustains values-in-use.

F

Fly-on-the-Wall Test A behavioral specificity standard for organizational norms and standards. A behavioral standard passes the test if a neutral observer could verify it through direct observation—"Debriefs run after every match, same agenda, same tone"—and fails if it requires inference about values—"We value accountability." If a behavior cannot be described in observable terms, it is not yet a behavioral standard. See also: Values-in-Use.

I

Institutional Amnesia The loss of organizational learning that occurs when cultural knowledge exists tacitly in individuals rather than in systems and is therefore lost at departure. Institutional amnesia is a structural vulnerability, not an individual failure. It is addressed through the custodianship cycle and distributed leadership. See also: Normalization of Deviance.

L

Learning Zone One of three performance zones (alongside Accountability and Selection Zones) in which errors are treated as data, feedback is descriptive, and psychological safety is high because mistakes carry no immediate consequences. Athletes in the learning zone voluntarily expose weakness. Conflating the learning zone with the accountability zone produces athletes who hide errors in training because they have learned that training is evaluation.

M

Measurement-to-Action Loop ("You Said/We Did") A feedback cycle in which organizational leaders visibly act on data and concerns surfaced through voice channels, and communicate that action back to contributors within a defined timeframe. Measurement without visible action trains silence: people learn that input is collected but not consequential. The loop is the primary credibility mechanism for sustaining Voice Normalization. See also: Voice Normalization.

N

Normalization of Deviance A gradual process in which the baseline for acceptable behavior shifts downward over time through incremental tolerance of unsafe or harmful practices (Vaughan, 1996). Each tolerance of a deviation becomes the new normal against which future deviations are assessed. High staff turnover and weak institutional memory are structural predictors of normalization of deviance.

O

Organizational Silence A learned pattern in which employees collectively withhold information, concerns, or feedback from organizational leaders, shaped by leadership response patterns rather than individual reluctance (Morrison & Milliken, 2000). Organizational silence is a system-level phenomenon; it is produced by the consequence architecture and sustained by vicarious learning. Three types require different interventions: acquiescent, quiescent (fear-based), and prosocial. See also: Silence Calculus.

Ownership Spine The minimum structural foundation for sustaining HPCOS implementation: named roles with explicit decision rights, a defined cadence for review and escalation, and documented triggers for intervention. The ownership spine ensures that the architecture survives the departure of any single champion. Without it, culture work is a program—it ends when the person who built it leaves. See also: Custodianship Cycle.

P

Prac-ademic The epistemological stance of the HPCOS: every theory earns its place by answering the question "What does this change on Tuesday morning?" Not a dismissal of foundational research—the architecture depends on it—but a filter for which research gets operationalized and how. Tools are presented with validation status declarations (validated instrument or practitioner-developed heuristic) so practitioners can calibrate confidence appropriately.

Prosocial Silence A form of organizational silence motivated by loyalty—staying quiet to protect teammates, the organization, or a coach, rather than from fear or futility. Common in elite sport culture. Prosocial silence can mask real harm under the guise of group solidarity. Intervention requires reframing: "reporting is not betrayal; concealment is the betrayal." See also: Acquiescent Silence; Quiescent Silence.

Psychological Safety A shared belief held by members of a team that the team is safe for interpersonal risk-taking (Edmondson, 1999). Three elements matter in sport contexts: it is shared (a team-level phenomenon, not one brave individual); it concerns interpersonal risk (speaking up, admitting error, challenging a decision); and it is a belief, not a permission. In HPCOS terms, psychological safety is the operating condition that determines whether truth travels fast enough for pressure to produce learning rather than silence.

Q

Quiescent (Fear-Based) Silence A form of organizational silence in which people withhold information because speaking carries real costs—to safety, status, or selection (Pinder & Harlos, 2001). Distinct from acquiescent silence (futility-based) and prosocial silence (loyalty-based). Intervention requires structural changes to the consequence architecture, not reassurance. See also: Organizational Silence; Silence Calculus.

R

Reinforcement Loop The cue → behavior → consequence sequence that makes organizational values observable or hollow. Behavior is maintained by its consequences, and those consequences are learned vicariously by everyone watching (Skinner, 1953; Bandura, 1977). When silence is reinforced, silence spreads. When voice is reinforced, voice normalizes. The reinforcement loop, not the values deck, determines what persists under pressure. See also: Consequence Architecture; Culture Hypothesis.

S

Selection Zone One of three performance zones (alongside Learning and Accountability Zones) positioned between them. Athletes are evaluated against known criteria, but the conversation remains forward-facing. Elite sport environments simultaneously operate across all three zones; the leader's task is to name which zone is active before a conversation begins so athletes can calibrate what honesty is safe and expected.

Silence Calculus The implicit cost–benefit assessment individuals perform when deciding whether to speak up. Variables include perceived probability of retaliation, belief that speaking will change anything, loyalty to teammates, and financial dependence on the decision-maker. The silence calculus is structural—it is shaped by the consequence architecture, not individual courage. Changing the calculus requires changing the consequences, not exhorting people to be braver.

Speed of Truth The first leading indicator of HPCOS function: the elapsed time between someone knowing something and the organization being able to act on it. In high-functioning systems, problems surface in hours; in dysfunctional ones, they fester for months. Speed of Truth is a proxy for whether the system is safe enough to speak into. A narrowing Speed of Truth signals improving safety; a widening one—especially after losses or leadership changes—is an early warning of cultural drift.

T

Toxic Triangle A model of organizational toxicity in which three mutually reinforcing elements sustain dysfunction: destructive leaders, susceptible followers, and conducive environments (Padilla et al., 2007; extended by Thoroughgood et al., 2018). The diagnostic value is identifying which corner is doing the most work—destabilizing any one corner begins to break down the system. Leader removal alone is insufficient when the conducive environment and follower-susceptibility corners are independently maintaining the pattern.

V

Voice Normalization The second leading indicator of HPCOS function: the degree to which concerns, bad news, and dissenting perspectives are raised before problems escalate—without the person who raises them paying a social or career cost. Voice Normalization is measured behaviorally (who speaks, when, and about what) and through Speed of Truth tracking. It is built through consistent reinforcement of voice and visible action on what people surface. See also: Measurement-to-Action Loop.

W

Weekly Diagnostic Triad A practitioner-developed heuristic (Chapter 3) providing a rapid, real-time decision-making format for diagnosing early toxicity signals across three domains: behavioral markers (silence, withdrawal, and hypervigilance), performance markers (error rates, load compliance, and strategic risk-taking), and retention markers (exit clustering and informal network thinning). Built-in escalation pathway traces source to coaching tier or executive cascade. Not a validated instrument.

INDEX

Note: Page numbers in *italics* indicate a figure and page numbers in **bold** indicate a table on the corresponding page.